CATULLUS, C. Valerius

EDITED BY

ELMER TRUESDELL MERRILL
LATE RICH PROFESSOR OF LATIN IN WESLEYAN UNIVERSITY

CAMBRIDGE, MASSACHUSETTS
HARVARD UNIVERSITY PRESS

SACRAE · MEMORIAE

CALVINI · SEARS · HARRINGTON

ANIMAE · CANDIDISSIMAE

PRAECEPTORIS

HVNC · LIBELLVM · QVALEMCVMQVE

ALVMNVS

D · D

FOREWORD

This reappearance of Merrill's *Catullus* perhaps calls for a word of explanation. A few years ago, when the book was allowed to go out of print, classical studies suffered a severe blow. For this was the only brief, sufficiently annotated edition available in English of the complete works of one of antiquity's most attractive poets.

Admittedly, one may always find fault with notes written in the knowledge and taste of half a century ago. For example, one may now tend to deplore the emphasis given to matters concerned with the chronology of the poems. But a later generation may not. Then, too, some today may possibly, on grounds of aesthetic improbability, reject Merrill's inclination to "partition the poet's Muse," so that two Catulluses emerge, the learned and the lyrical. More serious, certainly, is the considerable increase in our knowledge since 1893 of Catullus' relation to his Greek models. But our chief need is to have such basic commentaries as those of Ellis or Kroll brought up to date. Finally, some would inevitably have Merrill's text changed here and there. Still, in the case of so thorny a text *quot doctores tot lectiones*.

The alternative, then, to reprinting would have been a *novus libellus*—a new recension and commentary—and to that proposal the answer is simply *nummi desunt*. In any case Merrill's notes furnish ample and pertinent assistance on all points that are likely to bother the student, and for the instructor they offer now and then the not wholly undesirable challenge to differ from another scholar in interpretation and to try to supplement him in information. All in all, this edition indeed deserves to last *plus uno saeclo*, and one is very glad to have it back.

J. P. ELDER

CAMBRIDGE, MASSACHUSETTS
May, 1951

PREFACE.

THE text of this edition of Catullus is constituted upon the conviction that only *codices Sangermanensis* (*G*) and *Oxoniensis* (*O*) are of ultimate authority in determining the readings of the lost *codex Veronensis* (*V*), and that the readings of the other known MSS. (except *T*) that differ from those of *G* and *O* have the value of conjectural emendations merely.

In the Critical Appendix are exhibited in full the readings of *G* and *O*, with the omission, however, of such as present only unimportant orthographical peculiarities. For the readings of *G* I have depended mainly upon the published collations of Baehrens, Ellis, and Schwabe (in his last edition), together with the photolithographic fac-simile of the MS. published at Paris in 1890. For the readings of *O* I have followed a collation and complete transcript of that MS. made by me in July, 1889, by the courtesy of the Librarian of the Bodleian. This collation was carefully compared on the spot with the collations of Ellis and Schwabe, and is therefore, I trust, reasonably free from error.

A fac-simile of a page of *codex O*, reduced one-third in size, follows this preface.

My especial thanks are due to the editors-in-chief of this Series for their unfailing kindness and invaluable criticisms, and to my friend and associate, Mr. Frank W. Nicolson, for his assistance in proof-reading and in the preparation of the Critical Appendix.

E. T. M.

MIDDLETOWN, CONN.
Jan. 1, 1893.

teneramque uidit attin prope marmorea pelago

ferat impetum ille demens fugit in nemora fera

ibi semper omne uite spatium famula fuit

dea magna dea cybelle dea domina dindymei

procul a mea tuus sit furor omnis era domo

alios age incitatos alios age rapidos

Peliaco quondam prognate uertice pinus

dicuntur liquidas neptuni nasse per undas

phasidos ad fluctus et fines ceteos

cum lecti iuuenes argiue robora pupis

aurata optantes cholchis auertere pellem

ausi sunt uada salsa cita decurrere puppi

caerula uerrentes abiegnis equora palmis

illa quibus retines in summis urbibus arces

ipsa leui fecit uolitantem flamine currum

pinea coniungens inflexe texta carine

illa rude cursu prima inbuit amphitriten

que simul ac rostro uentosum proscidit equor

tortaque remigio spumis incanduit unda

emersere feri candenti e gurgite uultus

equoree monstrum nereides admirantes

illa atque alia uiderunt luce marinas

mortales oculis nudato corpore nymphas

nutricum tenus extantes e gurgite cano

tum thetidis peleus incensus fertur amore

tum thetis humanos non despexit hymeneos

tum thetidi pater ipse iugandum pelea sensit

o nimis optato seculorum tempore nati

heroes saluete deum genus o bona matrum

uos ego sepe meo uos carmine compellabo .

INTRODUCTION.

---·◦◦·---

EARLY LYRIC POETRY AT ROME.

1. The beginnings of lyric poetry among the Romans reach back to the prehistoric period of the city, and were as rude and shapeless as was the life of her people. Amid the rough farmer-populace of the turf-walled village by the Tiber the Arval Brethren and the Salii 'chanted their rude litanies to the rustic deities, — for even then religion was a prime cause in moving men toward poetry. In roughly balanced Saturnian verses men spoke regret and panegyric for the dead and praises for the valorous deeds of the living. The mimetic passion and rude wit of the Roman led him also into boisterous personal satire and into epigram more pungent than polished. But until the last few decades of the Republic these products of the Muse are either anonymous or connected with names well-nigh forgotten, and the remnants that have come down to us display no striking poetic excellence.

2. The progress of a national literature is perhaps rarely by fits and starts, even though it appears so to be. But the front advances in such a uniform line, that only now and then, when one wave sweeps out far beyond the rest, is the general advance of the tide remarked. So it would probably be unjust to the unknown poets of the Roman Republic to believe that their work did not mark a continual advance from period to period in lyric feeling and expression. Yet only in the first half of the last century before Christ did Latin poetry enter upon its first period of brilliancy. Amid the hot passions, the vigorous hatreds, the feasts and brawls, the beauty and the coarseness,

of life in the capital during this most active period in the history of Rome, there arose a school of writers who, though often conservatives in politics, were radicals in poetry. The tendencies of the traditional Roman past were by them utterly disregarded. Inspiration was drawn from the stirring life into which they were plunged, as well as from the sympathetic study of the sources of poetic art among both the earlier Greeks and the Alexandrians. As was to be expected, their models of rhythm were not the rude hexameters and ruder Saturnians of their Roman predecessors, but the more polished versification of the Greeks; and their subjects were sometimes their own personal experiences and emotions, and sometimes themes suggested by their Greek prototypes. So a new school of Roman poetry arose and flourished, to be superseded in turn by the polished Augustans, who cultivated the niceties of elegance, but at the expense of *verve*.

CATULLUS.

3. Of this new school of poets the most prominent and interesting figure is Catullus. It is possible to know him personally as only now and then an ancient writer can be known to us, and yet he gives us but few definite biographical facts concerning himself, while still fewer are given by other authors of his own and later ages. But the little body of poems that constitute his extant works is so replete with his intense personality, and shows forth so unreservedly his every emotion, that the man stands out before us as does no other man of the age with the exception of two or three of its political leaders. And all this is true, even though we acknowledge, as we are bound to do, that in many questions of importance concerning his life we must be content with a working hypothesis instead of a series of established facts, and that the biographer, as the interpreter of the poems of Catullus, must be understood to be presenting probabilities, and not certainties.

4. With regard to his full name we are left in some doubt. He refers to himself by name in his poems twenty-five times, but in each case only by the cognomen, *Catullus*, while the better manuscripts of his writings are inscribed simply *Catulli Veronensis Liber*. Yet there is no difficulty in ascertaining his gentile name from other writers. Varro (*L. L.* VII. 50), Suetonius (*Iul.* 73), Porphyrio (on Hor. *Sat.* I. 10. 19), Charisius (I. 97), Jerome (*Chron. a. Abr.* 1930), all give it as *Valerius*. There are fewer references to his praenomen. Four of the later and interpolated manuscripts give it in their titles as *Quintus*, and until lately it was supposed that to this indication might be added the testimony of the elder Pliny (*N. H.* XXXVII. 81). Relying upon such authority Scaliger went so far as to emend *c.* 67. 12 so as to bring in for the unintelligible words *qui te* the praenomen of the poet in the vocative, *Quinte;* and his suggestion won the approval of even so keen a critic as Lachmann. But it is now universally conceded that the initial *Q.* prefixed to the word *Catullus* in the passage specified from Pliny is an interpolation, the best MS., the *codex Bambergensis*, containing only the cognomen without prefix. There is, moreover, positive evidence in favor of a different praenomen. Jerome (*l.c.*), in speaking of the birth of the poet, calls him in full *C. Valerius Catullus*, and Apuleius (*Apol.* 10), whose accuracy, however, in the matter of names is not above suspicion, calls him *C. Catullus*. In the face, then, of the testimony of interpolated manuscripts only, his praenomen must stand established as Gaius.

5. Concerning the birthplace of Gaius Valerius Catullus there is abundant testimony. The titles of the best MSS. of his works call him *Veronensis*, and Jerome (*l.c.*) declares him born at Verona. In this testimony concur his admirers among the poets of the centuries immediately following (*e.g.* Ov. *Am.* III. 15. 7; Mart. I. 61. 1; X. 103. 5; XIV. 195; Auson. *Op.* 23. 1); and his own writings furnish confirmatory evidence of the same fact. He calls himself (*c.* 39. 13) *Transpadanus·* he

possessed a villa at Sirmio on the shore of Lacus Benacus near
Verona (*c.* 31) ; he was acquainted with Veronese society (*cc.*
67, 100) ; and he spent part of his time at Verona (*cc.* 35,
68ª).

DATE OF BIRTH AND OF DEATH.

6. The year of his birth and that of his death are stated by
Jerome in his edition of the Chronicles of Eusebius, probably
on the authority of the *De Poetis* of Suetonius.   Under date of
the year of Abraham 1930 (= B.C. 87) Jerome says, *Gaius
Valerius Catullus scriptor lyricus Veronae nascitur,* and under
that of 1960, or, according to some MSS., 1959 (= B.C. 57, or
58), he says, *Catullus XXX. aetatis anno Romae moritur.*
There is nothing to contradict Jerome's date for the birth of
the poet, but unfortunately for our belief in his entire accuracy,
a number of the poems of Catullus were clearly written later
than B.C. 57, — some of them at least as late as the end of the
year 55 B.C., or the beginning of the year 54 (*e.g. cc.* 11, 29, 53,
113).   Jerome is, therefore, certainly wrong about the date of
the poet's death, and hence about at least one of the two other
statements, the date of his birth and his age at death.   The
only scrap of evidence from other sources on these points is the
vague statement of Ovid that Catullus died young (*Am.* III. 9.
62 *obuius huic* [*in Elysio*] *hedera iuuenalia cinctus tempora
cum Caluo, docte Catulle, tuo*).

7. The poems of Catullus himself furnish us, however, with
some good negative evidence concerning the date of his death.
It probably occurred in the year 54 B.C.   In the first place,
there are no poems that clearly must have been written later
than the close of the year 55 B.C., or the earlier months of the
year 54, nor any that are even capable of more ready explanation, if a later date for their composition be supposed.   The remark about the consulship of Vatinius (*c.* 52), which did not
take place till the end of the year 47 B.C., forms no exception
to this statement (cf. Commentary), and the prosecution of

Vatinius by Calvus, mentioned in *c.* 53, may well have taken place in 56 B.C., instead of in the fall of 54. Furthermore, *c.* 11, which was surely written toward the close of 55 B.C., shows a decided change in the feeling of Catullus toward Cæsar, and accords well with the statement of Suetonius (*Iul.* 73), that after Catullus had angered Cæsar by his epigrams concerning him and Mamurra, a reconciliation with the poet took place, apparently at his father's house at Verona. It is hardly credible that if Catullus lived during the exciting years that followed 55 B.C., the only indication of his new feeling toward Cæsar should be the reference in *c.* 11, and that this was followed by silence. Such neutrality was not the fashion among the young friends whom Cæsar was constantly winning to himself from the ranks of his political opponents. There seems, indeed, to be an indication in *c.* 11 that Catullus might be expecting some post under the great commander. But the most satisfactory conclusion is that death came within a short time after the close of 55 B.C., and anticipated all hoped-for activities (cf., however, § 50).

8. Whether Jerome is wrong in one or in both of his other statements, remains, and must always remain, in doubt. All known facts concerning Catullus harmonize well with the hypothesis that he was born in 87, and died in 54 B.C., at the age of thirty-three, or that he was born in 84, and died in 54, at the age of thirty ; but nothing more definite can be said about the matter.

Family and Circumstances.

9. The only relative mentioned by Catullus is his brother, whose death was the occasion to him of such intense and lasting grief (*cc.* 65, 68, 101). But Suetonius (*l.c.*) speaks of the father as a host of Julius Cæsar even so late, apparently, as the close of the poet's life. Why he (to say nothing of the mother) is never mentioned by the poet, we cannot tell. Not improbably, however, he did not have the same active sympathy with the tastes and inclinations of Catullus as the father of Horace had with those of his son. Catullus, moreover, was not the only son, and was probably younger than the one whose untimely death in the Troad he records.

10. Yet there was apparently wealth enough in the family to enable even the younger brother to enjoy the advantages that wealth brought to the young Italian of that day. He was able early in his young manhood to go to Rome, and to make that city thenceforth his abiding-place (*c.* 68. 34 ff.). He owned a villa at Sirmio (*c.* 31), and another on the edge of the Sabine hills (*c.* 44). And there is no indication that while at Rome he was busy with any pursuit that could fill his purse, although, like many another young Roman, he later obtained a provincial appointment, and went to Bithynia on the staff of the governor Memmius in the hope of wealth (cf. § 29 ff.). The hope, he tells us (*cc.* 10, 28), proved abortive, but Catullus had yet money enough — perhaps even to purchase a yacht for his homeward journey like any millionnaire (cf. § 35 and introductory note to *c.* 4) — at any rate to continue his merry life at Rome, apparently without great pecuniary embarrassment. All these indications point to no financial inability or niggardliness on the part of his father. Possibly the villas, and an increase of income, came to him upon the death of his brother.

11. Whether Catullus, like Horace, was accompanied to Rome by his father is doubtful. On the whole, it seems hardly probable that he was. To say nothing of the considerations possibly connected with the interests of the elder son, the father was apparently resident in Verona at the time when Julius Cæsar was governor of Gaul (Suet. *Iul.* 73), and this fact may indicate that at no time was the family home at Verona broken up in favor of a new one at Rome.

EDUCATION.

12. Doubtless to the care of some friend of the family at Rome the youth was entrusted. And there were many

Transpadanes at Rome, — some of them making great names for themselves in the literary world. With some of these certainly a man of station prominent enough in Verona to be later, at least, the friend of Julius Cæsar, might command interest. Under the charge of one of them he might have placed so promising a young man as his son doubtless was. To which one the trust fell cannot now be determined, but as Catullus later (*c.* 1) addresses Cornelius Nepos as the friend and foster-father of his earlier poems, it seems not unlikely that to his guardianship (cf. § 63) Catullus owed his introduction into the society of Rome.

13. The purpose of his coming thither is nowhere stated, but may easily be divined. Rome was the school of Italy, at least to all who could pay for her tuition. And a youth with a poet's soul burning within him could hardly have been content with such schooling as a Transpadane town afforded, even to her wealthiest inhabitants. But whether Catullus did much studying of a serious sort may well be doubted. It cannot be quite true that his 'only books were woman's looks,' for his poems show an ardent and sympathetic study of the Greek poets. But his attainments in rhetoric and philosophy, if he had any at all, were certainly not of a scholastic character, and he apparently never cared to follow the students of the day to Athens or to Rhodes.

14. Not books, but life, exercised over him the preëminent charm. And this life was not the life of the past, but of the present, — the busy, delirious whirl of life in the capital of the world. Into it he plunged with all the ardor of a lively and passionate nature. Rome was from that first moment his home, the centre of all his beloved activities. Verona, his Sabine villa, and even Sirmio, became to him but hospitals or vacation haunts. Once only did he leave Italy, and even his joy at reaching Sirmio again on his return (*c.* 31) could not long detain him from Rome. And at Rome death met him.

15. In life at Rome, then, Catullus found his full development as a poet. Already from the donning of the *toga uirilis*,
so he tells us (*c.* 68. 15 ff.), he had been busied with love and
love-verses. But whether this period antedated or followed his
coming to Rome cannot be decided, since the date of publication of the Chronica of Nepos (*c.* 1. 8) is unknown, and on this
alone could a decision of the other point be based. Such
poems as those that concern Aufilena (*cc.* 100, 110, 111) may
possibly date from the Veronese period of the poet's life
(though *c.* 82 cannot possibly do so), and yet it is just as
possible that their scene was Rome (cf. introductory note to
c. 100), and the same may be said of the poems concerning
Ameana (*cc.* 41, 43). Much more likely is it, however, that
of the other poems that show some connection with Veronese
affairs *cc.* 17 and 67 date from his residence in his native city,
while *c.* 35 was surely written during only a temporary visit
there (cf. Commentary).

LESBIA.

16. But whenever these poems were written, they spring
from experiences that did not touch deeply the soul of the
writer. A passing fancy, a moment's passion, an evanescent
humor brought them forth. But at Rome, and not long after
he arrived at Rome, Catullus met the mastering passion of his
life, and beside the verses to which it gave birth the melodious
chamber ditties of Horace and the elaborated passions of the
elegiasts are but as tinkling cymbals. To the woman who exercised this wonderful power over him he gives the name of Lesbia.
But more often he is not content with a name, and the familiar
terms of endearment flow from his lips with a newer and deeper
meaning ; for he delights to feel that though his experience
is on the outside like that of other men, his mistress is peerless
in virtues and his love for her a love passing that of women.
On his side the passion was sudden and intense. He adopts
the words of Sappho, and tells Lesbia (*c.* 51) of the deadly

faintness that seizes upon him even while he feels himself a
god, and more than a god, in sharing her smile and her voice.
And with the swift passion comes the mad desire to win her
love. Lesbia is a married woman (*c.* 83. 1), but that consider-
ation demands only additional care and diplomacy on his part,
and is no bar to his efforts. He lays siege to her heart. His im-
portunate persistence, youth as he is, commands her attention
even amid a throng of lovers, but apparently only irritates her.
What does this youngster, lately come to Rome, hope for amid
so many of his betters? He sees that victory must be won over
this brilliant woman of the world by proving himself no mere
moon-calf. Therefore he curbs his sentiment, and matches wit
with wit. Even her own display of petulance is turned against
her in neat retort (*cc.* 83, 92). And meanwhile Catullus was
winning his way in the Roman world. The unknown young man
was becoming well known, and the haughty beauty finally surrendered, doubtless influenced by vanity rather than by passion.

17. Yet Catullus had no haunting fears concerning the genuineness of her love for him. He was so completely mastered
by his own passion that he could not doubt hers. Their meet-
ings, necessarily secret for the most part, on account of the
lady's position, took place at the house of a friend (*c.* 68. 68).
But not even the possibility of discovery restrained the ardor of
the poet's soul. He poured forth his feelings most simply and
unrestrainedly in a series of charming trifles. Mere childlike
delight in multitudinous kisses (*cc.* 5, 7), daintiest pretence of
lover's jealousy at the favors accorded Lesbia's sparrow (*c.* 2),
gentle, half-smiling sympathy with her over the untimely death
of her pet (*c.* 3), flow from his pen with a perfect freedom of
movement and yet with an exquisite grace and perfection in
every part. And the mere thought that any proud damsel could
once claim comparison with his Lesbia rouses him to hot scorn
(*cc.* 43, 86).

18. The sight of this young poet at her feet may have been
attractive to Lesbia, but it could not take the place of all other

attractions. The exclusive demand his love made upon her grew irksome. He might be so wholly swallowed up in love for her as to disregard everything else, but she was not so in love with him. It flattered her vanity to hold him thus in thrall, but was tiresome if she also must have her freedom limited by the same shackles. And so she gradually turned away from him toward other pleasures. He finally met her coldness by an attempt to assert his own independence (*c.* 8). But even in his self-exhortation to firmness in meeting indifference with indifference, he cannot forbear to dwell upon the happy days of the past, nor can he conceal his own hope for a reconciliation. Strangely enough, he seems not even to suspect infidelity on Lesbia's part with other lovers. Though he himself had made her unfaithful to her husband, he is troubled by no fear that she may be entering upon fresh fields of conquest. Though he cannot explain her present action, he is so utterly blinded by his own passion, that he even warns her to consider the desolate lot that awaits her, if she persists in breaking with him (*c.* 8. 14 ff.).

19. However misplaced was the confidence of Catullus in the force of his appeal to Lesbia, his independence of bearing was persevered in till it conquered, — at least to a certain extent. Lesbia saw that she had carried her coldness too far, and was likely to lose forever a lover whose talents and devotion were such that to be given up by him was a serious wound to her vanity. And with a shrewd calculation of the effect of such a course upon his wounded heart, she made her unexpected way into his presence, and prayed for reconciliation. As might be expected, the unsuspicious lover received her with a burst of rapture (*c.* 107).

20. But the relations of the two lovers never could be restored to their old footing. Neither of them felt precisely as before. Lesbia had no intention of confining herself to Catullus alone, but only of numbering him as still one of her slaves. Catullus, too, had won knowledge in a hard school, and the trustful confidence he had felt in Lesbia's full reciprocation of his love was gone. He does reproduce his former tone of joyous mirth in one poem celebrating the reconciliation (*c.* 36), but when Lesbia appeals to the gods to bear witness to her pledge of eternal fidelity (*c.* 109), though he joins in her prayer, it is clearly not with hearty faith, but only with a somewhat reserved desire. And with more experience, his heart is becoming a little hardened. However jesting the tone may be interpreted in which he answers Lesbia's protestations (*c.* 70), a strain of cynicism begins to make itself heard that is foreign to his former songs, though it has not yet become settled bitterness. But Catullus is fast learning to write epigram.

21. It was useless to suppose that he could long remain ignorant of the fact that Lesbia's favors were not confined to him. No one but himself had ever been ignorant of the true state of the case. Rumor now began to penetrate even his fast-closed ears, and that which he perhaps had already begun to fear came with no less a shock when presenting itself in the garb of fact. The emotions it aroused apparently varied from time to time. At one moment his old passion is strong within him, and in dwelling upon the happiness of the past he determines, with a pretence of philosophic carelessness that is supported by the broken staff of mythological precedent, to overlook the frailties of a mistress whose lapses from fidelity he believed were yet but occasional (*c.* 68. 135 ff.). At another moment he appeals in remonstrance and grief to the friends who have become his rivals (*cc.* 73, 77, 90).

22. And his perturbed soul was still further wrenched by another heavy blow that fell upon him at about the same time with these disclosures. His dearly loved brother was dead, and, to heighten the anguish of the moment, dead far away in the Troad, without a single relative near him to close his eyes, utter the last formal farewell, and place upon his tomb the customary funeral offerings. The news either reached Catullus when on a visit to his father's house at Verona, or summoned

him suddenly thither from Rome. For a time this emotion dulled his sensibility to every other. He could think of nothing else. He foreswore the Muses forever, save to express the burden of his woe (*cc.* 68. 19; 65. 12). To the request of the influential orator Hortensius for verses, he could send only a translation from Callimachus, and the story of his tears. He must even deny (*c.* 68ᵃ) an appeal from his friend Manlius for consolation on the death of his wife, — perhaps the same Manlius for whose happy bridal he had but a short time before written an exquisite marriage-song (*c.* 61). And even when Manlius sought to recall him to Rome by hints concerning the scandal aroused by Lesbia's misdoings, the only answer was a sigh (*c.* 68. 30).

23. Possibly other news also reached him concerning his faithless mistress. At all events when, shortly afterward, he did return to the capital, his eyes were fully opened. Not that he now ceased to love Lesbia, for that was beyond his power, and therein lay his extremest torture. He had lost all faith in her, he knew her now to be but an abandoned prostitute, and yet he could not break the chain of his old regard. 'I hate and love,' he cries, 'I know not how, but I feel the anguish of it' (*c.* 85).

24. Though he was condemned still to love Lesbia, the former connection with her was now broken off, never to be renewed. Yet he has for her words of sorrow rather than of scorn. Even now, as formerly (*c.* 104), he cannot malign her, although she has sunk so deep in degradation. In a simple, manly way he declares the fidelity of his love for her (*c.* 87), and the condition to which he has now been brought by her fault and not his own (*c.* 75). However difficult it be to associate the idea of pure affection with a passion like his, there is, nevertheless, an appeal of truth in his solemn asseveration at this moment of bitterest grief that his love for Lesbia was not merely the passion of any common man for his paid mistress, but was as the love of a father for his son (*c.* 72). Not

wholly evil, a heart that could feel such an impulse, even toward a mistaken object.

25. But however gentle his treatment of Lesbia, the rivals of Catullus found now no mercy at his hands. For them he had but bitter scorn and anger, since he mistakenly regarded them, and not Lesbia herself, as responsible for her downfall. Egnatius and his set of companions (*cc.* 37, 39), Gellius (*cc.* 74, 80, 88, 89, 90, 116), perhaps also Æmilius (*c.* 97), Victius (*c.* 98), and Cominius (*c.* 108), and other unnamed lovers (*cc.* 71, 78^b) suffer on this account from the stinging lash of his satire. Even Cælius Rufus, like Quintius an early friend of the poet (*c.* 100), and like Quintius the subject of remonstrance a short time before (*cc.* 77, 82), now finds no such gentle treatment (*cc.* 69, 71?). Possibly, also, the apparent fling at Hortensius in *c.* 95. 3, who was most kindly addressed in *c.* 65, may have been prompted by personal rather than by professional jealousy. Most significant, too (cf. § 28), is the bolt aimed at a certain Lesbius (*c.* 79).

26. The delights of vengeance were perhaps sweet, but they did not bring Catullus peace. The torment of his passion was still raging within him, and from that he longed to find freedom, not again in the arms of his mistress, but in victory over himself. For this he prayed most earnestly (*c.* 76), and this he finally attained, aided partly, no doubt, by absence from the country (cf. § 29), but more by the persistency with which he kept up the struggle within himself. It may well be, however, that in these months of mental anguish are to be found the beginnings of that disease that caused his untimely death. But the conviction evidently grew upon him that Lesbia had not been led astray by his false friends, but had always been deceitful above all things, and with the clearer insight came not only a gentler feeling toward the men he had judged traitors to friendship (cf. *e.g. c.* 58 to Cælius Rufus), but a horror and contempt, now unmixed with pity, for Lesbia herself. And when she tried once more, in the day of his reconciliation with Cæsar,

and the hope of budding fortune (cf. § 41), to win him back
to her, his reply was one of bitter scorn for her, though joined
with a touch of sorrowful reminiscence of departed joys.

27. As part of the history of Catullus after the break with
Lesbia has thus been anticipated in order to indicate the course
of his struggle with himself, it may be well to pause here a few
moments longer to ask who this Lesbia was. That we have in
the poems of Catullus a real and not an imaginative sketch of
a love-episode cannot be once doubted by him who reads.
Lesbia is not a lay figure, a mere peg on which to hang fancies,
like the shadowy heroines of Horace. That she was no *libertina*, but a woman of education and of social position, is equally
clear from the passages already cited. The name Lesbia, therefore, is immediately suggestive of a pseudonym ; and not only
the fashions of poetry, but the position of the lady herself,
appear at once to justify this expedient on the part of her poet-
lover. To this antecedent probability is added the direct testimony of Ovid, who says (*Trist.* II. 427), *sic sua lasciuo can-
tata est saepe Catullo femina cui falsum Lesbia nomen erat.*
Apuleius carries us a step further, saying (*Apol.* 10), *eadem
igitur opera accusent C. Catullum quod Lesbiam pro Clodia
nominarit.* The name Lesbia is the proper metrical equivalent
for Clodia, as the pseudonym of a mistress should be on the
lips of a Roman lover (cf. Bentley on Hor. *Carm.* II. 12. 13 ;
Acro on Hor. *Sat.* I. 2. 64).

28. It was reserved, however, for the Italian scholars of
the sixteenth century to identify this Clodia with the sister of
P. Clodius Pulcher, Cicero's foe, wife of Q. Cæcilius Metellus
Celer, who was prætor B.C. 63, then governor of Cisalpine
Gaul, consul for the year 60 B.C., and died in 59, not without
suspicion that his wife poisoned him (cf. Cic. *Cael.* 24. 60 ;
Quint. VIII. 6. 53). Among almost all Catullian scholars of
the present century this view has found acceptance, in spite
of the express dissent of a few. The general character and
course of life of this Clodia ' Quadrantaria ' (cf. Cic. *Cael.* and

Epp. passim; Drumann II. p. 376 ff.) coincide with those of Lesbia, and many minor details of reference in the poems of Catullus are thus explicable. Especially it may be noted that M. Cælius Rufus (cf. *cc.* 100, 77, 69, 58) was a lover of this Clodia (cf. Cic. *Cael. passim*) about the year 58 B.C., and within two years became her bitter enemy. There was all the more likelihood, then, of the reconciliation between him and Catullus marked by *c.* 58. And if Lesbia be this Clodia, then the Lesbius of *c.* 79 is her infamous brother, P. Clodius Pulcher, and the epigram becomes clear in the light of historic fact (cf. Commentary).

JOURNEY TO BITHYNIA.

29. But the first date in the life of Catullus that can be definitely fixed by the aid of his own poems is that of his absence from Italy after the final rupture with Lesbia (cf. § 24). He went to Bithynia (*cc.* 10. 7; 31. 5; 46. 4) on the staff of the governor, Memmius (*c.* 28. 9). Such expeditions on the part of young Romans of that day are so familiar that it is needless to cite other instances than those (*cc.* 9, etc., 28) of Veranius and Fabullus, the poet's friends. The ordinary motive was not only a love of adventure, but the desire for acquiring wealth at the expense of the provincials in one of the dozen ways possible under a friendly and not too conscientious official patron. Catullus apparently had not been poverty-stricken, however jestingly he claimed that common distinction of the society-man at the capital, though an increase of income may not have been without attractions for him. He had up to this time, too, apparently loved Rome above all other cities, and had not cared to leave it for any considerable period of time, even that he might visit Greece. But now there were two motives that might lead him to look with desire upon a journey to Bithynia. In the first place, it offered him an opportunity to visit the Troad and to pay the final offerings of love at the grave of his

brother (cf. § 22). In the second place, he had been passing
through a terrible mental struggle that was perhaps not yet over,
and Rome had become painful to him. In the distraction of
travel and residence in a foreign clime he might find that
absence from himself for which he sighed.

30. How he obtained the appointment we do not know, for
there is no earlier reference to Memmius in his poems, and
none but uncomplimentary references to him later. But it is
not strange that with all his circle of literary friends at Rome he
should command influence enough to secure such a post; nor
is it strange that C. Memmius, himself a learned man and a
verse-writer (Cic. *Brut.* 70. 247; Ov. *Trist.* II. 433; Plin. *Ep.*
V. 3. 5; Gell. XIX. 9. 7), was pleased to have the company in
his province of such men as Catullus and his poet-friend, C.
Helvius Cinna (*c.* 10. 31).

31. Memmius was prætor in 58 B.C., and therefore in all
probability ruled over Bithynia in 57–56 B.C., though this fact
cannot be substantiated from other sources. Of the journey
of Catullus to Bithynia and of his stay there we have no
record up to the period of his approaching return to Italy,
save in the one poem (*c.* 101) in which he commemorates the
funeral-offerings at the grave of his brother in the Troad, and
speaks the last farewell, — a farewell of infinite sadness because
spoken with no hope of a future reunion. To make these
offerings of pious affection was one of the motives of Catullus
in coming to this distant land, and doubtless the sad duty was
not long postponed after his arrival there. What were the
other occupations of his life in Bithynia we cannot tell. No
poems remain, at any rate, to mark the pleasures of social
intercourse, no squibs of raillery, no brilliant bits of fancy,
such as distinguish the Roman days of the poet. The year is
a long silence. Perhaps he was too sad to write; perhaps
the irksomeness and dulness of his official life wore hard
upon his Muse; perhaps, however, he was gathering inspiration from their native scenery and legend for those poems of

his matured genius, *cc.* 63 and 64, and had even then begun
to block them out. When they were published cannot be
determined.

32. Life in Bithynia was surely unsatisfactory from a financial point of view. The cobwebs in the poet's pockets were
not displaced by gold. Perhaps the shrewder men on the staff
learned better how to make hay while their brief sun was shin-
ing. Catullus, however, came back home poor, and blamed
Memmius for it. But whether Memmius really deserved the
exceedingly opprobrious epithets heaped upon him (cf. *cc.* 10,
28) may well be doubted. Virulence of language in invective,
especially in the use of terms applied to sexual impurity, was
by no means accompanied among the ancients by corresponding intensity of feeling, and is often to be understood as formal
and not literal.

33. Yet some pleasures in his Bithynian life Catullus must
have experienced; for when on the approach of spring (56
B.C.) he bids his companions adieu, it is with a tribute to the
delight he has taken in their company (*c.* 46. 9 *dulces comitum coetus*), and a reference perhaps to the expected pleasure
of a reunion with them in Italy (*c.* 46. 10–11).

34. But the pain of parting was very insignificant in comparison with the overwhelming joy of home-coming. The exquisite grace of the two sparrow-songs of Catullus (*cc.* 2, 3)
is matched by the most perfect delight that breathes through
the pair of poems (*cc.* 46, 31) that mark the beginning and
the end of his homeward voyage. They stand supreme among
the poems of home that have come down to us from antiquity,
thrilling and quivering with purest and most childlike passion.
With this pair of poems probably belongs a third (*c.* 4), which
followed speedily upon the two others.

35. The third of the triad (*c.* 4) indicates that Catullus
made this return voyage in a small vessel of Amastriac build
purchased by him for this purpose. It almost seems from his
account as if it were built to his order, and that he embarked in

it at Amastris rather than at the seaport of Nicæa. And all this indeed, may be true, in spite of the fact that *c.* 46 apparently speaks of Nicæa as the point of his immediate departure homeward ; for various reasons might be suggested to account for a journey to the eastern part of the province after bidding Nicæa a final farewell.

36. In *c.* 46. 6 the poet speaks of a plan of visiting *claras Asiae urbes* on his return voyage. He seems also to feel some joy at the prospect ; but this is the only passage in his writings that shows any susceptibility to the charm of historic associations connected with the ancient Greek cities. The course of the homeward voyage is but vaguely sketched in *c.* 4, and the only city actually mentioned there as visited on the journey is Rhodes (*c.* 4. 8), though we may infer from *c.* 46 that other famous sites between the Hellespont and Rhodes were not neglected by him. He may even have visited Athens, for his little ship probably was drawn across the Corinthian isthmus by the famous ship-railway instead of braving the dangers of the longer and rougher passage around the Malean cape. Yet no such mention of Athens exists in his writings as would suggest that he had ever visited, or cared to visit, that city. A similar doubt besets the question of his point of debarkation in Italy. If the expressions of *c.* 4 were to be taken literally, we must understand that the *phasellus* carried its master actually up the Po and the little Mincius into the Garda-lake, even to the shores of Sirmio itself. But this is well-nigh impossible; and even if possible, is it likely that the poet, so eager to reach home, would have submitted to the tedium of a tow-boat's voyage (for surely the *phasellus* could not *sail* up the Mincius), when a few hours by post from the mouth of the Po would have brought him to his desired haven? Apparently both the beginning and the end of the voyage of the *phasellus* as recounted in *c.* 4 are not to be interpreted with strict literalness. But the rapturous joy with which Sirmio is saluted in *c.* 31 forbids us to suppose that the poet first visited Rome, and later made his

way northward. Even the gaiety with which the dedicatory inscription of the model of the *phasellus* (*c.* 4) is struck off, — a poem after an entirely new style, — shows that at the time of its composition the first enthusiasm of delight had not yet evaporated.

LATER YEARS. RELATIONS WITH CÆSAR.

37. But even Sirmio could not long detain him from his loved Rome. His reappearance among his old friends is marked by a single poem (*c.* 10), whose gay and charming humor shows that even the vicinity of Lesbia had lost its power constantly to embitter his thoughts. And to the passion for Lesbia now appears to have succeeded that for a boy, Juventius, with the charms of whose company Catullus perhaps attempted to drive out the thoughts of his former love. How the intimacy began we cannot tell. The Juventian *gens* sprang from Tusculum, but inscriptions (C. I. L. vol. V. *passim*) show that people of that name also lived in the neighborhood of Verona. It may be, therefore, that the boy came to Rome under the guardianship of Catullus, as perhaps Catullus, years before, under that of Nepos. But nothing further is known of him beyond what may be inferred from the poems of Catullus that concern him (cf. introductory note to *c.* 15). His history is interwoven with that of a pair of friends, Aurelius and Furius, both at first friends of Catullus, to the former of whom the poet at one time was led to entrust temporarily the care of his ward (*c.* 15). The result might have been anticipated. Juventius learned to prefer them to Catullus, and in consequence Catullus vented his wrath upon them in a group of bitter poems (*cc.* 16, 21, 23, 26), though for Juventius he had only sorrowful remonstrance (*cc.* 24, 81).

38. Yet all this experience appears to have touched him in no wise deeply. It was but a passing diversion, and his jealousy not the bitter passion felt against his rivals with Lesbia. With far more earnestness did he throw himself into the political quarrel of his time. The year of his return from Bithynia

(56 B.C.) had witnessed the so-called renewal of the triumvirate at Luca, and Cæsar appeared to have won everything. In accordance with the agreement made at the Luca conference, Pompey and Crassus were consuls a second time for the year 55, and the senatorial party was at its wits' end. Catullus was apparently not an active political worker, but he did not hesitate to join his political friends in personal attacks upon the foe. Perhaps his earlier shafts were those aimed against Mamurra (cf. § 73), Cæsar's notorious favorite (cc. 29, 41, 43, 57), whom Catullus sometimes celebrates under the nickname of Mentula (cc. 94, 105, 114, 115), and these opened the way for the direct attack upon Cæsar himself (cc. 54, 93). But whatever the order of attack, that Cæsar was piqued by it we know from Suetonius (*Iul.* 73). That he made a successful effort to win over Catullus, as he did Calvus, we are also assured from the same source. Cæsar understood better than most Romans that political power in that city and that day must rest largely upon personal popularity, and he was not above exerting himself to win the good will of individuals of high or low degree. And aside from the fascination due to his great political and military success, he had personal traits that gave him a power over young men. It was the mysterious influence of a natural leader of men ; and in many more than these two instances the number of his friends was recruited from the ranks of the younger of his fiercest foes. There was another element also that must have tended to promote the reconciliation between Cæsar and Catullus. The father of Catullus was resident at Verona within the limits of Cæsar's Cisalpine province. He may not have taken an active part in politics, but at any rate he was a personal friend of Cæsar, and often his host (Suet. *l.c.*). This intimacy may well have led him to see clearly what the result of the approaching struggle for supremacy in Rome was likely to be, and to desire the more eagerly to see his son arrayed for Cæsar and not against him.

39. At all events, the reconciliation was brought about, and the lively pen of Catullus ceased to lampoon the great commander. Some have thought, however, that Mamurra was not included in the peace, and that the utmost Cæsar could effect in his favorite's behalf was that his personality should be there-after thinly veiled under the pseudonym Mentula.

40. But Cæsar was not to profit greatly from his new ally. Up to the end of the year 55 B.C. Catullus displays only hostility to Cæsar and the Cæsarians. The reconciliation apparently took place at the house of the father of Catullus at Verona during the winter visit of the governor to the nearer province in the early part of the year 54 (Cæs. *B. G.* V. 1). The only poem that shows the change of feeling toward Cæsar is *c.* 11, and this is connected with another marked incident in the life of the poet.

41. Catullus was now the friend of Cæsar. The great commander was entertained at his father's house, and perhaps even there was making his plans for future campaigns. The fortunes of the poet were rising. What might he not hope for from his great patron, and why should others not share in his success? Furius and Aurelius, scorned by him since their faithlessness in the matter of Juventius, were eager to crawl back into his favor. And they fancied they could bring him a message that would be joyfully greeted, and would secure them the favorable reception they sought for their own advances: Lesbia was willing to recall her recalcitrant lover. She had once before been successful when making the first advances herself (cf. § 19). Why should she fear defeat now? But both she and her ill-chosen emissaries were speedily undeceived. The broken chain of the old love could never be welded again. Catullus had won by absence, by self-discipline, and most of all, perhaps, by real knowledge of facts in the case, the freedom from his passion for which he had prayed (*c.* 76). He could once more believe in the friendship of Cælius Rufus, and to him acknowledge, with pain, indeed, but no longer with una-vailing torture, his true view of Lesbia's character (*c.* 58). And

these proffers now made to him through, and by, Furius and
Aurelius were definitely and disdainfully rejected (*c.* 11), —
with a manly, not a petulant disdain, for Catullus could not
even then forget that he had loved Lesbia.

42. This manly utterance was almost the last of the poet's
life. A few scattered verses there may have been, closing perhaps with the touching appeal written from Verona (cf. § 56)
to his brother-poet, Cornificius, for a word of consolation, but
that was all; and sometime in the year 54 B.C., in his beloved
Rome, so says the chronicler, the swiftly burning candle of his
life burned itself out.

43. With him died the clearest, if not the richest, poet-voice
ever lifted in Rome. He lacked the lofty grandeur of Lucretius, the polished stateliness of Vergil, the broad sympathies
of Horace. For on the one hand, he was no recluse to be
filled with heavenly visions, and on the other, his personality
was too intense to allow him to cultivate a tolerant spirit. He
delighted in life with a vigorous animal passion. Not without
charm to him was nature in her sylvan aspect (cf. *e.g. e.* 34. 9 ff.),
yet his highest enjoyment was in the life of men. And this life
he did not study, as did Horace, from the standpoint of a
philosopher. Indeed, he did not study it at all, but simply felt
it. For he was not outside of it, but a part of it to the fullest
degree, swayed by its ever-changing emotions. Such a nature
must of necessity ever remain in many essential aspects the
nature of a child. And such was the nature of Catullus
throughout his brief life, — warm in quick affections, hot in
swift hatreds, pulsing with most active red blood.

POEMS.

44. The great majority of his verses — all the most successful of them — are the direct expression of his own heart
at the moment. No poet was ever more unreserved, more
perfectly ingenuous. And yet, such is the facility of his genius
and the excellence of his taste, his verses show no ruggedness

or roughness, but glide along with the utmost ease and swift grace toward their mark. But he was no precisianist in metrics. His hexameters are less perfect and flexible than those of P. Varro or of Lucretius, his elegiacs less harmonious and melting than those of the Augustans, his logaœdics often less melodious than those of Horace. And nevertheless his rhythmical skill suggests constantly that it is the effect of great artfulness.

45. He studied with admiration both the Lesbian and the Alexandrian poets, though it is not easy to determine the precise limits of the influence of either school upon his genius. Part of this difficulty arise: from the meagreness of the remains of these Greek writers that have survived the Middle Ages, and part from the intense fire of his own personality that has metamorphosed into its own likeness all the material that came into contact with it. Even when he is professedly translating Sappho or Callimachus (cf. *cc.* 51, 66), his translation is full of original elements, and is worked out in a personal fashion. He is often Sapphic in his tendency to self-address, and in the warmth and tenderness of his emotions, and often Alexandrian in his liking for episode, for richness of mythological allusion, for striking turns of phrase (cf. especially *cc.* 63, 64, 68⁵ *passim*) ; and yet he is, after all, never other than distinctively Roman.

46. The speech Catullus employs is, as might be expected from what has already been said, the speech of every-day life. It will not be necessary to discuss here its phenomena in detail. It approximates closely in general to the speech of Plautus and Terence and of Cicero's letters, and suggests in some respects that of Petronius and other writers of the Silver Age, abounding as it does in diminutives (for the expression of tenderness, or of scorn, or even without any proper diminutive force), in words of Greek or of provincial extraction, in alliteration and anaphora. Yet in many instances in epic passages, or those of a more elevated tone than the majority of his lyrics, he does not hesitate to employ words and figures that suggest the earlier tragedians rather than the comedians.

47. Cicero, in his later years, professed contempt for the whole tribe of these *poetae noui* (like Catullus and his friends) who had forsaken all the traditions of Ennius (*Or.* 161 ; *Tusc.* III. 45 ; *Att.* VII. 2. 1) ; and Horace mentions Catullus but once, and then with definite disparagement (*Sat.* I. 10. 19) ; but even from these references it may be fairly inferred that the poetry of Catullus was well and acceptably known among his immediate generation of Romans, and had not to wait till the time of the elegiasts for a purely posthumous fame. It was, indeed, not so very long after his death that Cornelius Nepos ventured to rank him in quality alongside Lucretius (*Att.* 12. 4). His fame, then, was contemporary with himself. But even a cursory examination of his extant book of poems shows evidence that it was not published till after the poet's death. For although it has come down to us mutilated by the accidents of time in a most unseemly manner, no mutilation can account for the condition of *c.* 58[b], which is clearly but a rejected trial-sketch for the poem afterward elaborated as *c.* 55, and not a misplaced part of *c.* 55 itself (note the much greater frequency of dactyls in the second place in the verses of *c.* 58[b] than of *c.* 55). Would Catullus himself have published such a mere fragment? Still more, would he after the reconciliation with Julius Cæsar have published, or republished, the poems in which Cæsar is bitterly assailed? For this same reason, if for no other, it is also impossible to suppose, with certain critics, that Catullus himself arranged the book for publication, but was overtaken by death before it was actually published.

48. The only satisfactory hypothesis is that the book was both arranged and published, after the author's death, by some literary friend of his at Rome, where he ordinarily kept his books and papers (cf. *c.* 68. 33–36). The posthumous editor arranged the poems in three general groups. First come sixty shorter poems on various themes, all in iambic or logaœdic rhythms. Then follows the group of longer poems (*cc.* 61–68[b]), introduced by the three epithalamia (*cc.* 61, 62, 64), with their Eros accompanied by the Anteros of *c.* 63 ; this group of poems begins with glyconics (*c.* 61), continues with dactylic hexameters (*cc.* 62, 64), divided by passionate galliambics (*c.* 63), and concludes with elegiacs (*cc.* 65–68[b]). It is followed by a third group of shorter poems (*cc.* 69–116), all in the elegiac metre, but as varied in theme as the first group. This division was suggested entirely by the metres and length of the poems, and not at all by their subject-matter ; for the third group contains poems agreeing in subject and date with others in the first group (cf. *e.g. c.* 99 with *c.* 48, *c.* 81 with *c.* 24, *c.* 93 with *cc.* 29 and 57). Within each group poems on the same or similar themes occasionally stand together (*e.g. cc.* 2 and 3 ; *cc.* 61 and 62 ; *cc.* 88–91 ; *cc.* 110 and 111), but more frequently are divided by one or more poems on another, and often a contrasted theme (cf. *cc.* 5 and 7 ; *cc.* 21 and 23 ; *cc.* 62 and 64 ; *cc.* 69 and 71 ; *cc.* 70 and 72).

49. The editor certainly included one mere fragment (*c.* 58[b]) ; and perhaps more of the poems whose condition we attribute to the neglect of a later age (*e.g. cc.* 2. 11–13 ; 14[b] ; 54 ; 78[b]) may have been published by him in their present form, on account of his anxiety to omit no scrap found among his friend's posthumous papers.

50. Another possibility suggests itself. The editor certainly must have disregarded what would have been the wishes of Catullus in publishing, or republishing, the poems against Cæsar, especially if none had yet been written in his favor. The editor was doubtless one of the circle of literary friends of the poet at Rome, and so was, if not, like Catullus, a subject of sudden conversion, an anti-Cæsarian. Is it possible that he still further used his discretion, and served his own sympathies, by refraining from the publication of later poems favorable to Cæsar, and that by this theory, and not by that of the speedy death of the poet, we are to explain the absence in his works of all poems (except *c.* 11) showing a change of personal, if not of political, feeling? But this question may be reserved for another occasion.

51. It is not to be supposed, however, that all of these poems saw the light for the first time after the death of their author. The manifest point of most of the personal poems would have been utterly lost, had they not been published immediately after their composition, and the passage already cited from Suetonius (*Iul.* 73) shows clearly that Cæsar was acquainted before their author's death with some of the poems directed against him. One poem also (*c.* 16. 12) contains an evident reference to the earlier publication of *c.* 48 (or of *cc.* 5 and 7?). It seems likely, therefore, that many of the poems were published singly, at least among the circle of the poet's friends, while the extant dedication of a *libellus* to Cornelius Nepos suggests that a smaller collection of them was made and published by Catullus himself (cf. introductory note to *c.* 1).

52. Catullus undoubtedly wrote other poems than those included in the extant *liber*, but of the fragments attributed to him by the grammarians some are proved to have been falsely so ascribed, and the few remaining are, even if genuine, so slight as to be insignificant (cf. Commentary on *cc.* 18–21).

MANUSCRIPTS.

53. The popularity enjoyed by Catullus among the Augustan elegiasts did not preserve his memory alive through the declining centuries of the Roman empire. The scholars and poets of the latter half of the first millennium after Christ had forgotten even his name. Only Rather, bishop of Verona, in a sermon delivered there in 965 A.D., confesses that he had just become acquainted with his writings ; and an anthology of Latin poets written at about the same time (now *cod. Thuaneus, Parisinus 8071*) contains a single poem of Catullus (*c.* 62). Then he drops out of ken once more till the opening of the 14th century, when a writer of Vicenza, Benvenuto Campesani (who

died before 1330), celebrated in a few enigmatic verses (cf. Critical Appendix *ad fin.*) the rediscovery of the text of Catullus 'under a bushel,' apparently at Verona. From this MS., or from copies of it, numerous Italian scholars, among them Petrarch, early learned to know the poet. The original MS. soon disappeared, and has never been found ; but two descendants of it, apparently not more than one generation removed, are preserved to us, and form the basis of the present text of Catullus. One of these copies, ordinarily called *G* (now No. 14,137 in the National Library at Paris) was made in the year 1375, and the other, *O* (No. 30 of the Canonici Latin MSS. in the Bodleian Library) at about the same time. (Cf. also introductory note to Critical Appendix.)

54. The earlier editions of Catullus, however, were based upon interpolated MSS., and though displaying great erudition and classical taste left much to be desired in the way of true principles of textual criticism. The edition of Karl Lachmann (Berlin, 1829) first established the text of Catullus upon a scientific basis, though the two MSS. on which he mainly depended, *D* and *L* (in the Royal Library at Berlin), are far inferior to *G* and *O*. These became first known to the world, *G* in 1830 through I. Sillig (*Jahrb. für Philol.* xiii. p. 262 ff.), and *O* through Robinson Ellis in his first edition of Catullus (Oxford, 1867). During the last quarter of a century, then, the constitution as well as the elucidation of the text of Catullus has made its most marked advances.

FRIENDS AND FOES.

55. A few of the persons distinguished by the love or by the hatred of Catullus may conveniently be mentioned here. Some such persons, however, as Cæsar, Cicero, and Clodius, are so well known otherwise to the ordinary reader as to need no biographical notice in a work of this sort. Others, like Lesbia, have been sufficiently noticed in previous paragraphs of this Introduction. Still others are of so little present importance, or are so little known to us outside the mention of them by Catullus, that the brief references to them in the commentary on the individual poems may suffice. The names of all these, with references to the poems in which they are addressed or mentioned, may be found in the Index of Proper Names at the end of this volume.

56. It is a temptation to identify the Alfenus to whom the remonstrance of *c.* 30 is addressed with P. Alfenus Varus, *consul suffectus* 39 B.C., especially if he, in turn, can be identified with the Alfenus Varus who protected Vergil's property at Mantua (*Ecl.* 1, 6, 9), who was perhaps a native of Cremona (though falsely identified by the scholiasts on Horace with *Alfenus uafer* of *Sat.* I. 3. 130). For if Varus was at Cremona during the winter and spring of 55–54 B.C., while Catullus was at Verona (cf. § 40), we perhaps have a key to the difference in tone between *c.* 30 and *c.* 38. From Cornificius at Rome the poet could expect in his growing illness only written comfort, and that is all he asks. Alfenus Varus at Cremona was within easy reaching distance of Verona by a direct highway, the Via Postumia, and might have visited Catullus in person, but did not. Hence the deeper feeling of slight with which Catullus addresses him.

57. The '*Pollio frater*' of *c.* 12. 6 is very likely the only Pollio known to us from this period, C. Asinius, Cn. f. (born 75 B.C., died 5 A.D.), who became prætor in 45 B.C. and consul in 40, in which year he gained a triumph over the Parthini. At first a Cæsarian, he might have been won over to the senatorial party after Cæsar's death, but finally cast in his lot with Antonius, from whom, however, he became alienated, but without entering the circle of the intimate friends of Augustus. As orator, dramatic and lyric poet, historian of the first triumvirate, and literary critic, he gained lasting fame, and is frequently quoted by succeeding writers. Among his intimate friends were Vergil and Horace; cf. Verg. *Ecl.* 3. 84; 4; 8. 6; Hor. *Carm.* II. 1; *Sat.* I. 10. 42, 85.

58. Nothing further is known of the older brother of Pollio addressed in *c.* 12. The family of the Asinii sprang from Teate, the capital of the Marrucini, but it is doubtful whether *Marrucine* in *c.* 12. 1 is simply a distinguishing epithet. C. Asinius Pollio is the first of the family known to bear a cognomen, and perhaps that custom was introduced in his generation, his elder brother taking the cognomen Marrucinus from the seat of the family.

59. The Cælius of *c.* 58 is probably identical with the Cælius of *cc.* 82 and 100, and with the Rufus of *cc.* 69 and 77 (and also *cc.* 73 and 59?), the names and circumstances suggesting M. Cælius Rufus, born, according to Pliny (*N. H.* VII. 165), on the same day with C. Licinius Calvus, May 28, 82 B.C. (though perhaps this date is too late, by a few years, for the birth of Cælius). Cælius is well known as an ambitious politician and an orator (Cic. *Brut.* 79. 273 ; Quint. *Inst.* VI. 3. 69 ; X. 1. 115 ; 2. 25 ; Tac. *Dial.* 18, 21, 25). He was at first a partisan of the optimates ; but after filling the offices of tribune (52 B.C.), quæstor, and curule ædile (50 B.C.), and contracting immense debts by his extravagant life, he became a follower of Cæsar, and was by him made prætor for the year 48. But being shortly thereafter deposed for attempts at revolutionary legislation, he tried to seduce certain of Cæsar's troops, and was finally killed under the walls of Thurii. He was an active and interesting correspondent of Cicero, by whom he was defended (56 B.C.) in the famous speech *pro Caelio* against the charge of attempted poisoning brought by Clodia (Lesbia), whose favored lover he had been. He himself appears to have broken this connection, and perhaps to have opened the eyes of Catullus to Lesbia's real character, after which the friendship was again cemented between him and Catullus which had been severed by their rivalry (cf. §§ 25, 26). The poems addressed to him were apparently written in about the following order : *cc.* 100, 82, 77, (73), 69, (59), 58.

60. C. Licinius Macer Calvus, apparently the most intimate friend of Catullus, was the son of the annalist, Licinius Macer,

and was born May 28, 82 B.C. (cf. Plin. *l.c.*). He died in, or
not very long before, the year 47 B.C. (cf. Cic. *Fam.* XV. 21,
4). He was renowned as a most able and skilful orator,
though of low stature (cf. 53. 5 ; Sen. *Contr.* VII. 4. 7 ; Ov.
Trist. II. 431), and as a writer of epic, lyric, and epigram (cf.
Cic. *Brut.* 279, 283 ; Tac. *Dial.* 18 ; Quint. *Inst.* X. 1. 115 ;
Plin. *Ep.* I. 16. 5 ; Gell. XIX. 9. 7 ; Serv. on Verg. *Ecl.* 6. 47 ;
8. 4). On account of his intimacy with Catullus and the similarity of their political principles (cf. Suet. *Iul.* 73) and of
their writings they are often named together (cf. with above
Hor. *Sat.* I. 10. 19, and indexes to Propertius and Ovid).
The few extant fragments of his works are appended to the
editions of Catullus by Lachmann and L. Müller. The death of
Quintilia, apparently from the tone of *c.* 96 the wife of Calvus,
gave occasion for one of the finest and most touching of the
briefer poems of Catullus.

61. The Cornificius to whom Catullus addressed the pathetic
appeal of *c.* 38 was a poet (cf. vv. 7 and 8), and is doubtless
to be identified with the Cornificius mentioned by Ovid (*Trist.*
II. 436) in connection with other verse-writers of the period of
Catullus. It is not so clear, though quite possible, that he is
the Q. Cornificius to whom Cicero wrote friendly letters (*Fam.*
XII. 17–30), dated between 45 and 43 B.C. This Cornificius
was an active officer of Julius Cæsar, a member of the col-
lege of augurs, and later governor of the province of Africa,
which he endeavored to hold against T. Sextius, the general
of the second triumvirate. His death is mentioned by Jerome
under date of 41 B.C.: *Cornificius poeta a militibus desertus
interiit, quos saepe fugientes 'galeatos lepores' adpellarat.* If
this be the friend of Catullus, he may perhaps be counted as
another of the group of young writers won over by Cæsar from
the ranks of his political foes. His interest and activity in
rhetorical studies are distinctly indicated by Cicero, and there
seems to be no good reason to doubt that he is the *Cornificius
rhetor* not infrequently quoted by Quintilian. With but slightly

less probability may be attributed to him the work on the derivation of the names of the gods ascribed by Macrobius and
Priscian to an author of his name : but the verse in criticism
of a grammatical point in Vergil attributed by Cledonius (V.
43. 2) to Cornificius Gallus may have been written, as some
have thought, by Cornelius Gallus. Only two fragments of the
verses of Cornificius have been preserved, one a hendecasyllabic (Macr. VI. 4. 12), and the other the latter part of a
hexameter from his Glaucus (Macr. VI. 5. 13). They are
appended by L. Müller to his edition of Catullus.

62. The Cato to whom *c.* 56 is addressed was probably not
that pattern of ancient Roman strictness, M. Porcius Cato,
later called Uticensis, but the grammarian, Valerius Cato, who
was a countryman of Catullus (Suet. *Gram.* 11), and whose
amatory poems are mentioned by Ovid (*Trist.* II. 436) in
connection with those of Cinna (cf. § 63), Cornificius (cf.
§ 61), and Anser.

63. C. Helvius Cinna, a companion of Catullus on the staff
of Memmius (cf. *c.* 10. 30 and § 30), whose epic poem, the
Zmyrna, is praised in *c.* 95, was probably the Cæsarian tribune
mistaken for L. Cornelius Cinna, the anti-Cæsarian, in the riots
attending the funeral of Julius Cæsar, and killed by the popu-
lace (Plut. *Brut.* 20, *Iul.* 68 ; Suet. *Iul.* 85 ; cf. Shakspere *Jul.
Cæs.* III. 3). The insignificant extant fragments of his poems
are appended by L. Müller to his edition of Catullus.

64. The Cornelius of *c.* 1. 1 seems to be Cornelius Nepos, the
historian ; witness Ausonius, who says (XXIII. 1–3) ' *Cui . . .
libellum*' *Veronensis ait poeta quondam, inuentoque dedit statim
Nepoti.* Nepos (circ. 94–24 B.C.) was certainly a provincial
from Cisalpine Gaul (Plin. *N. H.* III. 127 *Nepos Padi accola*),
and probably a native of Ticinum (Plin. *Ep.* IV. 28. 1 ;
Mommsen in *Hermes* III. p. 62). His acquaintance with
Catullus, though nothing certain can be traced concerning it,
was doubtless fostered by their similarity of origin (cf. § 12).
Nepos was author not only of the work *De Viris Illustribus*, of

which a part, with lives of Cato and of Atticus, is still extant, but also of other historical works (cf. *c.* 1. 6 n.) and of poems (Plin. *Ep.* V. 3. 6).

65. Q. Hortensius Ortalus (114–50 B.C.), Cicero's greatest rival as an orator, was also somewhat of a historian (Vell. II. 16. 3), and wrote erotic poems (Ov. *Trist.* II. 441 ; Plin. *Ep.* V. 3. 5), which the Greeks at the banquet of Antonius Julianus (Gell. XIX. 9. 7) characterized as *inuenusta*, though they admitted that Catullus and Calvus wrote some verses comparable with those of Anacreon. Presuming, perhaps, upon his own gifts as a poet, Hortensius asked Catullus for a poem (*c.* 65. 18–19), and the poet complied with the request, though with an absence of compliment that indicates no intimate friendship with his petitioner, whose much greater age and high position gave him, however, the power to become an influential patron. That the friendship made no progress seems to be indicated by the uncomplimentary allusion to the verses of Hortensius in *c.* 95. 3 (cf. however § 25 *ad fin.*).

66. The Varus of *c.* 10 is apparently identical with the Varus of *c.* 22, who is a friend of Catullus and a critic of poetry, if not a poet himself. This may well be the distinguished Quintilius Varus, the Augustan critic (Hor. *A. P.* 438 ff.) and poet (Acro and Comm. Cruq. on *l.c.*). He is called a native of Cremona ; and his death in 23 B.C. (according to Jerome) drew from Horace a touching address of sympathy to Vergil (*Carm.* I. 24). Judged from the tone of the passage in the *Ars Poetica*, Quintilius must have been somewhat older than Horace, while yet he could hardly have been born long, if at all, before Catullus. The attempt to identify the Varus of *c.* 10 and *c.* 22 with Alfenus Varus of *c.* 30 is unsatisfactory.

67. The Manlius Torquatus, whose marriage with Vinia Aurunculeia is celebrated in *c.* 61, was perhaps the L. Manlius Torquatus whose father was consul in 65 B.C. (cf. Hor. *Carm.* III. 21. 1 ; Epod. 13. 6), and who was himself prætor in 49. He allied himself with the Pompeians, and was killed in Africa

in 47 (cf. *Bell. Afr.* 96). In 62 B.C. Manlius prosecuted P.
Cornelius Sulla on the charge of conspiracy with Catiline.
Cicero and Hortensius appeared for the defence and secured
an acquittal.   In Cicero's speech on that occasion (*Pro
Sulla*), and especially in his *Brutus* (76. 265), Manlius is
highly praised.

68. A certain Veranius is mentioned in *cc.* 12, 28, and 47
in connection with a Fabullus, evidently an intimate friend of
his, as both were of Catullus.   Beside these three references to
them jointly, *c.* 9 is addressed to Veranius alone, and *c.* 13 to
Fabullus alone, the equal recognition thus scrupulously given
them by Catullus suggesting the existence of a close bond of
intimacy between the two friends.   Nothing more is known of
them than can be gathered from Catullus himself.   Veranius
has in *c.* 9 just returned from a residence in Spain, and in *c.* 12
the presence there of Fabullus also is noted.   The 13th poem,
too, a jesting reference to a prospective dinner offered Fabullus,
appears to have been written while Fabullus was absent some-
where, or had just returned, and may well refer to the same
occasion as *c.* 9, the different tone of the individual poems, one
sportive, and one affectionate, corresponding to characteristic differences in the dispositions of the two friends.   In *cc.*
28 and 47 Veranius and Fabullus have been away from Rome
as members of the retinue of a certain Piso, a provincial governor.   They returned to Rome apparently not long after the
time of the return of Catullus himself from Bithynia (56 B.C.;
cf. § 31 ff.).

69. If, then, there be such a connection as indicated between *cc.* 9 and 13, the absence in Spain cannot have been that
with Piso, and must have preceded it by several years; for the
reference to Lesbia in *c.* 13. 11 clearly antedates the break
of Catullus with her, and that occurred before his journey to
Bithynia.   But it is not incredible that two friends so inti-
mately connected as Veranius and Fabullus should have been
together on more than one journey after fortune; and the

journey to Spain like the later one with Piso (cf. § 70) **may** well have been on the staff of a provincial governor, — probably about 60 B.C., as the reference to Lesbia indicates (cf. *c*. 13. 11 n.).

70. The Piso unfavorably commented upon in *cc*. 28 and 47 (cf. § 68) is probably L. Calpurnius Piso Cæsoninus, consul in 58 B.C. (the year of Cicero's exile), and in 57–55 governor of Macedonia, where he made an honorable record. After his return to Rome in 55 B.C. he attempted to reply to certain strictures of Cicero uttered in his absence, and drew down upon himself the overwhelming invective power of his adversary in the famous speech *In Pisonem*, in which the whole life, character, and actions of Piso were held up to undeserved obloquy.

71. The service of Catullus on the staff of C. Memmius, governor of Bithynia, has already been discussed (§ 29 ff.). Concerning Memmius himself we may add further that neither his political nor his personal character was above reproach. He was in 54 B.C. party to a most barefaced attempt to secure the consulship by bribing the consuls of that year (Cic. *Att*. IV. 18. 2), and was charged with the seduction of the wives of Lucullus (Cic. *Att*. I. 18. 3) and Pompey (Suet. *Gram*. 14). He appears to better advantage as a scholar and the patron of literary men, especially of Lucretius, who dedicated his great poem to him. Cicero (*Brut*. 70. 247) speaks well of his Greek scholarship, and of his ability in oratory, though blaming him for lack of application. Accused of *ambitus* in 53 B.C., on account of the operations of the preceding year, he went into exile in Greece (cf. Cic. *Fam*. XIII. 1), where he died about the year 49.

72. Prominent among the invective poems of Catullus is a group directed against a certain Gellius. This comprises *cc*. 74, 80, 88, 89, 90, 91, 116, but the poems are not arranged in chronological order. Apparently the earliest in composition is *c*. 116, and the second *c*. 91, — the first indicating that Catullus had tried to avert the hostility of Gellius by sending him translations from **Callimachus**, but declaring from that time open war, while the second asserts that Gellius had broken the bond of friendship with Catullus by becoming a lover of Lesbia. In *c.* 80. 1 the youth of Gellius is indicated, and in all the series except *c.* 116 he is charged with various abhorrent crimes. The most acceptable suggestion of his identity was originally made by Pantagathus (†1578), who judged him to be that son of L. Gellius Publicola (consul 72 B.C.) who is said by Valerius Maximus (V. 9. 1) to have been accused before the senate of *in nouercam* (cf. *c.* 88. 1, etc.) *commissum stuprum et parricidium cogitatum.* This younger Gellius was himself consul in 36 B.C., and his age therefore also accords with the intimations of Catullus. The *patruus* of *c.* 74 is identified by some critics with the Gellius Publicola attacked by Cicero in *Pro Sestio* 51. 110, while yet others have supposed, but with no sufficient reason, that this Gellius, and not the one of Valerius Maximus, is the Gellius assailed by Catullus.

73. The attacks of Catullus upon Mamurra have already been mentioned (§ 38). That he is identical with the 'Mentula' of *cc.* 94, 105, 114, and 115 we may be tolerably certain on noting the use of that name for Mamurra in *c.* 29. 13, and on comparing the wealth and extravagance of the two men (*cc.* 114 and 115 with *cc.* 29, 41, and 43), their literary pretensions (*c.* 105 with *c.* 57. 7), and their licentiousness (*cc.* 94 and 115. 7–8 with *cc.* 29. 7–8 and 57). These latter indications, however, but support that of *c.* 29. 13, and would not independently establish the identity.

74. A sufficient biography of Mamurra is given by Pliny (*N. H.* XXXVI. 6. 48), who says he was an *eques* of Formiæ and *praefectus fabrum* of Cæsar in Gaul, and quotes Nepos as authority for the statement that Mamurra first of the Romans incrusted the entire walls of his house on the Cælian with marble, and had within it none but solid marble columns. Cicero, too, mentions Mamurra's ill-gotten wealth (*Att.* VII. 7. 6), and in *Att.* XIII. 52. 1 (written in 45 B.C.) refers to the calm way

in which Cæsar received news of his death (so Nipperdey inter-
prets the allusion). The connection of Mamurra with the provincial Ameana (*cc.* 41, 43) may be assigned to the time when
he was in attendance upon Cæsar in his winter journeys to the
nearer province.

75. The poet Volusius of *cc.* 36 and 95 is probably not to be
identified with Tanusius Geminus, as Muretus and other later
writers would have it. The only ground for such identification
is a remark made by Seneca (*Ep.* 93. 11 *annales Tanusii scis
quam ponderosi sint et quid uocentur*). But of all the names
that appear in Catullus, Lesbia and Lesbius are the only ones
known to be pseudonyms (for Mentula is hardly a name, but an
easily recognized epithet). And the *quid uocentur* of Seneca
may readily refer to some other popular characterization of the
work of the annalist, and not to the *cacata charta* of *c.* 36. 1.

METRES.

The metres employed by Catullus are as follows : —

76. Dactylic Hexameter (*cc.* 62, 64) and Elegiacs (*cc.* 65–
116). The occurrence of spondaic verses is very frequent, and
doubtless is due to Alexandrian influence. In all, there are
42 such verses, of which 34 end in a quadrisyllable. In only
ten instances is this a proper name. In *c.* 64 there is a succession of three spondaic verses (vv. 78–80). — The tendency
to employ a succession of spondees in the same verse is striking. Thus *c.* 116. 3 is made up entirely of spondees, and 71
verses have spondees in the first four places. — The penthe-
mimeral caesura is by far the favorite, though the hephthe-
mimeral occurs occasionally ; and the feminine caesura in the
third foot is not unknown, though it is entirely excluded from
the fourth. — The hexameters end preferably in a dissyllable
or trisyllable, but in the ending of the pentameters greater
freedom is allowed. — Hypermeters are found in *c.* 64. 298
and *c.* 115. 5. On hiatus, see § 86 *d.*

77. Pure Iambic Trimeter (*c.* 4). Perhaps *c.* 29 is in the same metre; but cf. note on *Mamurram* in v. 3.

78. Iambic Trimeter (*c.* 52, and perhaps *c.* 29), with the optional substitution of a spondee for the first iambus of any dipody. The scheme, then, is, —

$$\| \bar{\cup} : \acute{\smile} \cup \_ \bar{\cup} \mid \acute{\smile} \cup \_ \bar{\cup} \mid \acute{\smile} \cup \_ \wedge \|.$$

79. Choliambic or Scazon (*cc.* 8, 22, 31, 37, 39, 44, 59, 60). The scheme is as follows : —

$$\| \bar{\cup} : \acute{\smile} \cup \mid \_ \bar{\cup} \mid \acute{\smile} \cup \mid \_ \cup \mid \acute{\angle} \mid \acute{\smile} \cup \|.$$

Thrice also the thesis is resolved (in *cc.* 22. 19; 37. 5; 59. 3, — unless in *c.* 37. 5 we read cōnfūtūēre as a quadrisyllable).

80. Iambic Tetrameter Catalectic, otherwise called Iambic Septenarius (*c.* 25). The scheme is, —

$$\| \bar{\cup} : \acute{\smile} \cup \mid \_ (\bar{\cup}) \mid \acute{\smile} \cup \mid \_ \bar{\cup} \mid \acute{\smile} \cup \mid \_ \cup \mid \acute{\angle} \mid \_ \wedge \|.$$

81. Phalaecean, often called Hendecasyllabic (*cc.* 1-3, 5-7, 9, 10, 12-16, 21, 23, 24, 26-28, 32, 33, 35, 36, 38, 40-43, 45-50, 53-58[b]). The scheme is, —

$$\| \overset{\acute{\smile}}{\cup} \overset{\bar{\cup}}{\_} \mid \_ \cup \cup \mid \acute{\smile} \cup \mid \_ \cup \mid \acute{\smile} \cup \|.$$

It may be remarked that while the verse most frequently opens with the irrational trochee (as always in Martial), there are nearly seventy exceptions to this rule, and they are about evenly divided between the regular trochaic opening and that with the iambus. The peculiar experiment with this metre tried in *cc.* 55 and 58[b] is noted in the introduction to *c.* 55.

82. Glyconic and Pherecratic series are combined by Catullus as follows : —

a. A second Glyconic catalectic followed by a second Pherecratic acatalectic forms the verse called Priapean, used in *c.* 17. The scheme is, —

$$\| \acute{\smile} \bar{\cup} \mid \_ \cup \cup \mid \acute{\smile} \cup \mid \_ \sqcup \| \acute{\smile} \bar{\cup} \mid \_ \cup \cup \mid \acute{\angle} \mid \_ \wedge \|.$$

The first series in this verse ends with a complete word, and does not allow hiatus after it : elision occurs there four times (vv. 4, 11, 24, 26).

b. The stanza of *c.* 34 is composed of four verses, of which the first three are second Glyconics catalectic, and the fourth a second Pherecratic acatalectic. The stanza of *c.* 61 is similar, but with four, instead of three, Glyconics. The scheme of the Glyconics thus arranged is, —

$$\| \underset{\smile}{\overset{\angle}{}} \underset{\underline{}}{\overset{\gtrless}{}} \mid \neg \smile \smile \mid \underset{\smile}{\angle} \smile \mid \underline{} \underline{} \|,$$

and that of the Pherecratics, —

$$\| \underset{\smile}{\overset{\angle}{}} \underset{\underline{}}{\overset{\gtrless}{}} \mid \neg \smile \smile \mid \underset{\smile}{\angle} \mid \underline{} \wedge \|.$$

Synapheia is observed throughout, as in the Priapean stanza. Once an irrational spondee takes the place of the cyclic dactyl (*c.* 61. 25).

83. GREATER ASCLEPIADIC verses compose *c.* 30. The scheme of each is as follows : —

$$\| \underset{}{\angle} > \mid \neg \smile \smile \mid \underset{}{\angle} \| \neg \smile \smile \mid \underset{}{\angle} \| \neg \smile \smile \mid \underset{\smile}{\angle} \smile \mid \underset{}{\angle} \wedge \|.$$

Contrary to the practice of Horace, caesura is not always observed between the successive series in each verse.

84. The SAPPHIC stanza (*cc.* 11, 51) as used by Catullus has the following scheme : —

$$\text{1. 2. 3} \| \underset{\smile}{\angle} \smile \mid \underline{} (\gtrless) \mid \neg \smile \smile \mid \underline{} \smile \mid \underset{\smile}{\angle} \smile \|$$
$$\text{4} \| \neg \smile \smile \mid \underset{}{\angle} \mid \underline{} \wedge \| \cdot$$

In allowing a trochee thrice in place of the irrational spondee (*cc.* 11. 6 ; 11. 15 ; 51. 13), and in indifference to the caesura. Catullus resembles Sappho more closely than does Horace.

85. In *c.* 63 the GALLIAMBIC verse is used. It is said to have originated as a lesser Ionic tetrameter catalectic, having, therefore, the following scheme : —

$$\| \smile \smile \vdots \underset{}{\angle} \underline{} \smile \smile \mid \underset{}{\angle} \underline{} \smile \smile \mid \underset{}{\angle} \underline{} \smile \smile \mid \underset{}{\boxminus} \overline{\wedge} \|.$$

But as used by Catullus anaclasis always occurs (except in vv

54 and 60?), and the resultant trochees are often, the last almost always, resolved. The scheme may therefore be written as follows (the regularly occurring caesura being indicated by a comma) : —

$$\| \overset{\smile}{\smile} : \overline{\smile\smile} \cup \mid \overline{\smile\smile} \cup \mid \angle \mid \_, \ \overset{\smile}{\smile} \mid \overline{\smile\smile} \cup \mid \overline{\smile\smile} \cup \mid \angle \wedge \|.$$

This scheme is not, to be sure, true to the theory of the Ionic series, but the result of anaclasis (*i.e.* the substitution of di-chorees for Ionics) seems to have been that the metre was treated as trochaic, and the anacrusis, therefore, became of necessity irrational. On no other theory is rhythmical recita-tion of the Galliambics of Catullus possible. The individual schemes of several verses of *c.* 63 are here given as specimens of the application of the general scheme : —

1. $\| \smile : \angle \cup \mid \_ \cup \mid \angle \mid \_, \ \smile \mid \angle \cup \mid \cup \cup \cup \mid \angle \wedge \|$
5. $\| > : \angle \cup \mid \_ \cup \mid \angle \mid \_, \ \smile \mid \angle \cup \mid \cup \cup \cup \mid \angle \wedge \|$
14. $\| \smile : \angle \cup \mid \_ \cup \mid \angle \mid \_, \ \smile \mid \angle \cup \mid \ \_ \cup \ \mid \angle \wedge \|$
18. $\| \smile : \angle \cup \mid \_ \cup \mid \angle \mid \_, \ > \mid \angle \cup \mid \cup \cup \cup \mid \angle \wedge \|$
23. $\| \smile : \cup \cup \cup \mid \_ \cup \mid \angle \mid \_, \ \smile \mid \angle \cup \mid \cup \cup \cup \mid \angle \wedge \|$
27. $\| \smile : \angle \cup \mid \cup \cup \cup \mid \angle \mid \_, \ \smile \mid \angle \cup \mid \cup \cup \cup \mid \angle \wedge \|$
63. $\| \smile : \cup \cup \cup \mid \cup \cup \cup \mid \angle \mid \_, \smile \mid \angle \cup \mid \cup \cup \cup \mid \angle \wedge \|$
91. $\| \smile : \angle \cup \mid \cup \cup \cup \mid \angle \mid \_, \ \smile \mid \cup \cup \cup \mid \_ \cup \mid \angle \wedge \|$
but 54. $\| \smile : \angle \mid \_ \cup \cup \mid \angle \mid \_, \ \ \smile \mid \angle \cup \mid \cup \cup \cup \mid \angle \wedge \|$
and 60. $\| \smile : \angle \cup \mid \_ \cup \mid \angle \mid \_, \ \smile \mid \ \angle \ \mid \_ \cup \cup \mid \angle \wedge \|$

PROSODY.

86. *a.* Catullus was unusually fond of ELISION, admitting it freely under almost every circumstance.

b. On the other hand, he admitted DIAERESIS only five times : *cc.* 2. 13 *soluit;* 61. 53 *soluunt;* 66. 38 *dissoluo;* 66. 74 *euoluam;* 95. 5 *peruoluent.*

c. SYNAERESIS occurs in *cc.* 40. 1 *Rauide;* 55. 10 *Camerium;* 62. 57 *conubium;* 64. 120 *praeoptarit;* 82. 3 *ei.*

d. HIATUS in thesis is found in *cc.* 66. 11 *nouo auctus;* 68. 158 *primo omnia;* 107. 1 *cupido optanti.* In *cc.* 27. 4, 66. 48, and 97. 2, it occurs in the MSS., but not in the emended text here presented. Hiatus in arsis occurs in *cc.* 10. 27 *mane inquii;* 55. 4 *te in;* 97. 1 *di ament;* 114. 6 *domo ipse.*

e. SYSTOLE of final *o* is not uncommon, especially in verbs. In 10. 26 *commodā* (imperative) occurs.

f. DIASTOLE occurs in *cc.* 64. 360 *tepēfaciet,* and 90. 6 *liquē-faciens* (but cf. 68. 29 *tepĕfactet*).

g. In *c.* 116. 8 *dabis* final *s* does not make position with the initial consonant following; and in *c.* 23. 27 the reading of *V, satis beatus,* is probably correct, representing *satis beatu's (i.e. beatus es).* In *cc.* 62. 4, 64. 20, and 66. 11 a final syllable ending in a single consonant is lengthened in thesis before *hymenaeus.* A final syllable ending in a short vowel is thrice lengthened in thesis before a mute followed by *r* (in *cc.* 4. 9, *Propontida trucem;* 4. 18 *impotentia freta;* 29. 4 *ultima Britannia*); and it is noticeable that all these instances occur in pure (?) iambics. A similar syllable is lengthened in thesis before initial *s* followed by a consonant in *cc.* 17. 24 *po'e stolidum;* 22. 12 *modo scurra;* 44. 18 *nefaria scripta;* 63. 53; *gelida stabula;* 64. 186 *nulla spes;* 67. 32 *supposita speculae.* But Catullus is not careful to follow out this rule of position in all cases, any more than he is consistent in instances of systole and diastole, or in such cases as *cc.* 43. 2 *nīgris,* but 68. 63 *nīgro;* and especially 71. 2 *podāgra,* but 71. 6 *podăgra.* In these minor matters he allows himself greater freedom than either Lucretius or the later poets, and the same liberty is seen in the greater matters concerned with his treatment of metres. His graceful command of rhythm was far removed from the fixed formalities adopted by the Augustans.

CATVLLI VERONENSIS
LIBER.

I.

Cui dono lepidum nouum libellum
Arido modo pumice expolitum?

1. A modest dedication to Cornelius. The poem probably served originally as an introduction to a part only of the extant *liber Catulli*. The entire collection is too large, and too varied in contents, to be described by the word *libellus* used in v. 1 (cf. Birt, Antike Buchwesen, pp. 22, 291, 401 ff.). The original *libellus* may have included, as Bentley and others after him have thought, *cc.* 1–60, but more likely was of undeterminable content, being incorporated in the entire *liber* published shortly after the poet's death (cf. Intr. 48, 51). — Metre, Phalaecean.

1–3. With the rhetorical question and answer, cf. 100. 5 *cui faueam potius? Caeli, tibi: nam,* etc.

1. **cui**: see Crit. App. — **dono**: the indicative present with future meaning is sometimes used to express the imminence of decision in questions implying great anxiety or eagerness; cf. 63. 55; Plaut. *Cas.* 384 *compressan palma an porrecta ferio?* Cic. *Att.* XIII. 40 *aduolone an maneo?* Verg. *Aen.* IV. 534 *en quid ago? rursusne procos experiar?* Sen. *Contr.* II. 3 (11). 19 *carnifex dicat, 'agon?'* — **lepidum nouum**: of the external rather than of the internal character of the

book; cf. 22. 6 *noui libri;* 78. 1 *lepidissima coniunx;* Plaut. *Pseud.* 27 *lepidis litteris, lepidis tabellis, lepida conscripta manu;* Stat. *Silu.* IV. 9. 7 *noster [libellus] purpureus nouusque charta;* Mart. IV. 10. 1 *dum nouus est, rasa nec adhuc mihi fronte libellus.* The tone is as if the young author held in his hands his first completed volume, and were charmed by its aspect; of its intrinsic merits he speaks modestly in vv. 8–10. — In 6. 17 *lepidus* refers to the dainty character of the verse itself (cf. Mart. VIII. 3. 19; XI. 20. 9 *lepidos libellos*), and Ausonius evidently understood it in that sense here; Aus. 23. 1–4 '*cui* . . . *libellum' Veronensis ait poeta quondam . . . at nos inlepidum, rudem libellum.* — **libellum**: especially used of a book of poetry, shorter than a prose *liber;* cf. Birt, *l.c.*

2. **arido**: a formal epithet of *pumex;* cf. Plaut. *Aul.* 297 *pumex non aequest aridus quam hic est senex;* Mart. VIII. 72. 2 *morsu pumicis aridi politus.* In 23. 12 ff. horn is mentioned as a typical dry substance. — **pumice**: the ends of the papyrus-roll were rubbed smooth with pumice-stone; cf. 22. 8 n.

Corneli, tibi ; namque tu solebas
Meas esse aliquid putare nugas,
5   Iam tum cum ausus es unus Italorum
Omne aeuum tribus explicare chartis,
Doctis, Iuppiter, et laboriosis !
Quare habe tibi quidquid hoc libelli

3. **Corneli**: *i.e.* Cornelius Nepos;
cf. Intr. 12, 64.— **solebas**: probably in the way of private friendship.

4. **aliquid**, *of some value :* cf.
Cic. *Tusc.* V. 36. 104 *eos esse aliquid
putare ;* Ov. *Fast.* VI. 27 *est aliquid
nupsisse Ioui ;* Prop. V. 7. 1 *sunt
aliquid Manes ;* Juv. 3. 230 *est
aliquid unius sese dominum fecisse
lacertae ;* Vulg. *Gal.* 2. 2 *qui ui-
debantur aliquid esse.* — **nugas**:
short, slight, sportive poems: cf.
Hor. *Sat.* I. 9. 2 *nescio quid medi-
tans nugarum ;* Mart. I. 113. 6 *per
quem perire non licet meis nugis ;*
Aus. 26. 1. 1 *latebat inter nugas
meas libellus ignobilis.*

5. **iam tum cum**, etc.: *i.e.* even
then, at the beginning of my career,
when you were already well known
and engaged on your great work.
The reference is probably not to a
direct mention of Catullus in the
projected book. — **unus Italorum**:
other Romans had written only an-
nalistic histories of their own country, or general histories covering
limited periods.

6. **omne aeuum**: *i.e.* the work
was a history of the world from the
earliest period to his own time, —
probably the (lost) *Chronica* mentioned by Ausonius in *Ep.* 16. 1
*Nepotis Chronica, quasi alios apolo-
gos (nam et ipsa instar sunt fabu-
larum) ad nobilitatem tuam misi.*
The *Chronica* was doubtless a
chronological work like the *An-
nalium Libri III.* of Varro, mentioned by Jerome, and the *Annalis*
of Atticus (cf. Nep. *Att.* 18. 1). —

chartis: single pieces of papyrus
prepared for writing: cf. 22. 6;
Hor. *Ep.* II. 1. 113 *calamum et
chartas et scrinia posco ;* then of
the writings themselves: cf. 36. 1,
20; 68. 46; Hor. *Carm.* IV. 8. 21
si chartae sileant quod bene feceris ;
Mart. V. 26. 2 *aliqua cum iocarer
in charta ;* then of divisions of the
writings, *books,* as here: cf. Q. Ser.
Samm. 721 *tertia namque Titi simul
et centesima Liui charta docet.*

7. **Iuppiter**: with this use as
an expletive, like *edepol, ecastor,
mehercule, medius fidius,* etc., cf.
66. 30; Plaut. *Merc.* 865 *Iuppiter,
estne illic Charinus ? Aul.* 241 *sed
pro Iuppiter, num ego disperii ?*
Ter. *Ad.* 757 *o Iuppiter, hancine
uitam !*

8. **habe tibi**: an expression of
the conveyance of rights in property,
to the formal effect of which the
preceding **quare** contributes: cf.
the formula of divorce quoted from
the Twelve Tables in Plaut. *Trin.*
266 *tuas res tibi habeto ;* Mart. X.
51. 16 *quae tua sunt, tibi habe ;
quae mea, redde mihi ;* Plaut.
Bacch. 1142 *si quam debes, te con-
dono ; tibi habe ;* Ter. *Phor.* 435 *te
oblectet ; tibi habe.* The familiarity
of the traditional order of the words
in these formulae may have given
rise to the unmetrical *tibi habe* of
V.— **quidquid . . . qualecumque**:
said with modest self-depreciation;
quare habe tibi, 'so take it,' **quidquid hoc libelli,** ''tis all thine,' **qualecumque,** 'such as it is.' With
quidquid hoc libelli as a quantita-

Qualecumque, quod, o patrona uirgo,
10   Plus uno maneat perenne saeclo.

2.

Passer, deliciae meae puellae,
Quicum ludere, quem in sinu tenere,

tive expression, cf. 31. 14; 37. 4 (like
quantum with a genitive in 3. 2;
9. 10); Liv. XXIII. 9 *iurantes per
quidquid deorum est;* Hor. *Epod.*
5. 1 *at o deorum quidquid in caelo
regit;* Sat. I. 6. 1 *Lydorum quidquid Etruscos incoluit fines, nemo
generosior est te;* Verg. *Aen.* I. 78
*tu mihi quodcumque hoc regni con-
cilias;* Tib. II. 2. 15 *gemmarum
quidquid felicibus Indis nascitur.*—
Est is to be supplied with **hoc** (cf.
Verg. *l.c.*), and then the **quidquid**
clause is modified by **qualecumque**
directly, in a politely deprecatory
tone: cf. Hor. *Sat.* I. 10. 88 *quibus
haec, sunt qualiacumque, adridere
uelim.*

9. **patrona uirgo**: the muse of
lyric poetry, to whom, as one of the
guardians of song, the poet prays
for the long life of his book: cf.
Suet. *Gram.* 6 *scriptores ac poetae sub clientela sunt Musarum;*
Sulpicia 11 *precibus descende clientis
et audi.* With **uirgo**, of the Muse,
cf. 65. 2; Prop. III. 30. 33 *nec tu
uirginibus reuerentia moueris ora.*
But some critics, with Guarinus, understand the reference of Pallas.

10. **plus uno saeclo**: a modest
statement of an indefinite extent of
time: cf. Hor. *Carm.* I. 32. 2 *quod
et hunc in annum uiuat et plures.*
With the modest prayer of Catullus
for abiding fame, cf. the proud reli-
ance of Horace upon the judgment
of his patron (*Carm.* I. 1. *fin.*),
and, later, his assurance of immortality (*Carm.* III. 30).

2. The poet envies Lesbia's pet
sparrow. — This poem appears to
date from the heyday of Catullus'
connection with Lesbia (cf. 3. 3 n.),
concerning whose identity, see Intr.
27 ff. — Metre, Phalaecean.

1. **passer**: the occurrence of
this word and its diminutive as pet
names in the works of Plautus shows
that even much earlier than this the
Romans were accustomed to make
pets of sparrows: cf. Plaut. *Cas.* I.
50 *meus pullus passer; As.* III. 3.
74 *dic igitur me tuum passerculum.*
Other names of birds are used in
the same way (cf. *ll. cc.*), and other
birds are mentioned as pets; cf. 68.
125 (*columbus*); Plaut. *Capt.* 1002
(*monedula, anas, coturnix*); Ov.
Am. II. 6. 1 *psittacus . . . occidit;*
Stat. *Silu.* II. 4. 1 *psittace . . . domini facunda uoluptas;* Mart. I. 7.
1 *Stellae delicium mei columba* (cf.
VII. 14. 5); XIV. 73 (*psittacus*);
XIV. 74 (*coruus*); XIV. 75 (*lusci-
nia*) ; XIV. 76 (*pica*), etc. The
sparrow was sacred to Aphrodite,
according to Sappho, and so an
especially fitting pet for Lesbia. —
deliciae: of a living object of endearment; cf. 6. 1; 32. 2; and
the repetition of this verse, 3. 4.
Elsewhere in Catullus *deliciae* is
used of inanimate objects (69. 4)
and of acts of endearment (45. 24;
68. 26; 74. 2). — **meae puellae**:
cf. 3. 3 n.

2. **quicum**: for *qui* as ablative
of the relative pronoun cf. 66. 77;
69. 8; 116. 3; and for the same

Cui primum digitum dare adpetenti
Et acris solet incitare morsus,
5   Cum desiderio meo nitenti
Carum nescio quid libet iocari
(Et solaciolum sui doloris,
Credo, ut tum grauis adquiescat ardor),

form as interrogative 67. 17 ; 72. 7.
— in sinu tenere, etc. : pressing
the sparrow to her bosom with one
hand, she holds him confined while
teasing him with, and provoking
him to peck at the extended forefinger of the other hand.

3. primum digitum, *finger-tip.*
— adpetenti : in hostile attack; cf.
Plaut. *Cist.* 208 *ita me amor . . .
agit adpetit raptat;* Tac. *Hist.*
IV. 42 *adpetitum morsu Pisonis
caput.*

5. desiderio : first of a passionate desire for something once enjoyed (cf. 96. 3; Hor. *Carm.* I.
24. 1 *quis desiderio sit pudor*), and
then of the object of desire (cf.
Hor. *Carm.* I. 14. 18 [*nauis*] *nunc
desiderium curaque non leuis*).
From this point the transition is
easy to a mere pet name, as here;
cf. Cic. *Fam.* XIV. 2. 2 *Hem, mea
lux, meum desiderium;* Petr. 139
tu, desiderium meum.— niteni :
of seductive beauty: cf. 61. 193;
Hor. *Carm.* I. 5. 12 *miseri, quibus
intemptata nites;* Prop. I. 2. 6
*sinere in propriis membra nitere
bonis.*

6. carum : here an almost color-
less word, somewhat as the Homeric
φίλον often is. It modifies nescio
quid, the object of iocari, which
takes this less marked sort of a cognate accusative; cf. Cic. *Fam.* IX.
14. 4 *haec enim iocatus sum;* Hor.
Sat. I. 5. 62 *in faciem permulta
iocatus.* The infinitive-phrase is
then the subject of libet.

7. et solaciolum : the general
sense is, ' My love in playing with
her sparrow finds amusement, — yes,
and comfort, too, for by this means
she stills the torturing flames of her
passion.' The play with the sparrow
is indulged in both for its own sake
and as a distraction from fiercer
passion. Vv. 7 and 8 contain,
therefore, a sort of rhetorical after-
thought, and may properly be considered parenthetical; and while a
noun could not stand directly as the
subject of libet, solaciolum may
yet, by virtue of the remote character of its modification in the after-
thought, be allowed as an appositive to the subject. See Crit. App.
— doloris : here used of the pain of
love-longing: cf. 50. 17 ; Ov. *Art.
Am.* II. 519 *litore quot conchae, tot
sunt in amore dolores;* Prop. IV.
20. 27 *quicumque solent in amore
dolores.*

8. ut tum : the constant confusion of *t* and *c* in the MSS. makes
entirely probable the emendation
of *cum* of *V* to tum. The *ut*-
clause carries on with specification
the sol. sui dol. of v. 7, the repetition being made less tautological by
the emphasis laid upon grauis; cf.
10. 7, 8, and 96. 3, 4, where there
are similar explications of preceding phrases. — grauis : cf. Prop.
IV. 21. 2 *ut me longa graui
soluat amore uia.* — ardor : the
fire of love; cf. 35. 15; 45. 16;
64. 93; 100. 7; and often in the
poets.

Tecum ludere sicut ipsa possem₁
10   Et tristis animi leuare curas!

•   •   •   •   •   •   •

Tam gratum est mihi quam ferunt puellae
Pernici aureolum fuisse malum,
Quod zonam soluit diu ligatam.

9. **ipsa**: this demonstrative is
sometimes used with even a more
remote reference, so that it is
equivalent to some such word as
dominus (cf. 64. 43 n.), but the
reference to *puellae* v. 1 is here
more immediate. — **possem**: op-
tative of ungratified wish.

10. **tristis animi curas**: of the
painful passion of love, as v. 7 *doloris ;* cf. 64. 72, 95; 68. 18; Hor.
Epod. 2. 37 *quas amor curas habet.*
With **animi** modifying **curas** cf. 64.
372 *animi amores ;* 68. 26 *delicias
animi ;* 102. 2 *fides animi.*

Some critics have judged that vv.
1–10 form a complete whole, or
that, at any rate, vv. 11–13 are the
conclusion of some other poem and
not of this (cf. Crit. App.). But
there seems to be no good reason
to doubt that the poem is not concluded with v. 10, while a study of
65 shows how naturally such a picture
as that of vv. 11–13 may conclude a
poem of warm emotion. Yet the
change of mood from **possem** (v.
9) to **est** (v. 11) makes it probable
that a lacuna exists here, though
perhaps of only a single verse, containing in the form of an infinitive-phrase some repetition of the

thought in **tecum ludere sicut
ipsa.**

11. **quam**, etc.: the comparison
is, of course, a limited one, extending only to the delight Atalanta
took in securing the apple. — **puellae pernici**: for the familiar story
of the victory of Hippomenes (or
Milanion) over the beautiful Atalanta in the foot-race by the help
of Aphrodite's golden apples, cf.
Apollod. III. 9. 2; Ov. *Met.* X.
560 ff.; Hygin. *Fab.* 185. Catullus
means us to understand, as does
Ovid (*Met.* X. 610 ff.), that not
only was the beautiful apple attractive to Atalanta, but she herself was not altogether unwilling
to be beaten.

12. **malum**: cf. 65. 19 n.

13. **zonam**: for similar reference see 61. 52; 67. 28; and cf.
Paul. Fest. p. 63 *cingulo noua nupta
praecingebatur, quod uir in lecto
soluebat, factum ex lana ouis.* The
figure is as old as Homer; cf. *Od.*
XI. 245. — **soluit**: on the diaeresis
see Intr. 86 *b.* — **diu ligatam**:
since she had long refused to marry;
cf. *Anth. Lat.* 1704. 48 Mey. *te uocant prece uirgines pudicae zonulam
ut soluas diu ligatam.*

3.

Lugete, o Veneres Cupidinesque
Et quantum est hominum uenustiorum !
Passer mortuus est meae puellae,
Passer, deliciae meae puellae,

3. The poet mourns the death of Lesbia's sparrow. — This daintiest of poems, a charming combination of gentle grace and half-smiling sympathy for the sorrow of the mistress, expressed under the outer form of pity for the fate of the sparrow, is a fit companion-piece to 2, and must be referred to the same period in the author's life. For imitations of this lament over the death of a pet, see the poems from Ovid, Statius, and Martial cited in note on 2. 1, and add the curious *titulus sepulcralis* of a pet dog in Wilmann's *Exempla Inscr. Lat.* 584. — Metre, Phalaecean.

1. **Veneres**: the plural is to be explained partly, perhaps, as an instance of a sort of attraction to the number of **Cupidines**, as Ellis and Schulze think (cf. 13. 12 with 36. 3), but more as resulting from the conception of the character of Venus and of Lesbia. In the type of Venus were summed up all graces and charms of mind and body. Lesbia was attractive for mental as well as for physical endowments (cf. 36 and 86); she therefore possessed *omnes Veneres* (86. 6); and Catullus calls upon all to share her sorrow who by the possession of similar characteristics (**quantum est hom. uen.**) can sympathize with her loss. Cf. Mart. IX. 11. 9; XI. 13. 6 *Veneres Cupidinesque.* — **Cupidines**: the conception already familiar to the Greeks of more than one Ἔρως is here extended to the

Latin tongue; cf. Hor. *Carm.* I. 19. 1; IV. 1. 5 *mater saeua Cupidinum ;* Ov. *Am.* III. 15. 1 *tenerorum mater Amorum ; Fast.* IV. 1 *geminorum mater Amorum.*

2. **quantum**, etc.: cf. 1. 8 n. *quidquid hoc libelli.* — **uenustiorum** : on the meaning see note on v. 1 *Veneres,* and cf. 13. 6; 22. 2. So far as there is any comparative idea in the word, it is that of comparison, not with other *homines uenusti,* but with other *homines,* ' and all ye men of any degree of grace.'

3. **meae puellae**: undoubtedly the Lesbia of the other poems : (1) so Martial thought (cf. VII. 14. 3 *plorauit amica Catulli Lesbia, nequitiis passeris orba sui ;* XIV. 77 *qualem dilecta Catullo Lesbia plorabat*), though Juvenal follows Catullus in mentioning no name (Juv. 6. 7 *nec tibi, cuius turbauit nitidos exstinctus passer ocellos*) ; (2) in the few other places where Catullus speaks of *his* 'puella,' no other than Lesbia is indicated (cf. 11. 15; 13. 11; 36. 2 ; 37. 11) ; (3) stronger than all other proof is the internal evidence from the poems themselves, for Catullus surely loved but one woman, and spoke of no other in words of such pure, tender, and all-absorbing passion as in 2 and 3.

4. The initial epanalepsis gives the mournfully iterative tone of a dirge, while the identity of v. 4 with 2. 1 connects the two poems skilfully, and heightens the effect of each by contrast with the other.

5   Quem plus illa oculis suis amabat;
    Nam mellitus erat, suamque norat
    Ipsa tam bene quam puella matrem,
    Nec sese a gremio illius mouebat,
    Sed circumsiliens modo huc modo illuc
10 Ad solam dominam usque pipiabat.
    Qui nunc it per iter tenebricosum
    Illuc unde negant redire quemquam.

5. **plus oculis suis amabat**: cf. 14. 1 *plus oculis meis amarem;* and similar expressions, 82. 2, 4 *carius oculis;* 104. 2 *carior oculis:* Shakspere, *Lear* I. 1 *I love you . . . dearer than eyesight.* Although the figure in *plus oculis amare* is not common in Latin, Terence uses twice the same expression (*Ad.* 701 *magis te quam oculos nunc ego amo meos;* 903 *qui te amat plus quam hosce oculos*), and so it is not altogether due to Alexandrian influence.

6. **mellitus**: Catullus uses this word in but two other places (48. 1; 99. 1), once of the kissable eyes of Juventius and once of the boy himself, so that it is seen to be with him exclusively a term of endearment; Plautus uses it but once, and in that sense (*Pseud.* 180 *quibus uitae estis, quibus . . . mammillae mellitae*); Cicero uses it but once, and in that sense (*Att.* I. 18. 1 *cum . . . mellito Cicerone*); while in Varro it appears first in the literal sense (*R. R.* III. 16. 22 *melliti faui*), as it does later in Horace (*Ep.* I. 10. 11 *pane egeo iam mellitis potiore placentis*) ; Plautus also twice uses the diminutive *mellitulus.* — **suam**: *puellam* is to be supplied from the genitives of the preceding verses, as shown by the *puella* of v. 7; cf. Tib. I. 4. 75 *pareat ille suae* (where *coniunx* has preceded) ; II. 5. 103 *nam ferus ille*

suae plorabat sobrius idem (where *puellae* has preceded).

7. **ipsa**: modifying **puella**, with a reference back to **suam**. — **puella**: *i.e.* Lesbia.

8. **illius**: with short penult, as always in Catullus in the case of this and similar genitives, with the exception of 67. 23 *illīus*.

9. **modo huc modo illuc**: cf. 15. 7; 50. 5 *modo hoc modo illoc;* 68. 133 *hinc illinc;* Sen. *Apoc.* 9 *modo huc modo illuc cursabat;* Cic. *Att.* XIII. 25. 3 *o Academiam uolaticam . . . modo huc modo illuc!*

11. **tenebricosum**: an unusual, though Ciceronian, word for the poetical *tenebrosum.* On the conception of the shadowy journey to Orcus, cf. v. 13 *tenebrae Orci;* Hor. *Carm.* IV. 2. 22 *nigro Orco;* Verg. *Geor.* III. 551 *Stygiis emissa tenebris;* Prop. V. 9. 41 *Stygias tenebras;* Ov. *Met.* V. 359 *tenebrosa sede tyrannus exierat;* I. 113 *tenebrosa in Tartara;* Calp. *Buc.* I. 52 *omnia Tartareo subigentur carcere bella immergentque caput tenebris.*

12. **unde**, etc.: quoted by Seneca (*Apoc.* 11 *fin.*) and imitated in *Anth. Lat.* 1704. 11 Mey. [*domus Auerni*] *unde fata negant redire quemquam.* The conception is thoroughly Greek, but from this time becomes common in Latin literature; cf. Verg. *Aen.* VI. 425 *ripam irremeabilis undae;* Hor. *Carm.* II. 3

At uobis male sit, malae tenebrae
Orci, quae omnia bella deuoratis ;
15   Tam bellum mihi passerem abstulistis.
O factum male ! io miselle passer !
Tua nunc opera meae puellae
Flendo turgiduli rubent ocelli.

27 *in aeternum exsilium ;* Prop. V.
11. 2 *panditur ad nullas ianua
nigra preces;* Shaksp. *Ham.* III. 1
*the undiscover'd country from whose
bourn no traveler returns.*

13. **at:** very rarely used in im-
precations in prose; but cf. 27. 5;
28. 14; 36. 18; Plaut. *Most.* 38 *at
te Iuppiter dique omnes perdant!*
Ter. *Eun.* 431 *at te di perdant;*
Hor. *Sat.* II. 6. 54 *at omnes di exa-
gitent me;* Verg. *Aen.* II. 535 *at
tibi pro scelere . . . di . . . praemia
reddant debita.* — **male sit:** cf. Cic.
Att. XV. 15. 1 *L. Antonio male sit!*
Phaedr. *App.* I. 21. 11 *at male tibi
sit!* For indicatives with *male* and
a dative see 14. 10; 38. 1. — **malae:**
observe the effect of the repetition
of **malae** after **male**, and below of
bellum after **bella**.

14. **Orci:** here not the god of
the under-world, as in Hor. *Carm.*
II. 18. 34 *satelles Orci;* but the
under-world itself, as in Hor. *Carm.*
IV. 2. 22 *mores aureos . . . nigro
inuidet Orco.* **tenebrae Orci** is,
then, equivalent to *tenebrosus Orcus;* cf. v. 11 n. — **devoratis:** Orcus
is ravenous ; cf. Hor. *Carm.* II. 18.
30 *rapacis Orci.*

15. **mihi:** another graceful touch
of tender sympathy; the grief suffered by Lesbia is Catullus' own
grief. — **abstulistis:** of removal by
violence; cf. 62. 32; 101. 5.

16. **o factum male :** cf. Ter.
Phor. 751 *male factum !* Cic. *Att.*
XV. 1a. 1 *o factum male de Alexi-*

one ! (in both instances of death);
and the inscription cited in the
introductory note to this poem,
Wilm. *Ex. Inscr. Lat.* 584. 4 *o
factum male, Myia, quod peristi !*
— **io:** an interjection expressing
deeper emotion than *o*, whether of
joy (cf. 61 *passim*), or of sorrow
(as here). — **miselle:** a colloquial
word from Plautus down, used by
Cicero only in his letters; especially
used of the dead ; cf. Tertull. *Test.
An.* 4 *cum alicuius defuncti recor-
daris, misellum uocas eum.*

17. The poem ends with the
graceful turning of sympathy back
from the dead sparrow to the sor-
rowing mistress, who is the chief
object of the poet's thought. — **tua
opera:** with gentle reproach, as if
the sparrow were responsible for
causing his tender mistress so much
pain; cf. Ter. *Andr.* 689 *sicin me
atque illam opera tua nunc miseros
sollicitari !*

18. In spite of his fondness for
diminutives, only twice elsewhere
does Catullus use the diminutive
form of both noun and adjective;
25. 2 *imula auricilla;* 64. 316 *aridulis labellis.* The complaint about
disfigurement of the eyes is especially fitting, since one of Clodia's
chief charms was her brilliant eyes;
cf. Cic. *Att.* II. 14. 1 *de conloquio
βοώπιδος ; Cael.* 20. 49 *flagrantia
oculorum ; Har. Resp.* 18. 38 *hos
flagrantis* [*oculos*] ; all references
to Clodia.

4.

Phasellus ille, quem uidetis, hospites,
Ait fuisse nauium celerrimus,
Neque ullius natantis impetum trabis
Nequisse praeterire, siue palmulis
5   Opus foret uolare siue linteo.
Et hoc negat minacis Hadriatici

4. A dedicatory inscription. —
On the return of Catullus from
Bithynia in 56 B.C. (see Intr. 33 ff.)
to his dearly loved home at Sirmio,
he suspended as a votive offering in a
shrine on his own property a model
of the yacht that had brought him
safely through his perils by sea,
and this poem is in the form of
a dedicatory inscription appended
thereto. It is needless, not to say
impossible, to suppose, as some
have done, that the actual yacht
was brought up the Po and the
Mincio, or by an overland route,
and beached in the Lago di Garda,
but the votive model is spoken of
as if the experiences of its prototype
were its own. (For a strong pre-
sentation of a different interpretation
of the poem cf. C. L. Smith in *Harvard Studies in Classical Philology*,
vol. III., p. 75.) Two other poems,
46 and 31, speak respectively of
the beginning and end of the homeward journey. A parody is found
in Verg. *Catal.* 8, and a number of
interesting parallels in the address
of Ovid on the vessel that carried
him into exile (*Trist.* I. 10). —
Metre, pure iambic trimeter.

   1. **phasellus**: a small and light
sail-boat, but large enough for cruis-
ing; cf. Hor. *Carm.* III. 2. 28 *ue-
tabo fragilem mecum soluat phase-
lon;* Verg. *Geor.* IV. 289 *circum
pictis uehitur sua rura phaselis.* —

quem uidetis: *sc.* in effigy. — **hospites** : the principal visitors at this
private shrine would be guests of
the master of the estate.

   2. **celerrimus**: an instance of
so-called attraction in case, more
common in Greek than in Latin,
but not so rare in the Augustan age
(especially in Ovid) and later ; cf.
Hor. *Ep.* I. 7. 22 *uir bonus et sapi-
ens dignis ait esse paratus.* The
adjective here is also attracted from
the gender of **nauium** into that of
phasellus; cf. Hor. *Sat.* I. 9. 4 *dul-
cissime rerum.*

   3. **neque . . . nequisse** : cf.
below *negat . . . negare.* — **trabis** :
a ship, as is made plain by **natantis** : cf. Verg. *Aen.* III. 191 *uastum
caua trabe currimus aequor ;* Hor.
Carm. I. 1. 13 *ut trabe Cypria Myr-
toum secet mare.*

   4. **palmulis** : cf. Fest. 220 Müll.
*palmulae appellantur remi a simi-
litudine manus humanae ;* Verg.
Aen. V. 163 *laeuas stringat sine
palmula cautes ;* also 64. 7 *palmis.*

   5. **uolare** : of the swift, skimming
motion of the ship : cf. 46. 6 ; Enn.
Ann. 379 Vahl. *uolat super impetus
undas ;* Verg. *Geor.* II. 41 *pelago
uolans da uela patenti ;* Ov. *Her.* 6.
66 *illa uolat, uentus concaua uela
tenet.*

   6 ff. Catullus retraces the course
of his homeward journey. — **hoc** :
object of **negare**, referring to the

Negare litus insulasue Cycladas
Rhodumque nobilem horridamque Thraciam
Propontida trucemue Ponticum sinum,
10   Vbi iste post phasellus antea fuit
Comata silua : nam Cytorio in iugo
Loquente saepe sibilum edidit coma.
Amastri Pontica et Cytore buxifer,
Tibi haec fuisse et esse cognitissima

goo̊d record of the ship just cited.
— minacis Hadriatici : a sea proverbially stormy; cf. Hor. *Carm.* I.
33. 15 *fretis acrior Hadriae;* III.
3. 5 *Auster, dux inquieti turbidus
Hadriae;* III. 9. 22 *improbo ira-
cundior Hadria.* The proper adjective is here used absolutely.

7. **insulas Cycladas** : a place of
danger to the mariner ; cf. Hor.
Carm. I. 14. 19 *interfusa nitentes
uites aequora Cycladas.*

8. **Rhodum nobilem** : in more
ancient times the island, with its
commanding position and excellent
harbor, had been a place of much
commercial importance, and now its
friendship with Rome, its delightful
climate, and the residence there of
distinguished teachers of philosophy and rhetoric had attracted
large numbers of Romans; cf. Hor.
Carm. I. 7. 1 (and Mart. IV. 55. 6)
claram Rhodon. — **horridam Propontida** : another sea of bad reputation among sailors; cf. the early
stories of the cruise of the Argo, and
Val. Flac. *Arg.* II. 645 *me fremens
tumido circumfluat ore Propontis;*
also of the adjacent strait, Hor.
Carm. III. 4. 30 *insanientem nauita Bosporum temptabo.* On the
lengthening of the final syllable, see
Intr. 86 *g.*

9. **trucem Ponticum sinum** :
cf. Ovid's account of the inhospita-
ble sea in *Trist.* IV. 4. 56-60.

10. **post** : a construction of adverb
with substantive common enough in
Greek, but very rare in earlier Latin,
though rather more frequent from
the Augustan age down.

11. **comata silua** : the figure is
as old as Homer ; cf. *Od.* XXIII.
195 ἀπέκοψα κόμην τανυφύλλου
ἐλαίης ; Hor. *Carm.* IV. 3. 11 *spis-
sae nemorum comae;* Verg. *Aen.*
VII. 60 *laurus sacra comam ser-
uata;* Prop. IV. 16. 28 *me tegat
arborea deuia terra coma;* Tib. I.
7. 34 *uiridem dura caedere falce
comam.* But *silua* of a single tree,
as apparently here, is a rare use.

12. **loquente coma** : cf. the sim-
pler and better figure in Verg. *Ecl.*
8. 22 *Maenalus pinos loquentes semper habet.*

13. **Amastri** : the city of Amastris, so named from its founder, the
wife of Dionysius, tyrant of the
Pontic Heraclea, was situated on
the Paphlagonian coast of the
Euxine Sea, not far from Mt. Cytorus, and on the site of the Homeric
city of Sesamus (*Il.* II. 853). The
younger Pliny praises its beauty
(*Trai.* 98). — **Cytore buxifer** : cf.
Verg. *Geor.* II. 437 *iuuat undan-
tem buxo spectare Cytorum.* The
adjective is ἅπαξ λεγόμενον.

14. **tibi** : Catullus combines Amastris and Cytorus in a single idea,
perhaps thinking of the city as built
on the mountain; cf. v. 18 n.

15 Ait phasellus; ultima ex origine
    Tuo stetisse dicit in cacumine,
    Tuo imbuisse palmulas in aequore,
    Et inde tot per impotentia freta
    Erum tulisse, laeua siue dextera
20 Vocaret aura, siue utrumque Iuppiter
    Simul secundus incidisset in pedem;
    Neque ulla uota litoralibus diis
    Sibi esse facta, cum ueniret a mari

16. **stetisse**: *i.e.* when a tree;
imbuisse: *i.e.* when a ship. The
course of the ship is now traced
again, but in the original direction,
from Cytorus to Sirmio.

18. **inde**: perhaps a case of poetic freedom with fact, for Catullus
was more likely to start on his
homeward journey from Nicaea (cf.
46. 5), and not from the extreme
eastern boundary of the province;
but cf. Intr. 35. — **impotentia**:
lacking self-control, *raging;* cf. 35.
12; Ter. *Andr.* 879 *adeo impotenti
esse animo;* Hor. *Carm.* III. 30. 3
Aquilo impotens. On the lengthening of the final syllable, see Intr.
86 *g.*

19. **erum**: Catullus himself. —
laeua siue dextera, etc.: whether
the wind was on the starboard or
port quarter or dead astern, it made
no difference to the craft, which
sailed straight ahead.

20. **uocaret aura**: the fair wind
'invites' the vessel to pursue its
course with hopes of a prosperous
voyage; cf. Verg. *Aen.* III. 70 *lenis
crepitans uocat Auster in altum;*
III. 357 *aurae uela uocant;* Ov.
Her. 13. 9 *qui tua uela uocaret uentus erat;* and for the converse, Verg.
Aen. IV. 417 *uocat iam carbasus
auras.* — **Iuppiter**: here = *aura;*
cf. Ov. *Met.* II. 377 *nec se* [*cycnus*]
caeloque Iouique credit.

21. **pedem**: the *pedes* (Gr. πόδες)
were the sheets, or ropes attached
one to each of the lower corners of
the square sail, whence they were
carried aft and belayed at either rail.
They were used to stretch the sail
taut, so as to secure the full effect
of the breeze. The *pedes* here stand
for the two halves of the sail itself,
and that was evenly filled only when
the vessel was sailing before the
wind; cf. Cic. *Att.* XVI. 6 *utrumque*
[*sinum*] *pedibus aequis transmisi-
mus;* Ov. *Fast.* III. 565 *nancta ratem pede labitur aequo.*

22. **neque**, etc.: not that the
vessel scorned the gods and their
power (cf. vv. 26, 27), but her sea-
worthiness kept her out of positions
of danger where appeals to them
were necessary. — **litoralibus diis**:
vows were made by sailors to Neptune, to Castor and Pollux, and to
Venus Marina (Hor. *Carm.* I. 5. 13
ff.; I. 3. 1, 2; IV. 11. 15), as well
as to lesser divinities; cf. Verg.
Geor. I. 436 *uotaque seruati soluent
in litore nautae Glauco et Panopeae
et Inoo Melicertae.*

23. **sibi**: dative of agent with
the perfect participle, as in 22. 4;
35. 18, etc. — **a mari nouissimo,**
from the most distant sea; cf. Ov.
Trist. III. 13. 27 *terrarum pars
paene nouissima, Pontus;* Tac. *Agr*
10 *oram nouissimi maris.*

Nouissimo hunc ad usque limpidum **lacum.**

25   Sed haec prius fuere : nunc recondita
     Senet quiete seque dedicat tibi,
     Gemelle Castor et gemelle Castoris.

5.

Viuamus, mea Lesbia, atque amemus,
Rumoresque senum seueriorum

24. limpidum lacum: *i.e.* the *lacus Benacus* (Lago di Garda), into the broader, southern end of which projects the peninsula of Sirmio (cf. 31), now Sermione, where stood the villa of Catullus. In the epithet is a thought of the contrast between the dark and turbulent sea over which the journey had been, and the beautifully blue and clear waters of the quiet lake.

25. sed haec prius fuere: *i.e.* all toil and danger has now become but a matter of quiet retrospect.

26. senet: a word of earlier Latin for the later *senescit.* — **se dedicat:** *sc.* in effigy. — **tibi:** Castor and Pollux were proverbially united, and were often spoken of, sometimes even as if they were a single person, under one name, — that of Castor being more frequently used, as in v. 27; cf. Hor. *Epod.* 17. 42 *Castor fraterque magni Castoris;* Stat. *Silu.* IV. 6. 15 *ab Elysiis prospexit sedibus alter Castor;* and the famous witticism of Bibulus in Suet. *Iul.* 10 *euenisse sibi quod Polluci; ut enim geminis fratribus aedes in foro constituta tantum Castoris uocaretur, ita suam Caesarisque munificentiam unius Caesaris dici:* but Hor. *Carm.* III. 29. 64 has *geminus Pollux.* — The Dioscuri were invoked as dispellers of storms by sailors, who took the electrical phe-

nomenon called still ' St. Elmo's [= Helena's?] fires ' for the stars affixed in ancient art to the foreheads of the brothers ; cf. 68. 65 and other poets *passim.*

5. To Lesbia; an exhortation to enjoy love and despise censure. — This utterance of the intoxication of passion must date, like 2 and 3, from the early days of the entire confidence of Catullus in Lesbia. With its companion piece, 7, it is cited by Ovid (*Am.* I. 8. 58), and by Martial (VI. 34. 7; XI. 6. 14; XII. 59. 3). — Metre, Phalaecean.

1. **uiuamus:** the key-note of the whole poem is struck in the first word; with *uiuere* in this pregnant sense, ' to enjoy life,' cf. Verg. *Copa* 38 *mors aurem uellens ' uiuite' ait, 'uenio';* Mart. I. 15. 12 *sera nimis uita est crastina; uiue hodie;* and the proverbial *dum uiuimus, uiuamus.* — **mea Lesbia:** so she is called again in 75. 1, but with a different feeling (cf. also 58. 1).

2. **rumores:** here not of unauthenticated report, but of direct observation and remark; cf. Ter. *Phor.* 911 *nam qui erit rumor, id si feceris!* — **senum seueriorum :** old men are proverbially censors of the young (cf. Hor. *A. P.* 174 [*senex*] *castigator censorque minorum*), and this is one type of old

Omnes unius aestimemus assis.

Soles occidere et redire possunt :

5   Nobis, cum semel occidit breuis lux,

Nox est perpetua una dormienda.

Da mi basia mille, deinde centum,

Dein mille altera, dein secunda centum,

Deinde usque altera mille, deinde centum,

10   Dein, cum milia multa fecerimus,

Conturbabimus illa, ne sciamus,

---

man in Plautus and Terence ; but cf. Cic. *De Sen.* 65 *seueritatem in senectute probo, sed eam (ut alia) modicam ; acerbitatem nullo modo.* With the comparative, cf. 3. 2 *uenustiorum.*

3. **unius aestimemus assis:** *i.e.* count as naught; cf. 42. 13 (*assis facere*) ; 10. 13 ; 17. 17 (*pili facere*); and, in the same sense, 23. 25 (*parui putare*). Catullus is the first to use in such phrases *assis* and *pili,* where Plautus and Terence have *flocci, nauci, pensi, nihili* (cf. however Plaut. *Capt.* 477 *neque ridiculos iam terrunci faciunt*).

4–6. On the general conception see 3. 11, 12 n.; Prop. III. 15. 24 *nox tibi longa uenit, nec reditura dies;* Hor. *Carm.* IV. 7. 13 ff. *damna tamen celeres reparant caelestia lunae; nos . . . puluis et umbra sumus;* and most beautifully in the Lament for Bion (Mosch. 3. 109 ff.), '*Ah me, when the mallows wither in the garden, and the green parsley, and the curled tendrils of the anise, on a later day they live again, and spring in another year ; but we men, we the great and mighty, or wise, when once we have died, in hollow earth we sleep, gone down into silence ; a right long, and endless, and unawakening sleep. And thou too, in the earth wilt be lapped in silence*' (Lang) : R.

Browning, *Toccata of Galuppi, Death stepped tacitly and took them where they never see the sun.*

5. **breuis lux:** a very unusual rhythm with which to end the verse ; cf. however 7. 7 *tacet nox,* and note the antithesis between *lux* at the end of v. 5 and *nox* at the beginning of v. 6.

7. **basia:** the word appears first here, but seems in later days to have supplanted entirely in the colloquial dialect both *sauia* and the more formal *oscula,* whence it made its way into the Romance languages. The lack of apparent congeners in Latin and Greek, and the occurrence of *buss* in early English, and of the nouns *buss, busserl,* and the verb *bussen* in early days in the conservative mountain dialects of South Germany and Austria, make it probable that this word was of Germanic origin, and made its way to Rome from the region of the Po. —**deinde:** the later, while *dein* is the earlier form of the word ; in both *ei* is regularly contracted into a single syllable.

9. **usque,** *straight on.*

10. **fecerĭmus:** with the original quantity of the penult, as occasionally in the poets.

11. **conturbabimus:** the confusion of the count is already effected in the poem by the hurrying suc-

Aut ne quis malus inuidere possit,
Cum tantum sciat esse basiorum.

6.

Flaui, delicias tuas Catullo,
Ni sint inlepidae atque inelegantes,
Velles dicere, nec tacere posses.
Verum nescio quid febriculosi
5 Scorti diligis : hoc pudet fateri.
Nam te non uiduas iacere noctes
Nequiquam tacitum cubile clamat

cession of *mille* and *centum*. — **ne sciamus**: for if not even we ourselves know the number, surely the eye of envy cannot determine it.

12. **inuidere**: *i.e.* to cast an evil eye, and so bring misfortune, upon a person or thing; cf. Accius ap. Cic. *Tusc.* III. 9. 20 *quisnam florem liberum inuidit meum?* The belief in 'the evil eye' is still widespread among eastern nations, and curious traces still survive among more highly civilized communities.

13. **tantum**, *just so many ;* cf. also 14. 7 *tantum impiorum.* From ancient times down it has been believed that a spell could be surely based only on some mathematically exact enumeration of particulars (cf. Hor. *Carm.* I. 11. 2 *Babylonios numeros*), and so it has been held unsafe to tell, or even to know, such details about one's precious things.

6. Flavius is rallied about an intrigue which he has in vain tried to conceal. With the general theme cf. 55 and Hor. *Carm.* I. 27 ; II. 4. — Metre, Phalaecean.

1. **Flaui**: otherwise unknown, though Baehrens suspects him to be the Fabullus of 12, 13, 28, and 47.

— **delicias**: see 2. 1 n. — **Catullo**: the poet is fond of referring to himself by name; cf. 7. 10; 11. 1 ; 13. 7; 14. 13; 38. 1; 44. 3; 49. 4; 56. 3; 58. 2; 68. 27, 135; 72. 1; 79. 3; 82. 1.

2. **ni sint . . . uelles**, *grantea that [your love] is not . . . you would surely be willing*, etc. The imperfect tense in both clauses would express at once a conclusion definitively arrived at after past deliberation ; the tenses as they here stand convey the idea of a pause for deliberation after laying down the chosen proposition (**ni sint**, etc.), and then a triumphant pounce upon the inevitable conclusion (**uelles dicere**, etc.). For other instances of this construction cf. 58[b] and Draeger *Hist. Synt.* II. p. 721. — **inlepidae atque inelegantes**: cf. similar phrases in 10. 4 ; 36. 17.

4. **febriculosi**: this word appears first, and only once, in Catullus, and but rarely later.

6. **uiduas noctes**: cf. Ov. *Ep.* 18. 69 *uiduas exegi frigida noctes ;* and similarly 68. 6 *in lecto caelibe.*

7. **nequiquam tacitum**: *i.e.* it is to no purpose that the bed lacks

Sertis ac Syrio fragrans oliuo,
Puluinusque peraeque et hic et ille
10   Attritus, tremulique quassa lecti
Argutatio inambulatioque.
Nam nil stupra ualet, nihil, tacere.
Cur ? non tam latera ecfututa pandas,
Ni tu quid facias ineptiarum.
15   Quare, quidquid habes boni malique,
Dic nobis : uolo te ac tuos amores
Ad caelum lepido uocare uersu.

the power of speech, for it tells as
emphatically and clearly (**clamat**)
as though it could speak; cf. 80. 7.

8. **Syrio**, etc. : cf. 68. 144 *fragrantem Assyrio odore;* and the
lament of Berenice's hair in 66.
75 ff. ; Hor. *Carm.* II. 7. 8 *corona-
tus nitentis malobathro Syrio capillos;* II. 11. 14 *rosa canos odorati
capillos, Assyriaque nardo uncti.*

15. **quidquid habes**, etc. : cf.
1. 8 n.; Hor. *Carm.* I. 27. 17 *quidquid habes, age, depone tutis auribus.*

16. **nobis** : = *mihi ;* the plural
for the singular of the first person
(though never of the second) often
occurs in Catullus in personal and
possessive pronouns and in verbs,
sometimes with a change from singular to plural even in the same sentence; cf. 77. 3-4; 91. 1-2. — **uolo,**
etc. : the tone of the poem is certainly different from that of 55, and
the raillery of the whole address
thus far suggests that these concluding words are not spoken seriously,
but after the spirit of Horace in the

odes cited in the introductory note.
— **amores** : of a *scortillum* also in
10. 1 and 45. 1 ; cf. the same word
of Juventius in 15. 1; 21. 4; 40. 7;
but of love itself in 38. 6; 64. 27,
etc. ; and never of a mere petted
friend, as in Cic. *Att.* XVI. 6. 4
*salutem dices Atticae, deliciis atque
amoribus meis.*

17. **ad caelum uocare** : phrases
like *ad caelum ferre, efferre, tollere*
are common enough in Latin, as is
uocare with *ad uitam, ad exitium,
ad salutem,* and the like; but this
particular phrase is rare, if not
unique, and its strangeness adds to
the mock-heroic, jesting tone of the
sentence. — **lepido** : not of external
character, as in 1. 1, but of internal;
cf. 36. 10 *lepide ;* 12. 8; 16. 7; 50.
7 *lepor,* etc. — **uersv** : = *carmine;*
Cicero says *uersum facere* as well
as *uersus facere ;* cf. also Verg.
Geor. III. 339 *quid tibi pastores
Libyae uersu prosequar ;* but the
collective use of the singular did
not become common till a later age.

7.

Quaeris quot mihi basiationes
Tuae, Lesbia, sint satis superque.
Quam magnus numerus Libyssae harenae
Laserpiciferis iacet Cyrenis,
5   Oraclum Iouis inter aestuosi

7. To Lesbia, in answer to a possibly somewhat petulant question mentioned in vv. 1–2. The poem is a companion-piece to 5, and was undoubtedly written at about the same time with it. — Metre, Phalaecean.

1. **quaeris**: perhaps after the appeal in 5 for sundry thousands of kisses. — **basiationes**: the word occurs in Catullus only here, and does not appear again before Martial, who uses it twice (II. 23. 4; VII. 95. 17). Abstract nouns in *-io* were common in colloquial speech in the time of Catullus.

2. **tuae**: subjective, as shown by comparison with 5.7 *da mi basia;* cf. also 8. 18. — **satis superque**: cf. the slight variation in v. 10; also Cic. *Rosc. Com.* 4. 11 *satis superque habere;* Hor. *Epod.* 1. 31 *satis superque ditauit;* 17. 19 *satis superque poenarum.*

3. **quam**: correlative with *tam* in v. 9. — **numerus harenae**, etc.: here is united a simplicity of figure that is even ante-Homeric with a precision of geographical and mythological allusion that smacks of the Alexandrian school. The sands of the seashore, the leaves of the forest, and the stars of the heavens, are the first types of infinite number that occurred to early man; cf. 61. 206 ff.; *Gen.* 13. 16 *I will make thy seed as the dust of the earth;* 15. 5 *look now toward heaven and tell the stars, if thou be*

able *to tell them; . . . so shall thy seed be;* Hom. *Il.* II. 800 φύλλοισιν ἐοικότες ἢ ψαμάθοισιν; Hor. *Carm.* I. 28. 1 *numero carentis harenae;* Ov. *Art. Am.* I. 254 *numero cedet harena meo;* I. 59 *quot caelum stellas tot habet tua Roma puellas;* Calp. *Buc.* 2. 72 *qui numerare uelit . . . tenues citius numerabit harenas.*

4. **laserpiciferis**: cf. Plin. *N. H.* XIX. 38 *laserpicium, quod Graeci* σίλφιον *uocant, in Cyrenaica prouincia repertum, cuius sucum laser uocant, magnificum in usu medicamentisque.* The plant was doubtless the *ferula asafoetida,* the exuded juice of which is still widely used as an antispasmodic. It held a prominent place among the products and exports of Cyrenaica, and is represented upon coins of the country. Pliny notes, however, that in his time it had ceased to be produced there, and our supply comes from Persia and the East Indies. — **Cyrenis**: Cyrenae (Gr. Κυρήνη) was the capital of the district of Libya, called Cyrenaica, that bordered upon the *Syrtis major.* It was founded, according to tradition, about the middle of the seventh century B.C., by Battus, otherwise called Aristotle, a Greek from the island of Thera, and attained great reputation as a centre of trade, and as the birthplace of Eratosthenes, Aristippus, and Callimachus.

5. **oraclum Iouis**: the Egyptian deity Ammon, or Hammon, origi-

Et Batti ueteris sacrum sepulcrum,
Aut quam sidera multa, cum tacet nox,
Furtiuos hominum uident amores,
Tam te basia multa basiare
10 Vesano satis et super Catullo est,
Quae nec pernumerare curiosi
Possint nec mala fascinare lingua.

8.

Miser Catulle, desinas ineptire,
Et quod uides perisse perditum ducas.

nally worshipped in Thebes under
the form of a ram, or of a human
figure with a ram's horns, had his
most famous temple and oracle in
the oasis of Siwah in the Libyan
desert, 400 miles from Cyrene (Plin.
l.c.).   He was identified by the
Greeks and Romans with Zeus and
Jupiter; cf. Prop. V. 1. 103 *hoc
neque harenosum Libyae Iouis ex-
plicat antrum.* — aestuosi : of
glowing heat, as in 46. 5 *Nicaeae
aestuosae;* cf. Hor. *Carm.* I. 22. 5
per Syrtes aestuosas; I. 31. 5 *aestuosae Calabriae.*

6. Batti: see v. 4 n. *Cyrenis.* —
sacrum sepulcrum: the tomb of the
founder stood in the city of Cyrene,
where he was reverenced as a god.

7. tacet nox: with the rhythm
cf. 5. 5 n.

9. tam : correlative with v. 3
quam. — te : subject, not object of
basiare ; cf. v. 2 n. — basia basiare : with the cognate accusative
cf. 61. 117 (*gaudia gaudere*), and,
less precisely, such expressions as
14. 3 *odissem odio*, etc.

10. uesano : of the mad passion
of love also in 100. 7 *uesana flamma*.

11–12. Cf. 5. 11–13 n. — curiosi: cf. Plaut. *Stich.* 208 *nam curi-*

osus nemost quin sit maleuolus. —
mala lingua : cf. Verg. *Ecl.* 7. 27
*baccare frontem cingite ne uati
noceat mala lingua futuro.*

8. The poet, somewhat vainly,
appeals to himself to return Lesbia's coldness with coldness.   The
puella of this poem is undoubtedly
Lesbia, for of no other does Catullus speak as in v. 5 (see note),
nor, indeed, as in the whole poem.
Catullus had evidently fallen in the
favor of his inconstant mistress, and
was ill able to put up with her coldness in a dignified manner.   While,
therefore, he complains of the un-
reasonableness of her treatment of
him, he seems to have one eye open
for a reconciliation.   Far different
is the swift and brief-worded bitterness that characterizes the poems
written after he had become convinced of Lesbia's utter unworthiness.   This was evidently written in
the time of temporary estrangement
which was ended by the voluntary
act of Lesbia (cf. 37, 107, 36, and
Intr. 18, 19). — Date, about 59 B.C.
Metre, choliambic.

1. Catulle : the poet is fond of
soliloquy in the form of self-address,
and of speaking of himself in the

Fulsere quondam candidi tibi soles,

Cum uentitabas quo puella ducebat

5 Amata nobis quantum amabitur nulla.

Ibi illa multa tum iocosa fiebant,

Quae tu uolebas nec puella nolebat.

Fulsere uere candidi tibi soles.

Nunc iam illa non uult : tu quoque, **impotens**, noli,

10 Nec quae fugit sectare, nec miser uiue,

Sed obstinata mente perfer, obdura.

Vale, puella ! iam Catullus obdurat,

Nec te requiret nec rogabit inuitam :

At tu dolebis, cum rogaberis nulla.

---

third person (cf. 6. 1 n.); but especially noteworthy in this poem is
the change from the second to the
third person (v. 12) and back again
(v. 19). — **ineptire** : a colloquial
word, occurring twice in Terence
(*Ad.* 934; *Phor.* 420), not at all in
Plautus, nor in any classical writer
after Catullus.

2. **perisse perditum** : cf. Plaut.
Trin. 1026 *quin tu quod periit
periisse ducis ?*

3. **candidi soles** : days of good
fortune and happiness ; cf. Hor.
Carm. IV. 5. 7 *gratior it dies et
soles melius nitent ;* and the opposite figure in *Sat.* I. 9. 72 *huncine
solem tam nigrum surrexe mihi !*

4. **cum uentitabas**, etc. : not of
a definite place, as into the house
of Allius (cf. 68. 68), but in general, when you were submitting to
her rule and guidance.

5. **amata nobis**, etc. : cf. 37. 12
and 87. 1, 2 for the same expression of his love for Lesbia, and
for similar comparisons of affection, 3. 5 n.

6. **ibi tum** : temporal, contrasted
with v. 9 *nunc iam ;* cf. Plaut. *Curc.*
648 *tum ibi nescio quis me arripit ;*

Ter. *Andr.* 634 *ibi tum eorum im-
pudentissuma oratiost;* Cic. *Caec.*
10. 27 *ibi tum Caecinam postulasse.*
Ibi is used alone in the temporal
sense in 63. 4, 42, 48, 76; 66, 33.
— **iocosa** : cf. Ov. *Trist.* II. 354
*uita uerecunda est, Musa iocosa
mea.*

9. **impotens** : if the emendation
impotens noli be correct, the adjective must mean ' weakling,' the
prey to his own passions; different from its meaning in 4. 18 and
35. 12.

10. **nec quae fugit sectare** : cf.
Theocr. 11. 75 τί τὸν φεύγοντα διώ-
κεις; which passage Catullus may
have had in mind, though in Theocritus the words retain more of their
literal meaning.

11. **perfer, obdura** : cf. Ov.
Trist. V. 11. 7 *perfer et obdura ;*
Hor. *Sat.* II. 5. 39 *persta atque obdura.* The asyndeton adds to the
tone of rugged determination.

14. **rogaberis** : as in v. 13, without the accusative of the thing desired. — **nulla** : a somewhat colloquial and emphatic use for *non ;* cf.
17. 20 ; Plaut. *Asin.* 408 *is nullus
uenit ;* Mil. *Glor.* 786 *nam cor non*

15   Scelesta, uae te! quae tibi manet uita!
      Quis nunc te adibit? cui uideberis bella?
      Quem nunc amabis? cuius esse diceris?
      Quem basiabis? cui labella mordebis?
      At tu, Catulle, destinatus obdura.

9.

Verani, omnibus e meis amicis
Antistans mihi milibus trecentis,

potest quod nulla habet (*i.e.* because she has none) ; Ter. *Hec.*
79 *si non quaeret, nullus dixeris;*
Cic. *Verr.* II. 2. 43 *hereditas ea,
quae nulla debetur.*

15. **scelesta:** Catullus fans his
anger and waxes more indignantly
reproachful, and yet so immediately
runs into the details of past happiness that in spite of his *uale, puella*
he almost seems to be wishing to
tempt Lesbia back to himself. Observe also from the rhetorical questions that he has yet no notion that
Lesbia's coldness to himself is connected with other intrigues. — **uae
te:** though the dative is commonly
used in connection with *uae* (cf. 64.
196 n. *uae miserae*), yet the accusative of exclamation is sometimes
found; cf. Plaut. *Asin.* 481 *uae te ;*
Sen. *Apocol.* 4 *uae me.* — **tibi manet:** *i.e.* will from now on continue
to be yours (cf. 61. 229 ; 76. 5);
while *te manet* would mean 'will
come upon you in the future' (cf.
Prop. III. 28. 58 *mors sua quemque
manet*).

17. **cuius esse diceris,** *who will
call you his own ?*

18. **cui labella mordebis:** cf.
Plaut. *Pseud.* 67 *teneris labellis molles morsiunculae ;* Hor. *Carm.* 1.
13. 12 *impressit memorem dente*

labris notam ; Tib. 1. 6. 14 *quem
facit impresso mutua dente Venus.*

19. As the verses that contain the
history of the past were closed by
the refrain in v. 8 which repeated
the opening in v. 3, so those that
declare the purpose of the future
close with the refrain in v. 19 in
repetition of the opening in v. 11.
— **destinatus:** the word first occurs here in the sense of *obstinatus ;*
it gives, as compared with *obstinata*
of the corresponding v. 11, the same
slight variety that is secured in vv. 3
and 8 by the change from *quondam*
to *uere.* A similar effort after variety
can be observed in other passages;
cf. *proponis* and *promittere* in 109.
1 and 3.

9. An expression of joy over the
return of Veranius from Spain. On
the date of composition and the
personality of Veranius, see Intr.
68, 69. With the poem, cf. Hor.
Carm. II. 7 on the safe return to
Italy of Pompeius. — Metre, Phalaecean.

1–2. **omnibus,** etc.: *i.e.* who
alone of all my friends art dearer to
me than all the rest put together,
however many they be. The ablative phrase is used in its ordinary
partitive sense, modifying the vocative directly, while **milibus** depends

Venistine domum ad tuos penates
Fratresque unanimos anumque matrem?
5 Venisti! o mihi nuntii beati!
Visam te incolumem audiamque Hiberum
Narrantem loca, facta, nationes,
Vt mos est tuus, applicansque collum
Iucundum os oculosque sauiabor.
10 O, quantum est hominum beatiorum,
Quid me laetius est beatiusue?

upon **antistans,** *amicis* being readily supplied from the partitive
phrase. — **mihi,** *in my feeling.* —
milibus trecentis: two numerals
commonly used independently of
indefinite multitude (for *milia* see
5. 7 ff.; 35. 8, etc.; for *trecenti,* 11.
18; 12. 10; 29. 14) are here combined for additional emphasis, as in
48. 3; cf. also 95. 3 *milia quingenta.*

4. unanimos: the word occurs
in Plautus only once (*Stich.* 729),
but was apparently a favorite with
Catullus, occurring thrice (9. 4; 30.
1; 66. 80), though it is not used
by Horace, the elegists, or Martial.
Vergil, however, employs it thrice.
— **anum**: cf. the adjectival use also
in 68. 46; 78b. 4. Plautus uses the
word as an adjective only once, but
the elegiasts and later prose writers
more frequently.

5. nuntii: plural, though of a
single message; cf. also the neuter
plural in 63. 75.

6. Hiberum: possibly used as
a general term for Spaniards, but
more likely indicating that
Veranius had been in the nearer
province.

7. loca, facta, nationes: the
country, its history, and the tribes
which inhabit it.

8. ut mos est tuus: as this was
not the last, so perhaps it was not

the first time that Veranius had visited foreign shores, and he apparently had some reputation among
his friends as a *raconteur.* — **appli-
cans collum**: *i.e.* pulling your face
toward mine, with arm around the
neck.

9. os oculosque sauiabor: the
union of the two nouns is common;
cf. Cic. *Phil.* 8. 7. 20 *ante os oculosque legatorum;* Verg. *Aen.* VIII.
152 *ille os oculosque loquentis lustra-
bat lumine;* also the English saying,
before my very face and eyes. On
the kissing of the eyes, cf. 45. 11-
12; 48. 1-2; (Q.) Cic. *Fam.* XVI.
27. 2 *tuos oculos dissauiabor.*

10. o: the interjection is used,
not with the *quantum*-clause as a
vocative, but with the exclamatory
clause following; cf. 31. 7. With a
similar triumphant appeal are closed
9 and 107, and with an indignant
appeal, 29, 47, 52, and 60. — **quantum,** etc. : a partitive clause modifying **quid** ; cf. Plaut. *Capt.* 835 *o
mihi quantumst hominum optumo-
rum optume;* and similar passages
cited in 1. 8 n. *quidquid hoc
libelli.*

11. quid, etc.: the neuter is not
very rare in Latin in similar sweeping appeals. With the general expression, cf. 107. 7 ; Ter. *Eun.*
1031 *ecquis me hodie uiuit fortu-
natior?*

10.

Varus me meus ad suos amores
Visum duxerat e foro otiosum,
Scortillum, ut mihi tunc repente uisum est,
Non sane inlepidum neque inuenustum.
5 Huc ut uenimus, incidere nobis
Sermones uarii, in quibus, quid esset
Iam Bithynia, quo modo se haberet,
Ecquonam mihi profuisset aere.

10. Catullus tells at his own expense how neatly he was shown up when attempting to put on airs about his supposed wealth acquired in Bithynia, whither he went in 57 B.C. in the retinue of the governor Memmius (see Intr. 29 ff.). As might be expected, the forms of expression are thoroughly colloquial.— Date of composition, about 56 B.C. Metre, Phalaecean.

1. **Varus:** cf. Intr. 66.— **amores:** cf. 6. 16 n.

3. **scortillum:** ἅπαξ λεγόμενον. — **repente,** *at first sight.* He professes to have changed his opinion later (see v. 33).

4. Cf. similar phrases in 6. 2 and 36. 17.

6–8. The three particular questions are given in a conversational asyndeton. The first concerns the general character of the province, and is carried on with specification (cf. 2. 8 n.) by the second, which concerns its particular condition, and by the third, which narrows the discussion down to the real point of interest, the influence of the province upon the purse of Catullus.

6. **quid esset iam Bithynia,** *what sort of a place Bithynia is nowadays.* Cf. Hor. *Ep.* I. 11. 7 *scis Lebedus quid sit;* Gell. IV. 1.

12 *hoc enim quis homo sit ostendere est, non, quid homo sit dicere.*

7. **iam:** not that the questioners had any precise knowledge of, or interest in, the past history of Bithynia, but only that the news at hand is from a freshly returned traveler. — **Bithynia:** the country was bequeathed to the Romans by Nicomedes III. in 74 B.C., and organized as a province. Western Pontus was added to it in 65 B.C., on the overthrow of Mithradates by Pompey. The united province was governed by propraetors till 27 B.C., when it was placed in the list of senatorial provinces, where it remained till the time of Trajan. Under the republic it could in no wise compare in importance with the neighboring province of Asia, being but thinly settled in the interior, and having only a scanty fringe of Greek culture along the coast. — **quo modo se haberet,** *how it is getting on.* Cf. Ter. *Phor.* 820 *ut meae res sese habent;* Cic. *Att.* XIII. 35. 2 *scire aueo quo modo res se habeat;* Tac. *Ann.* XIV. 51 *ego me bene habeo.*

8. **ecquonam,** etc., *whether I had made any money out of it.* *Ecquis* with an enclitic -*nam* both Plautine and Ciceronian ; cf. also 28. 6. The question is a com-

Respondi id quod erat, nihil neque ipsis
10   Nec praetoribus esse nec cohorti,
Cur quisquam caput unctius referret, —
Praesertim quibus esset irrumator
Praetor nec faceret pili cohortem.
' At certe tamen ' inquiunt, ' quod illic
15   Natum dicitur esse comparasti,
Ad lecticam homines.'   Ego, ut puellae

mentary on the frequent character
of Roman provincial administration.

9. **nihil neque ipsis**, etc. : the
three classes mentioned are the inhabitants themselves (**ipsis**), the
governors (**praetoribus**), and the
governor's staff (**cohorti**), and the
order is that of logical emphasis : —
not even the inhabitants have anything; how then can governors, to
say nothing of staff, ever get anything?

11. **cur**, etc. : the indirect question depends upon **nihil** regarded
as a cause. — **caput unctius referret**: *i.e.* be rolling in wealth on
his return ; a colloquial figure derived from the expensiveness of
fine ointments, which, therefore,
only the rich could use; cf. 6.
8 n.; Plaut. *Pseud.* 219 *numqui
quoipiamst tuorum tua opera hodie
conseruorum nitidiusculum caput?*
Cic. *Verr.* II. 2. 22. 54 *ita palaes-
tritas defendebat ut ab illis ipse unc-
tior abiret;* and an extension of
the same figure in 29. 22 *uncta patrimonia*. With the comparative
unctius *sc.* ' than those of men in
general '; cf. 3. 2 n. *uenustiorum;*
9. 10 *beatiorum*.

12. **quibus**: with oblique reference to **quisquam**, as though a
partitive *eorum* had preceded. —
irrumator, *a scurvy fellow;* the
word, like many others of similar
antecedents, has come to be used

not always in a literal sense, but as
a mere term of abuse; cf. v. 24; 28.
9, 10; Intr. 32.

13. **faceret pili**: cf. 5. 3 n.

14. **at**: *i.e.* in spite of the general poverty of the province, —
challenging the sweeping character
of the preceding statement.

15. **natum**: if Catullus means
that the custom of riding in a litter
originated in Bithynia, he tells us
what we learn from no other source,
— for the grammarian Probus, in
making a similar statement, probably borrowed it from him ; but
the custom was common there;
cf. Cic. *Verr.* II. 5. 11. 27 *ut mos
fuit Bithyniae regibus, lectica
octaphoro ferebatur.* Cappadocians
and Syrians, men of proverbially
great stature and strength, are often
mentioned as litter-bearers, as are
less frequently Thracians, Liburni-
ans and Moesians (Juv.), and in later
days Gauls (Clem. Alex.) and Ger-
mans (Tertull.) ; cf. Mart. VI. 77. 4
*quid te Cappadocum sex onus esse
iuuat?* Juv. 6. 351 *quae longorum
uehitur ceruice Syrorum.*

16. **lecticam**: a covered litter,
borne on the shoulders of slaves
(*lecticarii*), and used in Rome at
first by women and children, but
later by men also, as a vehicle in
the city (where carriages were not
allowed), and for short journeys
into the country.

Vnum me facerem beatiorem,
'Non' inquam, 'mihi tam fuit maligne,
Vt, prouincia quod mala incidisset,
20   Non possem octo homines parare rectos.'
At mi nullus erat neque hic neque illic
Fractum qui ueteris pedem grabati
In collo sibi conlocare posset.
Hic illa, ut decuit cinaediorem,
25   'Quaeso' inquit, 'mihi, mi Catulle, paulum
Istos commoda : nam uolo ad Sarapim

17. **unum beatiorem**, *the one man who was blest above his fellows;* for Catullus had said (vv. 9–13) that no staff — and especially not that of which he was a member — made anything out of the province; cf. 37. 17 *une*. — **me facerem**, *pass myself off as;* cf. Cic. *Flac.* 20. 46 *cum uerbis se locupletem faceret.*

18. **mihi fuit maligne**: cf. *male esse* with the dative of the person in 14. 10; 38. 1.

20. **homines rectos**, *straight-backed fellows* (as *lecticarii*). Eight appears to have been the maximum number of carriers, while six was common ; cf. the citations from Cicero and Martial on v. 15, and Martial often.

21–23. A confidential aside of the poet to the reader. — **at mi nullus**, etc. : *i.e.* but I hadn't, and never had had, a single one. — **hic** : *i.e.* in Rome now. — **illic** : *i.e.* in Bithynia then. — **grabati** : (Gr. κράββατος) a Macedonian word for a bedstead. It is sometimes mentioned as a possession of poverty, and such seems to be the idea here ; cf. Cic. *Diuin.* II. 63. 129 *utrum sit probabilius deosne immortalis concursare circum omnium mortalium qui ubique sunt non modo lectos uerum etiam gra·*

batos, etc. ; Sen. *Ep.* 20. 10 *leue argumentum est bonae uoluntatis grabatus aut pannus, nisi apparuit aliquem illa non necessitate pati sed malle.* And here not only is the couch a miserable thing to start with, but old and broken as well. No rich *lectica* had Catullus, — only a wretched bedstead as the nearest approach to it, — and no slave at all, far less eight.

24. **ut decuit cinaediorem**, *like the saucy jade she was;* cf. v. 12 n. The girl saw through the trick of Catullus (perhaps he intended she should), and took this witty way of compelling him to acknowledge himself a pretender.

26. **commoda** : with the short final *a*, cf. Plaut. *Cist.* 573 *commoda loquelam tuam* (at the beginning of a trochaic septenarius); so also more commonly in colloquial usage such pyrrhic imperatives as *ama, puta, roga,* etc. — **Sarapim** : an Egyptian deity, apparently at first identical with Osiris, and often later connected in worship with Isis. From Alexandria, where the great Sarapeum stood, the cult spread through Greece and Italy, reaching Rome perhaps as early as the time of Sulla, though it met there with

Deferri.' 'Mane,' inquii puellae,
'Istud quod modo dixeram, me habere,
Fugit me ratio : meus sodalis
30   Cinna est Gaius ; is sibi parauit.
Verum, utrum illius an mei, quid ad me?
Vtor tam bene quam mihi pararim.
Sed tu insulsa male et molesta uiuis,
Per quam non licet esse neglegentem.'

great opposition, and did not attain its height till the end of the first century after Christ. In 58 B.C., only about two years before this poem was written, the worship of the Egyptian divinities had been banished without the city walls. Upon the Campus Martius, however, Isis and Sarapis found a resting-place, and their temples were much frequented by the lower classes. Courtesans especially flocked to Isis, and invalids to Sarapis, whose priests were reputed to have wondrous powers of healing. But Sarapis may stand here for both divinities, and there is no need to suppose the girl was ill because of her professed destination or of her request for the use of a *lectica*. The spelling *Sarapis* instead of *Serapis* is well supported by inscriptions and by Greek usage.

27. **mane,** *hold on there; not so fast.* On the hiatus in arsis (with shortening of the final vowel, as always in Catullus) see Intr. 86 *d*.

28. **istud :** an accusative of specification, with which **me habere** is in apposition. Cicero in his letters generally uses a *quod*-clause without antecedent in such constructions. Note that not only with **habere**, but in each case below (*parauit, illius an mei, utor, pararim*) the word definitely indicating the *lecticarii* is omitted, since the

subject has become painfully embarrassing to the speaker.

29. **fugit me ratio,** *I did not think;* a colloquialism ; cf. Plaut. *Amph.* 385 *scibam equidem nullum esse nobis nisi me seruum Sosiam ; fugit te ratio ;* Auctor ad Herenn. II. 25. 40 *in mentem mihi si uenisset, hoc aut hoc fecissem ; sed me tum haec ratio fugit :* but *fugere* is more common in phrases of similar meaning, either absolutely or with other subjects than *ratio ;* cf. 12. 4 *fugit te.*

30. **Cinna Gaius :** *i.e.* C. Helvius Cinna, on whom see Intr. 63. The reversal of the formal order of *nomen* and *cognomen* is common enough in Latin, but the following here of the *praenomen*, added hastily after the familiar *cognomen*, indicates the embarrassment of the speaker.

31. **quid ad me :** *sc. attinet ;* cf. Cic. *Att.* XII. 17 *uelim appelles procuratores, si tibi uidetur ; quanquam quid ad me ?* Mart. XII. 30. 1 *sobrius est Aper ; quid ad me ?*

32. **quam mihi pararim :** *i.e. quam si mihi eos parauerim ;* cf. the ordinary comparative clauses introduced by *tamquam* without *si.*

33–34. Catullus has been stammering out his lame explanation with increasing embarrassment, and now detects, possibly by the ill-concealed merriment of his auditors, that the whole thing was a joke at his expense ; hence the sudden

11.

Furi et Aureli, comites Catulli,
Siue in extremos penetrabit Indos,
Litus ut longe resonante Eoa
       Tunditur unda,

5   Siue in Hyrcanos Arabasue molles,
    Seu Sacas sagittiferosue Parthos,

change to humorous petulance with
which he closes. — **male** : the word
has a detractive force which neu-
tralizes, like a negative, words of
good signification (cf. 16. 13 *male
marem*, 'no man at all'; Ov. *Trist.*
I. 6. 13 *male fidus*, 'faithless'), and
emphasizes words of bad signification, as here; cf. 14. 5; Ter. *Hec.* 337
male metuo, 'I'm horribly afraid';
Hor. *Sat.* I. 4. 66 *rauci male*, 'out-
rageously hoarse' (with similar anas-
trophe to that here). — **uiuis** : with
almost the bare sense of *es ;* cf.
Plaut. *Men.* 908 *ne ego homo uiuo
miser* (cf. 8. 10 *nec miser uiue*);
Tib. II. 6. 53 *satis anxia uiuas ;*
and similarly Tac. *Ann.* IV. 58. 4
ceterorum nescii egere.

11. A final answer to a proffer
of reconciliation from Lesbia, and
an offer of service from Furius and
Aurelius; see Intr. 41.— Date, the
end of 55, or beginning of 54 B.C.
(cf. v. 11). Metre, lesser Sapphic.

1. **comites** : the technical word
for members of the *cohors* of a provincial governor ; cf. 28. 1; 46. 9;
as Catullus may now hope to be a
comes of Caesar, Furius and Aurelius
have offered to be his humble and
useful friends, that they may profit
by his good fortune, and Catullus
ironically terms them his *comites.*

2. With vv. 2–12 cf. Hor. *Carm.*
I. 22. 5–8; II. 6. 1–4; *Epod.* 1. 11–
14. — **extremos Indos** : cf. Hor.

Ep. I. 1. 45 *impiger extremos cur-
ris mercator ad Indos ;* Prop. II. 9
29 *quid si longinquos retinerey
miles ad Indos ;* Stat. *Silu.* III. 2.
91 *uel ad ignotos ibam comes impiger Indos.*

3. **ut** : the rare locative use ; cf.
17. 10 ; Plaut. *Bacch.* 815 *in eopse
astas lapide, ut praeco praedicat ;*
Verg. *Aen.* V. 329 *labitur ut forte
[sanguis] humum super madefece-
rat.* — **longe resonante**, *far-echo-
ing.* — **Eoa unda**: *i.e.* the all-
encircling ocean-stream at the extreme East ; cf. Ov. *Fast.* VI. 474
uigil Eois lucifer exit aquis ; Tib.
IV. 2. 20 *proximus Eois Indus
aquis ;* Verg. *Geor.* II. 122 *quos
Oceano propior gerit India lucos.*

5. **Hyrcanos** : a people dwelling
by the southern end of the Caspian
Sea (*Mare Hyrcanum*), joined by
Vergil with the Arabians and Indi-
ans as distant enemies of Rome ;
cf. *Aen.* VII. 605 [*siue bellum*]
*Hyrcanis Arabisue parant seu ten-
dere ad Indos.* — **Arabas molles** :
so called from their proverbial riches
and luxury; cf. Verg. *Geor.* I. 57
molles sua tura Sabaei [*mittunt*];
Tib. II. 2. 3 *urantur odores quos
tener mittit Arabs.*

6. **Sacas** : a nomadic people,
called Scythians by the Greeks,
dwelling far to the north-east of
Parthia and Bactria; cf. Plin. *N. H.*
VI. 17. 50 *celeberrimi eorum [Scy-*

Siue quae septemgeminus colorat
   Aequora Nilus,

Siue trans altas gradietur Alpes
10 Caesaris uisens monimenta magni,
   Gallicum Rhenum, horribile aequor, ultimosque Britannos,

Omnia haec, quaecumque feret uoluntas
   Caelitum, temptare simul parati,
15 Pauca nuntiate meae puellae
   Non bona dicta.

---

tharum] *Sacae*, etc. — **sagittiferos
Parthos** : with reference, as very
often in Latin literature, to the traditional weapon and manner of fight-
ing of these most dreaded enemies
of Rome; cf. Hor. *Carm.* II. 13. 17
*miles [timet] sagittas et celerem fu-
gam Parthi ;* Ov. *Rem. Am.* 157
*uince Cupidineas pariter Parthas-
que sagittas ;* Stat. *Theb.* VI. 575
*[credas] Parthorum fuga totidem
exsiluisse sagittas.*

7. **septemgeminus** : as having
seven mouths ; cf. Verg. *Aen.* VI.
800 *septemgemini ostia Nili;* Ov.
Met. I. 422 *ubi deseruit madidos
septemfluus agros Nilus ;* V. 187
genitum septemplice Nilo. — **colorat aequora** : by its muddy waters,
which, in their overflow, still fertil-
ize the fields of Egypt ; cf. Verg.
Geor. IV. 291 *[Nilus] uiridem
Aegyptum nigra fecundat harena.*

10. In this and the two following
verses is a trace of the reconciliation of Catullus to Caesar; cf. Intr.
38 ff. The poet could not yet
sing Caesar's praises unreservedly,
though he might have done so had
he lived longer; but he has already
yielded from his earlier position of unmixed censure. — **monimenta** : the
places mentioned are themselves the
reminders of Caesar's greatness.

11. **Gallicum** : the Rhine is so
styled since it was the boundary of
Caesar's great conquests, and not
with reference to his passage of the
river from Gaul into Germany (cf.
Caes. *B. G.* IV. 16 ff.). — **horribile
aequor** : the proverbially rough
English channel. — **ultimos** : cf. 29.
4, 12 ; Hor. *Carm.* I. 35. 29 *serues
iturum Caesarem in ultimos orbis
Britannos ;* Verg. *Ecl.* 1. 66 *penitus
toto diuisos orbe Britannos.* The
preliminary invasion of Britain took
place in the late summer of 55 B.C.

13–16. Apparently Furius and
Aurelius, at the suggestion of Lesbia, tendered their services in bringing about a reconciliation with her;
but Catullus thoroughly despises
them for their actions in the past
(cf. Intr. 37), and employs them as
comites on only one, and that a
final, errand, — to convey to Lesbia
his decision against her appeal.

15. **meae puellae** : in half-scorn-
ful, half-mournful reminiscence of
such passages as 2. 1 and 3. 3 ; cf.
the tone of 58. Possibly Lesbia in
this appeal had called herself by the
endearing name that her lover used
to apply to her.

16. **non bona dicta** : the clearly-
worded and stinging, but controlled
bitterness of his reply carries the

Cum suis uiuat ualeatque moechis,
Quos simul complexa tenet trecentos,
Nullum amans uere, sed identidem omnium
20   Ilia rumpens ;

Nec meum respectet, ut ante, amorem,
Qui illius culpa cecidit uelut prati
Vltimi flos, praetereunte postquam
    Tactus aratro est.

12.

Marrucine Asini, manu sinistra
Non belle uteris in ioco atque uino :
Tollis lintea neglegentiorum.

expression of unalterable determination that is in marked contrast to
the tone of 8.

17. **uiuat ualeatque** : a decisive
utterance of farewell ; cf. Hor. *Ep.*
I. 6. 66 *uiuas in amore iocisque ;
uiue, uale.*

18. **tenet,** *holds in thrall ;* cf. 55.
17 ; Verg. *Ecl.* I. 31 *me Galatea
tenebat ;* Mart. XI. 40. 1 *formosam
Glyceram Lupercus solus tenet.* —
trecentos : colloquially used of
indefinite multitude ; cf. 9. 2 n. ;
Plaut. *Mil. Glor.* 250 *trecentae possunt causae colligi* (but *Trin.* 791
sescentae causae possunt colligi) ;
Hor. *Sat.* I. 5. 12 *trecentos inseris !*
and often elsewhere.

21. **respectet** : *i.e.* hope to win
back ; cf. Cic. *Planc.* 18. 45 *ne par ab
iis munus in sua petitione respectent.*
— **ut ante** : *i.e.* at the time mentioned in 107 and 36. 4, following
upon the break that prompted 8.

22. **uelut,** etc. : love then lan-
guished only, but is now dead and
cannot be recalled to life ; with the
figure, cf. Verg. *Aen.* IX. 433 *purpu-*

*reus ueluti cum flos succisus aratro
languescit moriens,* though Catullus
secures greater delicacy of expression by introducing *ultimi prati,*
and by using *tactus* instead of *succisus.*

12. On Asinius Marrucinus, a
napkin-thief, concerning whom see
Intr. 58. For the theme cf. 25, and
the well-known epigrams on Hermogenes, Mart. XII. 29, and on an
unnamed thief, VIII. 59. — On the
date of composition, see vv. 9 n.
and 15 n. Metre, Phalaecean.

1. **sinistra** : as the right hand
was given in token of friendship,
the left was proverbially the one
devoted to theft ; cf. Plaut. *Pers.*
227 *illa altera furtifica laeua ;*
Ov. *Met.* XIII. 111 [*nec clipeus*]
conueniet natae ad furta sinistrae :
the word occurs in 47. 1 in the figurative sense of ' accomplices ' in
thieving.

2. **in ioco atque uino** : cf. 50.
6 ; 13. 5.

3. **lintea** : no clear line seems to
have been drawn between handker-

Hoc salsum esse putas ?   Fugit te, inepte !

5   Quamuis sordida res et inuenusta est.

Non credis mihi ?   Crede Pollioni

Fratri, qui tua furta uel talento

Mutari uelit ; est enim leporum

Disertus puer ac facetiarum.

10   Quare aut hendecasyllabos trecentos

Exspecta, aut mihi linteum remitte,

Quod me non mouet aestimatione,

chiefs, napkins, and even towels, for *lintea, mantelia, mappae,* and *suda-ria* are used indiscriminately of all these articles. Sometimes the *map-pae* are mentioned as a part of the regular table-furnishing (cf. Varr. *L. L.* IX. 47 ; Hor. *Sat.* II. 4. 81), and sometimes each guest provides his own, as here, and in Mart. XII. 29. 11 *attulerat mappam nemo, dum furta timentur.*

4. fugit te, *that's where you're wrong;* cf. 10. 29 n. — **inepte,** *dunce,* since you apparently think this business funny ; cf. 25. 8 n., where the same word is used with slightly different application to characterize a similar thief of clothing.

5. quamuis, *utterly ;* used by Catullus in this sense only here ; but cf. Plaut. *Pseud.* 1175 *quamuis pernix hic homost,* and elsewhere.

6. Pollioni fratri : see Intr. 57.

7. talento : of an indefinitely large sum of money ; cf. Plaut. *Epid.* 701 *in meum nummum, in tuom talentum, pignus da.*

8. mutari uelit : as if it were a business transaction ; Pollio is so chagrined at your conduct that he would give a talent to change the facts. — **leporum ac facetiarum :** cf. the union of the same or similar words in one expression in 50. 7, 8; 16. 7.

9. disertus : *i.e.* Pollio has the feelings and training of a gentle-man ; for *disertus* implying, as here, distinctness of mental vision rather than of speech, see Ter. *Eun.* 1009 *numquam pol hominem stultiorem uidi nec uidebo ; at etiam primo callidum et disertum credidi homi-nem.* — **puer :** frequently used some-what loosely of a young man, as *puella* is of a young woman ; cf. 45. 11 ; 62. 47 ; 78. 4 ; Hor. *Carm.* I. 5. 1 *quis te puer urget, Pyrrha ?* Cic. *Phil.* 4. 1. 3 *nomen clarissimi adulescentis, uel pueri potius* (of Octavianus at the age of 19); Sil. Ital. XV. 33 *non digne puer* (of Sci-pio at the age of 20); cf. also 63. 63 n. As Pollio was born in 75 B.C., he might have been called *puer* up to the end of Catullus's life; but the date of this poem is estab-lished within narrower limits by vv. 14 ff.

10. hendecasyllabos : iambics like those of Archilochus were the traditional weapons of satire; cf. 36. 5; 40. 2 n.; 54. 6; but Catullus used hendecasyllables for the same pur-pose, as in 42; yet cf. Plin. *Ep.* V. 10. 2. — **trecentos :** cf. 9. 2 n.; 11. 18 n.

12. non aestimatione, etc.: *i.e.* the associations, and not the in-trinsic worth, of the napkin make it valuable.

Verum est mnemosynum **mei so**dalis.
Nam sudaria Saetaba ex Hiberis
15 Miserunt mihi muneri Fabullus
Et Veranius : haec amem necesse est
Et Veraniolum meum et Fabullum.

13·

Cenabis bene, mi Fabulle, apud me
Paucis, si tibi di fauent, diebus,
Si tecum attuleris bonam atque magnam
Cenam, non sine candida puella

13. **mnemosynum** : a Greek word, used only here for the pure Latin *monimentum*, as in Verg. *Aen.* V. 536 *cratera quem Anchisae Cisseus sui dederat monimentum.* — **mei sodalis** : the singular is used since the two friends, Veranius and Fabullus, are identified in the affections of Catullus ; note also how in vv. 15–17 all expression of preference is avoided by reversal of the order of two names, and by the reduction of Veranius to the diminutive form to correspond with Fabullus (cf. Intr. 68; 28. 3 n.).

14. **sudaria Saetaba** : cf. 25. 7; Saetabis (now Jativa) was a city of Tarraconensis near the eastern coast of Spain, and was noted for its manufacture of flax ; cf. Plin. *N. H.* XIX. 9.

15. **miserunt** : not far from 60 B.C. (cf. 9, and Intr. 68, 69), within a comparatively short time after which year, this poem, then, was probably written.

13. To Fabullus, an invitation to a dinner, where the guest is, however, to furnish the meal himself. Perhaps the dinner was to celebrate the return of Fabullus

from Spain with Veranius ; cf. 9 and Intr. 68, 69. — On the date of composition see v. 11 n. Metre, Phalaecean.

1. **cenabis** : to add to the humorous effect of what follows, the first two verses of invitation are phrased in a tone of lofty condescension, almost as if Catullus were conferring a munificent boon upon a humble friend. The verse is imitated in Mart. XI. 52. 1 *cenabis belle, Iuli Cerealis, apud me.*

2. The tone of dignity and condescension is kept up by the absurd twist of the modest phrase *si mihi di fauent*, and the effect is augmented by the extreme indefiniteness of the time set. Catullus has not quite yet determined the important question when he will offer his Barmecide feast. But some critics understand **paucis diebus** to imply that Fabullus is not yet in the city, and the time of his arrival is uncertain.

3. **bonam atque magnam cenam** : *i.e.* a dinner of fine quality and many courses.

4. **candida puella** : *i.e.* a *psaltria*, as in the invitation of Horace

5   Et uino et sale et omnibus cachinnis.
    Haec si, inquam, attuleris, uenuste noster,
    Cenabis bene ; nam tui Catulli
    Plenus sacculus est aranearum.
    Sed contra accipies meros amores
10 Seu quid suauius elegantiusue est :
    Nam unguentum dabo, quod meae puellae
    Donarunt Veneres Cupidinesque,
    Quod tu cum olfacies, deos rogabis
    Totum ut te faciant, Fabulle, nasum

to Hirpinus, *Carm.* II. 11. 21–24.
With the adjective cf. 68. 134 *candidus Cupido ;* 35. 8 *candida puella ;*
68. 70 *candida diua ;* 86. 1 *Quintia est candida ;* Hor. *Epod.* 11. 27
ardor puellae candidae.
   5. **et uino**, etc.: cf. 12. 2 n. —
sale, *wit*, as in 16. 7 ; 86. 4. —
omnibus cachinnis : cf. 31. 14
quidquid est domi cachinnorum.
   6. **uenuste** : the word indicates
the possession of a certain charm of
society breeding, as in 3. 2 ; 22. 2.
Cf. the similar vocative *iucunde* in
50. 16. — **noster** : also used in the
vocative for *mi* in 44. 1.
   7. **cenabis bene** : now that the
condition has been stated, the words
have a different expression from that
in v. 1. — **tui Catulli** : cf. 14. 13 *ad
tuum Catullum ;* 38. 1 *male est,
Cornifici, tuo Catullo.*
   8. **plenus aranearum** : denoting
utter abandonment and emptiness;
cf. 68. 49 ; Plaut. *Aul.* 83 *nam hic
apud nos nihil est aliud quaesti furi-
bus ; ita inaniis sunt oppletae atque
araneis ;* and more precisely Afran.
412 R. *tamne arcula tua plena est
aranearum ?* R. Browning, *Ring
and Book* V. 49 *when the purse he
left held spider-webs.*
   9. **contra**, *in return ;* cf. 76. 23
contra ut me diligat illa. — **meros**

amores : a term implying a perfection of charm; cf. Mart. XIV. 206.
1 *collo necte, puer, meros amores,
ceston.*
   10. **seu quid**, etc. : = *uel si quid,*
etc. ; *i.e.* or if there be a term implying greater delightfulness, it is
that. With the form of expression, cf. 22. 13 ; 23. 13 ; 42. 14 ;
82. 2, 4.
   11. **unguentum** : when fine, one
of the most expensive accompani-
ments of feasts; cf. 6. 8 n. Martial
(III. 12), apparently inspired by
this poem, chides a Fabullus for fur-
nishing his guests with good ointment, but nothing else. — **meae
puellae** : undoubtedly Lesbia ; cf.
3. 3 n. ; the lack of anything but
happy feeling in the memory indicates that this poem was written
while the love of Catullus for Lesbia
was still untroubled by disagreement
or suspicion, — therefore about 60
B.C.
   12. **Veneres Cupidinesque** : cf.
3. 1 n.; Prop. III. 29. 17 *adflabunt
tibi non Arabum de gramine odores,
sed quos ipse suis fecit Amor manibus.*
   14. Ellis quotes Ben Jonson, *Cynthia's Revels* V. 2 *you would wish
yourself all nose for the love on't* (a
perfume).

14.

Ni te plus oculis meis amarem,
Iucundissime Calue, munere isto
Odissem te odio Vatiniano :
Nam quid feci ego quidue sum locutus,
5   Cur me tot male perderes poetis ?
Isti di mala multa dent clienti
Qui tantum tibi misit impiorum.

14. To Calvus, on a Saturnalian
joke played by him upon Catullus.
— It was not uncommon for poets
to dedicate and send new writings
of their own to some friend as a
gift on the Saturnalia, or on a birth-
day ; cf. Mart. X. 17 ; Stat. *Silu.*
IV. 9 and pref.; II. 3. 62. Calvus
had sent a book to Catullus, who,
supposing it to be a choice bit of
new poetry of his friend's composition, sat down eagerly to read it,
but found, to his whimsical disgust,
that it was made up of wretched
specimens of some poetasters. On
the personality of Calvus cf. Intr. 60.
The allusion in v. 3 suggests that
the poem was not written till after
the great speech of Calvus against
Vatinius, recorded in v. 53. It cannot, therefore, be assigned to an
earlier date than the year 58 B.C.,
and probably was written on the
Saturnalia of 56 B.C. (cf. introductory note to 53.) On the Saturnalia
of the year 57, Catullus was apparently in Bithynia, and on that of 55,
quite possibly in Verona, while this
poem appears to have been written in
or near Rome. — Metre, Phalaecean.

   1. **ni te**, etc.: cf. the opening
verses of the address of Maecenas
to Horace quoted by Suetonius *Vit.
Hor.: ni te uisceribus meis, Horati,
plus iam diligo*, etc. — **plus oculis** :
cf. 3. 5 n.

   2. **iucundissime** : in about the
same sense as *carissime ;* Calvus is
addressed as *iucunde* in 50. 16 ; cf.
also 62. 47 ; 64. 215.
   3. **odissem**, etc.: *i.e.* I would
hate you as roundly as does Vatinius. Calvus had on more than one
occasion acted as the prosecutor of
Vatinius ; cf. introductory note to
53. With the collocation **odissem
odio,** cf. *Psalms* 139. 22 *I hate them
with perfect hatred.*
   5. **male perderes** : cf. 10. 33 n.,
and the converse in Hor. *Sat.* II. 1.
6 *pereām male.*
   6. **di mala multa dent**: a familiar formula of imprecation ; cf.
28. 14 ; Plaut. *Most.* 643 ; Ter.
Phor. 976 *malum, quod isti di deaeque omnes duint,* and the prayer
for blessing in Plaut. *Poen.* 208
multa tibi di dent bona. — **clienti** :
under the earlier Roman feudal system, one duty of the *patronus* was
to act as the legal representative of
the *cliens ;* the same terms were
now used to denote the legal
counsel and the man for whom
he incidentally appeared; cf. Hor.
Ep. II. 1. 104 *clienti promere iura.*
   7. **tantum impiorum,** *so many
scoundrels ;* such abominable poets
must be men of depraved character
(but of himself in 16. 5 *pium poetam*); with the partitive expression
cf. 5. 13.

Quod si, ut suspicor, hoc nouum ac repertum
Munus dat tibi Sulla litterator,

10 Non est mi male, sed bene ac beate,
Quod non dispereunt tui labores.
Di magni, horribilem et sacrum libellum,
Quem tu scilicet ad tuum Catullum
Misti, continuo ut die periret,

15 Saturnalibus, optimo dierum !

8. nouum ac repertum, *newly discovered,* for surely no one but a schoolmaster (**litterator**) would ever think of paying the *honorarium* of his legal counsel with books; but Sulla evidently thought he had found a kindred spirit in the poet-lawyer Calvus.

9. munus : the relation between lawyer and client was still construed to be that between the *patronus* and *cliens* of the earlier social system. Hence, as the *patronus* was bound to defend the *cliens* before the courts without the exaction of a special contribution of money from him, so the lawyer was still forbidden to accept a fee from his client. But the prohibition was usually evaded under the guise of gifts and legacies. — **Sulla litterator :** of this schoolmaster nothing further is known.

10. est mi male : cf. 38. 1 ; 3. 13 n. — **bene ac beate :** with the alliterative coupling cf. 23. 15 *bene ac beate ;* 37. 14 *boni beatique ;* so Cicero often, especially with an ethical meaning (= καλῶς κἀγαθῶς).

11. non dispereunt, etc. : schoolmasters were proverbially povertystricken (cf. of a later date Juv. 7. 203 ff.), and Calvus was lucky to get from Sulla even so much in return for his legal services.

12. di magni : the same words are used as an exclamation in 53. 5 also, but as a true invocation in 109. 3. — **sacrum,** *accursed,* as in 71. 1.

14. misti : for *misisti ;* cf. 66. 21 *luxti ;* 66. 30 *tristi ;* 77. 3 *subrepsti ;* 91. 9 *duxti ;* 99. 8 *abstersti ;* 110. 3 *promisti.* — **continuo die,** *on the very next day ;* cf. Ov. *Fast.* V. 733 *auferet ex oculis ueniens Aurora Booten, continuaque die sidus Hyantis erit ;* VI. 719 *tollet humo ualidos proles Hyriea lacertos, continua Delphin nocte uidendus erit.* **continuo** cannot be, as some suggest, an adverb, — if for no other reason, because *die Saturnalibus* alone is not Latin. The passage from Plaut. *Poen.* 497 *die bono Aphrodisiis,* is not in point, for *die* is there modified by an adjective. But the arrangement here makes improbable the direct modification of *die* by *optimo* and *dierum.* Calvus had evidently despatched the book the evening before, so that it might reach Catullus the first thing next morning.

15. Saturnalibus : a very ancient Latin festival, in commemoration of the golden age when Saturn dwelt among men. The especial day of the festival was Dec. 17 of each year, but the celebration was by popular usage extended over the week following. Presents were exchanged between friends, slaves were temporarily treated as if equals of their masters (cf. Hor. *Sat.* II. 7), and the utmost freedom and jollity prevailed.

Non, non hoc tibi, false, sic abibit:
Nam, si luxerit, ad librariorum
Curram scrinia, Caesios, Aquinos,
Suffenum, omnia colligam uenena,
20   Ac te his suppliciis remunerabor.
Vos hinc interea ualete, abite
Illuc unde malum pedem attulistis,
Saecli incommoda, pessimi poetae.

16. **non, non**: with this emphatic repetition, cf. Ter. *Phor.* 303 *non, non sic futurum est, non potest!* Prop. II. 3. 27 *non, non humani partus sunt talia bona.*— **non tibi sic abibit**, *you shall not get off so easily;* cf. Ter. *And.* 175 *mirabar hoc si sic abiret;* Cic. *Att.* XIV. 1. 1 *non posse istaec sic abire.* — **false**: keeping up the tone of humorously simulated indignation; the emendation to *salse* misses the point.

17. **si luxerit**, *as soon as the morrow dawns;* the conditional form points the restless impatience that can almost believe the morrow will never come. The day is spoiled for Catullus; but he must drag along a wretched existence through the tedious hours till next morning, when the shops of the booksellers will be opened once more, and he can take revenge in kind. — **librariorum**: generally used throughout this and the Augustan period of a mere copyist (*scriba;* cf. Hor. *A. P.* 354 *scriptor si peccat idem librarius usque*), but here of a copyist who is also a bookseller; in later Latin it is used of a true bookseller (*bibliopola*), who, however, usually employed a staff of copyists ; cf. Sen. *Ben.* VII. 6. 1 *libros dicimus esse Ciceronis; eosdem librarius suos uocat.*

18. **scrinia**: cylindrical boxes provided with a cover and used to hold each a number of MS. rolls

standing on end. — **Caesios, Aquinos**: the plural denotes such poets as those mentioned. The change to the singular in **Suffenum** (v. 19) is but for variety, or perhaps because Suffenus personally was an object of greater attention to Catullus (see 22). Caesius is otherwise unknown; Aquinus only through Cic. *Tusc.* V. 63 *adhuc neminem cognoui poetam* (*et mihi fuit cum Aquino amicitia*) *qui sibi non optimus uideretur.*

19. **omnia uenena**: *i.e.* everything that exists in the line of poisons.

21. **uos interea**, *while as for you, i.e.* not to make you wait too long for my commands while I am busying myself with other matters ; cf. 36. 18; 101. 7 n. — **ualete abite**: asyndetic, as in Hor. *Ep.* I. 6. 67 *uiue uale.* With this dismissal of worthless literature cf. Verg. *Catal.* 7. 1 *ite hinc, inanes, ite, rhetorum ampullae, inflata rore non Achaico uerba.*

22. **illuc**: *i.e. in malam rem*, as is made clear by the common form of objurgation in the comedians. — **malum pedem**: with a play upon the meaning of *pedem ;* cf. Ov. *Trist.* I. 1. 16 *uade, liber, uerbisque meis loca grata saluta; contingam certe quo licet illa pede.* — **attulistis**: cf. 63. 52 n. *tetuli pedem.*

23. **saecli incommoda**: pre eminent types of boredom.

14ᵇ.

Si qui forte mearum ineptiarum
Lectores eritis manusque uestras
Non horrebitis admouere nobis,

*

15.

Commendo tibi me ac meos amores,
Aureli.   Veniam peto pudentem,

14ᵇ. This fragment is so brief that it is almost impossible to determine its original character, though it is probably a modest and grateful recognition of attention at the hands of the public. By different critics it has been taken to be: the protasis to which 2. 11–13 is the apodosis, the whole thus forming a second, and general, introductory poem, while 1 is a special one; a fragment of the prologue to a *libellus* comprising 15–60, while 1 is the prologue to the *libellus* comprising 2–14; a fragment of the original epilogue to the *libellus* 2–14, while 1 is a prologue written expressly for the extant *liber*. Other less plausible theories have also found supporters.   But as it seems more likely that the existing *liber Catulli* is a rearranged complex of earlier *libelli* of undeterminable content, and was published by an unknown editor after the death of the author, it is quite possible that this scrap was found among his papers in its present condition, and was inserted in this arbitrary position upon the publication of the *liber*. See also Intr. 47 ff.

1. **ineptiarum**: cf. 1. 4 *nugas;* Mart. II. 86. 9 *turpe est difficiles habere nugas et stultus labor est ineptiarum;* XI. 1. 13 *qui*

reuoluant nostrarum tineas ineptiarum.

2. **manus admouere**: *sc. ut uolumen reuoluatis;* with friendly, not hostile intent; cf. Ov. *Met.* X. 254 *manus operi admouet.*

3. **non horrebitis**, *shall not disdain;* cf. Hor. *Ep.* I. 18. 24 *quem diues amicus odit et horret.* Others, who believe that 14ᵇ is really the first three verses of 16, thus strangely misplaced, would understand these words to mean 'shall have the impudence.'

15. To Aurelius, entrusting to his care a young boy, a favorite of the poet.   Evidently a poem of the Juventius cycle, which comprises also, directly or indirectly, 16 (?), 21, 23, 24, 26, 40 (?), 48, 81, 99 ; all of these poems are probably to be attributed to the later period of the residence of Catullus in Rome (56–54 B.C.); see Intr. 37. — Metre, Phalaecean.

1. **commendo tibi**: for some reason, perhaps the temporary absence of Catullus from town, Juventius is to be entertained by Aurelius. — **meos amores**: cf. 6. 16 n. *tuos amores.*

2. **Aureli**: see Intr. 37, 41. If not an intimate and warm friend, Aurelius must have been at this time on

Vt, si quicquam animo tuo cupisti
Quod castum expeteres et integellum,
5 Conserues puerum mihi pudice,
Non dico a populo : nihil ueremur
Istos qui in platea modo huc modo illuc
In re praetereunt sua occupati ;
Verum a te metuo tuoque pene
10 Infesto pueris bonis malisque.
Quem tu qua libet, ut libet moueto
Quantum uis, ubi erit foris paratum :
Hunc unum excipio, ut puto, pudenter.
Quod si te mala mens furorque uecors
15 In tantam impulerit, sceleste, culpam,
Vt nostrum insidiis caput lacessas,
Ah tum te miserum malique fati,
Quem attractis pedibus patente porta
Percurrent raphanique mugilesque.

good terms with Catullus, or Juventius would not have been entrusted
to his care. And, allowing for traditional grossness of language (cf.
Intr. 32), there is no tone of un-
friendliness in this poem. But
Aurelius (and his friend Furius;
cf. 23 and 24) betrayed the trust,
and from this occasion dates the
enmity of Catullus toward them.—
ueniam pudentem, *a modest favor*.

4. integellum: with the meaning of *integri* in 34. 2.

6. non dico . . . uerum: cf. 16.
10 *non dico . . . sed*. — ueremur:
for the first person singular, as not
infrequently also *nos* for *ego*, and *noster* for *meus* (cf. v. 16, and 6. 16 n.).

7. modo huc modo illuc: cf.
3. 9 n.

11. qua libet: locative, while *ut
libet* is modal; but cf. 40. 5; 76. 14.

14. mala mens, *infatuation*.

16. nostrum, etc.: *i.e.* a breach
of chastity toward Juventius would
be a treacherous crime against Catullus himself ; cf. 21. 7 *insidias mihi
instruentem*. — nostrum caput:
i.e. nos (= *me*), but with a more
definite reference to peculiar and
cherished interests; cf. 68. 120 *caput
seri nepotis* (= *serum nepotem*) ;
Plaut. *Capt.* 946 *propter meum caput;* Hor. *Carm.* I. 24. 2 *tam cari
capitis ; Sat*. II. 5. 94 *cautus uti
uelet carum caput;* Prop. II. 8. 16 *in
nostrum iacies uerba superba caput*.

17. te : accusative of exclamation. — mali fati: with this genitive of characteristic cf. 17. 7 *munus maximi risus; Juv. 3. 4 litus
amoeni secessus.*

18–19. On this punishment for
adultery cf. C. I. L. IV. 1261; Arist
Nub. 1083 ; Hor. *Sat.* I. 2. 133
Juv. 10. 317.

16.

Pedicabo ego uos et irrumabo,
Aureli pathice et cinaede Furi,
Qui me ex uersiculis meis putastis,
Quod sunt molliculi, parum pudicum.

5   Nam castum esse decet pium poetam
Ipsum, uersiculos nihil necesse est,
Qui tum denique habent salem ac leporem,
Si sunt molliculi ac parum pudici
Et quod pruriat incitare possunt,

10 Non dico pueris, sed his pilosis,
Qui duros nequeunt mouere lumbos.
Vos quod milia multa basiorum
Legistis, male me marem putatis?
Pedicabo ego uos et irrumabo.

16. Against Furius and Aurelius, who judge Catullus from his verses to be as bad as themselves. — The reference in v. 12 seems to fix the date of composition within the later period of the life of Catullus (see Intr. 37). Metre, Phalaecean.

1. **pedicabo**, etc.: the verbs are here not to be understood in the literal sense, but only as conveying vague threats, in the gross language of that day; cf. also Intr. 32.

5–6. With the sentiment cf. Ov. *Trist.* II. 354 *uita uerecunda est, Musa iocosa mea;* Mart. I. 4. 8 *lasciua est nobis pagina, uita proba;* Hadr. apud Apul. *Apol.* 11 *lasciuus uersu, mente pudicus eras;* Sen. *Contr. exc.* VI. 8 *quid tu putas poetas, quae sentiunt, scribere? Vixit modeste, castigate;* Plin. *Ep.* IV. 14. 5: Rob. Herrick *To his book's end this last line he'd have placed, Jocund his Muse was, but his life was chaste;* and *per contra* Sen.

Ep. 114. 3. — **pium poetam**: cf. the contrary epithet applied to worthless poets in 14. 7 *impiorum*.

7. **salem ac leporem**: cf. 12. 8 *leporum ac facetiarum;* 50. 7 *lepore facetiisque.*

10. **non dico . . . sed**: cf. 15. 6 *non dico . . . uerum.*

12. **milia multa basiorum**: with reference to 48, and perhaps to other poems like it, addressed to Juventius, but not included in the final *liber Catulli.* The words are a precise repetition of those in 5. 10, but there is no indication that Aurelius and Furius were at this time interested in the Lesbia episode (but for a later date cf. 11), while they were interested in Juventius (cf. 15, 21, 23, 24, and 81). That the reference is to Juventius rather than to Lesbia is indicated by the comparison of v. 13 *male marem* with Ov. *Art. Am.* I. 524 *et siquis male uir*

17.

O Colonia, quae cupis ponte ludere longo,
Et salire paratum habes, sed uereris inepta
Crura ponticuli assulis stantis in rediuiuis,
Ne supinus eat cauaque in palude recumbat,
5　Sic tibi bonus ex tua pons libidine fiat,
In quo uel Salisubsili sacra suscipiantur,

quaerit habere uirum. On this use of *male* see 10. 33 n.

14. The last verse is identical with the first also in 36, 52, and 57.

17. To the village of Colonia; a wish for the violent waking-up of an indifferent old Veronese who had a gay young wife. Very possibly written at Verona before Catullus came to Rome to live (cf. v. 8 n.) The frequency of alliteration is noteworthy. — Metre, Priapean.

I. Colonia: usually identified since Guarinus with the modern village of Cologna, a few miles eastward from Verona, the marshy situation of which fits well with the description in the text. — **ponte longo:** not the desired bridge, but the existing *ponticulus* (v. 3) itself. The village folk would fain hold their solemn ceremonials on their bridge, but fear its rottenness, and inability to bear the weight of so many people at once. *Pons,* often modified by *longus,* was the ordinary term for a causeway constructed across a morass, part bridge, and part corduroy road; cf. Hirt. *B. G.* VIII. 14. 4 *pontibus palude constrata legiones traducit;* Tac. *Ann.* I. 61 *ut pontes et aggeres umido paludum et fallacibus campis imponeret;* I. 63 *monitus pontes longos quam maturrime superare.* — **ludere:** on the religious ceremonials (cf. v. 6) connected with the bridging of streams by the early Latins, see

Preller *Röm. Myth.*³ II. p. 134 ff. The custom had apparently been carried northward by the Latin colonists.

2. **salire:** of the dance, at first priestly, but afterward popular. Cf. the rites of the Salii at Rome (Preller I. pp. 347, 355 ff.). — **paratum habes:** the use of *habere* almost as a simple auxiliary is not rare in any stage of the Latin language; cf. 60. 5; 67. 31; and Draeger *Hist. Syntax*² I. pp. 294 ff. — **inepta crura,** *shaky legs;* the noun is unique in this humorous application to inanimate objects, *pes* being commonly used in such connections.

3. **ponticuli:** the diminutive implies the general worthlessness of the whole structure. — **assulis rediuiuis,** *second-hand sticks.*

4. **supinus eat,** *tumble flat;* apparently a colloquial expression; the adjective is used in this sense of the sea in Plin. *N. H.* IX. 2, and of the alluvial plains of Egypt in Plin. *Pan.* 30. — **caua,** *deep;* cf. 95. 5 ; Ov. *Met.* VI. 371 *tota caua submergere membra palude.*

5–7. **sic fiat, . . . da:** with this form of conditional wish cf. Hor. *Carm.* I. 3. 1 ff. *sic te diua regat, Vergilium reddas;* Verg. *Ecl.* 9. 30 ff. *sic distendant ubera uaccae, incipe.* Martial imitates in VII. 93. 8 *perpetuo liceat sic tibi ponte frui.*

6. **Salisubsili:** the word is not found elsewhere, unless the quota-

Munus hoc mihi maximi da, Colonia, risus.
Quendam municipem meum de tuo uolo ponte
Ire praecipitem in lutum per caputque pedesque,
10 Verum totius ut lacus putidaeque paludis
Liuidissima maximeque est profunda uorago.
Insulsissimus est homo, nec sapit pueri instar
Bimuli tremula patris dormientis in ulna:
Cui cum sit uiridissimo nupta flore puella
15 (Et puella tenellulo delicatior haedo,

tion from Pacuvius given by Guarinus on this passage be genuine, *pro
imperio salisubsulus si nostro excubet.*
Here *Salisubsulus* apparently means
Mars; the derivation of the word is
evident. The rites of the Salii at
Rome were accompanied by violent
dances apparently survivals of the orgiastic rites of most ancient times (cf.
Preller *l.c.*), but even such rites as
these are not to shake the new bridge.

7. **maximi risus**: with this genitive of characteristic cf. 15. 17 n.

8. **municipem meum**: evidently, then, a Veronese; the keen
interest of Catullus in this local
affair (and perhaps even the metre,
used only here) point to a time
when he was yet residing at Verona;
cf. introductory note to 67.

9. **per caputque pedesque**: *i.e.*
over head and ears, soused completely under, — and that too (vv.
10–11) in the deepest part of the
slough. This marks the end of the
movement begun by *ire praecipitem.* Yet *per caput* in Liv. *Per.*
XXII. is explained in XXII. 3. 11
by *equus consulem super caput effu-
dit* to be equivalent to *praeceps* (cf.
Ov. *Ib.* 255 *ab equo praeceps deci-
dit*), and the Gr. κατωκάρα has the
same meaning.

10. **ut**: locative ; cf. 11. 3 n. —
totius lacus putidaeque paludis,
the brimming, stinking swamp.

11. **liuidissima**: of a dark gray
or bluish black color; cf. Verg. *Aen.*
VI. 320 *uada liuida ;* Hor. *Carm.*
II. 5. 10 *liuidos racemos.*

12. **insulsissimus est homo,**
he's the biggest ass of a man.

13. **tremula**: of the tremulous-
ness of age, as in 61. 51 ; 61. 161;
64. 307; 68. 142. Precision is not
attempted, or an aged man would
not be represented as the father of
so young a child; but, as in 61. 51;
64. 350 ; 68. 142, the poet emphasizes the traditional contrast between
age and youth by the juxtaposition
of the two extreme adjectives *bimuli*
and *tremuli.*

14. **uiridissimo flore,** *in her
freshest bloom;* cf. similar figures in
24. 1 *flosculus Iuuentiorum ;* 61. 57
floridam puellulam ; 61. 193 *ore
floridulo nitens ;* 63. 64 *gymnasi
flos ;* 64. 251 *florens Iacchus ;* 68. 16
*iucundum cum aetas florida uer
ageret ;* 100. 2 *flos iuuenum ;* Ter.
Eun. 318 *anni ? sedecim, flos ipse ;*
and more detailed similes in 61
22 n.

15. **et,** *and that too,* adding an
emphatic explanatory phrase ; cf.
Cic. *Verr.* II. 2. 21. 51 *hostis, et
hostis nimis ferus,* and often. —
delicatior, *livelier,* implying a tendency toward wantonness or sensu-
ality ; cf. Cic. *N. D.* I. 36. 102 *pueri delicati nihil cessatione melius*

Adseruanda nigerrimis diligentius uuis),
Ludere hanc sinit ut libet, nec pili facit uni,
Nec se subleuat ex sua parte, sed uelut alnus
In fossa Liguri iacet suppernata securi,
20 Tantundem omnia sentiens quam si nulla sit usquam,
Talis iste meus stupor nil uidet, nihil audit,
Ipse qui sit, utrum sit an non sit, id quoque nescit.
Nunc eum uolo de tuo ponte mittere pronum,
Si pote stolidum repente excitare ueternum
25 Et supinum animum in graui derelinquere caeno,
Ferream ut soleam tenaci in uoragine mula.

[*existimant*] ; *Att.* I. 19. 8 *odia illa libidinosae et delicatae iuuentutis.*

16. **nigerrimis:** *i.e.* dead-ripe, and so needing the most careful protection from thieves, as the young wife from lovers.

17. **pili facit:** cf. 10. 13; 5. 3 n.; Petr. 44 *nemo Iouem pili facit.* — **uni:** on this genitive form see Neue *Formenlehre* II.[2] p. 254.

18. **se subleuat,** *trouble himself; i.e.* he feels no decent jealousy, and no regard for the honor of his family.

19. **fossa:** perhaps a water-way constructed to float logs off; for Liguria abounded in ship-timber according to Strabo 202 ἔχουσι δ᾽ ὕλην ἐνταῦθα παμπόλλην ναυπηγήσιμον καὶ μεγαλόδενδρον. — **Liguri securi:** by transfer of epithet from **alnus;** cf. 31. 13 *Lydiae lacus undae;* 37. 20 ; 51. 11 ; Hor. *Carm.* I. 31. 9 *premant Calena falce quibus dedit fortuna uitem ;* III. 6. 38 *Sabellis docta ligonibus uersare glaebas ;* Verg. *Aen.* II. 781 *Lydius arua inter opima uirum fluit Thybris.*

20. **tantundem,** etc.: *i.e.* with no more feeling than if it had no existence at all. — **nulla:** cf. 8. 14 n.

21. **meus:** ironically; cf. Phaedr. V. 7. 32 *homo meus se in pulpito totum prosternit* (of a conceited

tibicen). — **stupor:** for *homo stupidus,* the abstract for the concrete; a common usage in colloquial speech from Plautus down.

23. **pronum:** with no more precise reference to attitude than in v. 4 *supinus.*

24. **pote** (sc. *est*) = *potest,* as always with this word in Catullus, except in case of the compound *utpote ;* cf. 45. 5 ; 67. 11 ; 76. 16 (twice); 98. 1. On the lengthening of the final syllable see Intr. 86 *g.* — **ueternum:** cf. v. 21 *stupor.*

25. **supinum:** with a play upon the actual position of the man in the mud.

26. **soleam:** there is no indication in ancient monuments or writers that the shoes were nailed on, though mules used as draught-animals, or on journeys, are several times mentioned as shod. Probably the metal sole (which in cases of great display was of silver, or even of gold ; cf. Suet. *Nero* 30 *soleis mularum argenteis ;* Plin. *N. H.* XXXIII. 140 *Poppaea, coniunx Neronis principis, soleas delicatioribus iumentis suis ex auro quoque induere iussit*) was attached to a sort of sock of leather or woven fibre, which was in turn fastened

21.

Aureli, pater esuritionum,
Non harum modo, sed quot aut fuerunt
Aut sunt aut aliis erunt in annis,
Pedicare cupis meos amores.
5   Nec clam : nam simul es, iocaris una,
Haerens ad latus omnia experiris.
Frustra : nam insidias mihi instruentem
Tangam te prior irrumatione.

by thongs about the fetlock. Such a shoe might readily be lost in strongly adhesive mud.

18–20. In the MSS., 17 is immediately followed by 21; but the earlier editors, influenced by the identity of metre, inserted as 18 the fragmentary address to Priapus beginning *hunc lucum tibi dedico*, and followed it, as 19 and 20, with two poems of similar character, beginning *hunc ego iuuenes locum*, and *ego haec ego arte fabricata rustica.* The first fragment is quoted by Terentianus Maurus (v. 2754) and ascribed by him to Catullus, though there is no other reason for connecting it with his name. It is published in *Anthol. Lat.* 1700 Meyer, and by many editors of Catullus among his fragmentary poems. The other two poems are generally acknowledged to be spurious. They are published in *Anthol. Lat.* 1699, 1698 Meyer, 775, 774 Riese; *App. Verg.* VI. 3, 2 Baehrens; *Priap.* 86, 85 Buecheler, 85, 84 Mueller.— But the numbering of the genuine poems as disturbed by these interpolations has become traditional, and is here followed.

21. The appeal made to Aurelius in 15 for a chaste guardianship of Juventius has apparently proved ineffective, and this is a final remonstrance with a threat of punishment if it be disregarded. — Metre, Phalaecean.

1. **Aureli**: see Intr. 37, 41.— **pater**: such a preëminent type of starvation is Aurelius that he might well pose as the parent, or presiding genius, among all similarly afflicted persons: cf. Mart. XII. 53 10 *huic semper uitio* [*rapacitati*] *pater fuisti.* — **esuritionum**: the word apparently occurs first in Catullus (cf. also 23. 14); it is also found in Petronius and Martial. With the use of abstract for concrete, cf. 47. 2 *scabies famesque mundi,* and often.

2. **non harum modo**, etc.: cf. 24. 2, 3 ; 49. 2, 3; Cic. *Red. Quir.* 7. 16 *Cn. Pompeius, uir omnium qui sunt, fuerunt, erunt, uirtute, sapientia, gloria princeps.*

4. **meos amores**: cf. 15. 1; 6. 16 n.

5. **simul**: sc. *cum eo ;* **una**, the common supplement (cf. Plaut. *Most.* 1022 *i mecum una simul*), follows in a second clause ; cf. 50. 13 *ut tecum loquerer simulque ut essem.*

7. **frustra nam**: cf. the same collocation in Hor. *Carm.* III. 7. 21 *frustra : nam uoces audit integer.* — **insidias mihi instruentem** : cf. 15. 16 ; and with the precise expression, Liv. VI. 23. 6 *insidiis instruendis locum.*

Atque id si faceres satur, tacerem :
10 Nunc ipsum id doleo, quod esurire,
Ah me me, puer et sitire discet.
Quare desine, dum licet pudico,
Ne finem facias, sed irrumatus.

22.

Suffenus iste, Vare, quem probe nosti,
Homo est uenustus et dicax et urbanus,
Idemque longe plurimos facit uersus.
Puto esse ego illi milia aut decem aut plura
5 Perscripta, nec sic, ut fit, in palimpsesto

11. **ah me me** : an exclamation of commiseration for Juventius. — **discet** : Aurelius is *pater esuritionum* (v. 1), and the boy will of course be taught bad habits by him; *i.e.* if the affection of Juventius is won away from Catullus so that the boy will not return to him, but prefers to live as the protégé of Aurelius, he will perforce have to share the privations that exist in the house of Aurelius. It sounds as if the poem were meant to toll back Juventius as much as to score Aurelius.

22. On Suffenus, a conceited and voluminous poetaster, though a good fellow in other relations. — Metre, choliambic.

1. **Suffenus**. mentioned as a bad poet in 14. 19, but otherwise unknown.—**Vare**: probably Quintilius Varus of Cremona, mentioned also in 10. 1; cf. Intr. 66. — **probe nosti**: apparently a colloquialism; cf. Ter. *Heaut.* 180 *hunc Menedemum nostin? Probe;* Cic. *De Or.* III. 50. 194 *Antipater, quem tu probe meministi.*

2. **uenustus, dicax, urbanus**: see Quintilian's definition of these three qualities in VI. 3. 17, 18, 21; and cf. Sen. *Const. Sap.* 17. 3.

3. **idem**, *at the same time, notwithstanding this ;* to point an unexpected contrast; cf. v. 15; 25. 4; 30. 9; 62. 43; 103. 4. — **longe plurimos**, *i.e.* an absolutely unprecedented number; *longe* is rare in the sense of *multo* before Cicero, but occurs frequently in his writings, and in later prose and poetry; cf. Caes. *B. G.* I. 2 *apud Heluetios longe nobilissimus fuit et ditissimus Orgetorix ;* Hor. *Sat.* I. 5. 2 *Heliodorus, Graecorum longe doctissimus.*

4. **milia**: cf. 9. 2 n. — **aut** . . . **aut**: when correlatives, usually introducing mutually exclusive alternatives, as in 12. 10–11 ; 64. 102 ; 69. 9–10 ; 103. 1–3 ; while only a single *aut* is used in the sense of ' or even,' as in 29. 14; and this is apparently the only instance where the latter *aut* of two correlatives has that meaning.

5. **sic** : with a strongly demonstrative force, pointing to what precedes, ' such being the case,' ' though the verses are so many ' ; cf. Liv. I. 5. 4 *crimini maxime dabant in Numitoris agros ab iis impetum fieri : sic ad supplicium Numitori*

Relata : chartae regiae, noui libri,
Noui umbilici, lora, rubra membrana,
Derecta plumbo et pumice omnia aequata.

Remus deditur. — ut fit, *as commonly ;* for mere scribbling, notes,
and first drafts, wax tablets were
generally used, or, especially when
the writing was considerable in
amount, parchment, on account of
the facility with which writing on
these substances could be erased.
Surely the enormous amount of the
verses of Suffenus must indicate that
they are but a first draft, to be greatly
reduced by revision, and therefore
calling for the use of cheap materials. But, behold, he actually pub-
lishes them all just as they stand,
and regardless of expense. — palimpsesto : writing-fabric from
which previous writing has been
erased, from a motive of economy,
to make room for later. Parchment
lent itself most readily to such erasure by washing, or erosion of the
surface, though palimpsests of papyrus were certainly not unknown (cf.
Marquardt *Privatleben der Römer* [2]
p. 815; Birt *Antike Buchwesen* pp.
57, 58, 63) ; but it is by no means
certain that they are referred to here.

6. relata : with especial reference to the form, as *perscripta* (v.
5) to the fact, of the writing. *Referre* commonly takes in this meaning the accusative with *in ;* but for
the ablative with *in* see Cic. *N. D.*
I. 12. 29 *Democritus imagines
earumque circuitus in deorum numero refert ; Rosc. Com.* 2. 5 *nomen
in codice accepti et expensi relatum*
(edd. *in codicem*) *;* and the ablative
may be justified by the fact that
here *relata* does not refer to technical entry in a book, but simply to
writing in general. — chartae regiae : the best quality of paper
appears to have been originally so

called, and later to have received
successively the names *hieratica*
and *Augusta* (Marquardt,[2] p. 810 ;
Birt, p. 247). — noui libri : *i.e.* no
cheap palimpsest, but the best of
paper, and that brand-new, 'new
books of royal paper'; and the emphasis effected by the parathetic
construction is supported by the
asyndeton preserved throughout the
following two verses.

7. umbilici : the rods, tipped
sometimes with bosses, on which the
rolls were wound (cf. the rollers with
bosses at the lower edge of modern
wall-maps) ; the name came originally from the central position of the
tip of the rod at the end of the roll.
— lora : probably the soft and elaborately decorated straps used instead
of common cords to fasten the roll
in shape when properly wound on the
umbilicus. — rubra membrana : the
cover of brightly colored parchment
in which the completed roll was enclosed for greater protection ; cf.
Ov. *Trist.* I. 1. 5 *nec te* [*librum*]
purpureo uelent uaccinia fuco ; Tib.
III. [Lygd.] 1. 9 *lutea sed niueum
inuoluat membrana libellum ;* Mart
III. 2. 10 *te* [*libellum*] *purpura
delicata uelet ;* X. 93. 4 *carmina
purpurea culta toga.*

8. derecta plumbo : for securing
greater regularity, a thin, circular
plate of lead guided by a ruler was
used to draw lines for the writing,
and to mark off the space reserved
for margins. derecta, like aequata, modifies omnia, and is
written rather than *directa* because
motion in a single, fixed direction is
indicated ; cf. 63. 56 *derigere aciem.*
— pumice omnia aequata : the
poet enumerates in detail and in

Haec cum legas tu, bellus ille et urbanus

10 Suffenus unus caprimulgus aut fossor

Rursus uidetur : tantum abhorret ac mutat.

Hoc quid putemus esse ? Qui modo scurra

Aut si quid hac re tritius uidebatur,

Idem infaceto est infacetior rure   .

15 Simul poemata attigit, neque idem unquam

Aeque est beatus ac poema cum scribit :

Tam gaudet in se tamque se ipse miratur.

logical order (**chartae . . . mem-brana**), as if with the author's own delight, the materials of this *édition de luxe*, and then sums up the particular operations upon them by mentioning the first and the last ; 'the whole thing ruled with the lead and smoothed off with the pumice.' On the last operation cf. I. 2 n.; Hor. *Ep.* I. 20. 2 [*liber*] *pumice mundus;* Prop. III. 1. 8 *exactus tenui pumice uersus eat;* Tib. III. (Lygd.) 1. 10 *pumicet et canas tondeat comas* [*libelli*] ; Ov. *Trist.* I. 1. 11 *nec fragili geminae poliantur pumice frontes;* Mart. I. 66. 10–12 *pumicata fronte si quis est non dum, nec umbilicis cultus atque membrana, mercare* (and I. 117. 16; IV. 10. 1; VIII. 72. 1).

9. **legas** : subjunctive of general statement (**tu** being unemphatic), as in Plautus and Cicero, and less commonly in other writers. — **bellus** : apparently here with no uncomplimentary meaning ; but cf. the satirical definition of a *bellus homo* in Mart. III. 63.

10. **unus**, *a mere;* cf. Cic. *Att.* IX. 10. 2 *me haec res torquet quod non Pompeium tanquam unus manipularis secutus sim ;* from this use developed the indefinite article of the Romance languages.

11. **rursus**, *on the contrary;* cf. **67.** 5. — **abhorret ac mutat**: *sc. a*

se ; with the absolute use cf. Cic. *De Or.* II. 20. 85 *sin plane abhorrebit et erit absurdus ; Or.* 31. 109 *an ego tragicis concederem ut crebro mutarent ?*

12. **modo**: on the lengthening of the final syllable, see Intr. 86 *g.* — **scurra**, *a wit*, in the older English sense of a polished town gentleman as distinct from a country booby; cf. Plaut. *Most.* 14 *tu, urbanus uero scurra, deliciae popli, rus mihi tu obiectas ?*

13. **aut si quid** : cf. 13. 10 n. — **tritius** : if the emendation be correct, the meaning must be 'more polished,' 'more fastidious in taste'; cf. Cic. *Fam.* IX. 16. 4 *ut Seruius facile diceret' hic uersus Plauti non est; hic est' quod tritas aures haberet consuetudine legendi.*

14. **infaceto** **rure**, *the stupid country*, as contrasted with the *urbanitas* of the city; cf. 36. 19 ; Plaut. *Most. l.c.;* Hor. *Ep.* II. 1. 158–160 *graue uirus munditiae pepulare, sed . . . hodie manent uestigia ruris.* With the collocation **infaceto infacetior** cf. 27. 4 *ebrioso ebriosioris ;* 39. 16 *inepto ineptior ;* 99. 2 *dulci dulcius;* 99. 14 *tristi tristius.*

15. **simul**: for *simul ac*, as in 51. 6; 63. 27, 45; 64. 31, 366; 99. 7; and often in poetry.

16. **aeque est**, etc.: with the sentiment cf. Hor. *Ep.* II. 2. 106

Nimirum idem omnes fallimur, neque est quisquam
Quem non in aliqua re uidere Suffenum
20 Possis.   Suus cuique attributus est error,
Sed non uidemus manticae quod in tergo est.

23.

Furi, cui neque seruus est neque arca
Nec cimex neque araneus neque ignis,
Verum est et pater et nouerca, quorum

ridentur mala qui componunt car-
mina ; uerum gaudent scribentes et
se uenerantur.

18 ff. Catullus falls here into an
unusually reflective vein, quite in
the style of Horace.

20. **attributus :** *i.e.* in the act of
creation. — **error :** *i.e.* some mental
idiosyncrasy.

21. Cf. Hor. *Sat.* II. 3. 299 *dixe-*
rit insanum qui me, totidem audiet
atque respicere ignoto discet penden-
tia tergo ; and Porph. on the passage, *Aesopus tradit homines duas*
manticas habere, unam ante se,
alteram retro : in priorem aliena
uitia mittimus, ideo et uidemus
facile ; in posteriorem nostra, quae
abscondimus et uidere nolumus.
Hoc Catullus meminit. To this Persius refers in 4. 23 *ut nemo in sese*
temptat descendere, nemo, sed praece-
denti spectatur mantica tergo. The
fable of Æsop is told in Babrius 66
and Phaedrus IV. 10.

23. An epigram of coarse irony
on the poverty of Furius, with
whom, as with Aurelius, Catullus
was now on no friendly terms, since
they had disregarded his injunctions
concerning Juventius (see Intr.
37, 41). Perhaps the immediate
inspiration to this poem came from
the fact that Furius, being utterly

bankrupt, as were many of the
young men about town at that day,
had become notorious among his
acquaintances for fruitless attempts
to negotiate a small loan, and in his
despair was trying to enlarge his
constituency by placating Catullus ;
cf. the similar attempt at a later
date commemorated in 11. With
the first verses cf. Mart. XI. 32. 1–4
nec toga nec focus est nec tritus
cimice lectus, nec tibi de bibula sarta
palude teges, nec puer aut senior,
nulla est ancilla nec infans, nec
sera nec clauis nec canis atque calix
(and XI. 56. 3–6). — Metre, Phalaecean.

1. **neque seruus :** cf. 24. 5.
Even a poor man could own a
slave, as, for instance, Horace, who,
when representing the extreme simplicity of his life, yet speaks of his
dinner as served by three slaves
(*Sat.* I. 6. 116). — **neque arca :** for
Furius has no money to keep in it.

2. **nec cimex :** for there is not a
bed to conceal one. — **neque ara-**
neus : for there is not a roof under
which he may spin his web. —
neque ignis : for there is no hearth
on which to build one.

3. **uerum :** with strongly contrasting adversation ; the things
Furius has are precisely those most

Dentes uel silicem comesse possunt,
5　Est pulchre tibi cum tuo parente
Et cum coniuge lignea parentis.
Nec mirum : bene nam ualetis omnes,
Pulchre concoquitis, nihil timetis,
Non incendia, non graues ruinas,
10　Non furta impia, non dolos ueneni,
Non casus alios periculorum.
Atqui corpora sicciora cornu
Aut si quid magis aridum est habetis
Sole et frigore et esuritione.
15　Quare non tibi sit bene ac beate ?

embarrassing to have in the absence
of what he has not. — **nouerca** :
proverbially an unpleasant relative;
cf. Verg. *Ecl.* 3. 33 *iniusta nouerca ;*
Hor. *Epod.* 5. 9 *quid ut nouerca me
intueris ?*

4. **dentes**, etc. : their fangs are
so sharpened by perpetual hunger.

5. **est pulchre tibi** : cf. v. 15,
and 14. 10 n.

6. **lignea** : the meaning is probably like that of *sicca* (v. 12), *dry,
withered,* and so *forbidding;* cf.
Lucr. IV. 1161 *neruosa et lignea
Dorcas.*

7. **nec mirum** : cf. 57. 3 ; 62.
14 ; 69. 7.

9. **non incendia**, etc. : because
there is no house to burn or col-
lapse. On the dangers in Rome at
a later date from such causes, cf.
Juv. 3. 6–8, 190–202.

10. **non furta impia** : because
there is nothing to steal : so Juvenal (14. 303–310) celebrates the
happiness of those who need take
no precaution against fire and
thieves, while other writers mention the torments that accompany
wealth; cf. Hor. *Sat.* I. 1. 76 ff. *an
uigilare metu exanimem, noctesque*

*diesque formidare malos fures, in-
cendia, seruos, ne te compilent fugientes, hoc iuuat ?* Mart. VI. 33. 3
*furta, fugae, mortes, seruorum, in-
cendia, luctus adfligunt hominem.*

11. **casus alios periculorum** :
cf. Cic. *Fam.* VI. 4. 3 *ad omnes casus subitorum periculorum obiecti
sumus.*

12. **atqui** : not like v. 3 *uerum*
to introduce a counterbalancing
affirmation, but to add a final particular that caps the climax; Furius
and his family are happiest of all in
their own bodily constitution, and
not by reason of external circumstances : with this use of *atqui* cf.
Cic. *Sen.* 19. 66 *quae aut plane
neglegenda est . . . aut etiam op-
tanda . . . atqui tertium certe nihil
inueniri potest.* — **sicciora** : cf. v. 6
lignea ; but *siccitas* is sometimes an
agreeable quality in a woman; cf.
43. 3 ; Plaut. *Mil.* 787 [*puellam*]
siccam et sucidam. — **cornu** : cf.
1. 2, where pumice-stone is mentioned as a typical dry substance.

13. **aut si quid**, etc. : cf. 13. 10 n.

14. **frigore**, etc. : cf. Mart. XII. 32.
7 *frigore et fame siccus.*

15. **bene ac beate** : cf. 14. 10 n.

A te sudor abest, abest saliua,
Mucusque et mala pituita nasi.
Hanc ad munditiem adde mundiorem,
Quod culus tibi purior salillo est,
20 Nec toto decies cacas in anno ;
Atque id durius est faba et lapillis,
Quod tu si manibus teras fricesque,
Non unquam digitum inquinare possis.
Haec tu commoda tam beata, Furi,
25 Noli spernere nec putare parui,
Et sestertia quae soles precari
Centum desine : nam satis beatu's.

24.

O qui flosculus es Iuuentiorum,
Non horum modo, sed quot aut fuerunt
Aut posthac aliis erunt in annis,
Mallem diuitias Midae dedisses

---

25. nec: the negative is repeated as if **noli spernere** were *ne sperne;* cf. Plaut. *Poen.* 1129 *mirari noli neque me contemplarier*, and elsewhere. — **putare parui**: cf. 5. 3 n.

26. sestertia centum: somewhat less than $5000, no great sum for a young man at that time to borrow, when one remembers the fabulous amounts owed by such men as Caelius, Curio, and Caesar. — **precari**: construed ἀπὸ κοινοῦ with **soles** and **desine**.

27. satis beatu's (for *beatus es*) : cf. Hor. *Carm.* II. 18. 14 *satis beatus unicis Sabinis.* See Crit. App.

24. To Juventius, a remonstrance on his intimacy with Furius ; cf. Intr. 37. — Metre, Phalaecean.

1. **flosculus**: cf. 17. 14 n. —

Iuuentiorum : perhaps with a play upon the apparent etymology, as if the word were equivalent to *iuuenum.*

2. **quot**, etc. : cf. 21. 2 n.

4. Not that Juventius was rich, nor that Furius had also tried to borrow money from him, but simply that the wealth of a Midas was to the mind of Catullus small in comparison with what Furius asked. — **Midae** : Midas shared with Croesus among the more ancient worthies, and Attalus among the more modern, the honor of standing as the typical possessor of boundless wealth : cf. 115. 3 *diuitiis Croesum superare;* Mart. VI. 86. 4 *heres diuitis esse Midae;* Ov. *Ex Pont.* IV. 37 *diuitis audita est*

5   Isti cui neque seruus est neque arca,
    Quam sic te sineres ab illo amari.
    'Quid ? Non est homo bellus?' inquies. Est :
    Sed bello huic neque seruus est neque arca.
    Hoc tu quam libet abice eleuaque :
10 Nec seruum tamen ille habet neque arcam.

25.

Cinaede Thalle, mollior cuniculi capillo
Vel anseris medullula uel imula auricilla

cui non opulentia Croesi? Hor. *Carm.* I. 1. 12 *Attalicis condicionibus nunquam dimoueas.*

5. **isti cui**, etc.: *i.e.* Furius ; cf. 23. 1.

7. **quid**: this familiar expression of surprise occurs also in 67. 37, and in slightly varied form in 62. 37 *quid tum ?* 52. 1, 4 *quid est ?* — **homo bellus**: cf. 22. 9 n. — **est**: *bellus* often refers to mere superficial attractiveness, and the sarcastic echo *bello huic* (v. 8) precludes the idea that Catullus was acknowledging in earnest any real excellence of Furius (cf. also note above) ; he means 'Yes, he is a fine fellow, forsooth, this starveling beggar.'

9. **hoc tu**, etc.: *i.e.* excuse and extenuate the thing as you please, the ugly fact remains, and you, as well as he, must acknowledge it ; and Catullus in the last verse rehearses the charge again to give it due effect.

25. On the thievery of a certain Thallus: cf. 12 on a similar subject. — Metre, iambic tetrameter catalectic.

1. **Thalle**: nothing further is known of him, though unsatisfactory attempts have been made to identify him with Asinius Marruci-

nus of 12, by reason of the similar charge against him, and even with Juventius, by reason of the characterization in vv. 1–2. His thieving may have been carried on at the baths (cf. the Vibennius of 33), but to judge from the articles taken, he more probably, like Asinius and Hermogenes, found his opportunity at a dinner where he was a guest. — **mollior**: the traditional adjective to characterize the peculiar unmanliness here charged upon Thallus ; cf. also 16. 4 ; Tac. *Ann.* XI. 2 *Suillio postremum mollitiam corporis obiectante.* — **cuniculi**: the Spanish rabbit described by Martial in XIII. 60 ; cf. also Varr. *R. R.* III. 12. 6 *tertii generis est, quod in Hispania nascitur, similis nostro lepori ex quadam parte, sed humilis, quem cuniculum appellant. . . . cuniculi dicti ab eo, quod sub terra cuniculos ipsi facere solent, ubi lateant in agris ;* Plin. *N. H.* VIII. 217. Catullus had doubtless been instructed in Spanish matters by Veranius (cf. 9. 6–7).

2. **anseris medullula**: the delicate inner feathers of the goose; cf. *Priap.* 64. 1 *quidam mollior anseris medulla.* — **imula auricilla**: the lobe of the ear; cf. Cic. *Q. Fr.*

Vel pene languido senis situque araneoso,
Idemque Thalle turbida rapacior procella,
5   Cum † diua mulier aries ostendit oscitantes,
Remitte pallium mihi meum quod inuolasti
Sudariumque Saetabum catagraphosque Thynos,
Inepte, quae palam soles habere tanquam auita.

II. 13. 4 *auricula infima mollio-*
rem (written in June, 54 B.C.); Bü-
cheler conjectures that Cicero cop-
ied the expression from the *liber*
Catulli, which must, therefore, have
been published before the middle
of the year 54 B.C. But the comparison is of precisely the homely
sort that might be proverbial ; cf.
for example Amm. Marc. XIX. 12.
5 *ima quod aiunt auricula mollior*,
where it is unsafe to judge that *quod*
aiunt points to a proverbial comparison that spread from a mere
invention of Catullus. **auricilla**
is a diminutive from *auricula*, itself
a diminutive, as *ocellus* (3. 18, etc.)
from *oculus*. With the diminutive
forms of noun and adjective in the
same phrase cf. 3. 18 *turgiduli*
ocelli ; 64. 316 *aridulis labellis*.

4. **idem**: cf. 22. 3 n. — **rapa-**
cior: indicating bold robbery ; cf.
Cic. *Pis.* 27. 66 *olim furunculus*,
nunc uero etiam rapax.

5. **diua**, etc.: the verse is unintelligible, and no satisfactory emendation has yet been suggested. The
general meaning seems to be that
Thallus does his thieving boldly, —
because there is nothing to fear,
since he chooses an occasion when
no one watches against thieves. If
oscitantes be the correct reading,
it must mean *off their guard,* rather
than *half-asleep,* as the thefts were
probably committed at dinners (see
v. 1 n.).

6. **pallium**: a Greek garment,
resembling somewhat the Roman
toga, but square-cornered, freer in

the arrangement of its folds, and
often brightly colored. — **inuolasti**,
pounced upon, when the wine went
round, and the *pallium* had been
thrown back from the shoulders of
the wearer; cf. Mart. VIII. 59. 9-10
lapsa nec a cubito subducere pallia
nescit, et tectus laenis saepe duabus
abit.

7. **sudarium Saetabum**: cf. 12.
3 n., 14 n.; perhaps this was one of
the set there mentioned. — **cata-**
graphos Thynos: the former word
is so little used as to make impossible its sure interpretation here ;
nor is it certain even which of the
two words is noun and which is adjective. But as *catagraphi* is used
of outline drawings (in Plin. *N. H.*
XXXV. 56), and as tablets were
commonly made of box (Prop. IV.
23. 8 *uulgari buxo sordida cera fu-*
it), a Bithynian wood (cf. 4. 13 n.),
it is quite possible that the objects referred to here were *pugil-*
lares, carved or otherwise decorated
on the outside, and so more valuable and tempting to a thief than
was the ordinary kind.   Perhaps
they were a memento of the journey
of Catullus himself to Bithynia.   It
would not be strange for the poet
to bring his tablets to some dinner
parties (cf. 50. 1-6). — **Thynos**:
cf. 31. 5 n.

8. **inepte**, *stupid*, in expecting to
be able to escape detection while
flaunting his spoils openly: by the
same word Asinius is addressed in
12. 4, but with a slightly different
application.

＊

Quae nunc tuis ab unguibus reglutina et remitte,
10   Ne laneum latusculum manusque mollicellas
Inusta turpiter tibi flagella conscribillent,
Et insolenter aestues uelut minuta magno
Deprensa nauis in mari uesaniente uento.

26.

Furi, uillula uestra non ad Austri
Flatus opposita est neque ad Fauoni

9. **reglutina**: as if whatever was touched by a thief's fingers stuck to them; cf. Lucil. XXVIII. 58–59 M. *omnia uescatis manibus leget, omnia sumet, crede mihi; presse ut dicam, res auferet omnis.*

10. **laneum**: a figure derived from the softness of wool; the meaning is doubtless the same as that of **mollicellas**, with a sneer at the unnatural *mollitia* of Thallus (v. 1–2), to which the sarcastic diminutives lend effect. — **manus**: as he tries with them to cover his back from the blows.

11. **inusta**: so Horace speaks of the burning of the lash in *Epod.* 4. 3 *Hibericis peruste funibus latus; Ep.* I. 16. 47 *habes pretium, loris non ureris.* — **turpiter**: *i.e.* with the punishment of a slave. — **conscribillent**: perhaps with a play upon the word, in that the lashes threatened are really those of satiric verse (cf. 12. 10–11 ; 42. 1–6 ; and the figure in Hor. *Carm.* III. 12. 4 *patruae uerbera linguae*), and not those at the hands of the law ; cf. Plaut. *Pseud.* 544–545 *quasi quom in libro scribuntur calamo litterae, stilis me totum usque ulmeis conscribito.* On *conscribillo* beside *scribo* see Lachmann on Lucr. I. 360.

12. **aestues**: *i.e.* bend into all sorts of shapes, like a school-boy

flinching from the lash. — **uelut** etc.: the poem, like several others in Catullus, ends with a comparison. — **minuta nauis**: so Cic. *Att.* XVI. I. 3 *minuta nauigia.*

13. **deprensa in mari**: *i.e.* unable to make harbor before the storm breaks ; cf. Verg. *Aen.* V. 52 *Argolico mari depensus ;* Hor. *Carm.* II. 16. 1 *in patenti prensus Aegaeo.* — **uesaniente uento**: observe the effect of alliteration and final consonance.

26. By itself this poem might well be taken as a mere jest at a friend's expense, or, if, with *G, nostra* be read in v. 1, at the expense of Catullus himself. But all other references to Furius are distinctly hostile in tone (cf. 11 ; 16 ; 23 ; 24), and there is no reason for premising a period of friendship in which Catullus might jest with Furius. *Vestra* should therefore be read, and the poem grouped with 23 and 24 as satirizing the extreme poverty into which Furius had doubtless brought himself. — Metre, Phalaecean.

1. **Furi**: see Intr. 37. — **uestra**: *i.e.* of Furius and the two unpresentable members of his family whom Catullus does not mean to have him forget, his father and step-mother ; cf. 23. 5–6.

2. **opposita**: with a play upon

Nec saeui Boreae aut Apeliotae,
Verum ad milia quindecim et ducentos.
5 O uentum horribilem atque pestilentem!

27.

Minister uetuli puer Falerni
Inger mi calices amariores,
Vt lex Postumiae iubet magistrae,
Ebrioso acino ebriosioris.

the meaning of ' to mortgage ' ; cf.
Plaut. *Pseud.* 87 *uix hercle opino*
[*me posse mutuam drachumam
unam dare*], *etsi me opponam
pignori ;* Ter. *Phor.* 661 *ager oppo-
situst pignori decem ob minas.*

3. **Apeliotae**: cf. Plin. *N. H.* II.
119 *ab oriente aequinoctiali subso-
lanus . . . illum Apelioten Graeci
uocant.*

4. **milia**, etc.: the sum was no
great one, when 10,000 sesterces
was a reasonable rent for merely
a house in Rome (cf. Cic. *Cael.* 7.
17); but as Furius was at the bottom of his pocket, it is probable
that he had mortgaged his house
for all that he could raise on it.
Catullus is scornfully indicating,
therefore, the meanness of the
house itself.

5. **o uentum**, etc., *O awful, fatal
draft.*

27. A drinking-song: the only,
and a very admirable, poem of Catullus in the vein afterward so success-
fully worked by Horace. — Metre,
Phalaecean.

1. **minister**: so Horace (*Carm.*
I. 38. 6) calls the *puer* (I. 38. 1)
who serves him with wine. — **Falerni**: generally esteemed by the
ancients as one of the best of the
Italian wines ; cf. Hor. *Carm.* II.
3. 8 *interiore nota Falerni.*

2. **inger**: for *ingere ;* the only
instance of the shortened imperative
form of this verb (unless *conger* be
right in Mart. VIII. 44. 9), though
fer is the regular form both in the
simple verb and in composition; cf.
also *dic, duc, fac.* Ellis quotes
other drinkers' abbreviations from
Meineke *Anal. Alex.* p. 131, πῖν for
πίνειν and πῶ for πῶθι. — **amariores**, *more pungent, i.e.* with no
longer any admixture of water; so
at the feast of Hor. *Carm.* I. 27
the drinking came at last to pure
wine (cf. I. 27. 9 *seueri Falerni*)
apparently by decree of the master
of the feast: cf. a similar figure for
unmixed wine in Hor. *Carm.* II.
11. 19 *pocula ardentis Falerni.*

3. **lex magistrae**: a ruler of the
feast was chosen (usually by lot),
and his decrees were absolute concerning the proportion of water to
wine in the mixing, and the proposal and drinking of toasts ; cf.
Hor. *Carm.* I. 4. 18 *nec regna uini
sortiere talis.* Here, in the un-
wonted *abandon* of the occasion, a
woman was ruler.

4. **ebrioso**, etc.: *i.e.* fuller of
grape-juice than the grape itself
is; so Damalis (Hor. *Carm.* I. 36.
13) was *multi meri.* With the
collocation *ebrioso ebriosioris* cf.
22. 14 n.

5   At uos quo libet hinc abite, lymphae,
    Vini pernicies, et ad seueros
    Migrate : hic merus est Thyonianus.

28.

    Pisonis comites, cohors inanis
    Aptis sarcinulis et expeditis,
    Verani optime tuque mi Fabulle,
    Quid rerum geritis ? Satisne cum isto
5   Vappa frigoraque et famem tulistis ?

5. **at:** introducing an imprecation ; cf. 3. 13 n. ; 28, 14 ; 36. 18.
— **quo libet hinc abite :** cf. Plaut.
Mil. 974 *quin tu illam iube abs te
abire quo libet.* Baehrens suggests
that *quo libet* is but politeness for
in malam rem ; cf. 14. 21 ff. With
the sentiment cf. Petron. 52 *aquam
foras, uinum intro !* — **lymphae :**
cf. the plural also in 64. 162.

6. **uini pernicies :** *i.e.* water
but ruins the wine. — **seueros,** *the
sober ;* cf. Hor. *Ep.* I. 19. 8 *forum
putealque Libonis mandabo siccis,
adimam cantare seueris.*

7. **hic :** with the word he raises
his cup on high. — **Thyonianus :**
Bacchus was called Thyoneus from
his mother, the Theban Semele or
Thyone. The adjective, being from
a Greek proper name, is in the masculine form, perhaps after the analogy of οἶνος.

28. An address of sympathy to
Veranius and Fabullus on their return in poverty from an absence in
Macedonia on the staff of Piso, the
governor. This absence of theirs is
not to be confounded with their
earlier trip to Spain mentioned in 9
and elsewhere (cf. Intr. 68 ff.). —
Date, about 55 B.C.   Metre, Phalaecean.

1. **Pisonis :** *i.e.* L. Calpurnius
Piso Caesonianus, on whom see
Intr. 70. — **comites :** *i.e.* members
of the *cohors,* or staff, of a provincial governor ; cf. 11. 1 ; 46. 9. —
inanis : *penniless,* for Piso cared
only to enrich himself, and Cicero
scores him for his avarice in *Pis.* 35.
86 ; cf. 64. 288 *uacuus.*

2. **aptis :** *i.e.* accommodated to
the circumstances of their bearers,
as definitely explained by **inanis ;**
the idea is carried out by the addition of **expeditis,** here in the
meaning of 'light,' but suggesting, from its commoner use, the
idea of soldiers in light marching
order.

3. The same careful recognition
of equality in esteem that has been
already noted (Intr. 68 ; 12. 13 n.)
is kept up here by calling Veranius
optime and Fabullus mi.

4. **quid rerum geritis :** a colloquial form of greeting ; cf. Plaut.
Aul. 117 *rogitant me ut ualeam,
quid agam, quid rerum geram.*

5. **uappa :** wine that has become
flat ; hence a colloquialism for a
good-for-nothing, and sometimes
for a totally depraved fellow ; cf.
Hor. *Sat.* I. 1. 104 *uappam ac nebu-
lonem.*

Ecquidnam in tabulis patet lucelli
Expensum, ut mihi, qui meum secutus
Praetorem refero datum lucello,
'O Memmi, bene me ac diu supinum
10   Tota ista trabe lentus irrumasti.'
Sed, quantum uideo, pari fuistis
Casu : nam nihilo minore uerpa
Farti estis.   Pete nobiles amicos.
At uobis mala multa di deaeque
15   Dent, opprobria Romuli Remique.

29.

Quis hoc potest uidere, quis potest pati,
Nisi impudicus et uorax et aleo,

6. ecquidnam: cf. 10. 8 n. —
tabulis, *account-books.* — lucelli :
modifying *ecquidnam.*

7. expensum : the word expected, if there was actually *aliquid
lucelli*, is *acceptum* (cf. Plaut. *Most.*
297 *ratio accepti atque expensi;*
Cic. *Rosc. Com.* I. 4 *in codice accepti et expensi*), but Catullus means
to indicate his presumption that all
accumulation was that of debt.

8. praetorem : *i.e.* provincial
governor, as in 10. 10, 13. — refero
datum lucello, *set down to my
credit;* cf. Hor. *Carm.* I. 9. 14 *lucro adpone.*

9. Memmi: see Intr. 71. —
bene me, etc.: *i.e.* you have most
scurvily abused me and betrayed
my hopes. See 16. 1 n.

11. pari: *sc. mecum.*

13. pete nobiles amicos : ironically spoken in self-apostrophe :
the suppressed conclusion is something like *sic irrumatus fueris.*
Neither the *Pisones* nor the *Mem-
mii* were new families ; the former
claimed descent from Numa (Hor.

A. P. 292 *uos [Pisones] o Pompi-
lius sanguis*), and the latter from
Mnestheus, the comrade of Aeneas
(Verg. *Aen.* V. 117 *Mnestheus, genus
a quo nomine Memmi*).

14. at uobis mala : cf. 3. 13 n.;
27. 5; 36. 18. — uobis : *i.e.* Piso and
Memmius. — mala, etc.: cf. 14. 6 n.

15. opprobria : *i.e.* you disgrace
to the noble origin of your nation;
cf. 34. 22 ; 49. 1; 58. 5.

29. A sharp attack upon Julius
Caesar for his patronage of Mamurra, with a snap at the end of
the lash for Pompey, whose conduct of affairs in the city was alien-
ating the optimates ; cf. Intr. 38.
The poem was written after the first
invasion of Britain (cf. vv. 4, 12, 20),
which took place in 55 B.C., and
during the lifetime of Julia, Caesar's
daughter and Pompey's wife (v. 24),
whose death, in the fall of the year
54, weakened the bond between the
two leaders. — Metre, pure iambic
trimeter (but see note on v. 3).

1–2. The writer has before his
mind the characteristics he believes

Mamurram habere quod comata Gallia
Habebat ante et ultima Britannia?
5 Cinaede Romule, haec uidebis et feres?
Et ille nunc superbus et superfluens
Perambulabit omnium cubilia
Vt albulus columbus aut Adoneus?
Cinaede Romule, haec uidebis et feres?
10   Es impudicus et uorax et aleo.

Caesar to possess, as v. 10 indicates: but cf. 16. 1 n. — **quis potest pati**: cf. 42. 5 *si pati potestis*.

3. **Mamurram**: perhaps with the first syllable long, as in 57. 2; Hor. *Sat.* I. 5. 37; Mart. IX. 59. 1; X. 4. 11; and in several derivatives from the same stem; though this would then be the only irrational foot in this poem, if vv. 20 and 23 be emended so as to introduce none but iambic feet. On the person see Intr. 73, 74. — **quod**, etc.: *i.e.* Mamurra has already absorbed and squandered all the proceeds of former conquests of Caesar (cf. vv. 18 and 19), and now shall the present conquests go the same road? — **comata Gallia**: *i.e. Gallia transalpina*, so called from the barbarian custom there prevailing of men wearing long hair; cf. Diod. V. 28; Cic. *Phil.* VIII. 9. 27 *Galliam togatam remitto, comatam postulo*; Plin. *N. H.* IV. 105 *Gallia omnis comata uno nomine appellata*; Suet. *Iul.* 22 *initio quidem Galliam cisalpinam . . . accepit . . . mox . . . comatam quoque*.

4. **ultima Britannia**: cf. v. 12; 11. 11 n. Caesar took command in Gaul in 58 B.C., and the first entry into Britain was made in the summer of 55 (cf. Caes. *B. G.* IV. 20 ff.). On the lengthening of the final syllable before initial *br*, see Intr. 86 g.

5. **cinaede**: here probably used simply as a word of general abuse (cf. Intr. 32), though Catullus may

have in mind such reports about Caesar as those set down by Suetonius in *Iul.* 49. — **Romule**: Caesar is apparently so termed because of his posing as the chief man of the state *domi et militiae*.

6. **et ille**, etc.: *i.e.* shall he come back to Italy newly enriched from the conquests in Gaul and Britain, and carry on more insolently than ever his life of debauchery? — **superbus et superfluens**: both adjectives refer to his wealth.

7. **perambulabit**: the word is selected to suit the comparison in *columbus* (v. 8).

8. **columbus**, etc.: *i.e.* a favorite of Aphrodite, and so an irresistible suitor. Doves were sacred to the goddess, and drew her chariot, and **Adoneus** is but another form for *Adonis;* cf. Plaut. *Men.* 144 *ubi Venus [raperet] Adoneum;* Auson. *Ep.* 30. 6 *Arabica gens [me existimant] Adoneum.*

9. The appeal is repeated from v. 5, because in vv. 3–4 the reference was only to the ill-gotten wealth of Mamurra, while in vv. 6–8 it was to the expected revival of his licentious career.

10. The verse embodies the stinging conclusion following upon the major premise implied in vv. 1–4, with 6–8, and the minor in vv. 5 and 9. — **impudicus** has a technical reference to *cinaede*. — **uorax** doubtless refers to gluttony and

Eone nomine, imperator unice,
Fuisti in ultima occidentis insula,
Vt ista uestra diffututa mentula
Ducenties comesset aut trecenties ?
15 Quid est alid sinistra liberalitas ?
Parum expatrauit an parum elluatus est ?
Paterna prima lancinata sunt bona ;
Secunda praeda Pontica ; inde tertia

wine-bibbing, and is not used in
the sense of 33. 4 and 57. 8, nor in
that of 80. 6 and 88. 8; yet Suetonius (*Iul.* 53) reports that Caesar
was abstemious in regard to food
and drink. — aleo : gambling had
grown to be such a passion among
the young Romans that it was
deemed a serious vice and restrained by law; cf. Cic. *Phil.* XIII.
11. 24 *in lustris, popinis, alea, uino
tempus aetatis omne consumpsisses ;
Cat.* II. 10. 23 *in his gregibus omnes aleatores, omnes adulteri, omnes
impuri impudicique uersantur.*

11. eo nomine, *on this account,*
one of the most frequent of the
phrases borrowed from book-keep-
ing. The demonstrative refers onward to the *ut*-clause in v. 13.
— imperator unice : in ironical
praise ; repeated in 54. 7.

12. ultima, etc. : cf. v. 4 n. —
Wildest rumors had long been afloat
about the vast wealth to be found in
the interior of Britain, and many
young Roman spendthrifts had desired to join Caesar's expedition
thither. He actually secured nothing of value, but evidently the true
news had not yet spread through
Italy.

13. ista uestra mentula : of a
debauchee, as 17. 21 *iste meus stupor,* of a dull fellow. Mamurra is
of course the man referred to (cf.
94, 105, 114, 115, and Intr. 73).
The possessive points to Pompey

as sharing blame with Caesar in the
matter ; cf. also vv. 21-24.

14. ducenties aut trecenties :
sc. centena milia sestertium, as
regularly with numeral adverbs in
the expression of sums of money.
Ducenti as well as *trecenti* (on
which cf. 9. 2 n.) is used of indefinitely large number ; cf. 37. 7;
Hor. *Sat.* I. 10. 60 *amet scripsisse
ducentos ante cibum uersus.* — comesset : cf. the same figure for squandering in v. 22 *deuorare.*

15. alid : for *aliud,* as 66. 28 *alis*
for *alius ;* so Plautus, Lucretius, and
others. Cf. 34. 8 n. — sinistra liberalitas : since the giving was made
possible by robbery (cf. 12. 1 n.);
see Cato's strictures (on Caesar ?) in
Sall. *Cat.* 52. 11 ff. *quia bona aliena
largiri liberalitas . . . uocatur* etc.
The question in this verse touches
upon the fitness of giving such gifts;
that in the next verse upon Mamurra's fitness to receive them.

17. Cf. 41. 4; 43. 5.

18. praeda Pontica : probably
not that brought back by Pompey
in 62 B.C. from the conquest of
Mithradates, but that from the capture of Mitylene in 79 B.C., when
Caesar was an officer in the army of
the governor of Pontus and Bithynia. Thus early was the patrimony
of Mamurra already squandered,
and thus early, when gains were
but small, did Caesar begin to lavish
wealth upon him.

Hibera, quam scit amnis aurifer Tagus.
20 Nunc Galliae timetur et Britanniae.
Quid hunc malum fouetis? aut quid hic potest
Nisi uncta deuorare patrimonia?
Eone nomine † urbis opulentissime
Socer generque, perdidistis omnia?

19. **Hibera:** *sc. praeda;* when
Caesar, in 61–60 B.C., governed
Further Spain as propraetor. —
scit, *is witness to;* cf. Verg. *Aen.*
XI. 258 *scelerum poenas expendi-
mus omnes; . . . scit triste Mineruae sidus;* Ov. *Met.* XII. 439 *ast
ego . . . scit tuus hoc genitor —
gladium spoliantis in ima ilia de-
misi.* — **aurifer Tagus:** the Tagus
had a reputation like that of the
Pactolus; cf. Ov. *Am.* I. 15. 34
auriferi ripa benigna Tagi; Mart.
X. 16. 4 *aurea diuitis unda Tagi;*
X. 96. 3 *auriferum Tagum.*

20. **nunc:** carrying on the series
of *prima . . . secunda . . . inde tertia;* reports have just arrived of the
completed conquest of Gaul and of
the invasion of Britain, and the
same fate now threatens them that
befell former conquests, — to be de-
voured by Mamurra. — **Galliae
timetur et Britanniae:** *sc. ab in-
colis;* cf. Sen. *Med.* 893 *iam domus
tota occidit, urbi timetur.*

21. **hunc malum,** *this rascal;*
cf. 64. 175 *malus hic;* Plaut. *Merc.*
974 *ut dissimulat malus;* Hor. *Sat.*
I. 4. 3 *siquis erat dignus describi,
quod malus ac fur.* — **fouetis:** *sc.*
Caesar and Pompey. — **quid hic
potest** nisi, *what is he good for
except,* etc.; *i.e.* it cannot be that
you favor him because of his effi-
cient services [Mamurra was *praefectus fabrum* under Caesar], for he
is utterly useless except to swallow
up money.

22. **uncta:** cf. 10. 11 n. —
deuorare: cf. v. 14 *comesset;*
Cic. *Phil.* II. 27. 67 *non modo
unius patrimonium sed urbes et
regna deuorare potuisset;* Vulg.
Marc. 12. 40 *qui deuorant* (Matt.
23. 14 *qui comeditis*) *domos uidua-
rum.* — **patrimonia:** of the wealth
that replaced the *paterna bona* (v.
17) first squandered.

23. **eone nomine,** etc.: *i.e.* was
it for the sake of Mamurra's pockets that this last deal for the final
ruin of Rome was made and cemented by a marriage? With this
final appeal cf. 9. 10 n.—**urbis,**
etc.: see Crit. App.

24. **socer generque:** perhaps
with a sneer at the political interests that dictated the marriage of
Caesar's daughter to a man over
twenty years her senior, who had
lately divorced his wife on suspicion
of adultery with Caesar himself. Yet
the marriage had actually proved a
very happy one on both sides. —
perdidistis omnia: the familiar
cry of the *optimates* at this time,
when they had become more es-
tranged from their former idol,
Pompey, by events following upon
the famous council of the so-called
triumvirs at Luca in 56 B.C., in accordance with which Pompey and
Crassus were this year consuls, with
the government of Spain and Syria
respectively to follow, while Caesar
had just had his command in Gaul
extended for five years.

30.

Alfene immemor atque unanimis false sodalibus,
Iam te nil miseret, dure, tui dulcis amiculi?
Iam me prodere, iam non dubitas fallere, perfide?
Nec facta impia fallacum hominum caelicolis placent;
5 Quae tu neglegis, ac me miserum deseris in malis.
Eheu, quid faciant, dic, homines, cuiue habeant fidem?
Certe tute iubebas animam tradere, inique, me
Inducens in amorem, quasi tuta omnia mi forent.
Idem nunc retrahis te ac tua dicta omnia factaque
10 Ventos irrita ferre ac nebulas aerias sinis.

30. A remonstrance addressed to Alfenus, on the ground that he had forsaken the poet in time of trouble. Attempts have been made by a forced interpretation of vv. 7–8 etc. to connect this poem with the Lesbia episode, proceeding on the theory that Alfenus had led Catullus into his intimacy with Lesbia, but refused assistance upon the arising of some difficulty in connection with the affair. But more probably these verses are but the morbidly exaggerated utterances of a distempered mind in, perhaps, a sick body, fancying itself deserted by former friends. Cf. 38, which is on a similar theme, and perhaps was written on the same occasion, though with a slight difference of tone; and see Intr. 56. — Date, probably 54 B.C. Metre, Asclepiadean major.

1. **immemor**: used absolutely, as in 64. 58. — **unanimis**: cf. 9. 4 n.

2. **dulcis amiculi**: perhaps adopting the phrase formerly used by Alfenus of Catullus.

3. With the arrangement of **me** and **non dubitas**, each joined with one of the two phrases with which they both belong, cf. 64. 336

adest . . . concordia; 68. 68 *domum . . . dedit;* Verg. *Aen.* IX. 12 *nunc tempus equos, nunc poscere currus.*

4. **nec**: by Plautus and other early writers *nec* is frequently used with no copulative force (= *non*), and perhaps is so used here; yet the idea may be 'you are injuring both me (vv. 2–3) and the gods (v. 4).'

5. **quae**: *sc. facta impia.* — **neglegis,** *make light of, i.e.* lightly commit; cf. Hor. *Carm.* I. 28. 30 *neglegis fraudem committere?* — me miserum, etc.: cf. Ter. *Heaut.* 258 *me in his deseruisti malis.*

6. **fidem**: with the thought cf. 64. 143; Ter. *And.* 425 *nullane in re esse quoiquam homini fidem.*

7. **certe**: *sc.* however so little you now remember it; cf. 64. 149. — **animam tradere**: *sc. tibi; i.e.* to surrender my whole being; cf. Cic. *Rosc. Am.* 50. 146 *omnia sua praeter animam tradidit.* — me **inducens in amorem,** *drawing my affections to yourself.*

8. **quasi,** etc.: *i.e.* assuring me I should never regret it.

9. **idem**: cf. 22. 3 n.

10. **uentos**: with the figure cf. 64. 59, 142; 65. 17; 70. 4 n.;

Si tu oblitus es, at di meminerunt, meminit Fides,
Quae te ut paeniteat postmodo facti faciet tui.

31.

Paene insularum, Sirmio, insularumque
Ocelle, quascumque in liquentibus stagnis
Marique uasto fert uterque Neptunus,
Quam te libenter quamque laetus inuiso,

Hom. *Od.* VIII. 408 ἔπος δ᾽ εἴ πέρ
τι βέβακται δεινὸν, ἄφαρ τὸ φέροιεν
ἀναρπάξασαι ἄελλαι; Theocr. 22.
167 τὰ δ᾽ εἰς ὑγρὸν ᾤχετο κῦμα
πνοιῇ ἔχοισ᾽ ἀνέμοιο (with which cf.
Hor. *Carm.* I. 26. 2 *tradam pro-*
teruis in mare Creticum portare
uentis); Verg. *Aen.* IX. 312 *aurae*
omnia discerpunt et nubibus irrita
donant; Ov. *Trist.* I. 8. 35 *cunc-*
tane in aequoreos abierunt irrita
uentos? Tib. I. 4. 21 *Veneris per-*
iuria uenti irrita per terras et freta
longa ferunt; Stat. *Ach.* I. 960 *ir-*
rita uentosae rapiebant uerba pro-
cellae.

   11. Cf. Verg. *Aen.* I. 542–3 *si*
genus humanum et mortalia temni-
tis arma, at sperate deos memores
fandi atque nefandi.

   31. On the delight of home-
coming. The poem is a most un-
artificial and joyous pouring out of
the poet's warmth of feeling at
reaching Sirmio after his year of
absence with Memmius in Bithynia
(v. 5), and forms a perfect conclusion to 46, while it is itself supple-
mented by the quieter reminiscent
strains of 4. With this and 101 cf.
Tennyson *Frater Ave atque Vale.* —
Date, summer of 56 B.C. Metre,
choliambic.

   1. paene: used adjectively, in
Greek fashion; cf. Cic. *Rep.* VI. 11
nunc uenis paene miles; Ov. *Her.*
15. 357 *paene puer.* Livy (XXVI.

42. 8) appears to be the first to
write *paeninsula.* — **Sirmio,** the
modern Sermione, is a long and
narrow peninsula running out into
the southern end of the Lago di
Garda (*Lacus Benacus*). The ruins
referred to by Tennyson (*l.c.*) are
of the age of Constantine, but are
called by the natives the Villa of
Catullus, in accordance with the
mediæval identification.

   2. ocelle, *the gem;* cf. in this
sense Aesch. *Eum.* 1025 ὄμμα πάσης
χθόνος; Pind. *Ol.* 2. ς Σικελίας τ᾽
ἔσαν ὀφθαλμός; Plaut. *Trin.* 245 *o*
ocelle mi (as a pet name); Cic. *Att.*
XVI. 6. 2 *ocellos Italiae, uillulas*
meas. — **liquentibus:** with the
same meaning as *liquidas* in 64. 2
and *limpidum* in 4. 24.

   3. uterque: as god of *stagna*
and of *mare;* so Mart. *Spect.* 13. 5
numen utriusque Dianae (as goddess both of the hunt and of birth;
cf. 34. 9–14).

   4. libenter . . . laetus: a not
infrequent collocation; cf. Plaut.
Trin. 821 *laetus lubens laudes ago*
(the speaker here also has just returned from a foreign shore); and
at the end of dedicatory inscriptions; *e.g.* C. I. L. VI. 533 . . . PO-
SVIT · L · L (*i.e. laetus lubens*). —
inuiso: in the sense of (poetical)
uideo, a rare use; cf. however 64.
233; Cic. *N. D.* II. 43. 110 *et natos*
Geminos inuises sub caput Arcti.

5 Vix mi ipse credens Thyniam atque Bithynos
   Liquisse campos et uidere te in tuto !
   O quid solutis est beatius curis,
   Cum mens onus reponit, ac peregrino
   Labore fessi uenimus larem ad nostrum
10 Desideratoque adquiescimus lecto?
   Hoc est quod unum est pro laboribus tantis.
   Salue, o uenusta Sirmio, atque ero gaude ;
   Gaudete uosque, o Lydiae lacus undae ;
   Ridete, quidquid est domi cachinnorum.

5. **Thyniam**: the Thyni, a people from Thrace, are said to have
settled that portion of Bithynia
which lay close to the Thracian
Bosphorus and was sometimes said
to be divided from Bithynia proper
by the river Psilis ; but the two
names, long before the time of
Catullus, had ceased to express any
actual distinction.

6. **liquisse**: for *reliquisse*, as
not infrequently in Catullus (cf. *e.g.*
46. 4); but in 35. 3 and elsewhere
relinquere occurs.

7. **quid est beatius**: cf. 9. 11.
— **solutis curis**: cf. Hor. *Carm.*
I. 22. 11 *curis expeditis.*

8. **peregrino labore fessi**: cf.
Hor. *Carm.* II. 6. 7 *lasso maris et
uiarum militiaeque.*

9. **larem**: the guardian deity of
the household, worshipped with the
penates at the hearth.   The plural
occurs but once in Plautus (*Rud.*
1206 *ut rem diuinam faciam lari-
bus familiaribus*), and the word not
at all in Terence; but from this time

down the plural is common as a
designation for the home, especially
in connection with *penates*, with
which divinities the *lares* came to
be practically identified.

11. **hoc est quod unum est,**
this is of itself reward enough.

12. **ero gaude**: probably an
imitation of the familiar χαῖρέ
μοι.

13. **Lydiae**: if the reading be
correct, the *lacus Benacus* was so
called from the well-known Etruscan settlements in the Po region.
The Etruscans were traditionally of
Lydian origin, and are often called
Lydians by the poets ; cf. Verg.
Aen. II. 781 *Lydius arua inter
opima uirum leni fluit agmine
Thybris ;* Hor. *Sat.* I. 6. 1 *Lydorum quidquid Etruscos incoluit
fines.*   With the transfer of epithet
from *lacus* to *undae* cf. Verg. *l.c.*
quidquid and 17. 19 n.

14. **quidquid est**, etc.: cf. 1. 8 n.
quidquid hoc libelli.   The whole
clause is to be taken as a vocative

32.

Amabo, mea dulcis Ipsithilla,
Meae deliciae, mei lepores,
Iube ad te ueniam meridiatum.
Et si iusseris illud, adiuuato,
5 Ne quis liminis obseret tabellam,
Neu tibi libeat foras abire ;
Sed domi maneas paresque nobis
Nouem continuas fututiones.
Verum, si quid ages, statim iubeto :
10 Nam pransus iaceo et satur supinus
Pertundo tunicamque palliumque.

33.

O furum optime balneariorum
Vibenni pater, et cinaede fili,
(Nam dextra pater inquinatiore,
Culo filius est uoraciore)

32. Contents, execrable. Date, undeterminable. Metre, Phalae-cean.

1. **amabo**: thus alone, and with *te*, often used in comedy and other colloquial writings with impera-tives ; the complete form is per-haps *sic amabo te*, as if in the expression of a conditioned wish ; cf. 17. 5 n.

2. **mei lepores**: plural, like *deli-ciae* and *amores* (21. 4, etc.) ; cf. Plaut. *Cas.* 217 *respice, o mi lepos.*

3. **ueniam**: the subjunctive with *iubere* is not common, but occurs occasionally from Terence down. — **meridiatum**: for the mid-day siesta; cf. 61. 118; 80. 3.

33. A bit of taunting advice to a notorious father and son, other-wise unknown, to go to the deuce. — Metre, Phalaecean.

1. **furum balneariorum**: thieves of clothing at the baths were trouble-some even in early Rome (cf. Plaut. *Rud.* 382 ff.), and the trouble con-tinued into later times; cf. Petr. 30 *subducta sibi uestimenta dispensato-ris in balneo.* — **optime**: *i.e.* most successful; with the ironical use cf. 36. 6 *electissima pessimi poetae scripta ;* 37. 14 *boni beatique.*

3. **dextra**: the left hand is the one traditionally appropriated to stealing (cf. 12. 1 n.), but here Catullus means simply the hand, and

5   Cur non exsilium malasque in oras
    Itis, quandoquidem patris rapinae
    Notae sunt populo, et natis pilosas,
    Fili, non potes asse uenditare?

34.

    Dianae sumus in fide
    Puellae et pueri integri ;
    Dianam pueri integri
      Puellaeque canamus.

5   O Latonia, maximi
    Magna progenies Iouis,

not the right as distinguished from the left.

5. cur non itis: an impatient exhortation; cf. Ter. *Eun.* 465 *quid stamus? quor non imus hinc?* Hor. *Carm.* III. 19. 18 *cur Berecyntiae cessant flamina tibiae?* — **exsilium**: perhaps the preposition with *oras* answers for both nouns, as in Hor. *Carm.* III. 25. 2 *quae nemora aut quos agor in specus:* but cf. Acc. 599 R. *proficisci exsilium.* — **malas in oras**: with a play between the idea of actual banishment (cf. Ter. *Phor.* 978 *publicitus hinc asportarier in solas terras*) and that of the familiar *in malam rem*.

8. asse: *i.e.* the most insignificant sum; cf. 5. 3 n.

34. A festival hymn to Diana, written, as usual, as if to be sung by a chorus of girls and boys, but whether responsively or not it is impossible to determine. If so, however, vv. 1-4 and 21-24 were doubtless sung by the united chorus, vv. 5-8 and 13-16 by the girls alone,

and vv. 9-12 and 17-20 by the boys alone. The composition was perhaps suggested by the annual festival to the Diana of the famous temple on the Aventine, held at the time of full moon (*i.e.* the Ides) in the month of August. To be compared with this are three odes of Horace : *Carm.* I. 21, IV. 6, and the *Carmen Saeculare,* — in all of which, however, Apollo is celebrated with Diana. — On the metre see Intr. 82 *b.*

1. **in fide**: cf. Hor. *Carm.* IV. 6. 33 *Deliae tutela deae.*

2. **integri** : modifying both nouns ; so also in v. 3. Cf. 61. 36 *integrae uirgines;* 62. 45 *uirgo intacta;* Hor. *C. S.* 6 *uirgines lectas puerosque castos.*

5. **Latonia** : Latona is often honored in hymns to her children; cf. Hor. *Carm.* I. 21. 3-4 [*dicite*] *Latonam supremo dilectam penitus Ioui;* IV. 6. 37 *rite Latonae puerum canentes.*

Quam mater prope Deliam
    Deposiuit oliuam,

    Montium domina ut fores
10 Siluarumque uirentium
    Saltuumque reconditorum
    Amniumque sonantum;

    Tu Lucina dolentibus
    Iuno dicta puerperis,
15 Tu potens Triuia et notho es
    Dicta lumine Luna.

7. **Deliam**, etc.: for the story
see Ov. *Met.* VI. 333 ff. (also XIII.
634–5).

8. **deposiuit**: one of the few
archaic forms in Catullus ; cf. 36.
16 *face;* 61. 42 n. *citarier;* 63. 47,
52 ; 66. 35 *tetuli;* 44. 19 *recepso;*
66. 28 *alis;* 29. 15 *alid;* 66. 37
coetu; 17. 17 *uni;* 51. 10 *suopte.*

9–12. **montium domina**, etc.:
cf. Hor. *Carm.* I. 21. 5–8 (which
verses, however, these of Catullus
far excel) ; III. 22. 1 *montium
custos nemorumque uirgo;* IV. 6.
33–34; *C. S.* 1 *siluarumque potens
Diana;* 69 *quaeque Auentinum
tenet Algidumque.*

13. **Lucina**, etc.: cf. Hor. *C. S.*
13–16 *rite maturos aperire partus
lenis, Ilithyia, tuere matres, siue tu
Lucina probas uocari seu Genita-
lis; Carm.* III. 22. 2–4.

14. **Iuno**: as the feminine coun-
terpart of the Diespiter (*Iuppiter
Lucetius*), who was worshipped in
the mid-months, Juno was regarded
as the deity who brought back the
moonlight after its monthly eclipse,
and so was worshipped on the Ka-
lends as Lucina, the light-bringing.
From this office she came to be

regarded as a goddess of birth. The
etymological connection of Juno and
Diana suggests how naturally the
latter, herself the moon-goddess,
became identified with the former
in other aspects also.

15. **potens Triuia**: cf. Verg.
Aen. VI. 247 *Hecaten caeloque Ere-
boque potentem;* Val. Flac. III. 321
*Triuiae potentis occidit arcana gene-
trix absumpta sagitta.* — It is not
strange to find Diana, as the moon-
goddess, identified with Ἑκάτη
Τριοδῖτις, the night-goddess (Lat.
Triuia), as was also Proserpina,
the goddess of the dark under-
world. — **notho es dicta lumine
Luna:** *i.e.* she is called *Luna* from
lumen, even though the light is not
her own; cf. Hor. *Carm.* IV. 6. 38
crescentem face Noctilucam; C. S.
35 *siderum regina bicornis, audi,
Luna, puellas;* Lucr. V. 575 *luna
notho fertur loca lumine lustrans.*
So Diana as the huntress and birth-
helper, as Luna, and as Triuia (=
Proserpina), is the threefold goddess; cf. Hor. *Carm.* III. 22. 4 *diua
triformis;* Verg. *Aen.* IV. 511 *ter-
geminam Hecaten, tria uirginis ora
Dianae.*

Tu cursu, dea, menstruo
Metiens iter annuum
Rustica agricolae bonis
20   Tecta frugibus exples.

Sis quocumque tibi placet
Sancta nomine, Romulique,
Antique ut solita es, bona
Sospites ope gentem.

35.

Poetae tenero, meo sodali
Velim Caecilio, papyre, dicas,
Veronam ueniat, Noui relinquens

---

17. **cursu menstruo**, etc.: cf.
Hor. *Carm.* IV. 6. 39–40 *prosperam
frugum celeremque pronos uoluere
menses.*

21. **quocumque . . . nomine**:
cf. Hor. *C. S.* 15–16 (quoted on
v. 13).

22. **Romuli**, etc.: cf. Hor. *C. S.*
47–48 *Romulae genti date remque
prolemque et decus omne.* With the
hypermeter cf. 64. 298; 115. 5; and
Hor. *l.c.*

35. An invitation to an otherwise unknown poet, Caecilius of
Como, to visit Catullus at Verona,
with incidentally a little pleasantry
about a love-affair of Caecilius, and
a neat compliment about his forth-
coming poem. This address could
not have been written before 59 B.C.
(cf. v. 4 n.), and was written while
Catullus was at Verona. Two occa-
sions only are surely known on which
he was at his ancestral home after
59, — once immediately on his return from Bithynia in the summer

of 56, and again somewhat more
than a year later, a few months before his death. The poem may well
date from one or the other of these
periods. — Metre, Phalaecean.

1. **tenero**: as a writer of love-
poetry; cf. Ov. (with whom it is a
favorite word) *Art. Am.* III. 333
teneri carmen Properti; Rem. Am.
757 teneros ne tange poetas; Mart.
IV. 14. 13 *tener Catullus;* VII. 14.
3 *teneri amica Catulli.* — **sodali**:
implying warm intimacy; cf. 10. 29;
12. 13; 30. 1; 47. 6.

2. **Caecilio**: possibly an ancestor
of C. Plinius Caecilius Secundus
(*circ.* 62–113 A.D.), whose home
was in Novum Comum, where inscriptions show that the Caecilii
flourished. — **papyre**: apostrophe
to his book by the author is not
uncommon, especially in Ovid (*e.g.
Trist.* I. 1) and Martial (*e.g.* VII.
84, also sent to a Caecilius).

3. **relinquens**: cf. 31. 6 n.
liquisse.

Comi moenia Lariumque litus :
5   Nam quasdam uolo cogitationes
    Amici accipiat sui meique.
    Quare, si sapiet, uiam uorabit,
    Quamuis candida milies puella
    Euntem reuocet manusque collo
10 Ambas iniciens roget morari,
    Quae nunc, si mihi uera nuntiantur,
    Illum deperit impotente amore :
    Nam quo tempore legit incohatam
    Dindymi dominam, ex eo misellae

4. Comi: in the year 59 B.C., in
accordance with the Vatinian law,
Julius Caesar settled 5000 colonists
at Comum, a town already established under Cn. Pompeius Strabo,
and called the place *Nouum Comum.* Como, the modern town,
lies at the southern end of the western arm of Lacus Larius (Lago di
Como), about thirty miles north of
Mediolanum (Milan).

5. cogitationes: Catullus desires
to entice his friend to visit him, and
so speaks with playful vagueness of
certain weighty matters that can be
communicated only by word of
mouth. The whole tone of the
poem is opposed to any serious interpretation of the phrase.

6. amici sui meique: the same
playful mysteriousness of expression
is kept up here, but Caecilius undoubtedly interpreted it correctly to
mean that the friend was the writer
himself. So Catullus speaks of himself to Alfenus in 30. 2 as *tui amiculi.*

7. uiam uorabit: an unusual,
but perfectly intelligible phrase, perhaps favored by the alliteration, and
augmenting by its exaggerated character the playfulness of the urgency.

8. candida: cf. 13. 4 n.

10. roget morari: for the more
usual construction of *rogare* with *ut*
see 13. 14.

12. illum deperit, *is dying for
him ;* cf. 100. 2 ; Plaut. *Cas.* 449
hic ipsus Casinam deperit; Nem.
Bucol. 2. 70 *rusticus Alcon te per-
eam ;* and in 45. 5 *perire* used
absolutely. — **impotente,** *violent ;*
cf. 4. 18 n.

13. quo tempore: denoting the
starting-point of a continued action,
as indicated by v. 14 *ex eo ;* cf. 68.
15 *tempore quo* with 68. 20, where
the continuance of activity from the
initial period is clearly indicated. —
legit: *sc. illa ;* she read the opening verses lent her by the author;
cf. 42, where Catullus was unable
to recover his tablets lent, perhaps,
under similar circumstances. The
custom of public recitation by the
author himself was introduced later
by Asinius Pollio (cf. 12. 6).

14. Dindymi dominam: *i.e.* a
poem, or play, based on the story of
Cybele; cf. 63. 13, 91, and introductory note to that poem. — **misellae** : she is pitied only as suffering
love's pleasing pain ; cf. 45. 21;
50. 9; 51. 5.

15   Ignes interiorem edunt medullam.
Ignosco tibi, Sapphica puella
Musa doctior : est enim uenuste
Magna Caecilio incohata Mater.

36.

Annales Volusi, cacata charta,
Votum soluite pro mea puella :
Nam sanctae Veneri Cupidinique
Vouit, si sibi restitutus essem

15. ignes: of the flames of love;
cf. **2. 8** n. *ardor ;* Verg. *Aen.* IV.
66 *est mollis flamma medullas ;* Ov.
Am. III. 10. 27 *tenerae flammam
rapuere medullae.* — **interiorem**:
cf. **64. 93** *imis medullis ;* **64. 196
extremis medullis ;** **66. 23** *penitus
exedit medullas.* — **medullam**: the
word occurs only here in Catullus in
the singular, but seven times in the
plural in the same sense ; cf. **25. 2**
medullula.

16. ignosco tibi: *sc.* for falling
deeply in love with Caecilius, and
therefore seeking to detain him. —
Sapphica musa: *i.e.* than the inspired Sappho herself ; perhaps with
a reminiscence of the frequency with
which, in the Palatine Anthology,
Sappho is ranked among the Muses.

17. doctior: an epithet commonly applied to poets, especially
of this school, which disdained the
rude simplicity of its predecessors,
and sought inspiration among the
polished Alexandrians (Catullus is
styled *doctus* by Ovid in *Am.* III. 9.
62, by Lygdamus in Tib. III. 6. 41,
and by Martial in VII. 99. 7 and
XIV. 152. 1) ; Catullus means that
a girl so appreciative of the best
poetry must have within herself the
attributes of a poet; so Propertius

calls Cynthia *docta* (III. 13. 11),
and in Catullus 65. 2 the Muses are
doctae uirgines.

18. magna Mater: *i.e.* Cybele;
cf. **63. 9** n. — **incohata**: there is
no reason to suppose, as some have
done, any playful implication that
Caecilius had been unwarrantably
long in getting beyond the beginning of his work.

36. Catullus calls upon the Annals of Volusius to aid him in the
discharge of a vow made by Lesbia,
invokes Venus to recognize the pay-
ment, and with the word throws the
Annals into the fire. — The poem
was evidently written about 59 or
58 B.C., in the short period of reconciliation after the temporary cool-
ness marked by **8** ; cf. Intr. 19, 20.
Metre, Phalaecean.

1. annales: probably chronicles
in verse, after the fashion of the
famous Annals of Ennius. — **Volusi**: cf. Intr. 75. — **cacata charta,**
defiled sheets ; the verses were so
wretched that they but spoiled good
paper.

2. mea puella: *i.e.* Lesbia; cf.
3. 3 n.

3. sanctae, *divine ;* cf. **68. 5**
sancta Venus ; **64. 95** *sancte puer*
[*Cupido*] ; **64. 298** *pater diuum*

5   Desissemque truces uibrare iambos,
     Electissima pessimi poetae
     Scripta tardipedi deo daturam
     Infelicibus ustilanda lignis.
     Et hoc pessima se puella uidit
10   Iocose lepide uouere diuis.
     Nunc, o caeruleo creata ponto,
     Quae sanctum Idalium Vriosque apertos,

sancta cum coniuge; 64. 268 *sanc-tis diuis.* — **Veneri Cupidinique:** cf. 3. 1 n.

5. **truces iambos:** the tradi-tional weapons of satire since the time of Archilochus ; cf. 12. 10 n. ; Hor. *Carm.* I. 16. 22 *me quoque pectoris feruor in celeres iambos mi-sit furentem ; A. P.* 79 *Archilochum proprio rabies armauit iambo :* the poems here meant are 8 and, per-haps, 37, possibly with others not included in the final *liber Catulli.*

6. **electissima,** *choicest* from their badness, the worst; with the irony of meaning cf. 33. 1 *optime ;* 37. 14 *boni beatique.* — **pessimi poetae:** so Lesbia had in a pet called Catul-lus, in that he made her uncomfort-able by his *truces iambi ;* and she would, of course, dedicate to Vulcan not the bad poetry of some undeter-mined poetaster, but the particular verses that had stung her, which would naturally be destroyed after a reconciliation as painful memorials (cf. Hor. *Carm.* I. 16 on a similar occasion). Catullus now playfully ignores the real meaning of her words, and pitches upon Volusius as the *pessimus poeta* of his acquaint-ance, whose works are therefore due to Vulcan.

7. **tardipedi deo:** *i.e.* Vulcan, who was lamed by the fall from heaven to Lemnos (Hom. *Il.* I. 586 ff.); cf. Tib. I. 9. 49 *illa uelim*

rapida Volcanus carmina flamma torreat; Quint. VIII. 6. 24 *Vulca-num pro igne uulgo audimus.*

8. **infelicibus lignis:** cf. Ma-crob. III. 20. 3 *arbores quae infe-rum deorum auertentiumque in tutela sunt, eas infelices nominant . . . quibus portenta prodigiaque mala comburi iubere oportet ; Legg. Regg.* ap. Liv. I. 26 *infelici arbori reste suspendito* [*perduellionem*].

9. **hoc:** *sc. uotum.* — **pessima puella:** spoken jestingly (cf. 55. 10), but in reminiscence of the same term applied by her to him (v. 6), which he now attempts to pass on to the unfortunate Volusius.

10. **iocose lepide:** Catullus as-serts (of course without foundation) that the vow was made sportively in the sense in which he has just interpreted it.

11. **nunc:** the moment of con-summation of the vow has come, and the poet as officiating priest stands ready with the offering, and begins the final prayer. — **caeruleo creata ponto:** by early tradition Aphrodite was born of the sea-foam : cf. Hes. *Theog.* 195; Anacr. 54, etc. Note the solemn effect of the mani-fold address, with which cf. the prayer of Chryses to Phoebus, Hom. *Il.* I. 37 ff., etc.

12. **Idalium:** a town and wooded mountain of Cyprus, whereon stood a renowned temple of Aphrodite;

Quaeque Ancona Cnidumque harundinosam
Colis, quaeque Amathunta, quaeque Golgos,
15   Quaeque Durrachium Hadriae tabernam,
Acceptum face redditumque uotum,
Si non inlepidum neque inuenustum est.
At uos interea uenite in ignem,
Pleni ruris et inficetiarum
20   Annales Volusi, cacata charta.

---

cf. 61. 17; 64. 96; Verg. *Aen.* I.
680 *hunc super alta Cythera aut
super Idalium recondam;* 692 *in
altos Idaliae lucos.* — **Vrios**: apparently an otherwise unknown parallel
form for *Vrium* (Ptol. III. 1. 17;
Strab. VI. 3. 9), the name of a town
which lay at the foot of Mons Gar-
ganus in Apulia, on the bay of Urias
(Mela II. 4. 66). Its connection
with the worship of Venus is unknown, though Ellis ascribes it to
the association of this district with
Diomedes (Verg. *Aen.* VIII. 9),
who founded cities (*e.g.* Venusia)
and temples in honor of Aphrodite
(Serv. on Verg. *Aen.* XI. 246). —
apertos, *storm-beaten;* Mela says
the bay was *pleraque asper accessu.*

13. **Ancona** (from the Greek
form Ἀγκών): this well-known city
of Picenum contained a temple of
Venus Marina; cf. Juv. 4. 40 *domum
Veneris, quam Dorica sustinet An-
con.* — **Cnidum**: in this famous
city at the extremity of the Cnidian
Chersonese in Caria were several
temples of Aphrodite, and the renowned statue of the goddess by
Praxiteles. — **harundinosam**: the
reeds of Cnidus were a great article
of export on account of their excellence for manufacture into paper ;
cf. Plin. *N. H.* XVI. 157; Aus. *Ep.* 7.
49 *nec iam fissipedis per calami uias
grassetur Cnidiae sulcus harundinis.*

14. **Amathunta**: a seaport town

of southern Cyprus, where the
Adonis-cult was especially carried
on; cf. 68. 51 *duplex Amathusia*
(of Venus). — **Golgos**: this town
of Cyprus held, according to Pausanias VIII. 5. 2, the oldest shrine of
Aphrodite; cf. Theocr. 15. 100 δέσ-
ποιν᾽ ἃ Γολγώς τε καὶ Ἰδάλιον ἐφί-
λασας.

15. **Durrachium**: formerly called
Epidamnus, a seaport in southern
Illyria, and the common port of
arrival and departure for the pas-
senger traffic between Italy and the
East ; hence **Hadriae tabernam.**

16. **acceptum face**: *i.e.* discharge the account, now that the
vow is to be paid ; cf. the commercial term in Cic. *Rosc. Com.* 1. 4. *in
codice accepti.* On **face** see 34. 8 n.

17. **si**, etc.: cf. 6. 2 and 10. 4 ;
if Catullus had not departed from
the strict form of the vow by offering a witty equivalent for the for-
feited pledge, there would be no
point to the *si*-clause. With *si* in
this sense, putting deferentially a
fact that must be generally conceded (= *si quidem*), cf. 76. 19.

18. **at**: turning from the previous thought and beginning the final
malediction, as in 3. 13; 27. 5; 28.
14. — **interea**: cf. 14. 21 n.

19. **pleni ruris**, etc.: cf. 22. 14 n.

20. **annales**, etc.: with the repetition of the opening verse cf. 16,
52, and 57.

37.

Salax taberna uosque contubernales,
A pilleatis nona fratribus pila,
Solis putatis esse mentulas uobis,
Solis licere quidquid est puellarum
5   Confutuere et putare ceteros hircos?
An, continenter quod sedetis insulsi
Centum an ducenti, non putatis ausurum
Me una ducentos irrumare sessores?
Atqui putate: namque totius uobis
10   Frontem tabernae sopionibus scribam.

37. Catullus abuses and threatens Egnatius and his companions, who aspire to be lovers of his *puella*. The expression concerning the *puella* in v. 11, and the repetition of v. 12 almost *verbatim* from 8. 5, make it fairly certain that Lesbia is meant, and that these verses were therefore written in the period of temporary estrangement (cf. 8, 107, 36, and Intr. 18, 19). It will be noted that, as in 8, there is no distinct censure of Lesbia on the ground of unfaithfulness with others. — Date, about 59 B.C. Metre, choliambic.

1. **taberna**: here probably a cook-shop with a bad reputation.

2. **pilleatis fratribus**: *i.e.* Castor and Pollux, who are often represented in ancient art wearing the *pilleus*. Their temple, usually called that of Castor alone (Suet. *Iul.* 10), stood on the southern side of the Forum, near its eastern end. From its restoration in 6 A.D., three Corinthian columns still stand with the ancient *podium.* — **pila**: the pillar at the door of each *taberna*, or shop, that served as a sign-post for advertisement of the goods within; cf. Hor. *Sat.* I. 4. 71 *nulla taberna*

meos habeat neque pila libellos; Mart. I. 117. 10 *contra Caesaris est forum taberna scriptis postibus hinc et inde totis.* Rows of *tabernae* stood even in the Forum from early times, while the streets of the vicinity abounded with them.

4. **quidquid est puellarum**: cf. I. 8 n. *quidquid hoc libelli.*

5. The first foot of the verse is probably a dactyl; but cf. Intr. 79. — **hircos**: *i.e.* creatures detestable to all women; cf. 69 and 71.

7. **an**: with ellipsis of the verb, the complete idea being *nescio* **centum** *sitis* **an ducenti**, *i.e.* 'a hundred of you, or, for all I care, two hundred'; cf. Cic. *Fam.* XIII. 29. 4 *non plus duobus an* [*i.e.* 'or possibly it was'] *tribus mensibus.* But cf. 29. 14 *ducenties aut trecenties.* — **ducenti**: cf. 29. 14 n.

10. **sopionibus scribam**: *i.e.* he will scrawl insulting pictures or inscriptions over the house-front, advertising to passers-by the disorderly character of the house, as some dwellings in Pompeii seem to have been treated. **sopio** is apparently a colloquial word for *penis.*

Puella nam mi, quae meo sinu fugit,
Amata tantum quantum amabitur nulla,
Pro qua mihi sunt magna bella pugnata,
Consedit istic.   Hanc boni beatique
15 Omnes amatis, et quidem, quod indignum est,
Omnes pusilli et semitarii moechi:
Tu praeter omnes une de capillatis,
Cuniculosae Celtiberiae fili,
Egnati, opaca quem bonum facit barba
20 Et dens Hibera defricatus urina.

38.

Male est, Cornifici, tuo Catullo,
Male est me hercule ei et laboriose,

11. **mi**: ethical dative. — *meo sinu fugit*: but cf. 44. 14 *in tuum sinum fugi*.

12. **amata**, etc.: cf. 8. 5, and introductory note to this poem.

13. **magna bella**: probably referring only in general to the great difficulties accompanying a successful *liaison* with a married woman, and one of Lesbia's social position.

14. **boni beatique**: ironical; cf. 33. 1 *optime ;* 36. 6 *electissima*. The alliterative coupling is common; cf. 14. 10 n.

15. **quod indignum est**: with the form of clause cf. 38. 4.

16. **semitarii**: cf. 58. 4.

17. **une**: with a specializing force; cf. 10. 17 *unum*. — **capillatis**: contrary to the old Roman custom, young city fops of the day affected long hair elegantly dressed as well as beards (v. 19); cf. Cic. *Cat.* II. 10. 22 *pexo capillo nitidos aut imberbis aut bene barbatos*.

18. **cuniculosae**: as the home of a particular species of rabbit: cf.

25. 1. Perhaps there is an oblique reference to the effeminacy of Egnatius in the choice of the adjective.

19. **Egnati**: cf. 39, directed against him expressly. Nothing further is known of him. — **bonum**, *pretty;* said sneeringly; cf. Cic. *l.c., bene barbatos*. — **barba**: cf. v. 17 n.

20. **dens**: collective, as in 39. 20. — **Hibera**, *after the Spanish fashion*, with a transfer of epithet to **urina** from **defricatus**; cf. 17. 19 n. — **defricatus**: cf. 39. 17 ff.

38. An appeal to Cornificius for the consolation of some verses from him. Catullus was apparently ill, perhaps with his last illness, and, with the exaggerated fancies of a sick man, thinks himself deserted by his friends; cf. *c.* 30, and Intr. 42 and 56. — Date, probably 54 B.C. Metre, Phalaecean.

1. **male est**: of bodily illness; cf. Plaut. *Amph.* 1058 *animo male est* (of feeling faint); and, on the

Et magis magis in dies et horas.

Quem tu, quod minimum facillimumque **est,**

5 Qua solatus es adlocutione?

Irascor tibi.   Sic meos amores?

Paulum quid libet adlocutionis,

Maestius lacrimis Simonideis.

39.

Egnatius, quod candidos habet dentes,

Renidet usque quaque.   Si ad rei uentum est

other hand, Cic. *Fam.* XVI. 5. 1 *cum meliuseule tibi esset* (to Tiro, left ill at Patrae). — **Cornifici**: see Intr. 61.

2. **laboriose**: used of physical suffering ; cf. Cic. *Phil.* XI. 4. 8 *dolores maiores quos laboriosos solemus dicere.*

3. **magis magis**: cf. the same phrase in 64. 274, and Verg. *Geor.* IV. 311; but more commonly as in 68. 48. — **in dies et horas**: cf. *Bell. Afr.* 1. 2 *omnes in dies horasque parati.*

4. **quod minimum**, etc.: with the form of the clause cf. 37. 15 *quod indignum est.*

6. **meos amores**: not of a person (cf. 6. 16 n.), but of the affection itself: 'is it thus you treat my love for you?' Cf. 64. 27 n. With the ellipsis of the verb in a question of surprise cf. Cic. *Att.* XIII. 24 *nihil igitur ne ei quidem litterarum?*

7. **paulum quid libet**, *just one little word* (Ellis); with the ellipsis of the imperative cf. 55. 10 (*sc. reddite*); Ter. *And.* 204 *bona uerba, quaeso* (*sc. dicas*).

8. **maestius**, *and let it be sadder,* — for Catullus is so disconsolate that he has ceased to desire encour-

agement, and yearns only for what is in accordance with his own mood. — **lacrimis Simonideis**: Simonides (556–467 B.C.), the celebrated poet of Ceos, excelled especially in plaintive themes, and so won even from Aeschylus the prize offered for an elegy upon the Athenians who fell at Marathon.

39. Egnatius, who was singled out for especial attack in 37. 17–20, is again satirized in the vein there indicated. Cf. also Martial's satire on the continual grin of Canius Rufus (III. 20). The poem was doubtless written at about the same time as 37, and the metres are identical.

1. **candidos habet dentes**: cf. 37. 19–20.

2. **rei subsellium**, *the defendant's bench;* cf. Cael. ap. Cic. *Fam.* VIII. 8. 1 *inuocatus ad subsellia rei occurro.* Egnatius was one of the friends gathered (*aduocati*) to lend the defendant their support at the trial, and ought to have assumed the expression of countenance that would have accorded with the pathetic character of the counsel's speech and have aided in influencing the judges, — but he grins.

> Subsellium, cum orator excitat fletum,
> Renidet ille.   Si ad pii rogum fili
> 5 Lugetur, orba cum flet unicum mater,
> Renidet ille.   Quidquid est, ubicumque est,
> Quodcumque agit, renidet.   Hunc habet morbum
> Neque elegantem, ut arbitror, neque urbanum.
> Quare monendum est te mihi, bone Egnati.
> 10 Si urbanus esses aut Sabinus aut Tiburs
> Aut parcus Vmber aut obesus Etruscus
> Aut Lanuuinus ater atque dentatus
> Aut Transpadanus, ut meos quoque attingam,
> Aut qui libet qui puriter lauit dentes,
> 15 Tamen renidere usque quaque te nollem ;

5. lugetur: he is one of the friends attending the funeral, and should of all men show in his face his sympathy with the bereaved mother, — but he only grins.

6. quidquid est, *whatever is going on.*

7. morbum: cf. 76. 25 ; Sen. *Clem.* II. 6. 4 *morbum esse, non hilaritatem, semper adridere ridentibus et ad omnium oscitationem ipsum quoque os diducere.*

8. neque elegantem, etc.: *i.e.* it isn't a nice habit at all.

9. monendum est te: this impersonal construction of the neuter gerundive of a transitive verb with a direct object occurs only once in comedy (Plaut. *Trin.* 869 *mi agitandumst uigilias*), but is fairly common in Lucretius and Varro, though nowhere found in Caesar. It rarely occurs in Cicero and in the Augustan and later writers. — **bone:** this vocative is generally used ironically, in more or less mild disparagement; cf. Ter. *Andr.* 616 *eho dum bone uir, quid ais ? uiden me consiliis tuis miserum*

impeditum esse ? So also Plato's ὦ 'γαθέ.

10 ff. The meaning is: if you were, not to say a native of Rome, but even anything else than what you are, your grinning would be more decent, though yet objectionable enough ; but from a Spaniard it is utterly nauseating. The instances cited are not chosen because of any especial qualities, but as types of Italian provincials from near and far, and the descriptive adjectives are therefore but formal epithets.

11. parcus, *frugal.* — **obesus:** the monuments of the Etruscans show them to have been a short and thick-set people.

12. ater, *dark-complexioned ;* cf. 93. 2. — **dentatus:** *i.e.* having fine teeth; cf. Mart. I. 72. 3 *dentata sibi uidetur Aegle emptis ossibus Indico-que cornu.*

13. meos, *my countrymen,* as Verona was a Transpadane town.

14. puriter: an antique word, used also in 76. 19; cf. such forms as 63. 49 *miseriter.*

Nam risu inepto res ineptior nulla est.
Nunc Celtiber es : Celtiberia in terra,
Quod quisque minxit, hoc sibi solet mane
Dentem atque russam defricare gingiuam,
20 Vt quo iste uester expolitior dens est,
Hoc te amplius bibisse praedicet loti.

40.

Quaenam te mala mens, miselle Rauide,
Agit praecipitem in meos iambos?
Quis deus tibi non bene aduocatus
Vecordem parat excitare rixam?
5   An ut peruenias in ora uuigi?
Quid uis? qua libet esse notus optas?

16. **inepto ineptior**: on the collocation cf. 22. 14 n.

20. **uester**: *i.e.* the teeth of Egnatius as representative of those of his countrymen. — **dens**: collective, as in 37. 20.

40. An unknown Ravidus is threatened with the pillory of verse for playing the rival to Catullus. — The resemblance of this poem to 15, including the use of the phrase *meos amores* (v. 7), suggests that it too is one of the Juventius cycle, and was written at about the same time (see Intr. 37). Metre, Phalaecean.

1. **mala mens**: cf. 15. 14. — **miselle**: in feigned commiseration. — **Rauide**: undoubtedly dissyllabic (cf. such forms as *lautus* from an apparent *lauitus*, *audeo* from an apparent *auideo*, *eicit* dissyllabic in Lucretius, etc.); there are no cases of synapheia in Phalaecean verse.

2. **iambos**: these very verses, though Phalaecean, are perhaps those threatened, iambics being

used as a general term for all verses of personal satire; cf. 54. 6; 12. 10 n.

3. **tibi**: ἀπὸ κοινοῦ with *aduocatus* and *excitare*. — **non bene aduocatus**: pointing to the older belief that a slight mistake in the observance of the ceremonials of invocation might bring down the wrath of the deity instead of his goodwill.

4. **uecordem rixam**: cf. 15. 14 *furor uecors.*

5. **peruenias in ora uulgi**: cf. Ov. *Trist.* III. 14. 23 *populi peruenit in ora ;* Ennius' Epitaph *uolito uiuos per ora uirum.*

6. **quid uis**: a colloquial question of indignant expostulation, more common with *tibi* expressed ; cf. Ter. *Heaut.* 61 *pro deum atque hominum fidem, quid uis tibi?* Cic. *De Or.* II. 67. 269 *quid tibi uis, insane?* Hor. *Sat.* II. 6. 29 *quid uis, insane?* Prop. I. 5. 3 *quid tibi uis, insane?* — **qua libet,** *in any possible way ;* cf. 76. 14; but in a locative sense in 15. 11.

Eris, quandoquidem meos amores
Cum longa uoluisti amare poena.

41.

Ameana puella defututa
Tota milia me decem poposcit,
Ista turpiculo puella naso,
Decoctoris amica Formiani.
5   Propinqui, quibus est puella curae,
Amicos medicosque conuocate:
Non est sana puella, nec rogare
Qualis sit solet aes imaginosum.

7. eris: *sc. notus.* — **meos amores**: probably of Juventius (cf. 15. 1), who had been exposed to the approaches of Ravidus by his residence with Aurelius.

8. cum longa poena: cf. 77. 2 *magno cum pretio atque malo.* Catullus expects long life for his verses (cf. 1. 10).

41. A scornful attack upon the greed for gold, joined with lack of personal attractions, of a certain Ameana, against whom 43 is also directed. On her connection with Mamurra see Intr. 74. — Date, 60–58 B.C. (cf. introductory note to 43). Metre, Phalaecean.

2. tota: emphatic; cf. Verg. *Aen.* I. 272 *ter centum totos annos.* — **milia decem**: *sc. sestertium* (= *decem sestertia*); the coincidence of this sum with that mentioned in 103. 1 suggests that the two epigrams concern the same event.

4. decoctoris Formiani: *i.e.* Mamurra, whose native city was Formiae (cf. 57. 4; Hor. *Sat.* I. 5. 37), and who is scored in 29 for squandering his ancestral estates

and the large gifts of his patrons. Cf. 43. 5.

5. propinqui, etc.: early legislation in Rome provided for investigation into the question of a person's sanity, and for the interests of relatives in such a case; cf. XII. Tabb. ap. Cic. *Inu.* II. 50. 148 *si furiosus escit, adgnatum gentiliumque in eo pecuniaque eius potestas esto;* Hor. *Sat.* II. 3. 217 *interdicto huic omne adimat ius praetor et ad sanos abeat tutela propinquos.*

7. nec rogare, etc.: the passage is hopelessly difficult (cf. Crit. App.), but the emendation of Froelich departs least from the MSS., and is otherwise more nearly satisfactory than any other attempt. The idea is that if the girl would only consult her mirror (cf. Mart. II. 41. 8 *si speculo mihique credis*), she would herself be convinced of the folly of expecting ten sestertia. With **aes** (= *speculum*) cf. χαλκός in Aesch. *Frag.* 384 κάτοπτρον εἴδους χαλκός ἐστ', οἶνος δὲ νοῦ.

8. imaginosum: ἅπαξ λεγόμενον, but it must be used of the mirror because it pictures (*imagines red-*

42.

Adeste, hendecasyllabi, quot estis
Omnes undique, quotquot estis omnes.
Iocum me putat esse moecha turpis
Et negat mihi uestra reddituram
5   Pugillaria, si pati potestis.
Persequamur eam, et reflagitemus.
Quae sit quaeritis ?   Illa quam uidetis
Turpe incedere, mimice ac moleste

dit) everything presented before it;
cf. gloss. Labb. p. 87ᶜ *imaginosus
εἰκονώδης.*

42. An unknown woman, apparently a courtezan with whom Catullus has quarrelled, refuses to return
to him his tablets, and hence these
verses are marshalled to enforce the
demand.   The woman was certainly
not Lesbia, for on no occasion does
Catullus speak of her or to her in a
tone of careless brutality, without
any trace of former regard.   Some
critics, especially comparing v. 9
with 43. 3, 6, have thought her to
be Ameana, but the position of 42
between two others concerning her
is perhaps an indication that such
was not the opinion of the original
editor of the *liber Catulli ;* see Intr.
48.   Metre, Phalaecean.

1. **hendecasyllabi**: as the vehicle of satire; cf. 12. 10 n. — **quot
estis**, etc. : *i.e.* every single one of
you, no matter how many ye are.

3. **iocum**, *her laughing-stock ;* in
the sense of *ludibrium ;* cf. Prop.
III. 24. 16 *me fallaci dominae
iam pudet esse iocum ;* Petron. 57
*spero me sic uiuere ut nemini iocus
sim.*

4. **uestra**: since they contained
verses.   With the close conjunction
of *mihi uestra* note the repeated

identification throughout of the
poet with his own verses.

5. **pugillaria**: perhaps a colloquialism for the more commonly
occurring *pugillares ;* cf. also Gell.
XVII. 9. 17 *pugillaria noua, nondum etiam cera illita.*   The tablets in question may have contained
the first sketch of a poem lent the
woman for perusal before the quarrel
intervened (cf. 35. 13 n.), or may
have been used by Catullus for ex-
tempore composition at an enter-
tainment at her house (cf. 25. 7;
50. 1–6), and kept by her. — **si pati
potestis**: *i.e.* only imagine it, if you
can; cf. 29. 1 *quis potest pati.*

6. **reflagitemus**: ἅπαξ λεγόμενον.

8. **turpe incedere**: even her
gait betrays her wanton character;
so Cicero speaks of Clodia (*Cael.*
20. 49), *si denique ita sese geret non
incessu solum sed ornatu . . . ut
meretrix uideatur ;* and Vergil of
a different character (*Aen.* I. 405),
uera incessu patuit dea ; cf. Prop.
II. 2. 6 *incedit uel Ioue digna soror.*
— **mimice ac moleste ridentem**:
i.e. wearing the sickening grin of a
mime; and the characterization is
still more offensively pushed by
comparison with the unjoyous grin
of a dog (cf. also v. 17).   With

Ridentem catuli ore Gallicani.

10 Circumsistite eam, et reflagitate :
'Moecha putida, redde codicillos,
Redde, putida moecha, codicillos.
Non assis facis ? o lutum, lupanar,
Aut si perditius potes quid esse.

15 Sed non est tamen hoc satis putandum.
Quod si non aliud potest, ruborem
Ferreo canis exprimamus ore.
Conclamate iterum altiore uoce
'Moecha putida, redde codicillos,

20 Redde, putida moecha, codicillos.'
Sed nil proficimus, nihil mouetur.
Mutanda est ratio modusque nobis,
Si quid proficere amplius potestis,
'Pudica et proba, redde codicillos.'

moleste in this sense cf. 10. 33.
Note the alliteration.

9. **Gallicani**: perhaps used because the woman was of *Gallia prouincia*, though the adjective may
be only a chance one, since Gallic
dogs were a breed approved in Italy.

13. **assis facis**: cf. 5. 3 n. —
lutum: cf. the similar use as a
term of abuse in Plaut. *Pers.* 413
*possum te facere ut argentum acci-
pias, lutum?* Cic. *Pis.* 26. 62 *o
tenebrae, o lutum, o sordes!*

14. **aut si**, etc.: with the form of
expression cf. 13. 10 n.

15. **sed non**, etc.: *i.e.* we are
evidently accomplishing nothing by
simply calling her bad names ; let
us shout more loudly, that for very

shame of public scandal, she may
comply with our demand.

16. **potest**: *sc. fieri;* for similar easy ellipses with *posse* see 72.
7; 76. 16, 24.

17. **ferreo**, *brazen*, showing none
of the mobility of sensitiveness ; cf.
Cic. *Pis.* 26. 63 *os tuum ferreum
senatus conuicio uerberari noluisti.*
— **canis ore**: cf. the Homeric epithet κυνώπης ; and among other
nations the dog has been the type
of shamelessness.

22. **mutanda**, etc.: *i.e.* perhaps
success is impossible, but if there is
any chance, it lies in a complete
change of front.

24. Cf. the similar irony in the address to Canidia, Hor. *Epod.* 17. 38 ff.

43.

Salue, nec minimo puella naso
Nec bello pede nec nigris ocellis
Nec longis digitis nec ore sicco
Nec sane nimis elegante lingua,
5　Decoctoris amica Formiani.
Ten prouincia narrat esse bellam?
Tecum Lesbia nostra comparatur?
O saeclum insapiens et infacetum!

44.

O funde noster seu Sabine seu Tiburs
(Nam te esse Tiburtem autumant quibus non est

43. Another uncomplimentary address to the Ameana of 41 (cf. vv. 1 and 5 of 43 with 3 and 4 of 41). It seems to have been composed while Catullus was still on good terms with Lesbia (hence in 60–58 B.C.), for it is well-nigh impossible that he should defend her, even as a paragon of beauty only, after the settled bitterness of their final separation. — Metre, Phalaecean.

2. **nigris ocellis**: cf. Hor. *Carm.* I. 32. 11 *Lycum nigris oculis nigroque crine decorum; A. P.* 37 *spectandum nigris oculis nigroque capillo.*

3. **longis digitis**: cf. Prop. II. 2. 5 *fulua coma est longaeque manus, et maxima toto corpore, et incedit uel Ioue digna soror.* Even the absurdly long fingers pictured in the older vase-paintings may indicate the partiality of the ancients for this mark of beauty.

4. **nec nimis elegante**, *none too refined*; cf. the similar use of *nimis*

and *nimium* in 56. 4; 60. 5; 64. 22; 93. 1; and on the litotes also Mart. IX. 81. 3 *non nimium curo.* — **lingua**: after mentioning details that appeal to the eye, Catullus passes to that which offends the ear, — for *elegans* is apparently not used of the shape of features. The slobbering lips (v. 3) were naturally accompanied by a thick and awkward tongue that disfigured the speech.

5. Cf. 41. 4.

6. **prouincia**: *i.e.* Gallia Cisalpina, commonly called simply *Prouincia.*

7. **comparatur**: it may be that the city-man Mamurra himself had inflamed the vanity of the provincial Ameana by comparing her with the popular beauty of the capital. It is not likely that the relations between Catullus and Lesbia were discussed in the Province.

44. Sestius, following the custom of interchange of literary productions among friends (cf. 14), had sent Catullus a copy of his

Cordi Catullum laedere: at quibus cordi est
Quouis Sabinum pignore esse contendunt),
5 Sed seu Sabine siue uerius Tiburs,
Fui libenter in tua suburbana
Villa malamque pectore expuli tussim,
Non immerenti quam mihi meus uenter,
Dum sumptuosas adpeto, dedit, cenas.
10 Nam, Sestianus dum uolo esse conuiua,
Orationem in Antium petitorem
Plenam ueneni et pestilentiae legi.
Hic me grauido frigida et frequens tussis
Quassauit usque dum in tuum sinum fugi

newly-composed oration, and had
accompanied it with an invitation
to a dinner, from which the poet
was unexpectedly detained by a
sudden attack of influenza. After
his recovery he sends Sestius these
verses in excuse for his absence,
humorously attributing his illness
to the frigid quality of the oration,
which he had felt forced to read in
expectation of being called upon
for his opinion concerning it. —
Metre, choliambic.

3. **cordi**: cf. 64. 158; 81. 5;
95. 9. — **laedere**: for Tibur was
a fashionable place of summer
abode, while Sabinum was noted
only as the country of frugal peas-
ant life.

4. **pignore contendunt**: cf.
Verg. *Ecl.* 3. 31 *tu dic, mecum quo
pignore certes.*

6. **tua**: since the villa was a part
of the *fundus.* — **suburbana**: Tibur
(now Tivoli) was but 18 miles from
Rome, and indeed, being placed on
the abrupt edge of the Sabine hills
as they descend to the plain, was
visible from the city itself.

7. **malam**, *wretched;* cf. Hor.
A. P. 453 *mala scabies.* — **expuli**:

cf. Hor. *Ep.* II. 2. 137 *expulit elle
boro morbum.*

8. **uenter**: the stomach inflicted
a penalty for contemplated gluttony,
instead of lending itself to the expected gratification.

10. **Sestianus**: referring probably to P. Sestius, a man especially
helpful to Cicero at the time of his
exile, and defended by him in a
speech still extant when prosecuted
in 56 B.C. on a charge of *uis.* He
was apparently a man of irritable
temper and vigorous tongue; with
v. 12 cf. Cic. *Quint. Fr.* II. 4. 1, etc.
— **dum uolo**, etc.: *i.e.* I joyfully
planned to accept the invitation,
and under the circumstances dared
not postpone the reading of the oration sent by my prospective host.

11. **Antium**: otherwise unknown. — **petitorem**: probably (as
in Hor. *Carm.* III. 1. 10 *hic generosior descendat in campum petitor*)
of a candidate for public office; but
the occasion of the attack cannot
be determined.

12. **plenam**, etc.: with a jesting
double meaning; the speech was
full of *uenenum* and *pestilentia* for
the reader as well as for the unfor·

15 Et me recuraui otioque et urtica.

Quare refectus maximas tibi grates

Ago, meum quod non es ulta peccatum.

Nec deprecor iam, si nefaria scripta

Sesti recepso, quin grauedinem et tussim

20 Non mi, sed ipsi Sestio ferat frigus,

Qui tunc uocat me cum malum librum legi.

45.

Acmen Septimius suos amores

Tenens in gremio 'Mea' inquit, 'Acme,

Ni te perdite amo atque amare porro

Omnes sum adsidue paratus annos

---

tunate Antius; cf. 14. 19 (where *uenena* is used of wretched verses), and the collocation of *uenenum* and *pestis* in 77. 5–6.

15. **urtica**: nettles were a light article of vegetarian diet (cf. Hor. *Ep.* I. 12. 7 *abstemius herbis uiuis et urtica*), and thus well fitted for a patient with influenza; cf. concerning them Plin. *N. H.* XXII. 35 *utilissimam cibis coctam conditamu: arteriae tussi cum tisana pectus purgare.*

16. **tibi**: *i.e.* the villa (cf. v. 17 *ulta*), to which the address turns from the *fundus*.

17. **ulta**: *sc.* by refusing to grant me relief from the punishment which the *uenter* had inflicted.

18. **nefaria scripta**: on the lengthening of the final short syllable in thesis see Intr. 86 *g*.

19. **recepso**: a sigmatic aorist form, which came to be used like the ordinary future-perfect, which was itself of similar origin. Cf. 34. 8 n.

20. **non mi, sed ipsi Sestio**:

a παρὰ προσδοκίαν. — **frigus**: of a cold also in Hor. *Sat.* I. 1. 80 *tentatum frigore corpus.*

21. **uocat**: *sc. ad cenam;* cf. 47. 7 *uocationes;* Plaut. *Capt.* 76 *quos nunquam quisquam uocat.*

45. A love-idyl, marked by a most charming simplicity and *abandon* of sentiment and expression. It is impossible to determine whether the poem is purely ideal, or was written in honor of the love of some actual friend (cf. 6. 16–17). With it cf. the less intensity of Hor. *Carm.* III. 9. — Date, 55 B.C. (cf. v. 22 n.). Metre, Phalaecean.

1. **Acmen**: the Greek name suggests a *libertina*, while **Septimius** is the *nomen* of an honored Roman family. — **amores**: cf. 6. 16 n.

2. **tenens in gremio**: he was reclining on a couch, and she sitting on its edge close to him, and resting back in his arms; cf. the well-known illustrations of *symposia*.

3. **perdite amo**: cf. 104. 3; Ter. *Phor.* 82 *hanc amare coepit perdite.* — **porro**, *in time to come;* cf. 68. 45.

5   Quantum qui pote plurimum perire,
    Solus in Libya Indiaque tosta
    Caesio ueniam obuius leoni.'
    Hoc ut dixit, Amor, sinistra ut ante,
    Dextra sternuit adprobationem.
10 At Acme leuiter caput reflectens
    Et dulcis pueri ebrios ocellos
    Illo purpureo ore sauiata
    'Sic' inquit, 'mea uita, Septimille,

5. **pote**: for *potest;* cf. 17. 24 n.
— **perire**: usually with the person
loved as direct object ; cf. Plaut.
Poen. 1095 *earum hic alteram
efflictim perit* (cf. *deperire* in 35.
12 ; 100. 2) ; or as instrumental
ablative, a construction common in
the Augustan poets.

6. **solus**, etc.: cf. Hor. *Carm.*
III. 27. 51 *utinam inter errem
nuda leones.* — **Libya**: *i.e.* Africa;
on its lions cf. Hor. *Carm.* I. 22.
15 *Iubae tellus, leonum arida nutrix ;* Plin. *N. H.* VI. 195. — **India
tosta**: cf. Verg. *Geor.* IV. 425
rapidus [*rabidus?*] *torrens sitientis
Sirius Indos ardebat caelo;* Tib. II.
3. 55 *comites fusci, quos India torret.*

7. **caesio leoni**: cf. Hom. *Il.*
XX. 172 [λέων] γλαυκιόων δ' ἰθὺς
φέρεται μένει ; Ellis quotes Plin.
N. H. VIII. 54 *leonum omnis uis
constat in oculis.*

8-9 (= 17-18). The reading
seems correct as it stands here, so
far as the contrast of *sinistra* and
dextra is concerned, but a satisfactory interpretation of **sinistra ut
ante** is impossible. Sneezing was
apparently a good omen, however
occurring, and there is no indication
that Amor had sneezed before at all,
or that he had ever been unpropi-
tious (*sinister*) toward the lovers.
ut ante may be corrupt, but none
of the emendations proposed (see

Crit. App.) are at all satisfactory.
Bonnet suggests that the difficulty
may lie in our lack of detailed
knowledge of the interpretation of
this omen among the ancients.

9. **sternuit adprobationem** :
sneezing was early regarded as a
good omen ; cf. Hom. *Od.* XVII.
541 ff.; Xen. *Anab.* III. 2. 9 πτάρ-
νυταί τις · ἀκούσαντες δ' οἱ στρατιῶ-
ται πάντες μιᾷ ὁρμῇ προσεκύνησαν
τὸν θεόν ; Ov. *Epist.* 18. 152 *sternuit, et nobis prospera signa dedit;*
Prop. II. 3. 24 *candidus argutum
sternuit omen Amor.*

10. **caput reflectens**: *i.e.* bend-
ing backward so as to turn her face
upward toward that of Septimius.

11. **pueri**: cf. 12. 9 n. *puer.* —
ebrios: *i.e.* swimming with passion,
drunk with love; so Dido ' drank '
love (Verg. *Aen.* I. 749 *longum
bibebat amorem*). — **ocellos**: on
the kissing of the eyes cf. 9. 9 n.

12. **purpureo**: = *roseo* (64. 49
tincta roseo purpura fuco); cf. 63.
74 ; 80. 1 *rosea labella* (as a mark
of youthful and almost feminine
beauty) ; Verg. *Aen.* II. 593 *roseo
haec insuper addidit ore ;* Ov. *Am.*
III. 14. 23 *purpureis condatur
lingua labellis ;* Apul. *Apol.* 9 *oris
sauia purpurei.*

13. **mea uita**: cf. 68. 155; 104.
1 ; 109. 1, and many instances in
colloquial and amatory writers.

Huic uni domino usque seruiamus,
15   Vt multo mihi maior acriorque
Ignis mollibus ardet in medullis.'
Hoc ut dixit, Amor, sinistra ut ante,
Dextra sternuit adprobationem.
Nunc ab auspicio bono profecti
20   Mutuis animis amant amantur.
Vnam Septimius misellus Acmen
Mauult quam Syrias Britanniasque :
Vno in Septimio fidelis Acme
Facit delicias libidinesque.
25   Quis ullos homines beatiores
Vidit, quis Venerem auspicatiorem ?

14. **huic domino**: *i.e. Amori.* — **usque**: *i.e.* from now on forever ; cf. 48. 2. — **seruiamus**: cf. 61. 134 *seruire Talasio.*

16. **medullis**: cf. 35. 15 n.

17–18 (= 8–9). Amor declines to decide which loves the more ardently, and impartially sneezes his approbation of the professions of each.

20. **amant amantur**: for similar collocations of active and passive see Cic. *Cat.* II. 10. 23 *amare et amari ;* Phaedr. II. 2. 2 *ament amentur ;* Tac. *Germ.* 38 *ut ament amenturue.*

21. **misellus**: cf. 35. 14 ; 51. 5.

22. **Syrias Britanniasque**: the allusion suggests that the poem was composed in 55 B.C., for in that year Caesar invaded Britain and Crassus took command in Syria. Syria was proverbially a country of great wealth, and Britain was supposed to be so till the expedition of Caesar

proved it otherwise (cf. Cic. *Fam.* VII. 7. 1 *in Britannia nihil esse audio neque auri neque argenti* (to Trebatius after the expedition); *Att.* IV. 16. 7 *Britannici belli exitus exspectatur ; . . . etiam illud iam cognitum est, neque argenti scripulum esse ullum in illa insula neque ullam spem praedae nisi ex mancipiis*). The plural is used to indicate, not the several parts of the countries themselves, but such rich countries as Syria and Britain ; cf. Prop. III. 16. 10 *alias Illyrias.*

24. **facit**, etc.: *i.e.* centres all her affections. — **delicias**: see 2. 1 n., and cf. 68. 26; 74. 2; Cic. *Cael.* 19. 44 *amores autem et hae deliciae, quae uocantur.*

25. **quis**, etc.: with a similar triumphant appeal close 9 and 107, and with an indignant appeal, 29. 47, 52, and 60.

26. **auspicatiorem**: cf. v. 19.

46.

Iam uer egelidos refert tepores,
Iam caeli furor aequinoctialis
Iucundis Zephyri silescit auris.
Linquantur Phrygii, Catulle, campi
5   Nicaeaeque ager uber aestuosae :
Ad claras Asiae uolemus urbes.
Iam mens praetrepidans auet uagari,
Iam laeti studio pedes uigescunt.
O dulces comitum ualete coetus,

46. Farewell to Bithynia! An unmatched expression of pure joy at the prospect of home-coming. Written in the spring of 56 B.C., when Catullus was concluding his year of absence in Bithynia with Memmius (see Intr. 29 ff.). The other poems of this little cycle are 31 and 4. — Metre, Phalaecean.

1. **egelidos**: the prefix here has the privative meaning, as in Colum. X. 282 *nunc uer egelidum, nunc est mollissimus annus;* but the prefix is intensive in Verg. *Aen.* 8. 610 *procul egelido secretum flumine uidit.*

2. **furor aequinoctialis**: the ancients had long noted that the period of the autumnal and vernal equinoxes were accompanied by storms; cf. Plin. *N. H.* XVIII. 221.

3. **Zephyri**: the spring-wind of the Romans ; cf. Hor. *Carm.* I. 4. I *soluitur acris hiems grata uice ueris et Fauoni ;* Verg. *Geor.* II. 330 *(uere) Zephyri tepentibus auris laxant arua sinus.*

4. **Phrygii campi**: cf. 31. 5 *Bithynos campos.*

5. **Nicaeae**: Strabo (XII. 564) says of Nicaea, the capital of Bithynia, περικεῖται δὲ κύκλῳ πεδίον μέγα (cf. *Phrygii campi*) καὶ σφόδρα

εὔδαιμον (cf. *ager uber*) οὐ πάνυ δὲ ὑγιεινὸν τοῦ θέρους (cf. *aestuosae*). Homer mentions the fertility of the region in *Il.* XIII. 793 ἐξ Ἀσκανίης ἐριβώλακος. — **aestuosae**: cf. 7. 5 n. The unhealthy character of the region as summer came on rendered departure even more agreeable.

6. **claras Asiae urbes**: *i.e.* the famous Greek cities on the Aegean coast of Asia proper. — **uolemus**: the figure of flying for sailing is prompted by the eagerness of the desire to be gone ; cf. 4. 5 of the same voyage.

7. **praetrepidans** : tremulous with eager anticipation ; cf. 63. 43 *trepidante sinu.*

8. **pedes**: not that Catullus was contemplating, as some have thought, a land journey, but the passionate eagerness for departure is most unaffectedly pictured by its influence upon the physical feelings.

9. **dulces**: the social intercourse among the *comites* had been pleasant, but far outweighing the pain of separation was the delight of home-coming. — **comitum**: *i.e.* the other members of the governor's *cohors;* cf. 11. 1; 28. 1.

10 Longe quos simul a domo profectos
    Diuersae uariae uiae reportant.

47.

Porci et Socration, duae sinistrae
Pisonis, scabies famesque mundi,
Vos Veraniolo meo et Fabullo
Verpus praeposuit Priapus ille?
5   Vos conuiuia lauta sumptuose
De die facitis? mei sodales
Quaerunt in triuio uocationes?

10. longe: modifying profectos; the companionship had been endeared by their very distance from home.

11. diuersae: contrasted with simul profectos. — uariae: the homeward paths were not only pursued separately, but were varied in character, Catullus, for instance, making a detour to visit the clarae Asiae urbes.

47. An expression of indignation that two unworthy men should have enriched themselves as members of the cohors of Piso in Macedonia (cf. 28), while Veranius and Fabullus came back poor. With the interrogative form throughout cf. 60, and see 9. 10 n. — Date, about 55 B.C. (see Intr. 68). Metre, Phalaecean.

1. Porci et Socration: otherwise unknown, though the good Roman name of the former may indicate that he was a man of some social position, while the latter, being a Greek, was perhaps one of the favorites mentioned by Cicero, Pis. 27. 67 Graeci stipati quini in lectis, saepe plures. — sinistrae: i.e. accomplished assistants in plundering rascality; cf. 12. 1 n., and the familiar English expression ' his right-hand men.'

2. Pisonis: see Intr. 70. — scabies: referring to their generally dissolute character. — fames: referring to their greed for whatever they could lay hands on. — mundi: i.e. they are the pre-eminent types of rascally greed; cf. expressions of similar character in 14. 23 ; 21. 1. If mundus is here used, as seems probable, in the sense of orbis terrarum rather than of κόσμος, this is its first appearance with that meaning.

3. Veraniolo et Fabullo: cf. Intr. 68, 69; on the affectionate diminutive cf. 12. 17.

4. uerpus Priapus: Cicero (Pis. 28. 69) calls Piso an admissarius. — praeposuit: i.e. favored them above the others by giving them a chance to enrich themselves.

6. de die: to begin a feast during the working part of the day for the sake of spending a longer time at it was a mark of most excessive luxury ; cf. Plaut. Asin. 825 aa amicam de die potare; Ter. Ad. 965 adparare de die conuiuium; Hor. Sat. II. 8. 3 de medio potare die; Liv. XXIII. 8. 6 epulari coeperunt de die . . . ut in domo diti ac luxuriosa.

7. quaerunt, etc.: i.e. compelled to play the parasite like Ergasilus

48.

Mellitos oculos tuos, Iuuenti,
Siquis me sinat usque basiare,
Vsque ad milia basiem trecenta,
Nec unquam uidear satur futurus,
5   Non si densior aridis aristis
Sit nostrae seges osculationis.

49.

Disertissime Romuli nepotum,
Quot sunt quotque fuere, Marce Tulli,
Quotque post aliis erunt in annis,

in Plaut. *Capt.* 461 ff., in order to
get a mouthful of food. — **in triuio**:
as a general lounging place, where
men rich enough to furnish a dinner
might be found; cf. 58. 4 *quadriuiis.* — **uocationes**: not found elsewhere in the sense of 'invitations
to dinner,' though this interpretation
is justified by the use of the nouns
uocatus and *uocator*, and of the verb
uocare (cf. 44. 21), and by the point
of the contrast thus drawn between
the lots of the two pairs of friends.

48. One of the earliest poems of
the Juventius cycle; cf. introductory
note to 15, and with the theme the
address to Lesbia, 7. — Metre, Phalaecean.

1. **mellitos** : the same epithet is
applied to Juventius in 99. 1. —
oculos: cf. 9. 9 n.

2. **usque**, *continually ;* cf. 45. 14.

3. **milia trecenta**: of indefinite
multitude; cf. 9. 2 n.

5. **non si**: following a negation,
as in 69. 3; 70. 2; 88. 8. — **aridis
aristis**: cf. Aug. *Ciu. Dei* IV. 8
*quamdiu seges ab initiis herbidis
usque ad aridas aristas peruueniret.*

49. An expression of thanks to
M. Tullius Cicero on some unknown
occasion. It is, however, mistakenly
(see notes below) understood by
many critics to be ironical in tone.
— Metre, Phalaecean.

1. **disertissime** : Cicero himself
often uses this epithet, and always
as one of high praise. — **Romuli
nepotum** : cf. 28. 15; 34. 22; 58. 5.
In none of these passages do the
words themselves convey any tone
of disparagement (see 58. 5 n.) ;
cf. also Hor. *Carm. Saec.* 47 *Romulae genti date decus omne ; Carm.*
IV. 5. 1 *Romulae custos gentis ;
Epod.* 7. 19 *Remi sacer nepotibus
cruor.*

2. **quot sunt**, etc.: cf. 21. 2–
3; 24. 2–3; in the latter instance
the expression is connected with
high praise. — **Marce Tulli**: the
formal address suits the formal expression of thanks to a *patronus ;*
cf. Cic. *Att.* VII. 7. 7 *ad summam
'dic, M. Tulli': adsentior Cn. Pompeio, id est T. Pomponio ; Cat.* I. 11.
27 *si res publica loquatur 'M. Tulli,
quid agis ?'*

Gratias tibi maximas Catullus
5 Agit pessimus omnium poeta,
Tanto pessimus omnium poeta
Quanto tu optimus omnium patronus.

50.

Hesterno, Licini, die otiosi
Multum lusimus in meis tabellis,
Vt conuenerat esse delicatos.
Scribens uersiculos uterque nostrum
5 Ludebat numero modo hoc modo illoc,
Reddens mutua per iocum atque uinum.
Atque illinc abii tuo lepore

4. **gratias**: apparently, from v. 1 *disertissime* and v. 7 *patronus*, for some legal assistance or oratorical effort, though it is impossible to say what.

5. **pessimus omnium poeta**: the self-depreciation heightens the praise of v. 7; Catullus also speaks of himself with excessive modesty in addressing his patron Nepos in 1.

6. With the epanalepsis cf. that in 3. 3–4.

7. **optimus omnium patronus**: the construction of *omnium* with *pessimus* in v. 5 makes it impossible to suppose a double meaning here by construing *omnium* with both *optimus* and *patronus*.

50. At a banquet (v. 6), perhaps at the house of Calvus, perhaps at that of some friend (v. 7), Catullus and Calvus had engaged in a contest of improvisation, in which Catullus was so newly charmed with his friend's genius that he begs for a speedy repetition of the enjoyment. — Date uncertain, but perhaps not far removed from that of 14. Metre, Phalaecean.

1. **Licini**: *i.e.* Calvus, on whom see Intr. 60.

2. **lusimus**: of lyric, especially amatory, verse composition; cf. 61. 232; 68. 17; Hor. *Carm.* I. 32. 1 *si quid uacui sub umbra lusimus tecum, barbite;* Verg. *Ecl.* I. 10 *ludere quae uellem calamo agresti;* Aus. *Epist.* 7. 1 *ut rescriberes ad ea quae ioculariter luseram.* — **tabellis**: *i.e. pugillaribus;* cf. 42. 5 n.; 25. 7 n.

3. **conuenerat**, *we had agreed.* — **esse delicatos**: *i.e.* to compose amatory verse; cf. Cic. *N. D.* I. 40. 111 *seiunctum a delicatis et obscenis uoluptatibus; Pis.* 29. 70 *ut omnes libidines . . . delicatissimis uersibus expresserit.*

5. **ludebat numero**: cf. Verg. *Ecl.* 6. 1 *ludere uersu.* — **modo hoc modo illoc**: cf. the close of 3. 9.

6. **reddens mutua**: probably each improvising on a theme suggested by the other's verses. — **per iocum atque uinum**: cf. 12. 2.

7. **illinc**: perhaps meaning only 'from the contest,' though more

Incensus, Licini, facetiisque,
Vt nec me miserum cibus iuuaret,
10   Nec somnus tegeret quiete ocellos,
Sed toto indomitus furore lecto
Versarer cupiens uidere lucem,
Vt tecum loquerer simulque ut essem.
At defessa labore membra postquam
15   Semimortua lectulo iacebant,
Hoc, iucunde, tibi poema feci,
Ex quo perspiceres meum dolorem.
Nunc audax caue sis, precesque nostras,
Oramus, caue despuas, ocelle,
20   Ne poenas Nemesis reposcat a te.
Est uehemens dea : laedere hanc caueto.

likely indicating that the banquet was not at the house of Catullus. — **lepore facetiisque:** cf. 12. 8; 16. 7.

9. **miserum:** cf. 35. 14 n. *misellae.*

10. **somnus,** etc. : cf. 63. 37 *piger oculos sopor operit;* Verg. *Geor.* IV. 414 *incepto tegeret cum lumina somno.*

11. **toto:** modifying **lecto**; cf. Juv. 13. 218 *toto uersata toro iam membra quiescunt.* — **indomitus furore:** *i.e.* unable to quiet my feelings; but cf. 64. 54 *indomitos furores.*

13. **simul:** cf. 21. 5.

14. **postquam:** found only here in Catullus with the imperfect, though he uses it with the perfect six times, and with the pluperfect subjunctive in indirect discourse once (84. 11). In the comedians it occurs only once with the imperfect (Plaut. *Most.* 640), but this use becomes more frequent with Cicero, Sallust, and Livy.

16. **iucunde:** cf. 14. 2 n. *iucundissime Calue.*

17. **dolorem:** of longing passion; cf. 2. 7 n.

18. **audax:** with the meaning of *superbus.* — **caue:** cf. the same quantity in v. 19 and 61. 152, and frequently in the comedians and later. The verb occurs in Catullus but four times, and yet with three different constructions dependent upon it; the simple subjunctive in this and the following verses, the present infinitive in v. 21, and the subjunctive with *ne* in 61. 152. — **preces:** as expressed in v. 13.

19. **ocelle:** cf. 31. 2 n.

20. **Nemesis:** the *Rhamnusia uirgo* (64. 395 ; 66. 71 ; 68. 77) also appears as the avenger of slighted love in the episode of Narcissus, Ov. *Met.* III. 406 ff.

21. **uehemens,** *severe, inexorable;* cf. Cic. *Cat.* IV. 6. 12 *si uehementissimi fuerimus, misericordes habebimur.* The adjective is dissyllabic here, and apparently elsewhere, except in a verse of M. Aurelius to Fronto.

51.

Ille mi par esse deo uidetur,
Ille, si fas est, superare diuos
Qui sedens aduersus identidem te
　　Spectat et audit

5　Dulce ridentem, misero quod omnis
Eripit sensus mihi : nam simul te,
Lesbia, adspexi, nihil est super mi

　　　　.　　　.　　　.　　　.

Lingua sed torpet, tenuis sub artus
10　Flamma demanat, sonitu suopte
Tintinant aures, gemina teguntur
　　Lumina nocte.

51. A free translation of the ode
of Sappho given below, which is preserved in Longinus *De Sublim.* X. 2.

φαίνεταί μοι κῆνος ἴσος θέοισιν
ἔμμεν ὤνηρ, ὅστις ἐναντίος τοι
ἰζάνει καὶ πλασίον ἆδυ φωνεί-
　　σας ὑπακούει

καὶ γελαίσας ἰμερόεν, τό μοι μάν
καρδίαν ἐν στήθεσιν ἐπτόασεν·
ὡς γὰρ εὔιδον βροχέως σε, φώνας
　　οὐδὲν ἔτ' εἴκει.

ἀλλὰ καμ μὲν γλῶσσα ἔαγε, λεπτόν δ'
αὔτικα χρῶ πῦρ ὑπαδεδρόμακεν,
ὀππάτεσσι δ' οὐδὲν ὄρημ', ἐπιρρόμ-
　　βεισι δ' ἄκουαι.

ἀ δέ μ' ἵδρως κακχέεται, τρόμος δέ
πᾶσαν ἄγρει, χλωροτέρα δὲ ποίας
ἔμμι, τεθνάκην δ' ὀλίγω 'πιδεύης
　　φαίνομαι ἄλλα.

It will be noticed that for the
fourth stanza of Sappho Catullus
substitutes one entirely his own, and
that elsewhere he adds, omits, and
modifies details at his pleasure. —
Written at about the same time as
2 and 3, and perhaps the earliest

of the poems addressed to Lesbia,
and the one which first drew her
regard.　Metre, lesser Sapphic.

2. **si fas est** : a not infrequent,
and peculiarly Roman, expression;
cf. Cic. *Tusc.* V. 13. 38 *humanus
animus . . . cum alio nullo nisi
cum ipso deo, si hoc fas est dictu,
comparari potest.*

5. **dulce ridentem** : cf. 61. 219;
Hor. *Carm.* I. 22. 23 *dulce ridentem
Lalagen amabo, dulce loquentem.* —
misero : cf. 35. 14 n. *misellae.*

6. **eripit sensus** : cf. 66. 25 *sensibus ereptis.* — **simul** : cf. 22. 15 n.
With the thought cf. Plaut. *Mil.*
1271 *dum te optuetur, interim linguam oculi praeciderunt;* Publ. Sy-
rus 40 *amor, ut lacrima, ab oculis oritur, in pectus cadit;* Shaksp.
Merch. Ven. III. 2 (of Fancy) *it is
engender'd in the eyes, With gazing fed.*

8. See Crit. App.

10. **suopte** : cf. 34. 8 n.

11. **gemina** : by transfer of epithet from *lumina;* cf. 17. 19 n. —
teguntur nocte : cf. Ernst Schulze

Otium, Catulle, tibi molestum est :
Otio exsultas nimiumque gestis.
15   Otium et reges prius et beatas
      Perdidit urbes.

52.

Quid est, Catulle ? quid moraris emori ?
Sella in curuli struma Nonius sedet,

*Aber wenn du nah gekommen, Kann
ich doch dich nimmer sehn, Weil
vor Freud' und Schmerz und Za-
gen Mir die Augen übergehn.*

13–16. The prisoner of love is
torn with conflicting emotions ; he
rejoices in his chains and yet shrinks
from the power of his own passion,
which he perceives has been fostered by his lack of active occupations. With the thought cf. Ov.
Rem. Am. 138 [*otia*] *sunt iucundi
causa cibusque mali, Otia si tol-
las, periere Cupidinis arcus.* —
otium : a similar emphatic repetition of *otium* at the beginning
of closely connected verses is
found in Hor. *Carm.* II. 16. 1,
5, 6.

13. **molestum** : of a disease, as
in Hor. *Ep.* I. 1. 108 *pituita molesta
est.*

14. **exsultas . . . gestis** : similar phraseology is used by Cicero,
speaking of the slave to passion, in
Tusc. V. 6. 16 *exsultans et temere
gestiens.*

15–16. Probably Catullus had no
especial case in mind, but Croesus
and Sybaris might have served him
as well-known examples of such
ruined kings and cities.

52. This epigrammatic address
is evidently one of the series of attacks upon the Caesarians, and was
perhaps written in 55 B.C., when

the excitement against Vatinius was
at its height, and Catullus wrote 29
and other poems of the same general character. — Metre, iambic trimeter.

1. **quid est** : an appeal of impatient indignation, cf. Plaut. *Amph.*
556 *quid est ? quo modo ? . . . tibi
. . . linguam abscidam.* — **quid
moraris emori** : *i.e.* what pleasure
can you take in life when such dis-
graceful things are possible? cf.
Hor. *Carm.* III. 27. 58 *quid mori
cessas ?* Ov. *Her.* 9. 146 *impia quia
dubitas Deianira mori ?*

2. **sella in curuli** : apparently
indicating that Nonius had just attained the first of the curule offices,
— the curule aedileship, — perhaps
as part of the program settled upon
at the conference at Luca in 56
B.C. This would very well fit Nonius
Asprenas, who was an officer of
Caesar in the African War in 46
with the title of proconsul (*Bell.
Afr.* 80. 4 ; *Bell. Hisp.* 10. 2), and
perhaps not so well M. Nonius Sufe-
nas, who so late as 56 was only
tribunus plebis. — **struma** : a scrof-
ulous tumor, used here as an uncomplimentary nickname, from the
manner in which rascals were attaching themselves to the high offices
of the state; cf. Cic. *Sest.* 65. 135
strumam ciuitatis ; Plin. *N. H.*
XXXVII. 81 *Nonius senator, filius*

Per consulatum perierat Vatinius:
Quid est, Catulle? quid moraris emori?

53.

Risi nescio quem modo e corona,
Qui, cum mirifice Vatiniana
Meus crimina Caluus explicasset,

'*strumae Noni*' *eius quem Catullus poeta in sella curuli uisum indigne tulit*, where the reproduction of the order of the words in Catullus seems to indicate that Pliny understood **struma** to be an epithet and not a true cognomen.

3. **perierat**: παρὰ προσδοκίαν, for *iurat*. — **Vatinius**: in the year 55 the Caesarians succeeded in electing Vatinius praetor over Cato. Already in 56 Cicero had charged him with impudent assurance regarding a future consulship, and to the same characteristic Catullus refers here. But the coveted advancement was doubtless promised by Caesar at Luca, and this promotion to the praetorship was regarded but as a step thereto by Vatinius and by Catullus as well, whose indignation was all the more fired by it.

4. The first verse is identical with the last also in 16 and 36.

53. An anecdotal jesting compliment to the oratorical power of Calvus, as 50 was a compliment to his poetical talent. Tacitus (*Dial.* 21) speaks of the orations of Calvus against Vatinius as still read, *praecipua secunda ex iis oratio*, as if there were at least three of them. He also says (*Dial.* 34) that Calvus was not much more than 22 years old when he attacked Vatinius *iis orationibus quas hodie quoque cum*

admiratione legimus. This remark may well apply to the prosecution mentioned by Cicero (*Vat.* 14) as occurring in 58 B.C., when Calvus was 24 years old. No records exist of any further prosecution of Vatinius by Calvus until that of August, 54 B.C., when Cicero appeared for the defence. But when Cicero in 56 B.C. cross-examined Vatinius (see *In Vatinium*) while conducting the defence of Sestius, Calvus promised to indict Vatinius, apparently at once (Cic. *Quint. Fr.* II. 4. 1), and the trial may well have come off speedily, though doubtless an acquittal was secured by the same influences that immediately gave Vatinius the praetorship for 55 B.C., and hurried him into office (Cic. *Quint. Fr.* II. 7. 3) to escape further prosecution. At this unrecorded trial in 56 B.C. the famous second speech of Calvus was probably delivered, and to it Catullus doubtless refers here. — Metre, Phalaecean.

1. **corona**: a circle of auditors, especially at a trial; cf. Cic. *Flac.* 28. 69 *a iudicibus oratio auertitur, uox in coronam turbamque effunditur;* Hor. *Ep.* I. 18. 53 *scis quo clamore coronae proelia sustineas campestria.*

2. **Vatiniana**: the adjective is here equivalent to an objective genitive, while in 14. 3 it is subjective.

Admirans ait haec manusque tollens
5   'Di magni, salaputium disertum!'

54.

Othonis caput oppido est pusillum,
*
Et eri rustica semilauta crura,
Subtile et leue peditum Libonis,
*
Si non omnia, displicere uellem
5   Tibi et Fuficio, seni recocto
*
Irascere iterum meis iambis
Immerentibus, unice imperator.

4. manus tollens: the instinc-
tive gesture of amazement ; cf. Cic.
Acad. II. 19. 63 *uehementer admirans . . . ut etiam manus saepe
tolleret.*

5. di magni: cf. 14. 12 n. —
salaputium: apparently a comical
slang word, referring to the short
stature of Calvus; cf. Ov. *Trist.* II.
431 *exigui licentia Calvi ;* Sen.
Contr. VII. 4 *erat enim [Caluus]
paruulus statura, propter quod
etiam Catullus in hendecasyllabis
uocat illum 'salaputtium disertum.'*
Except in these two places the word
nowhere occurs, though *Salaputis*
is found as a man's name in an
African inscription (C. I. L. VIII.
10570). The etymology is uncertain.

54. Apparently an attack upon
Caesar, but exhibiting, in spite of
attempts at emendation, an extremely un-Catullian blindness and
awkwardness, which fact, together
with the repetition in the MSS. of
50. 16–17 after v. 1, makes it altogether probable that the tradition of
the text is incurably defective. The
persons mentioned by name are all

unknown. — Date, 55 B.C. (cf. v. 7)
Metre, Phalaecean.

1. **oppido**: colloquial for *ualde ;*
especially frequent in Terence. —
pusillum: the insinuation is probably like that of our proverb, ' Little
head, little wit.'

2. **et eri**: unmetrical and unintelligible, the latter possibly because
of a *lacuna* between vv. 1 and 2, as
indicated by the repetition there of
50. 16–17 ; but perhaps a proper
name lies hid under the words. —
rustica: cf. the references to the
country in uncomplimentary char-
acterizations in 22. 14; 36. 19.

5. **tibi**: probably referring to the
person addressed below as *unice
imperator.* — **recocto**: *i.e.* rejuve-
nated, an old man with all the vices
of a young one ; cf. the story of
Medea, Aeson, and Pelias in Ov.
Met. VII. 159 ff.; Hor. *Sat.* II. 5.
55 *recoctus scriba ex quinqueuiro*
Petron. frag. 21 B. *anus recocta
uino trementibus labellis.*

6. **iambis**: perhaps in general of
satirical verses in whatever metre;
cf. 40. 2 n.; 12. 10 n.

7. **immerentibus**: since they

55·

Oramus, si forte non molestum est,
Demonstres ubi sint tuae tenebrae.
Te campo quaesiuimus minore,
Te in circo, te in omnibus libellis,
5   Te in templo summi Iouis sacrato.

tell nothing but the plain truth.—
unice imperator: comparison with
29. 11 *imperator unice* and v. 6 *ite-rum* suggests forcibly that Julius
Caesar is meant, and that 54 fol-
lowed soon after 29 in composition,
and here refers to it.

55. An appeal to an otherwise
unknown Camerius to disclose his
whereabouts to his friend, who has
been searching through Rome for
him. Similar descriptions of an anxious search for a friend through the
city are not wanting in the comedians ; cf. Plaut. *Amph.* 1009 ff. ;
Epid. 196 ff. ; Ter. *Ad.* 713 ff.
The poem appears to be an unfinished experiment in a not very
pleasant modification of the Phalaecean verse, and was perhaps, with
the accompanying fragment, 58ᵇ,
found among the papers of Catullus
after his death and published by the
original editor of the *Liber*. The odd
verses (and also v. 8) through v. 13,
and from that point the even verses,
have a spondee in the second place.
In 58ᵇ, however, only vv. 1 and 9
have a spondee in the second place.
— Date, 55 B.C. (cf. v. 6 n.).

1. **si forte**, etc.: a bit of colloquial politeness ; cf. Ter. *Ad.* 806
*ausculta paucis, nisi molestumst,
Demea ;* Cic. *Cluent.* 60. 168 *tu
autem, nisi molestum est, paulisper
exsurge ;* Mart. I. 96. 1 *si non molestum est teque non piget . . . dicas.*

2. **tenebrae**, *lurking-place ;* cf.
Prop. IV. 15. 17 *saepe illam immun-
dis passa est habitare tenebris.*

3. **campo minore**: probably so
called to distinguish it from the
great *campus Martius ;* and Paulus
(Fest. p. 131) mentions a *campus
Martialis* on the Caelian, where
horse-races were held when the
Tiber overflowed the *campus Martius* (cf. also Ov. *Fast.* III. 519–
522). This is possibly the place
meant, as the search passed from
it through the Circus Maximus, by
the shops near the Forum (cf. 37.
2 n.), over the Capitoline, to Pompey's portico in the Campus Martius. There were yet other *campi ;*
cf. Prop. III. 23. 6 *campo quo mouet
illa pedes ?* Not. et Cur. App. I.
Campi VIII., etc. On the ablative
without *in* cf. Ov. and Prop. *ll.cc.;*
Liv. XXI. 8. 7 *iustae acies uelut
patenti campo constiterant.*

4. **circo**: *i.e.* the Circus Maximus, a haunt of idlers ; cf. Hor.
Sat. I. 6. 113 ff. — **tĕ**: not elided,
for no trochee stands in the second
place ; while the hiatus with systole
is supported by that in 10. 27; 97.
1 ; 114. 6; cf. Intr. 86 *d.* — **libellis**,
book-shops, as perhaps in Mart. V.
20. 8 *libelli, campus, porticus . . .
haec essent loca semper.*

5. **templo summi Iouis**: the
triple Etruscan temple of Jupiter
Capitolinus with Juno and Minerva,
ascribed to Tarquinius Priscus, was
burned in 83 B.C. Sulla began, and
Q. Lutatius Catulus in 69 B.C. completed, the new temple, which was
itself burned in 69 A.D. under Vitel-
lius (cf. Tac. *Hist.* III. 72).

   In Magni simul ambulatione
   Femellas omnes, amice, prendi,
   Quas uultu uidi tamen serenas.
   † A uelte sic ipse flagitabam :
10 'Camerium mihi, pessimae puellae!'
   Quaedam inquit nudum † reduc . . .
   'En hic in roseis latet papillis.'
   Sed te iam ferre Herculi labos est :
   Tanto ten fastu negas, amice ?
15 Dic nobis ubi sis futurus, ede
   Audacter, committe, crede luci.
   Nunc te lacteolae tenent puellae ?
   Si linguam clauso tenes in ore,

6. **Magni ambulatione** : in the summer of 55 B.C., the year of his second consulship, Pompey threw open to the public his stone theatre on the Campus Martius, with a magnificent *porticus* adjoining it in the rear of the stage. He is frequently mentioned by his contemporaries under the title *Magnus*, conferred by Sulla in 81 for his African victories.

7. **femellas** : ἅπαξ λεγόμενον. — **prendi**, *hailed;* cf. Ter. *Phor.* 620 *prendo hominem solum ; 'quor non' inquam, 'Phormio,'* etc.

8. **uultu serenas** : *i.e.* showing no guilty confusion.

10. **Cāmerium** : the first foot is an iambus, with the second syllable long by position of its vowel before *r* followed by consonantal *i* ; for a resolution of the normal trochee in a tribrach in this metre would be unique. With the construction (*sc. reddite ?*) cf. 38. 7. — **pessimae puellae**, *you naughty girls* (Munro) ; cf. the jesting sense of *pessima* in 36. 9.

11. The general character of the gesture is clear, despite the diffi-

culty of emendation. See Crit. App.

13. **te ferre** : *i.e.* to endure with patience your conduct. — **Herculi labos est** : with the figure cf. Prop. III. 23. 7 *ubi pertuleris, quos dicit fama, labores Herculis.* The genitive in -*i* from Greek proper names in -*es* is not infrequent in the earlier period and in Cicero.

15. **ubi sis futurus**, *where you are to be (found)*, that I may come thither at an appointed time and meet you.

16. **crede luci** : in contrast with v. 2 *tenebrae.*

17. The sportive manner of the girl (vv. 11–12) has awakened the poet's suspicions, and he is anxious to learn the truth from his friend's own lips. — **lacteolae** : apparently not occurring again till Aus. *Epist.* 7. 2. 46 *carnem lacteoli uisceris* (of an oyster), where it plainly = *candidi* (cf. 64. 65 *lactentis papillas ;* Hor. *Carm.* I. 13. 2 *lactea Telephi bracchia*); see, then, 13. 4 n. *candida puella.*— **tenent** : cf. 11. 18 n.

18–20. With the sentiment cf. 6. 1–3. — **tenes** : this repetition with

Fructus proicies amoris omnes :
20   Verbosa gaudet Venus loquella.
Vel si uis, licet obseres palatum,
Dum ueri sis particeps amoris.

56.

O rem ridiculam, Cato, et iocosam
Dignamque auribus et tuo cachinno.
Ride, quidquid amas, Cato, Catullum :
Res est ridicula et nimis iocosa.
5   Deprendi modo pupulum puellae
Trusantem : hunc ego, si placet Dionae,
Pro telo rigida mea cecidi.

different meaning immediately after
tenent of the preceding verse is but
another mark of the unfinished
character of the poem.

21–22. The poet declares himself, however, more interested in
the true happiness of his friend
than in the satisfaction of his own
curiosity. — **palatum:** not as the
organ of taste, but of the voice ;
cf. Hor. *Sat.* II. 3. 274 *balba feris
annoso uerba palato ;* Ov. *Am.* II.
6. 47 *ignauo stupuerunt uerba palato.* — **ueri amoris:** *i.e.* sincerely
requited love ; cf. Mart. XI. 26. 5
Veneris gaudia uera.

56. On the Cato to whom these
coarse verses are addressed see Intr.
62. — Metre, Phalaecean.

2. tuo : modifying both nouns,
though agreeing with the second.

3. quidquid amas Catullum :
i.e. in proportion to the love you
bear Catullus ; a variation on the

colloquial phrase *si me amas* in ex-
hortations ; cf. Plaut. *Trin.* 244 *da
mihi hoc, mel meum, si me amas, si
audes ;* Ter. *Heaut.* 1031 *caue posthac, si me amas, unquam istuc
uerbum ex te audiam ;* Cic. *Att.* V.
17. 5 *si quicquam me amas, hunc
locum muni.*

4. nimis : cf. 43. 4 n.

6. si placet Dionae : a variation
on the phrase *si dis placet,* sometimes used in the sense of *dis iu-
uantibus* of completed actions ; cf.
Plaut. *Capt.* 454 *expediui ex serui-
tute filium, si dis placet.* **Dione**
is mentioned in Hom. *Il.* V. 370 as
the mother of Aphrodite, but Catullus apparently has in mind Venus
herself ; cf. Bion 1. 93 ; Theocr. 7.
116 ; Plaut. *Mil.* 1414 ; and the
Augustan and later poets often, as
Verg. *Ecl.* 9. 47 *ecce Dionaei processit Caesaris astrum ;* Hor. *Carm*
II. 1. 39 *Dionaeo sub antro.*

57.

Pulchre conuenit improbis cinaedis,
Mamurrae pathicoque Caesarique.
Nec mirum : maculae pares utrisque,
Vrbana altera et illa Formiana,
5 Impressae resident nec eluentur :
Morbosi pariter gemelli utrique,
Vno in lecticulo erudituli ambo,
Non hic quam ille magis uorax adulter,
Riuales socii puellularum :
10 Pulchre conuenit improbis cinaedis.

57. Like 29, an attack upon Julius Caesar and his favorite Mamurra, and apparently written at about the same time with that poem, *i.e.* in late 55 B.C. With the sentiment cf. Mart. VIII. 35 *cum sitis similes paresque uita, uxor pessima, pessimus maritus, miror non bene conuenire uobis.* — Metre, Phalaecean.

2. **Mamurrae**: see Intr. 73, 74.

3. **nec mirum**: cf. 23. 7 n. — **utrisque**: found in Catullus in the plural only here and in v. 6; and in general the plural is much more common in prose than in poetry.

4. **urbana**: *i.e. Romana ;* cf. 29. 23 *urbis* (= *Romae*). — **Formiana**: cf. 41. 4 n.

6. **morbosi**: probably merely a translation of παθικοί ; cf. gloss. Labb. p. 116ᵃ *morbosus παθικός.* — **gemelli**: sneeringly, of their similarity in character ; cf. Hor. *Ep.* I.

10. 3 *cetera paene gemelli fraternis animis,* where, however, there is no irony.

7. **lecticulo**, *study-couch :* ἅπαξ λεγόμενον, but the feminine *lecticula* occurs in this sense in Suet. *Aug.* 78, and the masculine is not strange by analogy with *lectulus* (cf. Plin. *Ep.* V. 5. 5). — **erudituli**: Caesar was not only a historian, but a grammarian (Suet. *Iul.* 56; Cic. *Brut.* 72. 253) and a poet (Suet. *l.c.;* Tac. *Dial.* 21; Plin. *Ep.* V. 3. 5). On Mamurra's attempts at poetry see 105.

9. **riuales socii**: here it appears better to take **riuales** in its original implication of not unfriendly rivalry, the two friends vying with each other in the number of their mistresses ; v. 9 thus completes v. 8; cf. Tac. *Hist.* I. 13 [*Otho erat*] *gratus Neroni aemulatione luxus.*

10. The first and last verses are identical also in 16, 36, and 52.

58.

Caeli, Lesbia nostra, Lesbia illa,
Illa Lesbia, quam Catullus unam
Plus quam se atque suos amauit omnes,
Nunc in quadriuiis et angiportis
5 Glubit magnanimi Remi nepotes.

58b.

Non custos si fingar ille Cretum,
Non si Pegaseo ferar uolatu,
Non Ladas ego pinnipesue Perseus,

58. To Caelius, on the debasement of Lesbia ; see Intr. 41.— Date, probably 55 B.C.   Metre, Phalaecean.

1. **Caeli**: see Intr. 59. — **nostra**: for *mea*, as it is absurd to suppose, with some critics, that Catullus recognizes in Caelius an equal interest with himself in Lesbia.

3. **plus quam se**, etc. : cf. 8. 5 ; 3. 5 n.

4. **quadriuiis**: cf. 47. 7 n. *triuio.* — **angiportis**, *alley-ways ;* cf. Hor. *Carm.* I. 25. 9 *inuicem moechos anus adrogantes flebis in solo leuis angiportu.*

5. **magnanimi Remi nepotes**: *i.e.* the descendants of the Romans of a noble day have fallen thus low. There is indignation but not sarcasm in the phrase; cf. 49. 1 n.

58b. These few verses on the same theme as 55 are evidently a fragment, and were inserted here by the original editor of the *liber Catulli* quite in accordance with his usual habit of separating poems on similar themes by two or three others of a different character. See Intr. 48, and introductory note to 55. — Metre, Phalaecean.

1. **custos ille Cretum**: *i.e.* the bronze giant Talus, devised by Daedalus and made by Hephaestus for King Minos, who strode from headland to headland, making the circuit of the island thrice daily; cf. Apoll. Rh. IV. 1638 ff.; Apollod. I. 9. 26. 3 ff. — **fingar**, *be molded into ;* cf. 66. 50 *ferri fingere duritiem.*

2. **Pegaseo uolatu**: for the story of the winged horse, Pegasus, who sprang from the blood of Medusa as her head was severed by Perseus, see Apollod. II. 4. 2. 9 ; 3. 2. 1.

3. **Ladas**: Pausanias mentions by this name two victors in the Olympic foot-races, one of Sparta, and the other, less famous, an Achaean (Paus. III. 21. 1; X. 23. 14); cf. Mart. X. 100. 5 *habeas licebit alterum pedem Ladae ;* Juv. 13. 96 *pauper locupletem optare podagram nec dubitet Ladas.*   There is a manifest anacoluthon ; the idea of v. 1 *si fingar* is the one in mind. — **pinnipes Perseus**: in order to attack Medusa in safety, Perseus had borrowed of the Nymphs the winged shoes like those of Hermes, as well as Pluto's

Non Rhesi niueae citaeque bigae :
5　Adde huc plumipedes uolatilesque,
Ventorumque simul require cursum,
Quos uinctos, Cameri, mihi dicares :
Defessus tamen omnibus medullis
Et multis langoribus peresus
10　Essem te mihi, amice, quaeritando.

59.

Bononiensis Rufa Rufulum fellat,
Vxor Meneni, saepe quam in sepulcretis

helmet of invisibility and the magic wallet; see Apollod. II. 4. 2. Cf. Prop. III. 30. 3 *non si Pegaseo uecteris in aere dorso, nec tibi si Persei mouerit ala pedes.* **pinnipes** is ἅπαξ λεγόμενον.

4. Rhesi: Rhesus was the king of Thrace whose famous horses Ulysses and Diomed stole on the night of his arrival to help the Trojans ; cf. Hom. *Il.* X. 438 ff.; Ov. *Met.* XIII. 249 ff. There is a similar anacoluthon to that in v. 3; *si ferar* fills out the idea.

5. plumipedes : ἅπαξ λεγόμενον; the reference is clearly not to flying men like Daedalus and the sons of Boreas (for Perseus in v. 3 is a type of such swiftness), but to birds, thus interposed between horses and winds. — **uolatiles:** carrying further the picture in the preceding adjective; *feather-footed* (Ben Jonson) *and flying fowl.*

7. uinctos: with reference to the story of Aeolus and Ulysses (cf. Hom. *Od.* X. 17 ff.); the idea being only that if he were by their master put in possession of the winds to rule them at his pleasure, their unwearied swiftness would not suffice

him. — **dicares** = *dares,* as in Verg. *Aen.* I. 73 *propriam dicabo.*

8. defessus omnibus medullis : cf. Plaut. *Stich.* 340 *at ego perii, quoi medullam lassitudo perbibit.* With **defessus . . . quaeritando** cf. Plaut. *Amph.* 1014 *sum defessus quaeritando, nusquam inuenio Naucratem.*

9. langoribus peresus: cf. Serenus Samm. 62 *languore peresus.*

10. essem: with this sequence after v. 1 *fingar* and v. 2 *ferar* cf. 6. 2 n.

59. A skit upon a certain woman named Rufa, who, from the fact that she is especially mentioned as a Bolognese, must have been living elsewhere, probably at either Verona or Rome. The persons mentioned are otherwise unknown, though some suppose that Rufulus is M. Caelius Rufus (Intr. 59). — Metre, choliambic.

1. Rufa Rufulum : perhaps the similarity in name denotes some relationship (cf. Lesbius and Lesbia in 79), the diminutive being used sneeringly.

2. sepulcretis: ἅπαξ λεγόμενον; apparently used of common and

Vidistis ipso rapere de rogo cenam,
Cum deuolutum ex igne prosequens panem
5 Ab semiraso tunderetur ustore.

60.

Num te leaena montibus Libystinis
Aut Scylla latrans infima inguinum parte
Tam mente dura procreauit ac taetra,
Vt supplicis uocem in nouissimo casu
5 Contemptam haberes, ah nimis fero corde?

cheap places of burial; with the form cf. *arboretum, rosetum, busticetum*, etc.

3. **rapere**, etc.: *i.e.* pilfer the food placed on the funeral pyre to be burned with the body (cf. Verg. *Aen.* VI. 224 *congesta cremantur turea dona, dapes, fuso crateres oliuo*). On such *bustirapi* (Plaut. *Pseud.* 361) cf. Ter. *Eun.* 491 *e flamma petere te cibum posse arbitror;* Ov. *Ib.* 20 *hic praedam medio raptor ab igne petit;* Mart. XI. 54. So poverty and hunger are satirized in 21 and 23.

4. **prosequens**: *i.e.* stooping down to grasp it.

5. **semiraso**: *i.e.* careless about shaving, and hence 'squalid'; cf. 54. 2 *semilauta;* Luc. *Phar.* VIII. 738 *sordidus ustor.* — **tunderetur**: caught in the act and beaten by the *ustor*, commonly a slave of low degree belonging to the *libitinarii* who attended to the burning of bodies.

60. This brief complaint over the want of sympathy of some friend in the poet's extremity is apparently a bit of incomplete verse, but in

tone is very like 30, while its language suggests the complaint of Ariadne in 64. 154 ff. Perhaps it was the last verse penned by Catullus as his strength failed him and death came on. — Date, 54 B.C. (?). Metre, choliambic..

1. **leaena**: perhaps the first occurrence in Latin of the Greek word for the early *leo femina* (Plaut.) and *lea* (Varro). — **Libystinis**: rare form of the adjective; cf. 7. 3 *Libyssae*.

2. **latrans**, etc.: Catullus, like most, if not all, of the Latin poets that mention her, evidently thinks of Scylla with a woman's body ending below in a group of fierce dogs; but Homer (*Od.* XII. 85 ff.), as might be expected in an earlier conception, describes her as a monster entirely without human form.

4. **in nouissimo casu**, *at his supreme trial;* the phrase may well imply apprehended death; cf. Tac. *Ann.* XII. 33 *nouissimum casum experitur* (*i.e.* tries the forlorn hope).

5. **contemptam haberes**: cf. 17. 2 n. — **nimis**: cf. 43. 4 n.

61.

Collis o Heliconii
Cultor, Vraniae genus,
Qui rapis teneram ad uirum
Virginem, o Hymenaee Hymen,
5   O Hymen Hymenaee,

61. With 61 begins the group of
longer poems of Catullus which extends through 68. Of these 61, 62,
and (after the interposition, as commonly, of a poem on a different
subject) 64 are on marriage themes,
and in certain MSS. as well as by
earlier editors are called *Epithalamia*. 61 is written in honor of the
marriage of Manlius Torquatus and
Vinia Aurunculeia (cf. v. 16 n.), but
is in no sense a true *epithalamium*,
sung by a chorus outside the marriage chamber. The poet himself,
on the contrary, speaks throughout,
acting as a sort of *choragus*, and,
yielding fully to the joyous enthusiasm of the occasion, in a tone of
purest inspiration joins in each part
of the ceremonial. The poem is,
then, a graceful combination of lyric
reminiscences of the ceremonies attending a Roman marriage, rather
than a precise dramatic representation of any of them. Hence the
poet allows himself certain liberties
with the rites, omitting all reference
to some, altering others, and introducing a Greek flavor, especially by
the invocation to Hymen, and by
the singing of a true *epithalamium*
at the end. — For a description of
Roman marriage-rites see Becker
Gallus (English translation[5]) p.
160 ff.; Marquardt *Privatleben der
Römer*[2] p. 42 ff. — Date uncertain,
though it hardly seems possible that
Catullus could have sung another's
love with so clear a note after his
love for Lesbia had ended in such

bitter disappointment. Metre, Glyconic (Intr. 82 *b*).

1–35. Invocation to Hymen. The
poet speaks as if standing before the
bride's home, awaiting her coming
forth for the procession to the house
of the bridegroom.

1. collis Heliconii: Mt. Helicon
in Boeotia was from most ancient
times known as the seat of the
Muses (cf. Hes. *The.* 1 Μουσάων
Ἑλικωνιάδων), of one of whom Hymen was the son.

2. cultor: for *incola;* cf. 64. 300
cultricem montibus Idri; 63. 72
siluicultrix. — **Vraniae**: by other
writers Hymen is called the son
of Calliope, or of Terpsichore, or
even of Bacchus and Venus (cf.
Serv. on Verg. *Aen.* IV. 127). —
genus: for *filius;* cf. 64. 23.

3. rapis: cf. the same traditional
sentiment in 62. 20 ff. And though
perhaps not directly referred to here,
the prehistoric marriage by capture
is traceable in the Roman custom
of taking the bride from her mother's arms with a show of force, and
of carrying her over the threshold
of her new home (cf. 166–167). —
teneram: in contrast with the idea
of violence in *rapis.* — uirum uir-
ginem: with the favorite alliation-
tive contrast; cf. Verg. *Aen.* I. 493
audet uiris concurrere uirgo.

4. Hymen: the Greek god of
marriage addressed under the
double name Ὑμήν Ὑμέναιε (or in
reverse order) ; cf. Eur. *Tro.* 311 ;
Arist. *Pax* 1335 ; Theocr. 18. 58 ;

Cinge tempora floribus
Suaue olentis amaraci,
Flammeum cape, laetus huc,
Huc ueni niueo gerens
10   Luteum pede soccum,

Excitusque hilari die
Nuptialia concinens
Voce carmina tinnula
Pelle humum pedibus, manu
15   Pineam quate taedam.

Namque Vinia Manlio,
Qualis Idalium colens

Plaut. *Cas.* 752 *io Hymen Hymenaee;*
Ov. *Her.* 14. 27 *Hymen Hymenaee;*
and also 62. 5, etc.

6–10. The attributes of Hymen
are those of marriage ; here, the
wreath, veil, and slippers of the
bride; in v. 15, the torch.

6. **floribus** : cf. Paul. Fest. p. 63
*corollam noua nupta de floribus,
uerbenis, herbisque a se lectis sub
amiculo ferebat;* Ov. *Her.* 6. 43
*pronuba Iuno adfuit et sertis tem-
pora uinctus Hymen.*

7. **suaue olentis amaraci,** *sweet
marjoram* (Gr. σάμψυχον) ; cf.
Verg. *Aen.* I. 693 *mollis amaracus
illum floribus et dulci adspirans
complectitur umbra.*

8. **flammeum** : the long mantle
(= *palla ?*) drawn up to serve as a
head-covering; in the case of brides
and of the wife of the *flamen* it was
of a brownish-yellow color (*luteum*); cf. Luc. *Phar.* II. 361 *lutea
demissos uelarunt flammea uultus.*
—**cape,** *don;* cf. v. 9 *gerens.* — **huc,
huc** : cf. 64. 195.

9. **niueo** : to contrast with v. 10
luteum.

10. **soccum** : unlaced slippers,

used commonly for house-wear, and
so especially by women. In the
apparel of the bride in the Aldo-
brandini marriage scene they are
yellow in color.

12. **concinens** : of a single voice
also in 65. 13; but v. 123 *concinite
in modum.*

13. **tinnula** : of a clear, high-
pitched tone like the ring of a resounding bar of metal ; cf. 64. 262 ;
Pomponius ap. Macrob. VI. 4. 13
uocem reddam tenuem et tinnulam.

14. **pelle humum pedibus** : of
dancing, as in Lucr. V. 1402 *duro
terram pede pellere;* Hor. *Carm.* I.
37. 1 *pede libero pulsanda tellus;*
III. 18. 15 *pepulisse ter pede terram.*

15. **pineam quate taedam** : on
torches in the marriage procession
cf. Verg. *Aen.* VII. 397 *ipsa flagrantem feruida pinum sustinet ac
canit hymenaeos; Ciris* 439 *pronuba
nec castos accendet pinus honores;*
Ov. *Fast.* II. 561 *conde tuas, Hymenaee, faces.*

16. **Vinia Manlio** : the bride is
called Aurunculeia in v. 86, a fact
which Scaliger rightly explained as
due to an adoption, Vinia being the

Venit ad Phrygium Venus
Iudicem, bona cum bona
20   Nubet alite uirgo,

Floridis uelut enitens
Myrtus Asia ramulis,
Quos hamadryades deae
Ludicrum sibi rosido
25   Nutriunt umore.

Quare age huc aditum ferens
Perge linquere Thespiae

present legal name corresponding
to the formal *nomen gentile* of the
bridegroom, in immediate connection with which it stands, while
Aurunculeia was the name before
adoption. Both names are common
enough, but the personality of the
bride can be no further determined.
On Manlius Torquatus (cf. vv. 216
and 222) see Intr. 67.

17. qualis: the comparison extends only to the all-conquering
beauty of the bride. — Idalium
colens: cf. 36. 12 n.

18. Phrygium iudicem: *i.e.*
Paris, whose decision in giving the
golden apple as the prize of beauty
to Aphrodite rather than to Hera or
Pallas brought in its train all the
woes of the Trojan War ; cf. Hom.
Il. XXIV. 28 ff.; Hor. *Carm.* III.
3. 18 *Ilion, Ilion fatalis incestusque
iudex et mulier peregrina uertit in
puluerem.*

19. bona uirgo: the thought
turns from beauty to character ; cf.
v. 186 *bonae feminae;* v. 226 *a bona
matre.* — cum bona alite: of the
ominous flight of birds ; cf. Hor.
Carm. I. 15. 5 *mala ducis aui domum;* Cic. *Diuin.* I. 16. 28 *nam
ut nunc extis, sic tum auibus, magnae res impetriri solent.*

22. myrtus Asia: the myrtle
flourished in damp places, and the
thought here is probably of the
famous fertile region about the Cay-
ster in Lydia; cf. Hom. *Il.* II. 461
Ἀσίῳ ἐν λειμῶνι Καϋστρίου ἀμφὶ
ῥέεθρα; Verg. *Geor.* I. 383 *uolucres
quae Asia circum dulcibus in stagnis rimantur prata Caystri.* The
myrtle bore white blossoms (Arist.
Au. 1099 ἠρινὰ παρθένια λευκότροφα
μύρτα), and was sacred to Venus
(Phaedr. III. 17. 3 *myrtus Veneri
placuit*); similarly Ariadne is compared to a myrtle-branch in 64. 89,
and Vinia herself in v. 91 ff. to the
hyacinth, and in v. 193 ff. to the white
parthenice and the flame-red poppy.

23. hamadryades deae: *i.e.*
tree-nymphs ; cf. Serv. on Verg.
Ecl. 10. 62 *quae una cum arboribus nascuntur et pereunt;* Apol.
Rhod. II. 479 ff.

24. rosido: for the later *rorido*
(Prop. III. 30. 26) or *roscido* (Plin.
N. H. IX. 10. 38 *roscido umore*).

25. The place of the cyclic dactyl
is in this verse taken by an irrational
spondee (Intr. 82 *b*); cf. the similar
substitutions in the experimental
metre of 55 and 58 *b*.

26. quare age: cf. v. 38 ; 64.
372. — aditum ferens: cf. v. 43 ;

Rupis Aonios specus,
Nympha quos super irrigat
30 Frigerans Aganippe,

Ac domum dominam uoca
Coniugis cupidam noui,
Mentem amore reuinciens
Vt tenax hedera huc et huc
35 Arborem implicat errans.

Vosque item simul, integrae
Virgines, quibus aduenit
Par dies, agite in modum
Dicite 'O Hymenaee Hymen,
40 O Hymen Hymenaee,'

Vt libentius, audiens
Se citarier ad suum

63. 47 *reditum tetulit;* 63. 79 *reditum ferat.*

27. **Thespiae rupis:** the town of Thespiae lay at the foot of Helicon.

28. **Aonios specus:** Aonia was the name of the district about Helicon, whence the Muses were called Aonides (Ov. *Met.* V. 333; Juv. 7 59). On caves as quiet retreats of the Muses cf. Hor. *Carm.* III. 4. 40; Juv. *l.c.*

29. **nympha Aganippe:** her fountain is described by Paus. IX. 29. 3. — **super:** for *desuper;* cf. Verg. *Aen.* IX. 168 *haec super e uallo prospectant Troes;* Tib. III. 2. 10 *ossa super nigra fauilla teget.*

31. **dominam:** for the Roman wife was *domina* wherever her husband was *dominus,* according to the marriage formula *ubi tu Gaius ego Gaia.*

32. **coniugis cupidam noui:** the bride displays proper maidenly reluctance (cf. vv. 83–85), yet feels the drawings of love (cf. vv. 176–178).

34. **hedera,** etc.: cf. the similar familiar figure in v. 106 ff. — **huc et huc:** cf. Hor. *Epod.* 4. 9 *huc et huc euntium.*

36–45. Exhortation of the *choragus* to the waiting maidens to join in singing the praises of Hymen.

36. **integrae:** cf. 34. 2 n.

37. **aduenit,** *is close at hand,* while the future would mean 'will sometime come.'

38. **par dies:** *i.e.* their own wedding-day. — **agite:** expletive, as in v. 26 *age;* v. 123 *ite;* cf. 63. 12; 64. 372. — **in modum:** *i.e.* in the unison of prescribed rhythm; cf. v. 123; Hor. *Carm.* IV. 6. 43 *docilis modorum uatis Horati.*

42. **citarier:** with this earlier infinitive form cf. v. 65, etc. *compararier;* v. 68 *nitier;* 68. 141 *componier,* and see 34. 8 n. — **suum munus:** explained by vv. 44–45.

Munus, huc aditum **ferat**
Dux bonae Veneris, boni
45   Coniugator amoris.

Quis deus magis anxiis
Est petendus amantibus?
Quem colent homines magis
Caelitum? o Hymenaee **Hymen,**
50   O Hymen Hymenaee.

Te suis tremulus parens
Inuocat, tibi uirgines
Zonula soluunt sinus,
Te timens cupida nou**us**
55   Captat aure maritus.

Tu fero iuueni in manus
Floridam ipse puellulam
Dedis a gremio suae

---

43. **aditum ferat**: cf. v. 26 n.

44. **dux**: as the presiding deity
of marriage. — **bonae Veneris,**
honorable love; cf. vv. 61–63; v. 202
bona Venus.

45. **coniugator**: ἅπαξ λεγόμενον; with the figure cf. 68. 118 n.

46–75. The *choragus* leads the
maidens in singing the praises of
Hymen.

46. **anxiis**: *i.e.* fretting with
eager passion; cf. Stat. *Silu.* I. 2.
81 *quantos iuuenis premat anxius
ignes.*

51. **te parens inuocat**: the aged
parent desires to see his daughters
established under the protection of
husbands before his death; cf. 62.
58; 66. 15–16. — **tremulus**: *sc.*
with the palsy of age; cf. 17.
13 n.

53. **zonula**, etc.: *i.e.* maidens
willingly submit to thy sway; with

the figure cf. 2. 13 n. — **soluunt**:
on the diaeresis see Intr. 86 *b.*

54. **timens**: contrasted with the
following word, **cupida**; the bridegroom's eagerness is so great as to
be somewhat allied to fear, almost
like that of the traditional bride;
so he trembles even while he listens
anxiously to catch the music of the
bridal procession.

55. **captat aure**: cf. Verg. *Aen.*
III. 514 *auribus aera captat.*

56. **in manus**: perhaps with a
reminiscence of the legal *conuentio
in manum.*

57. **floridam**: cf. 17. 14 n.; the
idea is of the bride's tender, youthful bloom, and contrasts with that
in v. 56 *fero.*

58. **a gremio suae matris**: of
the guarded peacefulness of the
bride's former life; cf. v. 3 n. *rapis;*
62. 21–22; 64. 87–88.

Matris, o Hymenaee Hymen,
60   O Hymen Hymenaee.

Nil potest sine te Venus
Fama quod bona comprobet
Commodi capere : at potest
Te uolente.   Quis huic deo
65   Compararier ausit ?

Nulla quit sine te domus
Liberos dare, nec parens
Stirpe nitier : at potest
Te uolente.   Quis huic deo
70   Compararier ausit ?

Quae tuis careat sacris
Non queat dare praesides
Terra finibus : at queat
Te uolente.   Quis huic deo
75   Compararier ausit ?

Claustra pandite ianuae,
Virgo adest.   Viden ut faces

61. nil commodi capere: cf.
Ter. *Eun.* 971 *hoc capio commodi.*

65. compararier: on the form
see v. 42 n. *citarier.*

67. liberos: by the formula that
embodied the strict Roman reverence for the family, a wife was taken
liberorum quaerendorum gratia,
and Gaius remarks (I. 64), *si quis
nefarias atque incestas nuptias con-
traxerit, neque uxorem habere uidetur, neque liberos.*

68. stirpe nitier: with the figure
cf. Plin. *Ep.* IV. 21. 3 *unus ex tribus liberis superest domumque pluribus adminiculis paulo ante fun-
datam desolatus fulcit ac sustinet.*

71. careat: the change with this
stanza from direct to hypothetical
statement corresponds to the absence of probability that an entire
land would be without marriage-
rites.

72. dare praesides: in the
older days only Roman citizens
could serve in the legions, and no
man could be born a Roman citizen
save within the strictly guarded mar-
riage-laws.

76–120. The hymn to Hymen
finished, the bride is now urged to
come forth and take her place in
the procession to the bridegroom's
house, and to dry her tears (v. 85)

Splendidas quatiunt comas?

80   .   .   .   .   .

        .   .   .   .   .

        .   .   .   .   .

Tardet ingenuus pudor :
Quem tamen magis audiens
85   Flet quod ire necesse est.

Flere desine.   Non tibi, Aurunculeia, periculum est
Ne qua femina pulchrior
Clarum ab Oceano diem
90   Viderit uenientem.

Talis in uario solet
Diuitis domini hortulo

by thoughts of her own conquering
beauty (vv. 86–100), which the poet
skilfully extols by prophesying her
entire and lasting influence over her
husband (vv. 101 ff.).

77. **uiden ut**, etc. : addressed to
the bride, who may look out through
the now opened doors and see the
procession ready to escort her on
her way to her new home. The
phrase is used in Catullus, as regularly in early Latin, in the sense of
quo modo, without affecting the mood
of the verb (cf. v. 98 ; 62. 8), the
ut being more exclamatory than interrogative. In 62. 8 it is addressed
to more than one person. In later
writers the subjunctive becomes the
rule ; cf. also v. 171 ff. *aspice ut
immineat.*

79–82. The two concluding verses
of the first defective stanza doubtless contained an exhortation to the
bride to come forth, vv. 79–80 perhaps being *ne moreris, abit dies :*

prodeas noua nupta (cf. v. 94 and
the urgent repetitions in vv. 95,
96, 100, 110, 120), while vv. 81–
82 referred to her evident reluctance, for which vv. 83–85 assign
the reason.

83. **ingenuus pudor** : *i.e.* the
natural modesty of a maiden gently-
bred ; cf. Plin. *N. H.* Praef. 21
*est plenum ingenui pudoris fateri
per quos profeceris;* Prop. I. 4. 13
*ingenuus calor et multis decus arti-
bus;* Plin. *Ep.* I. 14. 8 *ingenua
totius corporis pulchritudo et quidam senatorius decor.*

84. **tamen** : referring to *ingenuus;* it is a becoming modesty,
but is indulged too far. — **magis** :
sc. quam nostra uerba. — **audiens,**
minding; cf. Verg. *Geor.* I. 514
neque audit currus habenas; Hor.
Carm. I. 13. 13 *si me satis audias.*

85. **flet** : on the genuineness of
the bride's tears cf. 66. 15–18.

89. **diem** : *i.e.* the morrow's day.

Stare flos hyacinthinus.
Sed moraris, abit dies :
95   Prodeas, noua nupta.

Prodeas, noua nupta, si
Iam uidetur, et audias
Nostra uerba.   Vide ut faces
Aureas quatiunt comas :
100   Prodeas, noua nupta.

Non tuus leuis in mala
Deditus uir adultera
Probra turpia persequens
A tuis teneris uolet
105   Secubare papillis,

Lenta quin uelut adsitas
Vitis implicat arbores,
Implicabitur in tuum
Complexum.   Sed abit dies :
110   Prodeas, noua nupta.

O cubile quod omnibus

.   .   .   .

93. **flos hyacinthinus**: cf. Verg. *Aen.* XI. 69 *florem languentis hyacinthi ;* not our hyacinth, but the blue iris or the larkspur. On the comparison with a flower cf. v. 22 n.

98. **uide**: perhaps with more impatience than v. 77 *uiden.*

99. **aureas**: of fire also in Lucr. VI. 205 *liquidi color aureus ignis ;* cf. Pind. *Ol.* I. I ὁ δὲ χρυσὸς αἰθόμενον πῦρ.

103. **probra turpia**: cf. 91. 4 *a turpi probro.*

106. **quin**, *nay rather.* — **uelut**, etc.: with the comparison cf. Hor.

Carm. I. 36. 20 *lasciuis hederis ambitiosior ; Epod.* 15. 5 *artius atque hedera procera adstringitur ilex, lentis adhaerens bracchiis ; Gall. Epithal.* 3 (Anth. Lat. 232 Mey.) *bracchia nec hederae uincant.*

108. **implicabitur**: as of the middle voice.

111. **cubile**, etc.: the Epithalamium of Ticidas evidently contained a similar address of congratulation to the *lectus genialis ;* cf. the quotation by Priscian (I. 189) *felix lectule.*

112–114. These verses perhaps stood in the archetype at the bottom

. .
. .

115　Candido pede lecti,

Quae tuo ueniunt ero,
Quanta gaudia, quae uaga
Nocte, quae medio die
Gaudeat!　Sed abit dies:
120　Prodeas, noua nupta.

Tollite, o pueri, faces:
Flammeum uideo uenire.
Ite, concinite in modum
'O Hymen Hymenaee io,
125　O Hymen Hymenaee.'

Ne diu taceat procax
Fescennina iocatio,

or top of a page, with vv. 79–82
standing in a corresponding position
on the other side of the leaf, and
were lost by the same mutilation
that destroyed vv. 79–82.

115. candido pede lecti: the
feet of the bed were frequently of
ivory; cf. 64. 45, 48; Hor. *Sat.* II.
6. 103 *tincta super lectos canderet
uestis eburnos;* Plat. Com. κλίνη
ἐλεφαντόπους.

117. gaudia gaudeat: with the
figura etymologica cf. 7. 9 n. —
uaga, *fleeting* (Ellis) ; of the elu-
siveness of the constant onward
movement of time ; cf. 64. 271 n.
uagi solis.

118. medio die: of the mid-day
siesta; cf. 32. 3; 80. 3.

121–125. The bride yields to the
persuasion and comes forth, and
the procession begins to move.

121. tollite faces: in preparation for departure.

122. flammeum: the bright-
tinted mantle catches the eye first
as the bride comes forth.

123. ite: expletive; cf. v. 38 n.;
Prop. IV. 4. 7 *ite agite, date lintea.*
— concinite: cf. v. 12 n.; Spenser
*Epithal. The boys run up and down
the street, Crying aloud with strong
confused noise, As if it were on̬
voice, Hymen! io Hymen! Hymen! they do shout.* — in modum:
cf. v. 38 n.

124. io: as in the familiar cry *io
Triumphe.*

126–155. The *uersus Fescennini,*
sung on the way to the bridegroom's
house, which are addressed successively to the (perhaps imaginary)
former slave-favorite of the bridegroom, to the bridegroom himself,
and to the bride.　Antiquarian accuracy is not observed, for the
bridegroom (according to v. 171 ff.)
is with his friends awaiting at his

Nec nuces pueris neget
Desertum domini audiens
'30 Concubinus amorem.

Da nuces pueris, iners
Concubine: satis diu
Lusisti nucibus: libet
Iam seruire Talasio.
135 Concubine, nuces da.

Sordebant tibi uilicae,
Concubine, hodie atque heri:

own home the arrival of the bride, and therefore not present to hear the verses addressed to him; while in place of the bridegroom (v. 128 n.) the *concubinus* is present and scatters the nuts.

127. **Fescennina iocatio**: cf. Paul. Fest. 85 *Fescennini uersus, qui canebantur in nuptiis, ex urbe Fescennina dicuntur allati, siue ideo dicti quia fascinum putabantur arcere* (cf. 5. 12 n.); Hor. *Ep.* II. 1. 145 *Fescennina licentia uersibus alternis opprobria rustica fudit;* Sen. Rh. p. 223 B. *inter nuptiales Fescenninos in crucem generi nostri iocabantur.* Similar licentious catches directed against the general were sung by his soldiers in the triumphal procession (cf. Suet. *Iul.* 49 and 51).

128. **nuces pueris**: as a part of the marriage ceremonies the bridegroom scattered nuts among the crowd of bystanders; cf. Verg. *Ecl.* 8. 29 *tibi ducitur uxor; sparge, marite, nuces,* and the comments thereupon by Servius, who gives several explanations of the custom.

129. **desertum**, etc.: *i.e.* perceiving that his love for his master is now slighted.

130. **concubinus**: the *puer delicatus* to whom the (traditionally libellous) fescennines represent the bridegroom as having been devoted.

131. **iners**: the favorite has thus far enjoyed a life of idleness; cf. Cic. *N. D.* I. 36. 102 *Epicurus quasi pueri delicati nihil cessatione melius existimat.*

132. **satis diu**: *i.e.* you have long enough by favor of your master enjoyed a child's free life (cf. Servius *l.c.*) ; now scatter nuts to show that the life of irresponsibility is over for you.

134. **seruire**: contrasted with *lusisti;* you have thus far played; now your master chooses the service of Talasius, and sport is over. — **Talasio**: for the traditional origin of this distinctively Roman marriage-cry that corresponded to the Greek cry of *Hymen,* see Liv. I. 9. 12.

136. **sordebant**, etc.: *i.e.* at your master's country-seat even the wives of the bailiffs, so much above common slaves like yourself, were but mean in your eyes.

137. **hodie atque heri**, *but yesterday;* cf. Gr. χθές καὶ πρώην and ἐχθὲς καὶ σήμερον (Ep. Heb. 13. 8).

　　　Nunc tuum cinerarius
　　　Tondet os.　Miser ah miser
140　Concubine, nuces da.

　　　Diceris male te a tuis
　　　Vnguentate glabris marite
　　　Abstinere : sed abstine.
　　　O Hymen Hymenaee io,
145　O Hymen Hymenaee.

　　　Scimus haec tibi quae licent
　　　Sola cognita : sed marito
　　　Ista non eadem licent.
　　　O Hymen Hymenaee io,
150　O Hymen Hymenaee.

　　　Nupta, tu quoque quae tuus
　　　Vir petet caue ne neges,
　　　Ne petitum aliunde eat.
　　　O Hymen Hymenaee io,
155　O Hymen Hymenaee.

138. cinerarius: the slave who acted as hair-dresser; cf. Varr. *L. L.* V. 129 *calamistrum quod his cale-factis in cinere capillus ornatur. Qui ea ministrabat a cinere cine-rarius est appellatus.*

139. tondet os: *i.e.* the days of your childhood, and with them the charm of your young beauty, and your life of idle luxury are past; cf. Mart. XI. 78. 3 *flammea texuntur sponsae, iam uirgo paratur ; ton-debit pueros iam noua nupta tuos.* — miser ah miser: cf. 63. 61.

141. The verses are now directed to the bridegroom. — male: modi-fying abstinere, with the meaning of *aegre*, as in Verg. *Geor.* I. 360

iam sibi tum curuis male temperat unda carinis. — te abstinere : with the verb in this reflexive construc-tion cf. Ter. *Hec.* 139 *sese illa ab-stinere ut potuerit ?*

142. unguentate : as frequently, with an idea of excessive and effemi-nate luxury. — glabris : *i.e. pueris delicatis,* plural as though, forsooth, the bridegroom had kept many *con-cubinos.*

146. licent, etc.: the sentiment intimated concerning the license allowed by society to an unmarried man is true to ancient life.

151. The chorus now turns to the bride with equally, though less bru-tally, plain words.

En tibi domus ut potens
Et beata uiri tui :
Quae tibi sine seruiat
(O Hymen Hymenaee io,
160   O Hymen Hymenaee)

Vsque dum tremulum mouens
Cana tempus anilitas
Omnia omnibus adnuit.
O Hymen Hymenaee io,
165   O Hymen Hymenaee.

Transfer omine cum bono
Limen aureolos pedes,

156–235. The procession reaches the bridegroom's house (–165), the bride is assisted over the threshold without stumbling (–170), and finds the bridegroom awaiting her (–180). She is then duly conducted to the *lectus genialis* (–190), the bridegroom allowed to enter the apartment (–205), and outside the door the chorus sings its congratulations and prophecies of present and future happiness (–235). Many small details of the usual marriage ceremonies are untouched by the poet.

156. ut: modifying potens (*sc. est*). — potens: cf. Hor. *Carm.* I. 35. 23 *potentis domos.*

157. beata: cf. 51.15 *beatas urbes.*

158. sine seruiat: for you come to be *domina*, and the house offers its lasting allegiance for your acceptance.

161. tremulum: cf. v. 51 n.

162: cana anilitas: cf. 108. 1 *cana senectus.* — tempus: for *caput*, as in Prop. V. 8. 15 *iacuit pulsus tria tempora ramo Cacus.* The singular rarely occurs in the sense of 'one of the temples' except when

so modified as to distinguish between them ; but cf. Auct. ad Herenn. IV. 55 *dubitanti Graccho percutit tempus.*

163. omnia omnibus adnuit: *i.e.* by the constant palsied motion of the head.

166. transfer: apparently addressed to the bride, who here steps over (not upon) the threshold, instead of being lifted across it ; cf. Plaut. *Cas.* 767 ff. *i, sensim superattolle limen pedes, noua nupta; sospes iter incipe hoc, ut uiro tuo semper sis superstes, ut potior sis pollentia, uictrixque sis, superetque tuum imperium.* — omine cum bono: the custom of lifting the bride across the threshold is doubtless traceable to the original marriage by capture, as certain even of the ancients suggested, but its origin had been almost lost sight of, and the Romans explained it generally as due to fear that the bride might stumble, and so offend Vesta, to whom the threshold was sacred (Varro ap. Serv. on Verg. *Ecl.* 8. 29), or begin her new life

Rasilemque subi forem.

O Hymen Hymenaee io,

170   O Hymen Hymenaee.

Adspice unus ut accubans

Vir tuus Tyrio in toro

Totus immineat tibi.

O Hymen Hymenaee io,

175   O Hymen Hymenaee.

Illi non minus ac tibi

Pectore uritur intimo

Flamma, sed penite magis.

O Hymen Hymenaee io,

180   O Hymen Hymenaee.

under an evil omen (Plaut. *Cas.
l.c.;* Ov. *Met.* X. 452 *ter pedis
offensi signo est reuocata*).

167. **aureolos**: perhaps only of
the color of the shoes (cf. v. 10
luteum soccum with 2. 12 *aureolum
malum*) ; but cf. ἀργυρόπεζα of
Thetis (Hom.) and Aphrodite
(Pind.), χρυσοπέδιλος of Hera
(Hom.), χρυσέη Ἀφροδίτη (Hom.),
etc.

168. **rasilem forem**, *the polished doorway.*

171. **adspice**: the bride now
stands within the dwelling at the
entrance to the *atrium,* where the
bridegroom has been celebrating
with his friends the *cena nuptialis;*
cf. Plaut. *Curc.* 728 *tu, miles, apud
me cenabis; hodie fient nuptiae;*
Cic. *Quint. Fr.* II. 3. 7 *eo die apud
Pomponium in eius nuptiis eram
cenaturus.* — **unus** : the bridegroom is the one object upon which
her eyes rest, while he in turn has
eyes for her alone (v. 173). — **ac-**

cubans: *sc. in lecto tricliniari,* in
connection with which *accubare* is
especially used.

172. **Tyrio in toro**: *i.e.* a couch
with crimson draperies ; cf. 64. 49,
163 ; Hor. *Sat.* II. 6. 103 (cf. v.
115 n.) ; Tib. I. 2. 75 *Tyrio recu-
bare toro.*

173. **totus**, *with his whole being;*
cf. 64. 93. — **immineat**, *is intent
upon;* cf. Ov. *Met.* I. 146 *imminet
exitio uir coniugis.*

177. **uritur**: rare, if not unique,
in the passive with such a subject
as **flamma**; but cf. the not infrequent use in Greek of δαίεσθαι in
similar constructions.

178. **penite**, *secretly;* he shows
no sign of his passion to curious
eyes; cf. Tib. IV. 5. 17 *optat idem
iuuenis quod nos, sed tectius optat,*
but for the contrary view Ov. *Art.
Am.* I. 276 *uir male dissimulat;
tectius illa cupit.* The adverb is
ἅπαξ λεγόμενον from the adjective
penitus of Plautus and late Latin.

Mitte bracchiolum teres,
Praetextate, puellulae :
Iam cubile adeat uiri.
O Hymen Hymenaee io,
185   O Hymen Hymenaee.

O bonae senibus uiris
Cognitae bene feminae,
Conlocate puellulam.
O Hymen Hymenaee io,
190   O Hymen Hymenaee.

Iam licet uenias, marite :
Vxor in thalamo tibi est
Ore floridulo nitens
Alba parthenice uelut
195   Luteumue papauer.

182. **praetextate :** the poet speaks unprecisely of but one boy leading the bride to the door of the *thalamus,* and giving her into the hands of the *pronubae;* but cf. Fest. 245ᵃ *patrimi et matrimi pueri tres nubentem deducunt, unus qui facem praefert ex spina alba, quia noctu nubebant, duo qui tenent nubentem.*

186. **bonae feminae**; cf. v. 19 *bona uirgo;* Aug. *Nupt.* I. 9 *progrediente autem genere humano iunctae sunt quibusdam bonis uiris bonae feminae.* — **senibus** uiris : the *pronubae* were wives of one husband, and of the dignity of character that comes with honored age; cf. Serv. on Verg. *Aen.* IV. 166 *Varro pronubam dicit quae ante nupsit quaeque uni tantum nupta est, ideoque auspices deliguntur ad nuptias.*

187. **cognitae bene :** *i.e.* of approved uprightness established on intimate knowledge, as in 91. 3.

188. **conlocate :** *sc. in lecto geniali;* the technical term.

193–195. So the blushing Lavinia is described in Verg. *Aen.* XII. 67 ff. *Indum sanguineo ueluti uiolauerit ostro siquis ebur, aut mixta rubent ubi lilia multa alba rosa, talis uirgo dabat ore colores.*

193. **floridulo :** cf. 17. 14 n.; the adjective is apparently ἅπαξ λεγόμενον.

194. **parthenice :** perhaps a sort of feverfew or artemisia.

195. **luteum papauer :** but poppies are not always described as flame-colored ; cf. Prop. I. 20. 38 *lilia candida purpureis mixta papaueribus;* Anth. Lat. 775. 12 R. *luteae uiolae lacteumque papauer.*

At, marite, (ita me iuuent
Caelites) nihilo minus
Pulcher es, neque te Venus
Neglegit.   Sed abit dies :
200   Perge, ne remorare.

Non diu remoratus es,
Iam uenis.   Bona te Venus
Iuuerit, quoniam palam
Quod cupis cupis et bonum
205   Non abscondis amorem.

Ille pulueris Africi
Siderumque micantium
Subducat numerum prius,
Qui uestri numerare uult
210   Multa milia ludi.

Ludite ut libet, et breui
Liberos date.   Non decet
Tam uetus sine liberis
Nomen esse, sed indidem
215   Semper ingenerari.

Torquatus uolo paruulus
Matris e gremio suae

196. ita me iuuent caelites:
cf. 66. 18; 97. 1 n.
    198. Venus: the giver of beauty
as well as of love.
    202. bona Venus: of authorized
love ; cf. v. 44 n.; v. 204 *bonum
amorem;* vv. 61–63.
    203. quoniam, etc.: since your
love now has received the sanctions
of law and religion, and does not
need concealment.
    206. pulueris, etc.: cf. 7. 3 n.

213. tam uetus nomen: the
Torquati were proud of their long
line of patrician ancestry ; cf. Cic.
Sull. 8. 24, where a Torquatus is
reproved for such overweening
haughtiness.
    214. indidem, *from the same
stock,* instead of being strengthened,
as so many old Roman families had
to be, by adoptions.
    216–220. The best antique pic-
ture of infant life ; cf. Verg. *Aen.*

Porrigens teneras manus
Dulce rideat ad patrem
220   Semihiante labello.

Sit suo similis patri
Manlio et facile insciis
Noscitetur ab omnibus
Et pudicitiam suae
225   Matris indicet ore.

Talis illius a bona
Matre laus genus adprobet
Qualis unica ab optima
Matre Telemacho manet
230   Fama Penelopeo.

Claudite ostia, uirgines:
Lusimus satis.   At, boni
Coniuges, bene uiuite et
Munere adsiduo ualentem
235   Exercete iuuentam.

IV. 328 *siquis mihi paruulus aula luderet Aeneas, qui te tamen ore referret.*

219. **dulce rideat**: cf. 51. 5 n.

224. **pudicitiam indicet ore**: *i.e.* by his resemblance to her husband ; cf. Hor. *Carm.* IV. 5. 23 *laudantur simili prole puerperae;* Mart. VI. 27. 3 *est tibi quae patria signatur imagine uultus, testis maternae nata pudicitiae.*

226. **talis**, etc.: *i.e.* may the virtues of his mother be reflected in the boy, and win him such renown as came to Telemachus from the character of his mother, Penelope. The sentence is a somewhat awkwardly expressed double compliment to the mother, directly in its praise of her virtue, and indirectly in its prophecy of the future character and renown of her son.

229. **manet**: cf. 8. 15 n.

231. **ostia**: for *fores (sc. thalami).*

232. **lusimus**: here of singing amatory verses, as in 50. 2, 5 and 68. 17 of writing them.

233. **bene uiuite;** cf. 5. 1 n.

62.

Vesper adest : iuuenes, consurgite : Vesper Olympo
Exspectata diu uix tandem lumina tollit.
Surgere iam tempus, iam pinguis linquere mensas ;
Iam ueniet uirgo, iam dicetur hymenaeus.
5 Hymen o Hymenaee, Hymen ades o Hymenaee.

62. An epithalamium, but, un-
like 61, apparently without reference to a particular marriage, and,
like 61, without archaeological precision. The form is that of a song
divided between a chorus of youths
and one of maidens singing alter-
nately, but not always in precisely
equal strophes, the former the
praises of Hesperus and of marriage, the latter the fears and sor-
rows of surrendered maidenhood.
The youths sing vv. 1–5, 11–19, 26–
31, 33–38 (with lost verses preceding v. 33), 49–66; and the maidens,
vv. 6–10, 20–25, 32 (and lost verses
following it), 39–48. The setting
throughout is Greek rather than
Roman, though the fragments of
Sappho and the Epithalamium of
Helen by Theocritus (18) furnish
no ground for postulating direct
imitation on the part of Catullus.
On the place of action cf. vv. 1, 3,
7 nn. — Date, uncertain.   Metre,
dactylic hexameter.

1. **Vesper**: cf. Plin. *N. H.* II.
36 *sidus appellatum Veneris . . .
ante matutinum exoriens Luciferi
nomen accipit . . . contra ab oc-
casu refulgens nuncupatur Vesper ;*
Cic. *N. D.* II. 20. 53 *stella Veneris,
quae* Φωσφόρος *Graece, Lucifer La-
tine dicitur, cum antegreditur solem, cum subsequitur autem,* Ἑσπε-
ρος; Censor. *Die Nat.* 24. 4 *eius
stellae quam Plautus* [*Amph.* 275]
*Vesperuginem, Ennius Vesperum,
Vergilius Hesperon appellat.* — **consurgite**: *sc. a mensis ;* cf. v. 3 n. —

Olympo lumina tollit: the appearance at twilight of the evening
star, though of course in the west,
is by analogy spoken of as its rising; cf. Hor. *Carm.* II. 9. 10 *nec
tibi Vespero surgente decedunt amores nec rapidum fugienti solem.*
Here the star stands above the
Thessalian (cf. v. 7 *Oetaeos*) Olympus; though the poets also speak
of Vesper as leaving Olympus (the
dwelling of the gods) or Oeta to
usher in the night ; cf. Verg. *Ecl.*
6. 86 *inuito processit Vesper Olympo ;
Cul.* 203 *piger aurata procedit Vesper ab Oeta ; Cir.* 350 *gelida uenientem ignem ab Oeta.* For the ablative with *tollere* without a preposition cf. Ov. *Met.* XV. 192 *clipeus
terra cum tollitur ima.*

3. **surgere . . . linquere mensas**: cf. Verg. *Aen.* VIII. 109 *relic-
tis consurgunt mensis.* — **pinguis**:
here = *opimas,* as in Verg. *Aen.* III.
224 *dapibusque epulamur opimis.*
— **mensas**: the feast is doubtless
that spread at the house of the
bride's parents.   Contrary to the
usual Greek custom, women were
present, but were seated at tables
by themselves.   From the house
of her parents the bridegroom at
evening escorted the bride to her
new home in solemn procession to
the music of hymeneal songs, which
were also sung outside the closed
door of the bride-chamber.

4. **iam ueniet uirgo**: *sc.* from
her chamber, to take her seat beside
the bridegroom in the carriage in

Cernitis, innuptae, iuuenes ? consurgite contra :
Nimirum Oetaeos ostendit Noctifer ignes.
Sic certe est : uiden ut perniciter exsiluere ?
Non temere exsiluere ; canent quod uincere par est.
10 Hymen o Hymenaee, Hymen ades o Hymenaee.

Non facilis nobis, aequales, palma parata est :
Adspicite, innuptae secum ut meditata requirunt.
Non frustra meditantur ; habent memorabile quod sit.
Nec mirum, penitus quae tota mente laborant.

which she is to be drawn to his house. — **hymenaeus,** *the marriage-hymn ;* with this meaning first in Hom. *Il.* XVIII. 491 ἐν τῇ μέν [πόλει] ῥα γάμοι τ' ἔσαν ... πολὺς δ' ὑμέναιος ὀρώρει; elsewhere in Catullus of the god Hymen (61. 4; 62. 5, and often), and of marriage itself (66. 11, etc.). On the lengthening of the preceding short syllable see Intr. 86 *g.*

5. Cf. Theocr. 18. 58, where the dactylic hexameter opens in the same way, and 61. 4 n.

6. **innuptae:** for *uirgines,* as in 64. 78. — **contra,** *on your side, i.e.* from your position at a table opposite theirs.

7. **nimirum :** *i.e.* it must be that the youths have already caught sight of the evening star, and that is the reason for their rising. — **Oetaeos :** Mt. Oeta is the name of the range in the district of Oetaea, just at the head of the Maliac Gulf, between Thessaly and Aetolia. Upon it the funeral pyre of Heracles was erected. It is sometimes connected with the Thessalian Olympus ; cf. v. 1 n. *Olympo.* — **ostendit ignes:** cf. Hor. *Carm.* III. 29. 17 *iam clarus occultum Andromedae pater ostendit ignem.* — **Noctifer:** cf. Calp. *Buc.* 5. 120 *iam sole fugato frigidus aestiuas impellit Noctifer horas.*

8. **sic certe est:** the explanation at first only suggested appears convincing, and is reaffirmed as sure ; cf. 80. 7. — **uiden ut:** cf. 61. 77 n. — **perniciter exsiluere :** *i.e.* they show the eager swiftness of confidence in their ability to surpass their competitors in song.

9. **non temere :** *i.e.* not in mere bravado, nor in baseless self-confidence. — **quod:** direct object of **uincere.** The two choruses will vie with each other in responsive song, as do the swains in the bucolics of Theocritus and Vergil. — **par** (*sc. nobis*), *it is our task.*

11. **palma :** *i.e.* victory. — **parata :** cf. Petron. 15 *nec uictoria mi placet parata.*

12. **secum meditata requirunt :** *i.e.* they are conning verses already learned and practised, and are not depending, like us (v. 15), merely upon ability in improvisation.

13. **non frustra meditantur:** *i.e.* their study will not prove fruitless. *Meditari* is almost the technical word for poetic composition; cf. Verg. *Ecl.* 6. 82; Hor. *Sat.* I. 9. 2; *Ep.* II. 2. 76. The verse corresponds closely with v. 9.

14. **nec mirum:** cf. 23. 7 n. — **quae laborant:** but cf. the subjunctive mood in similar causal clauses in vv. 21 and 27. So Plautus and Terence apparently use the

15 Nos alio mentes, alio diuisimus aures :
    Iure igitur uincemur ; amat uictoria curam.
    Quare nunc animos saltem conuertite uestros :
    Dicere iam incipient, iam respondere decebit.
    Hymen o Hymenaee, Hymen ades o Hymenaee.

20 Hespere, qui caelo fertur crudelior ignis ?
    Qui natam possis complexu auellere matris,
    Complexu matris retinentem auellere natam
    Et iuueni ardenti castam donare puellam.
    Quid faciunt hostes capta crudelius urbe ?
25 Hymen o Hymenaee, Hymen ades o Hymenaee.

indicative and subjunctive indiscriminately with the causal relative,
and even change from one to the
other, as here, while in later Latin
the subjunctive becomes the rule.

15. nos : with strong emphasis
upon the contrast with the absorp-
tion of the maidens in their coming
task. — alio mentes, alio aures :
i.e. while they have practised earnestly, following their leader *tota
mente* (v. 14), we have attended to
our leader with our ears only, while
our thoughts have been far from him
and from the task that lay before
us ; alio . . . alio are correlative,
referring to distinct directions. —
diuisimus : cf. in slightly different
meaning Verg. *Aen.* IV. 285 (and
VIII. 20) *atque animum nunc huc
celerem nunc diuidit illuc.*

17. saltem : with nunc. — con-
uertite : *sc. ad rem ;* cf. Cic. *N. D.*
I. 27. 77 *quo facilius animos impe-
ritorum ad deorum cultum a uitae
prauitate conuerterent.*

20. Hespere : the same form of
the name is followed in vv. 26, 32,
and 35, and in 64. 329; but cf. v. 1
Vesper (and the yet different name
Noctifer in v. 7). With the sentiment of the strophe cf. 61. 3–4. —

caelo fertur, *traverses the heavens ;*
Baehrens cites Germ. *Progn.* II. 2
*per idem Cythereius ignis fertur
iter.* — ignis : cf. Hor. *Carm.* I.
12. 47 *uelut inter ignes luna mino-
res ;* Germ. *l.c.*

21. possis : cf. v. 14 n. *laborant.*
— complexu matris : cf. 61. 58 ;
64. 88. — auellere : not with direct
reference to the show of force with
which in the Roman ceremony the
bride was taken from her mother's
arms, but in general of the rude in-
terruption of the peaceful simplicity
of her life of maidenhood; cf. 61. 3
rapis.

22. retinentem, *clinging.*

23. iuueni ardenti : cf. 61. 56
fero iuueni, and observe the sequence of the contrasted epithets
ardenti castam.

24. capta urbe : the comparison
of great woes to those endured by a
conquered city was traditional; cf.
Hom. *Il.* IX. 592 κήδε' ὅσ' ἀνθρώ-
ποισι πέλει τῶν ἄστυ ἀλώῃ; Verg.
Aen. II. 746 *quid in euersa uidi
crudelius urbe ?* Prop. V. 8. 56 *spec-
taclum capta nec minus urbe fuit ;*
Ov. *Met.* XIV. 578 *et sonus et ma-
cies et pallor et omnia captam quae
deceant urbem.*

Hespere, qui caelo lucet iucundior ignis?
Qui desponsa tua firmes conubia flamma,
Quae pepigere uiri, pepigerunt ante parentes,
Nec iunxere prius quam se tuus extulit ardor.
30 Quid datur a diuis felici optatius hora?
Hymen o Hymenaee, Hymen ades o Hymenaee.

Hesperus e nobis, aequales, abstulit unam
　　　　　　　　　　*
Namque tuo aduentu uigilat custodia semper.
Nocte latent fures, quos idem saepe reuertens,

27. **desponsa**: ordinarily used only of the betrothed maiden. — **firmes**: cf. v. 14 n. *laborant.*

28. **uiri . . . parentes**: *i.e.* marriage-contracts arranged by husbands on the one side and parents on the other. **viri** is used by anticipation as in v. 65 *genero;* cf. also 64. 328 *maritis.* With the change of form of the repeated tense for metrical reasons and for variety cf. Lucil. III. 11–12 Müll. *uerum haec ludus ibi susque omnia deque fuerunt, susque haec deque fuere inquam, omnia, ludu' iocusque;* Verg. *Ecl.* 10. 13 *illum etiam lauri, etiam fleuere myricae, pinifer illum etiam sola sub rupe iacentem Maenalus et gelidi fleuerunt saxa Lycaei;* Lucr. VI. 2–5 *dididērunt, recreauērunt, rogarunt, dedērunt, genuēre.*

29. **iunxere**: cf. 78. 3 *dulces iungit amores.*

30. Cf. similar sentiments at the end of 9, 45, and 107.

32 ff. Of this strophe, sung by the maidens, only the first verse remains, but the comparison of its key-note with vv. 33 ff., sung by the youths, indicates that the two fragmentary strophes stood in immediate succession. The strophe of the maidens ended, of course, with the refrain *Hymen o Hymenaee*, etc.

33 ff. The maidens had complained of Hesperus for robbing them of a companion, and in general for ushering in the night, the time of fear and depredation. The youths denied in the lost verses that Hesperus is the harbinger of danger, and in vv. 33–36 support their denial by two reasons and by an *argumentum ad hominem :* possible danger at night is averted by ordinary watchfulness; Hesperus himself acts as thief-taker by ushering in the unexpected dawn; and finally, maidens themselves but feign fear of the darkness.

33. **custodia**: for *custodes ;* cf. Verg. *Aen.* VI. 574 *cernis custodia qualis uestibulo sedeat?* Ov. *Met.* XIV. 371 *abest custodia regi.* — Neither in this nor in the two following verses is there any reference to *furtiuos hominum amores* (7. 8) save by merest indirection ; the maidens complained, and the youths are responding to the charge, that the darkness makes possible acts of violence.

34. **nocte latent fures** : perhaps quoted *verbatim* from the song of the maidens, but neutralized as far

35 Hespere, mutato comprendis nomine eosdem.

At libet innuptis ficto te carpere questu.

Quid tum, si carpunt tacita quem mente requirunt?

Hymen o Hymenaee, Hymen ades o Hymenaee.

Vt flos in saeptis secretus nascitur hortis,

40 Ignotus pecori, nullo conuulsus aratro,

Quem mulcent aurae, firmat sol, educat imber,

as it is a charge against Hesperus,
by the following clause. — idem . . .
mutato nomine: the poet disre-
gards the scientific fact that the
same planet is not both morning
and evening star at the same season
of the year. The identity of Hesperus and Lucifer (cf. Cic. *l.c.* on
v. 1) was known about the time of
Pythagoras, whether established by
him or by Parmenides, and is frequently alluded to by the Romans;
cf. Varr. *R. R.* III. 5. 17 *stella Lucifer interdiu, noctu Hesperus; Cir.*
350 [*ignem*] *quem pauidae alternis
fugitant optantque puellae* (*Hespe-
rium uitant, optant ardescere
Eoum*); Cinna *Zmyrna* (ap. Serv.
on Verg. *Geor.* I. 288) *te matutinus
flentem conspexit Eous, et flentem
paulo uidit post Hesperus idem:*
also Tennyson *In Mem.* 121 *Sweet
Hesper-Phosphor, double name For
what is one.* — saepe: modifying
comprendis.

35. comprendis: if the thefts
were *furtiui amores, deprendis*
would be the more natural term,
but the prime reference in *fures* is
the patent one, and Hesperus acts
as constable. — eosdem: to correspond to v. 34 *idem.*

36. ficto questu: cf. 66. 16 *falsis lacrimulis.*

37. requirunt: as if filled with
longing for the return of what
was once offered and rejected; cf.
8. 13.

39. ut flos, etc.: the comparison
of blooming maidenhood to a flower-
ing plant is a favorite one; cf. 61.
22 n. Ellis cites the fuller imitation
of this passage by Ben Jonson in
The Barriers, and by Rob. Browning *Ring and Book* III. 233 ff.

40. conuulsus: the feelings of
the maidens lead them to use a
word implying more than ordinary
violence (cf. 64. 40), while in 11.
24, for a different reason, the light-
est possible word is used of the
action of the plough upon a tender
plant.

41. mulcent aurae: on the gen-
erative and nourishing power of the
breezes cf. 64. 90, 282; Lucr. I. 11
*reserata uiget genitabilis aura Fa-
uoni; Hor. Carm.* I. 22. 17 *nulla
arbor aestiua recreatur aura;* Prop.
V. 7. 60 *mulcet ubi Elysias aura
beata rosas;* Ov. *Met.* I. 107 *uer
erat aeternum, placidique tepentibus auris mulcebant Zephyri natos
sine semine flores; Fast.* V. 209 *est
mihi fecundus hortus . . . aura
fouet.* — The exact correspondence
of v. 42 to v. 41 as of v. 44 to v. 43
(*quem . . . illum; idem cum . . .
illum*), and comparison with the
next strophe, where v. 53 *hanc* follows immediately upon vv. 49–52 *ut
uidua uitis . . . contingit*, make it
unreasonable to suppose a lacuna
of one verse after v. 41, as required
by a fictitious theory of precise correspondence in the number of verses

Multi illum pueri, multae optauere puellae ;
Idem cum tenui carptus defloruit ungui,
Nulli illum pueri, nullae optauere puellae :
45 Sic uirgo, dum intacta manet, dum cara suis est ;
Cum castum amisit polluto corpore florem,
Nec pueris iucunda manet nec cara puellis.
Hymen o Hymenaee, Hymen ades o Hymenaee.

Vt uidua in nudo uitis quae nascitur aruo
50 Nunquam se extollit, nunquam mitem educat uuam,

between this and the following
strophe.

42. Imitated by Ovid in *Met.* III.
353 *multi illum iuuenes, multae
cupiere puellae.*

43. idem: subject of defloruit;
cf. 22. 3 n. *idem.*— tenui carptus
ungui: cf. Verg. *Aen.* XI. 68 *uirgineo demessum pollice florem;*
Prop. I. 20. 39 *decerpens tenero
pueriliter ungui florem;* Ov. *Her.*
4. 30 *tenui primam delegere ungue
rosam.*

45. dum . . . dum: Quintilian
explains as follows (*Inst.* IX. 3.
16) *Catullus in Epithalamio ' dum
. . . est,' cum prius dum significet
quoad, sequens usque eo.* In illus-
tration of his view might be cited
Plaut. *Truc.* 232 *dum habeat dum*
(MSS. *tum*) *amet; ubi nil habeat,
alium quaestum coepiat* (cf. Haupt
Opusc. II. p. 473). But comparison
with v. 56 indicates that Quintilian
misunderstood the meaning of Catullus as much as did the less learned
emendators of *V* and *T*, who
changed the second dum to *tum*.
The two *dum*-clauses are not correlative, but coördinate, both modifying sic uirgo (*sc. est*), while sic is
emphatic, referring to v. 42. Thus
v. 45 corresponds alone to vv. 39–42,
while vv. 46–47 correspond to vv. 43–
44. — intacta: cf. 34. 2 n. *integri.*

— cara suis : the maidens use the
second *dum*-clause as a sort of definition of the first, and so indicate
their belief in the dependence of
family and friendly affection upon
the virginity of its object. The sentiment is more definitely declared
in vv. 46–47. Observe the neat way
in which the youths in v. 56 repeat
after the maidens the first *dum*-
clause, but define it very differently
by the second.

46. The fierce virginity of the
chorus views even marriage as a
compromise of chastity. — castum
florem = *castitatis florem ;* cf. Cic.
Balb. 6. 15 *ipsum florem dignita-
tis infringere;* and cf. the indication of chastity as the crowning
virtue in the familiar euphemism
flos aetatis (Liv. XXI. 2. 3 ; Suet.
Iul. 49).

47. iucunda: with substantially
the same meaning as the following
cara ; cf. 14. 2 n.

49. uidua (= *caelebs*) *unwed, i.e.*
not trained upon a tree; more frequently used of trees themselves; cf.
Hor. *Carm.* IV. 5. 30 *uitem uiduas
ducit ad arbores;* Mart. III. 58. 3
uidua platano ; Juv. 8. 78 *stratus
humi palmes uiduas desiderat ulmos ;* Hor. *Carm.* II. 15. 4 *platanus
caelebs.* — nudo : *i.e.* bare of trees ;
cf. Ov. *Trist.* III. 10. 75 *aspiceres*

Sed tenerum prono deflectens pondere corpus
Iam iam contingit summum radice flagellum,
Hanc nulli agricolae, nulli accoluere iuuenci ;
At si forte eadem est ulmo coniuncta marito,
55 Multi illam agricolae, multi accoluere iuuenci :
Sic uirgo, dum intacta manet, dum inculta senescit ;
Cum par conubium maturo tempore adepta est,
Cara uiro magis et minus est inuisa parenti.

Et tu ne pugna cum tali coniuge, uirgo.
60 Non aequum est pugnare, pater cui tradidit ipse,
Ipse pater cum matre, quibus parere necesse est.
Virginitas non tota tua est, ex parte parentum est :

---

nudos sine fronde, sine arbore campos.

50. **mitem,** *ripe;* cf. Verg. *Geor.* I. 448 *heu male tum mitis defendet pampinus uuas.*

51. **prono pondere:** cf. *Cir.* 26 *prono grauidum prouexit pondere currum;* Val. Fl. III. 564 *detrahit; adiutae prono nam pondere uires.*

52. **iam iam:** cf. Verg. *Aen.* II. 530 *iam iamque manu tenet et premit hasta;* Hor. *Epod.* 2. 68 *iam iam futurus rusticus.* — **contingit radice flagellum :** a peculiar inversion for *contingit radicem flagello.* — **flagellum:** a young vine-shoot; cf. Varro *R. R.* I. 31. 3 *uitem, quam uocant minorem flagellum, maiorem et iam unde uuae nascuntur palmam.*

53. **accoluere iuuenci:** of 'cultivating' between the rows of vines; cf. Varro *R. R.* I. 8. 5 [*uineae*] *interualla pedamentorum qua boues iuncti arare possint.*

54. **ulmo:** cf. v. 49 n. *uidua.* The elm is most frequently mentioned by the poets as the tree on which the vine is trained; cf. Hor. *Ep.* I. 16. 3 *amicta uitibus ulmo;*

Verg. *Geor.* I. 2 *ulmis adiungere uites;* Ov. *Am.* II. 16. 41 *ulmus amat uitem, uitis non deserit ulmum;* Calp. *Buc.* 2. 59 *inter pampineas ulmos.* — **marito:** with the figure cf. *ll.cc.* and Cato *R. R.* 32 *arbores facito uti bene maritae sint.* Catullus apparently uses the masculine (as appositive) instead of the concordant feminine for the sake of the figure.

56. **dum . . . dum:** cf. v. 45 n.

57. **par conubium:** *i.e.* a marriage with one of equal station; cf. Ov. *Her.* 9. 32 *siqua uoles apte nubere, nube pari.* On the synaeresis see Intr. 86 *c.*

58. **magis:** the comparison is not with reference to her husband's love for her, but to her condition before marriage (v. 45 *sic*) ; she has gained affection instead of losing it, for a husband is better than a friend, and there is no danger of her presence becoming irksome to her father (who desires to see his daughters settled in marriage ; cf. 61. 51–52; 66. 15–16).

59. **et:** connecting the general expression of approval of marriage

Tertia pars patri, pars est data tertia matri,
Tertia sola tua est.   Noli pugnare duobus,
65 Qui genero sua iura simul cum dote dederunt.
Hymen o Hymenaee, Hymen ades o Hymenaee.

63.

Super alta uectus Attis celeri rate maria
Phrygium ut nemus citato cupide pede tetigit

with its application to this specific case.

63. **tertia** : cf. Lucilius (on Virtus) *commoda patriae prima putare, deinde parentum, tertia iam nostra.*

64. **noli pugnare duobus** : Passerat cites the proverbial Platonic expressions from *Leg.* XI. 119 πρὸς δύο μάχεσθαι καὶ ἐναντία χαλεπόν; *Phaedr.* 89 πρὸς δύο οὐδ' Ἡρακλῆς. Catullus is the first to use *pugnare* with a dative, but he is followed by the later poets, who admit the same construction with other verbs of contest (cf. Gr. μάχεσθαί τινι); cf. Verg. *Aen.* IV. 38 *placitone etiam pugnabis amori?* Hor. *Epod.* 11. 18 *desinet imparibus certare.*

65. **genero** : used by anticipation, as v. 28 *uiri;* 64. 328 *maritis.*

63. The self-mutilation and subsequent lament of Attis, a priest of Cybele. The centre of the worship of the Phrygian Κυβέλη or Κυβήβη, was in very ancient times the town of Pessinus in Galatian Phrygia, at the foot of Mt. Dindymus, from which the goddess received the name Dindymene. Cybele had early become identified with the Cretan divinity Rhea, the Mother of the Gods, and to some extent with Demeter, the search of Cybele for Attis being compared with that of Demeter for Persephone. The especial worship of Cybele was conducted by emasculated priests called *Galli* (or, as in vv. 12 and 34, with reference to their physical condition, *Gallae*). Their name was derived by the ancients from that of the river Gallus, a tributary of the Sangarius, by drinking from which men became inspired with frenzy (cf. Ov. *Fast.* IV. 361 ff.). The worship was orgiastic in the extreme, and was accompanied by the sound of such frenzy-producing instruments as the *tympana, cymbala, tibiae,* and *cornu,* and culminated in scourging, self-mutilation, syncope from excitement, and even death from hemorrhage or heart-failure (cf. Lucr. II. 598 ff.; Varr. *Sat. Men.* 131 ff. Büch.; Ov. *Fast.* IV. 179 ff.). The worship of the Magna Mater, or Mater Idaea, as she was often called (perhaps from identification with Rhea of the Cretan Mt. Ida rather than from the Trojan Mt. Ida), was introduced into Rome in 205 B.C. in accordance with a Sibylline oracle which foretold that only so could 'a foreign enemy' (*i.e.* Hannibal) be driven from Italy. Livy (XXIX. 10, 14) gives an interesting account of the solemnities that accompanied the transfer from Pessinus to Rome of the black stone that represented the divinity, and of the

Adiitque opaca siluis redimita loca deae,
Stimulatus ibi furenti rabie, uagus animis

establishment of the Megalensia ; cf. also Ov. *Fast.* IV. 247 ff. The stone itself was perhaps a meteorite, and is thus described by Arnobius (*Adu. Gent.* VII. 46) : *lapis quidam non magnus, ferri manu hominis sine ulla impressione qui posset ; coloris furui atque atri, angellis prominentibus inaequalis, et quem omnes hodie . . . uidemus . . . indolatum et asperum.* Servius (*Aen.* VII. 188) speaks of it as *acus Matris Deum*, and as one of the seven objects on which depended the safety of Rome.

The early connection of Attis with the Mother of the Gods seems to point to the association of an original male element with an original female element as the parents of all things. But in the age of tradition Attis appears as a servant instead of an equal, and the subordination of the male to the female element is further emphasized by the representation of Attis, like the Galli of historic times, as an emasculated priest. Greek imagination pictured him as a beautiful youth who was beloved by the goddess, but wandered away from her and became untrue ; but being sought and recalled to allegiance by her, in a passion of remorse he not only spent his life in her service, but by his own act made impossible for the future such infidelity on his part, thus setting the example followed by all the *Galli* after him (cf. Ov. *Fast. l.c.*). Catullus departs from this form of the Attis myth, and makes Attis a beautiful Greek youth who in a moment of religious frenzy sails across seas at the head of a band of companions to devote himself to the already long-established service of the goddess (vv. 1–3). On

reaching the shores of Trojan Ida he consummates the irrevocable act of dedication (vv. 4–5), and with his companions rushes up the mountain to the sanctuary of the goddess (vv. 6–38). But on awaking next morning he feels the full awfulness of his act (vv. 39–47), and gazing out over the sea toward his lost home, bewails his fate (vv. 48–73), till the jealous goddess unyokes a lion from her car and sends him to drive her wavering votary back to his allegiance (vv. 74–*fin.*). The story is told with a nervous vigor and swing of feeling that are unequalled in Latin literature, and to it the galliambic metre (Intr. 85), the one traditionally appropriated to such themes, lends great effect. The date of composition is uncertain, but Catullus may have found his immediate inspiration in his contact with the Cybelian worship in its original home during his residence in Bithynia in 57–56 B.C. (see Intr. 29 ff.). Or it may have been found in his studies in the Alexandrian poets; for Callimachus certainly used the galliambic metre, though no distinct title of a poem by him on this theme is extant. Caecilius of Comum was also engaged on a poem based on the worship of Cybele (cf. 35. 13 ff.), and Varro and Maecenas both exercised their talents in the same direction (cf. Varr. *Sat. Men. l.c.;* Maec. in Baehr. *Fragm. Poet. Rom.* p. 339).

The poem abounds in rhetorical devices to add to its effect ; such are the frequent employment of alliteration (vv. 2, 6, 7, 8, 9, 10, 13, etc.), of strange and harsh compounds (vv. 23 *hederigerae,* 34 *properipedem,* 41 *sonipedibus,* 51 *erifu*

5 Deuoluit ili acuto sibi pondera silice.
  Itaque ut relicta sensit sibi membra sinę uiro,
  Etiam recente terrae sola sanguine maculans
  Niueis citata cepit manibus leue typanum,
  Typanum, tubam Cybelles, tua, mater, initia,

gae, 72 *nemoriuagus*), and the repetition of words of agitated movement and feeling (*e.g. rapidus* three
times, *citatus* four times, *citus* twice,
rabidus three times, *rabies* once).

1. **celeri**: indicating his eagerness for arrival.

2. **Phrygium nemus**: that clothing the slopes not of Dindymus but
of Ida (cf. vv. 30, 52). — **citato
cupide pede**: emphasizing the
eager haste of the traveller, rather
than indicating a land journey after
reaching the shores of Asia (cf. vv.
47, 89); the poet is not writing as
a geographer. Cf. v. 30 *properante
pede*.

3. **opaca**: cf. v. 32. The mad
rush of the new devotees is contrasted with the silent mysteries of
the abode of the goddess.

4. **ibi**, *thereupon;* cf. vv. 42, 48,
76; and 66. 33; 8. 6 n. — **furenti
rabie**: cf. v. 38 *rabidus furor*. —
uagus animis: the plural to indicate his divided, distorted emotions;
cf. Verg. *Aen.* VIII. 228 *ecce furens
animis aderat Tirynthius*.

5. **ili**: genitive from the stem
ilio-, a rare but legitimate variant
for the more frequent *ili-;* cf.
Cels. IV. 1 *iliis* (dat. plur.); Gloss.
Labb. *ilium* λαγών; Marc. Emp.
36 [*ilium*].

6. **sine uiro**: *i.e. sine uirilitate*.

7. **terrae sola** (plural, as in v. 40
sola dura): cf. Lucr. II. 592 *nam
multis succensa locis ardent sola
terrae*.

8. **niueis manibus**: cf. v. 10 n.
teneris digitis. Adjectives descriptive of feminine beauty are employed

to accord with the change of gender
under which Attis is now spoken of,
and himself speaks of his companions (vv. 12 *Gallae*, 15 *exsecutae*, 34
rapidae Gallae); cf. Hor. *Carm.* II.
4. 3 *niueo colore* (of Briseis) ; III.
27. 25 *niueum latus* (of Europe);
Verg. *Aen.* VIII. 387 *niueis lacertis*
(of Venus). — **citata**: Attis is from
henceforth a *notha mulier* (v. 27),
and is described by feminine adjectives; cf. vv. 11 *adorta, tremebunda,*
31 *furibunda*, 32 *comitata*, etc.;
but when he returns to himself and
thinks with sorrow and loathing
upon his condition, the masculine
adjective is resumed ; cf. vv. 51
miser, 78 *hunc*, 88 *tenerum*, 89 *ille*.
The emendations by which all these
later masculines (except v. 78 *hunc*)
have been transformed to feminines
are based on incorrect feeling. —
leue: the *tympanum* is probably
called *leue* because it is *cauum* (v.
10). — **typanum**: Gr. poet. form
τύπανον, *metri gratia* (cf. v. 21, etc.
tympanum, Gr. τύμπανον); from
representations in vase- and wall-
paintings, an instrument like the
modern tambourine, but with the
rattling disks of metal suspended at
intervals from its edge by short
cords.

9. **tubam Cybelles**: as the blare
of the *tuba* is the summons and in-
citement to warriors, so is the beat
of the *tympanum* to the votaries
of Cybele ; the phrase is further
explained by **tua initia**. The
famous norm of Bentley (on Lu-
can I. 600) that when the penult is
short the form *Cybele* should be

10 Quatiensque terga tauri teneris caua digitis
     Canere haec suis adorta est tremebunda comitibus.
     'Agite ite ad alta, Gallae, Cybeles nemora simul,
     Simul ite, Dindymenae dominae uaga pecora,
     Aliena quae petentes uelut exsules loca
15 Sectam meam exsecutae duce me mihi comites
     Rapidum salum tulistis truculentaque pelagi
     Et corpus euirastis Veneris nimio odio,
     Hilarate erae citatis erroribus animum.

written, but when it is long the
form *Cybebe, Cybelle* being discarded
altogether, is not well supported by
either Greek or Latin usage. *Cybelle*
(Gr. Κύβελλα) is found in many
good MSS. — **mater**: Cybele was
the *Magna Mater Idaea* of the
Romans, as well as *mater deorum;*
cf. intr. note; *Hymn. Cyb.* μήτερα
μοι πάντων τε θεῶν, πάντων τ' ἀν-
θρώπων. — **initia**: technically used
only of the mysteries of Demeter
(cf. Varr. *R. R.* III. 1. 5 *initia
uocantur potissimum ea quae Cereri
fiunt sacra*), but here of the symbol
of the secret worship of Cybele,
perhaps by reason of the popular
confusion of Cybele with Demeter.

10. **teneris digitis**: cf. v. 8 n.
niueis manibus; Ov. *Ib.* 456 [*ut
Attis*] *quatias molli tympana rauca
manu; Fast.* IV. 342 *feriunt molles
taurea terga manus.* — **caua**: the
word *tympanum* also denoted a
kettle-drum with a hemispherical
resounding cavity and a single head
of hide, and so *caua*, which would
properly characterize it, is here used
of its cognate instrument, the tambourine; cf. Ov. *Fast.* IV. 183 *ina-
nia tympana tundent;* Aus. *Epist.*
24. 21 *caua tympana.*

11. **tremebunda**: in the quivering of nervous excitement.

12. **agite**: cf. 61. 38 n. — **Gallae**: cf. v. 34, and intr. note. —

Cybeles: Gr. Κυβέλη ; cf. v. 9 n.
Cybelles.

13. **Dindymenae dominae**: cf.
v. 91; 35. 14. — **uaga**: of the pur-
poseless wanderings of the crazed
devotees ; cf. vv. 18 *erroribus;* 25
uaga cohors; 31 *uaga uadit.* —
pecora: cf. Ov. *Ib.* 457 *pecus
Magnae Parentis* (of the Galli)

15. **sectam meam exsecutae,**
under my rule; Attis acts as re-
cruiting officer, and then (**duce
me**) guides the new devotees to
their place of service. **comites**
implies here a certain subordination
as in the case of the *comites* of a
provincial governor; cf. 28. 1 ; 11.
1. Apparently *exsequi* is used with
sectam only here, though Cicero
uses *sectam persequi* (*Verr.* II. 5.
70. 181), and *sectam sequi* is frequently found (cf. Liv. XXIX. 27.
2 *qui meam sectam secuntur*, a formal expression in an invocation).

16. **rapidum**: of the rushing
waves of the sea, as explained in
truculenta pelagi ; cf. 64. 358 *rapido Hellesponto.* — **truculenta pelagi**: with the construction cf. Verg.
Aen. IX. 81 *pelagi alta;* Hor. *Carm.*
IV. 4. 76 *acuta belli ;* with the sentiment, Hor. *Carm.* I. 3. 10 *truci
pelago.*

18. **hilarate**, etc.: *i.e.* haste to
gladden the heart of the goddess by
the presence of this new accession

Mora tarda mente cedat ; simul ite, sequimini
20 Phrygiam ad domum Cybelles, Phrygia ad nemora deae,
Vbi cymbalum sonat uox, ubi tympana reboant,
Tibicen ubi canit Phryx curuo graue calamo,
Vbi capita maenades ui iaciunt hederigerae,
Vbi sacra sancta acutis ululatibus agitant,
25 Vbi sueuit illa diuae uolitare uaga cohors,

of enthusiastic votaries. — **erroribus** : the *rabidus furor animi* (v.
38) would lead the band, not directly
to the temple, but in Maenad-like
tortuousness of course.

21. **cymbalum** : *cymbala* were
hollow hemispheres of metal a few
inches in diameter, held one in each
hand by the aid of small rings or
thongs attached to the centre of
their convex surfaces. Struck together, they gave a sharp, clanging
sound that fitted well with that of
the *tympana* and *tibiae;* cf. 64. 262
tereti tenuis tinnitus aere ciebant;
Ov. *Fast.* IV. 184 *aera tinnitus
aere repulsa dabunt;* 189 *sonus
aeris acuti;* Aus. *Epist.* 24. 23 *tinnitus aëni.* — **reboant**: cf. Aus.
Epist. 24. 21 *tentis reboant caua
tympana tergis.*

22. **Phryx** : the *tibiae* were said
to be a Phrygian invention ; cf. 64.
264; Lucr. II. 620 *Phrygio stimulat
numero caua tibia mentis;* Tib. II.
I. 86 *obstrepit et Phrygio tibia curua
sono ;* Ov. *Fast.* IV. 181 *inflexo Be-
recyntia tibia cornu.* — **curuo calamo** : the *tibia* was originally made
of a reed. The curved variety appears from bas-reliefs to have been
shaped sometimes like the *lituus,*
straight and of uniform diameter
from the mouth-piece till near the
bell, where it curved sharply back
upon itself, but sometimes to have
had a gentle double curve and an
increasing diameter from mouth-
piece to bell, like a cow-horn. The

straight varieties, more commonly
used, were generally played in pairs,
one with each hand, being often
supported in position at the player's
mouth by a band admitting the two
mouth-pieces and fastened at the
back of the head. — **graue**: cf.
Stat. *Theb.* VI. 113 *signum luctus
cornu graue mugit adunco tibia.*

23. **maenades**: the poet bor-
rows for the priests of Cybele the
name appropriate to the frenzied
maidens that attended upon the
similar rites of Dionysus. — **capita
ui iaciunt**: frequent wall-paintings
and engraved gems show the bac-
chanals beating the tympana and
swaying the head violently back and
forth; cf. 64. 255 *capita inflectentes;*
Maec. *frag.* 4 Baehr. *sonante typano
quate flexibile caput;* Varr. *Sat.
Men.* 132 Buech. *semiuiri teretem
comam uolantem iactant;* Ov. *Met.*
III. 726 *ululauit Agaue, collaque
iactauit, mouitque per aera crinem.* — **hederigerae**: ἅπαξ λεγόμενον.

24. **acutis ululatibus**: cf. v. 28;
Maec. *frag.* 5 Baehr. *comitum chorus ululet;* Ov. *Fast.* IV. 341 *exu-
lulant comites; Met. l.c.*

25. **illa**: the demonstrative characterizes as well-known the whole
statement ; in this use *ille* corresponds closely to our definite article.
— **uolitare uaga**: so of Bacchus in
64. 251, 390. — **cohors**: *i.e. comites;* cf. v. 11 and 28. 1 *Pisoni
comites, cohors inanis.*

Quo nos decet citatis celerare tripudiis.'
Simul haec comitibus Attis cecinit notha mulier,
Thiasus repente linguis trepidantibus ululat,
Leue tympanum remugit, caua cymbala recrepant,
30 Viridem citus adit Idam properante pede chorus.
Furibunda simul anhelans uaga uadit animam agens
Comitata tympano Attis per opaca nemora dux,
Veluti iuuenca uitans onus indomita iugi :
Rapidae ducem secuntur Gallae properipedem.
35 Itaque, ut domum Cybelles tetigere lassulae,
Nimio e labore somnum capiunt sine Cerere.
Piger his labante langore oculos sopor operit :

26. **tripudiis** : of the wild, rhyth-mic dance connected with the wor-ship.

27. **simul** : *sc. atque ;* cf. v. 45 and 22. 15 n. — **notha mulier** : cf. Ov. *Fast.* IV. 183 *semimares* (of the Galli); *Ib.* 453 *nec femina nec uir* (of Attis) ; Varro *Sat. Men.* 132 Buech. *semiuiri* (of the Galli).

28. **thiasus** : of a band of raving devotees, as in 64. 252, and often, of the attendants of Iacchus. — **trepidantibus** : as v. 11 *treme-bunda*, of the quivering of nervous excitement; cf. Verg. *Aen.* VII. 395 *aliae tremulis ululatibus aethera complent* (of the Bacchic worship-pers). — **ululat** : cf. v. 24 n. *ulula-tibus*.

29. **leue tympanum** : cf. v. 8 *leue typanum.* — **recrepant** : the word apparently occurs only here and in *Ciris* 108 *lapis recrepat Cyllenia murmura pulsus.*

30. **uiridem Idam** : cf. v. 70 ; *Culex* 311 *iugis Ida patens fronden-tibus ;* Ov. *Art. Am.* I. 289 *sub umbrosis nemorosae uallibus Idae ; Fast.* VI. 327 *in opacae uallibus Idae ; Met.* XI. 762 *umbrosa sub Ida ;* Stat. *Silu.* III. 4. 12 *pinifera*

Ida. — **properante pede** : cf. v. 34 *properipedem.*

31. **animam agens** : to be ex-plained from **anhelans** of the almost fainting condition resulting from haste, excitement, and exhaus-tion, *gasping.* It usually means ' to give up the ghost'; cf. Cic. *Fam.* VIII. 13. 2 *Q. Hortensius, cum has litteras scripsi, animam agebat.*

32. **comitata** : usually with an ablative of person instead of thing when, as here, it has a personal sub-ject.

33. **ueluti iuuenca**, etc. : the comparison is usually employed by the poets of the yoke of love ; cf. 68. 118 n.

35. **domum Cybelles** : appar-ently the shrine of the goddess on the mountain-top.

36. **Cerere** : cf. Cic. *N. D.* II. 23. 60 *fruges Cererem appellamus, uinum autem Liberum ; ex quo illud Terenti ' sine Cerere et Libero friget Venus '* (from Ter. *Eun.* 732). — The fasting in this case was probably not due to a require-ment of ritual, but simply to the utterly exhausted condition of the new Galli.

Abit in quiete molli rabidus furor animi.
Sed ubi oris aurei Sol radiantibus oculis
40 Lustrauit aethera album, sola dura, mare ferum,
Pepulitque noctis umbras uegetis sonipedibus,
Ibi Somnus excitam Attin fugiens citus abiit:
Trepidante eum recepit dea Pasithea sinu.
Ita de quiete molli rapida sine rabie
45 Simul ipsa pectore Attis sua facta recoluit,
Liquidaque mente uidit sine quis ubique foret,
Animo aestuante rusum reditum ad uada tetulit.

38. quiete molli, etc.: cf. v. 44.
—rabidus furor; cf. v. 4 *furenti
rabie.*

39. oris aurei: doubtless to be
construed with Sol rather than with
oculis; cf. Lucr. V. 461 *aurea . . .
matutina rubent radiati lumina
solis;* Verg. *Geor.* I. 232 *sol aureus;*
Ov. *Met.* VII. 663 *iubar aureus ex-
tulerat sol.* — radiantibus oculis:
cf. Ov. *Trist.* II. 325 *radiantia
lumina solis;* and with the figure in
oculis, F. W. Bourdillon, *The night
has a thousand eyes and the day but
one.*

40. lustrauit, *surveyed,* rather
than 'illumined,' as the figure in
oculis shows. — aethera album,
etc.: the adjectives album, dura,
ferum describe permanent characteristics and not those peculiar to
the morning, and hence album
must be understood not merely of
the sky brightened by dawn, but of
the bright, fiery aether ; cf. Cic.
N. D. I. 13. 33 *caeli ardorem;* II.
15. 41 *in ardore caelesti qui aether
uel caelum nominatur.* — sola:
plural, since the sun views every
region of earth. — dura, *solid,* to
distinguish the earth from the fluid
aether and sea. — ferum : a traditional epithet of the sea ; cf. v.
16 n. *truculenta pelagi.*

41. sonipedibus: first in Lucil.
XV. 15. Muel. *Campanus sonipes;*
also in Cic. *De Or.* III. 47. 183
paeon . . . sicut . . . sonipedes; and
frequently in later poets.

42. ibi: temporal, as in v. 4 (see
note). — Somnus, etc.: the morn
having come, Somnus is released
from duty and flies eagerly (citus)
back to Pasithea, whose reciprocal
eagerness of longing is indicated by
v. 43 trepidante sinu. Pasithea
was one of the lesser Graces, and
was promised to Sleep as a wife by
Hera in Hom. *Il.* XIV. 267 ff.

45. simul: cf. v. 27 n. *simul.*

46. liquida mente : of passion-
less calm ; cf. Plaut. *Epid.* 643
*animo liquido et tranquillo's : tace !
Pseud.* 232 *nihil curassis : liquido's
animo : ego pro me et pro te curabo.*
— sine quis: cf. v. 5. — ubique:
the quantity of the penult shows the
equivalence to *et ubi.*

47. animo   aestuante :   contrasted with *liquida mente;* there
was but a moment of clear and
calm mental vision succeeded by
the torture of recollection. — rusum : so sometimes in earlier Latin
(including Lucretius) for later *rursus.* — reditum tetulit: cf. v. 79
uti reditum ferat; 61. 26 *aditum
ferens;* 61. 43 *aditum ferat.*   On

Ibi maria uasta uisens lacrimantibus oculis
Patriam adlocuta maesta est ita uoce miseriter:
50 'Patria o mei creatrix, patria o mea genetrix,
Ego quam miser relinquens, dominos ut erifugae
Famuli solent, ad Idae tetuli nemora pedem,
Vt apud niuem et ferarum gelida stabula forem
Et earum omnia adirem furibunda latibula,
55 Vbinam aut quibus locis te positam, patria, reor?
Cupit ipsa pupula ad te sibi derigere aciem,
Rabie fera carens dum breue tempus animus est.
Egone a mea remota haec ferar in nemora domo?
Patria, bonis, amicis, genitoribus abero?
60 Abero foro, palaestra, stadio, et gymnasiis?
Miser ah miser, querendum est etiam atque etiam,
anime.
Quod enim genus figurae est ego non quod obierim?

the archaic form of the verb cf. v.
52; 34. 8 n.

48. maria uasta: cf. 31. 3 *mari
uasto;* 64. 127 *pelagi uastos aestus.*

49. miseriter: for *misere*, as
puriter for *pure* in 39. 14; 76. 19.

51. miser: while under the influence of his mad enthusiasm, Attis
gloried in his emasculation, but
now, in his recovered senses, he
speaks of his condition only with
loathing, using feminines (v. 68)
to point this feeling, but of course
not using a feminine adjective in
this expression of passionate longing
for his home.

52. tetuli: see 34. 8 n.

53. ferarum gelida stabula: cf.
Verg. *Aen.* VI. 179 *itur in anti-
quam siluam, stabula alta ferarum.* On the lengthening of the
final syllable before initial *st* see
Intr. 86 *g.*

55. reor: indicative present with
future meaning; cf. 1. 1 n. *dono.*

56. pupula: cf. Cic. *N. D.* II.
57. 142 *acies ipsa, qua cernimus,
quae pupula uocatur.* — derigere:
so, rather than *dirigere,* of the fixed
gaze in a single direction; cf. 22. 8
derecta plumbo.

57. carens est: for *caret;* cf.
64. 317 n. *fuerant exstantia.*

59. genitoribus: *i.e. parenti-
bus;* cf. Lucr. II. 615 *ingrati genitoribus* (of the Galli).

60. foro: the poet here employs
the corresponding Latin word for
the Greek ἀγορά.

61. miser ah miser: cf. 61. 139.
— etiam atque etiam: cf. Plaut.
Trin. 674 *te moneo hoc etiam atque
etiam;* Ter. *Eun.* 56 *etiam atque
etiam cogita;* and often in later
writers.

62. figurae: under the word is
the Greek feeling for the beauty of
the human form that had made Attis
the object of so much adoration; cf.
Cic. *N. D.* I. 18. 47 ff.

Ego mulier, ego adulescens, ego ephebus, ego puer,
Ego gymnasi fui flos, ego eram decus olei:
65 Mihi ianuae frequentes, mihi limina tepida,
Mihi floridis corollis redimita domus erat,
Linquendum ubi esset orto mihi sole cubiculum.
Ego nunc deum ministra et Cybeles famula ferar?

63. mulier: starting with the torturing thought of his present hateful condition, he retraces the steps of his former career as the passionate admiration of a whole city. — **adulescens**: cf. 12. 9 n. *puer;* Censor. *Die Nat.* 14. 2 [*Varro putat*] *usque annum* XV. *pueros dictos . . . ad tricensimum annum adulescentes . . . usque quinque et quadraginta annos iuuenis . . . adusque sexagensimum annum seniores . . . inde usque finem uitae senes.* — **ephebus**: cf. Censor. *Die Nat.* 14. 8 *de tertia autem aetate adulescentulorum tres gradus esse factos in Graecia prius quam ad uiros perueniatur, quod uocent annorum xiiii.* παῖδα, μελλέφηβον *autem xv.,* δεῖν *sedecim* ἔφηβον, *tunc septemdecim* ἐξέφηβον.

64. gymnasi flos : with the figure cf. 17. 14 n. — **olei** : *i.e.* palaestrae, as the contestants were well rubbed with oil before the sports; cf. Cic. *De Or.* I. 18. 81 *nitidum . . . genus uerborum . . . sed palaestrae . . . et olei.*

65. ianuae frequentes: devoted admirers flocked to his doors by day. — **limina tepida**: finding no entrance, his lovers spent the night in complaints on his door-stone; cf. Plat. *Symp.* 183 A οἱ ἐρασταὶ . . . ποιούμενοι . . . κοιμήσεις ἐπὶ θύραις; Aristaenetus 2. 20 ὅτε μὲν γὰρ αὐτοὶ ποθεῖτε, ἀστρώτους καὶ χαμαιπετεῖς κοιμήσεις ἐπὶ θύραις ποιεῖσθε; Hor. *Carm.* III. 10. 20 *non hoc semper erit liminis patiens*

latus; Prop. I. 16. 22 *tristis et in tepido limine somnus erit;* Ov. *Met.* XIV. 709 *posuit in limine duro molle latus.*

66. corollis: the door-posts and threshold were decorated with garlands by the lovers in token of their devotion; cf. Lucr. IV. 1177 *at lacrimans exclusus amator limina saepe floribus et sertis operit;* Ov. *Met.* XIV. 708 *interdum madidas lacrimarum rore coronas postibus intendit;* Prop. I. 16. 7 *mihi non desunt turpes pendere corollae.*

67. linquendum ubi, etc.: the proudly careless boy affected so completely to disregard the attentions of his lovers as to be aware of them only as he left the house in the morning for the stadium and palaestra. — **esset**: only one earlier instance of the subjunctive of repetition with *ubi* can be cited (Plaut. *Bacch.* 431). In the silver age the construction becomes more frequent; cf. Hor. *Carm.* III. 6. 41 *sol ubi montium mutaret umbras.*

68. deum ministra: not specifically a servant of the general pantheon, but simply *a temple servant,* an unknown priest instead of the beloved of a city: the needful specification follows in **Cybeles famula**; cf. Tac. *Ann.* I. 10. 5; IV. 37. 5 *effigie numinum.* — **ministra, famula**: not content with the contrast between the lord of a cityful of lovers and the slave of a mysterious divinity, Attis brands his present disgrace by using the feminine form.

Ego maenas, ego mei pars, ego uir sterilis ero ?
70 Ego uiridis algida Idae niue amicta loca colam ?
Ego uitam agam sub altis Phrygiae columinibus,
Vbi cerua siluicultrix, ubi aper nemoriuagus ?
Iam iam dolet quod egi, iam iamque paenitet.'
Roseis ut huic labellis sonitus citus abiit
75 Geminas deorum ad aures noua nuntia referens,
Ibi iuncta iuga resoluens Cybele leonibus
Laeuumque pecoris hostem stimulans ita loquitur.

69. **maenas**: cf. v. 23 n. *maenades.*

70. **uiridis Idae**: cf. v. 30 n.

71. **altis Phrygiae columinibus**: the following verse makes it
clear that mountain-summits are
meant, though the form appears to
be used only here in that sense ;
but the form *culmen* is so used by
Caesar (*B. G.* III. 2) and by Suetonius (*Dom.* 23), and perhaps *columinibus* is here used *metri gratia.*

72. **siluicultrix, nemoriuagus**:
each adjective is ἅπ. λεγ., though
Vergil (*Aen.* X. 551) uses *siluicola*,
and Lucretius (II. 597) *montiua-
gum.*

73. **iam iam**: with the repetition
cf. Cic. *Phil.* II. 34. 87 *iam iam
minime miror te otium perturbare;*
Verg. *Aen.* XII. 875 *iam iam lin-
quo acies.* — **iam iamque**: not = *et
iam iam,* for the passionate exclamation of sorrow demands an asyndeton; the phrase rather = *iam et
iam;* cf. Cic. *Att.* VII. 20. 1 *at illum ruere nuntiant et iam iamque
adesse;* XVI. 9 *iam iamque uideo
bellum :* and in Catullus himself 38.
3 and 64. 274 *magis magis* beside
68. 48 *magis atque magis.*

74. **roseis labellis**: the youthful
beauty of Attis is thus contrasted
with the intensity of his suffering
and the bitterness of his plaint ; cf.
45. 12 n. *purpureo ore.*

75. **geminas**: cf. 51. 11 *gemina
teguntur lumina nocte* (where, however, there is a transfer of epithet);
Culex 150 *geminas aures;* Verg.
Aen. V. 416 *temporibus geminis;*
Ov. *Fast.* II. 154 *geminos pedes;*
Stat. *Silu.* IV. 4. 26 *geminas aures;*
Mart. X. 10. 10 *geminas manus.* —
deorum aures: somewhat loosely
said, as if Cybele were not alone on
the summit of Ida, but in the company of the other gods. — **nuntia**:
the neuter singular in the sense of
'news' is very unusual, and the
neuter plural in the same sense is
still more rare ; cf. however Sedul.
II. 474 *grandia nuntia.*

76. **iuga resoluens**: while un-
fastening the lion from the yoke
she addresses him. Cybele is often
depicted by the poets as riding in a
chariot drawn by yoked lions ; cf.
Lucr. II. 600 *hanc ueteres Graium
docti cecinere poetae sedibus in curru
biiugos agitare leones;* Verg. *Aen.*
III. 113 *et iuncti currum dominae
subiere leones;* X. 253 *biiugi ad
frena leones.*

77. **laeuum**: the 'nigh' lion ;
the specification is doubtless introduced for the sake of increasing the
realistic effect of the lion's attack by
details of word painting. — **pecoris
hostem**: probably with reference
to the Greek descriptions of the lion
as ταυροβόρος (Anth. Plan. 94)

'Agedum' inquit, 'age ferox i, fac ut hunc furor agitet,
Fac uti furoris ictu reditum in nemora ferat,
80 Mea libere nimis qui fugere imperia cupit.
  Age caede terga cauda, tua uerbera patere,
  Fac cuncta mugienti fremitu loca retonent,
  Rutilam ferox torosa ceruice quate iubam.'
  Ait haec minax Cybelle religatque iuga manu.
85 Ferus ipse sese adhortans rabidum incitat animo,
  Vadit, fremit, refringit uirgulta pede uago.
  At ubi umida albicantis loca litoris adiit
  Tenerumque uidit Attin prope marmora pelagi,

ταυροκτόνος (Soph. *Ph.* 400), ταυρο-
λέτωρ (Man. *Chron.* 252), ταυρο-
σφάγος (Lyc. 47), ταυροφόνος
(Orph. *Hym.* 14. 2); for *pecus* indicates neat cattle as well as sheep;
cf. Varro *R. R.* II. 1. 12 *de pecore
maiore, in quo sunt . . . boues,
asini, equi.* — stimulans : probably
not with a goad, but with her words.

78. agedum, age : with the repetition cf. Ter. *And.* 310 *age age.* —
fac ut : with the construction cf. v.
79 ; 64. 231 ; 109. 3 ; but for *fac*
and subjunctive without *ut*, v. 82 ;
68. 46.

79. reditum ferat : cf. v. 47 *reditum tetulit.*

81. caede terga cauda : this
habit of the lion in rage is noted
by Plin. *N. H.* VIII. 16. 49, and by
Luc. *Phar.* I. 208 *mox ubi se saeuae
stimulauit uerbere caudae erexitque
iubam et uasto graue murmur hiatu
infremuit.*

82. fac retonent : with the construction cf. 68. 46 and v. 78 n.
retonent is ἅπαξ λεγόμενον.

84. minax : of Cybele's attitude
toward Attis. — religat iuga, *frees
the lion from the yoke*, completing
the action begun in v. 76 *iuncta
iuga resoluens ;* with this conjunction of *resoluere* and *religare* in the

same meaning cf. Pallad. Rut. III.
13 *prouidendum est omnibus annis
uitem resolui ac religari.* For *religare* in the other sense cf. 64. 174.

85. rabidum : Cybele's exhortation was to arouse the lion to fury
rather than to haste, and that is
the characteristic passion of his
subsequent action; hence *rapidum*,
the reading of *V*, must be an error
for *rabidum*, as *rapidos* for *rabidos*
in v. 93, where a similar collocation
occurs, *incitatos rabidos* being like
rabidum incitat.

86. pede uago : the lion rushes
now here, now there, in search of
his prey; otherwise in 64. 277.

87. albicantis : not of the general color of sea-sand, but of the
whiteness and sparkle of a foam-
wet beach, as the position and use
of umida indicate. — loca litoris :
cf. v. 70 *Idae loca.*

88. tenerum : not of the beauty,
but of the present effeminate condition of Attis ; cf. Juv. 1. 22 *tener
spado.* — marmora pelagi : cf.
Hom. *Il.* XIV. 273 ἅλα μαρμαρέην.
The word seems to describe the
sparkling of the sea that occurs
when it is covered with ripples only,
and hence to convey the idea of a
calm expanse (*nitens aequor*).

Facit impetum : ille demens fugit in nemora fera :
90 Ibi semper omne uitae spatium famula fuit.

Dea magna, dea Cybelle, dea domina Dindymi,
Procul a mea tuus sit furor omnis, era, domo :
Alios age incitatos, alios age rabidos.

64.

Peliaco quondam prognatae uertice pinus
Dicuntur liquidas Neptuni nasse per undas

89. **demens** : *sc.* with present fear, not with past recollections.

90. **famula** : repeating the feminine used by Attis himself in v. 68, and leaving with the reader, as the final thought, the irrevocable character of the awful self-consecration with which the poem opened.

91–93. The epilogue is a brief hymn to the dread goddess herself.

91. **dea magna**: cf. Prop. IV. 17. 35 *dea magna Cybelle*. — **domina Dindymi**: cf. v. 13; 35. 14.

92. **procul**, etc.: cf. Ov. *Fast.* IV. 116 *a nobis sit furor iste procul*.

93. **age**: with the verb in this sense with an adjective expressing, as it were, the result of the action, cf. Ov. *Met.* V. 13 *quae te, germane, furentem mens agit in facinus?* Tac. *Agr.* 41 *sic Agricola . . . in ipsam gloriam praeceps agebatur.* — **incitatos . . . rabidos** ; cf. the same collocation in v. 85 *rabidum incitat.*

64. This poem, often called in the later MSS. and earlier editions the Epithalamium of Peleus and Thetis, is rather a brief epic, or epyllion, after the Alexandrian style, having for its basis the wedding of Peleus and Thetis, and for one of its divisions the marriage-song of the Parcae. But into this

epyllion is wrought another which details the story of Theseus and Ariadne under the guise of describing the embroidered drapery of the marriage-couch of Thetis. This second epyllion is even longer than the first, covering vv. 50–266, while the entire poem contains but 408 verses. — The date of composition is uncertain, though the finish of thought and expression seem to point to maturity of development on the part of the author. Metre, dactylic hexameter.

1–30. Introductory, explaining the circumstances that led to the marriage of Peleus and Thetis.

1. **Peliaco**: cf. the imitation of this proem by Ovid, *Am.* II. 11. 1 *prima malas docuit, mirantibus aequoris undis, Peliaco pinus uertice caesa uias;* Prop. IV. 22. 11 *tuque tuo Colchum propellas remige Phasin, Peliacaeque trabis totum iter ipse legas.* — **prognatae**: cf. the similar figure in Hor. *Carm.* I. 14. 12 [*pinus*] *siluae filia nobilis.*

2. **dicuntur**: the poet makes it clear that he is repeating an ancient tradition ; cf. vv. 19 *fertur*, 76 and 124 *perhibent*, 212 *ferunt.* — **liquidas** : not an otiose epithet, but indicating the unstable water as unfitted to support a heavy body ;

Phasidos ad fluctus et fines Aeeteos,
Cum lecti iuuenes, Argiuae robora pubis,
5 Auratam optantes Colchis auertere pellem
Ausi sunt uada salsa cita decurrere puppi,
Caerula uerrentes abiegnis aequora palmis.
Diua quibus retinens in summis urbibus arces
Ipsa leui fecit uolitantem flamine currum,
10 Pinea coniungens inflexae texta carinae.
Illa rudem cursu prima imbuit Amphitriten.

cf. Verg. *Aen.* V. 859 *liquidas pro-*
iecit in undas praecipitem ; Nemes.
Buc. 2. 76 *nec tremulum liquidis*
lumen splenderet in undis. —
nasse: cf. 4. 3 *natantis trabis ;*
66. 45 *iuuentus per medium nauit*
Athon.

3. **Phasidos**: the chief river of
Colchis, rising in the Caucasus and
flowing into the Euxine Sea at its
eastern end. — **Aeeteos**: Gr. Αἰη-
τείους : Aeetes was king of Colchis
and father of Medea.

4. **lecti iuuenes**: so the Argonauts are called by Ennius (*Med.*
Exsul 209 R. *Argiui delecti uiri*)
and Vergil (*Ecl.* 4. 34 *altera quae*
uehat Argo delectos heroas); cf. also
Theocr. 13. 18 πασᾶν ἐκ πολίων
προλελεγμένοι (of the Argonauts).

5. **auratam pellem**: for the
story of the Argonautic expedition
see Hom. *Od.* XII. 69; Hes. *Theog.*
992; Apollod. I. 9. 16 ff.; and the
poems by Pindar (*Pyth.* 4), Apollonius, and Valerius Flaccus. — **auer-**
tere, *to win ;* especially used of
plunder ; cf. Caes. *B. C.* III. 59. 4
praedam omnem domum auerte-
bant ; Cic. *Verr.* II. 3. 69. 163
innumerabilem frumenti numerum
auersum ab re publica esse ; Verg.
Aen. VIII. 207 *quattuor a stabulis*
tauros auertit.

6. **uada salsa**: cf. Verg. *Aen.*
V. 158 *longa sulcant uada salsa*

carina. — **cito decurrere puppi**
cf. Ov. *Fast.* VI. 777 *celeri decurrite*
cumba.

7. **caerula uerrentes aequora**:
cf. Verg. *Aen.* III. 208 *adnixi*
torquent spumas et caerula uer-
runt. — **palmis**: cf. 4. 4 n. *pal-*
mulis.

8. **diua retinens**, etc.: *i.e.*
Athena Polias ; cf. Verg. *Ecl.* 2.
61 *Pallas quas condidit arces ipsa*
colat. — **quibus**: referring to v. 4
lecti iuuenes. — **summis**: with the
partitive force.

9. **ipsa fecit**: Catullus here follows the tradition of Apollonius I.
111 αὐτὴ γὰρ καὶ νῆα θοὴν κάμε,
with which cf. Phaedr. IV. 7. 9
fabricasset Argus opere Palladio ra-
tem ; Sen. *Med.* 368 *non Palladia*
compacta manu Argo ; Val. Flac. I.
94. — **currum**: the newly invented
vehicle for the sea is described by
its similarity to those in use on land;
cf. Cic. *N. D.* II. 35. 89 *diuinum et*
nouum uehiculum Argonautarum ;
and v. 6 *decurrere.*

11. **cursu imbuit**: cf. Val. Flac.
I. 69 *ignaras Cereris qui uomere*
terras imbuit ; Sil. Ital. III. 64 *iu-*
uenem primo Hymenaeo imbuerat
coniunx. — **Amphitriten**: *i.e.* the
sea, as in Ov. *Met.* I. 14 *bracchia*
porrexerat Amphitrite. For the
descent of the goddess see v. 29 n.
Tethys.

Quae simul ac rostro uentosum proscidit aequor
Tortaque remigio spumis incanduit unda,
. Emersere freti candenti e gurgite uultus
15 Aequoreae monstrum Nereides admirantes.
Illa, siqua alia, uiderunt luce marinas
Mortales oculis nudato corpore nymphas
Nutricum tenus exstantes e gurgite cano. .
Tum Thetidis Peleus incensus fertur amore,
20 Tum Thetis humanos non despexit hymenaeos,
Tum Thetidi pater ipse iugandum Pelea sensit.

12. uentosum aequor : cf. Verg.
Aen. VI. 335 *a Troia uentosa per
aequora uectos ;* Ov. *Her.* 16. 5
uentosa per aequora uectum.

13. torta : cf. Verg. *Aen.* III. 208,
cited on v. 7.— incanduit unda : cf.
Ov. *Met.* IV. 530 *percussa recanduit
unda ;* and with incanduit in this
sense Plin. *Pan.* 30 *pars magna terrarum alto puluere incanduit.*

14. With the general picture cf.
Sil. Ital. VII. 412 ff. *ac totus multo
spumabat remige pontus, cum trepi-
dae fremitu uitreis e sedibus antri
aequoreae pelago simul emersere
sorores.* — freti : the MS. *feri*
hardly describes the beautiful faces
and forms of Thetis and her companions, being usually joined with
such adjectives as *immanis, inhu-
manus, immansuetum ;* but on freti
cf. *Oct.* 720 *talis emersam freto spu-
mante Peleus coniugem accepit The-
tim.* — candenti e gurgite : cf. v.
13 *incanduit unda ;* v. 18 *e gurgite
cano ;* Lucr. II. 767 [*mare*] *uerti-
tur in canos candenti marmore
fluctus ;* Sil. Ital. XIV. 362 *spumat
canenti sulcatus gurgite limes.*

15. monstrum admirantes : cf.
the wonder expressed by the shepherd at the sight of the Argo in
Accius ap. Cic. *N. D.* II. 35. 89. —
Nereides : sea-nymphs, daughters

of Nereus and Doris ; cf. v. 29 n.
Tethys.

17. oculis : emphasizing the re-
ality of the wonderful sight; cf.
Ter. *Eun.* 677 *hunc oculis suis nostrarum nunquam quisquam uidit.*

18. nutricum : the word occurs
only here in the sense of *papilla-
rium.* — tenus : with the genitive,
as in Cic. *Arat.* 83 *lumborum tenus,*
Verg. *Geor.* III. 53 *crurum tenus.*
— gurgite cano : cf. v. 14 n.;
Ciris 514 *cano de gurgite.*

19. tum : Catullus represents this
as the first meeting of Peleus and
Thetis; but, according to Apollonius
(I. 558), Peleus, though an Argo-
naut, was long since married; while
Valerius Flaccus (I. 130) represents
the wedding of Peleus and Thetis as
pictured among the adornments of
the Argo itself, and Achilles as
brought by Chiron to bid his father
good-by before the sailing (I. 255).
— fertur : cf. v. 2 n. *dicuntur.*

20. hymenaeos : plural, as in
v. 141; but singular with the same
meaning in 66. 11. On the lengthening of the preceding short syllable
see Intr. 86 *g.*

21. pater ipse : *i.e.* Zeus, who
had himself intended to wed Thetis; but being warned by the Fates
(or, according to other stories. by

O nimis optato saeclorum tempore nati
Heroes, saluete, deum genus, o bona matrum
23b Progenies, saluete iterum . . .
Vos ego saepe meo, uos carmine compellabo,
25 Teque adeo eximie taedis felicibus aucte
Thessaliae columen Peleu, cui Iuppiter ipse,
Ipse suos diuum genitor concessit amores.
Tene Thetis tenuit pulcherrima Nereine?
Tene suam Tethys concessit ducere neptem
30 Oceanusque, mari totum qui amplectitur orbem?

Themis, or by Prometheus) that the
son of Thetis would be greater than
his father, he gave up his purpose,
and furthermore, fearing that his
own throne might be endangered
by the existence of a rival, declared
that Thetis should wed no immor-
tal; cf. Aesch. *Prom.* 167 ff., 907 ff.;
Ov. *Met.* XI. 221 ff.

22. nimis optato: cf. 43. 4 n.
nimis, and with the general sentiment of the verse, Verg. *Aen.* VI.
649 *magnanimi heroes, nati meli-
oribus annis.*

**23 f. saluete . . . saluete ite-
rum**: cf. Verg. *Aen.* V. 80 *salue,
sancte parens; iterum saluete,* etc.
— **matrum**: either there is hypallage of the adjective, or *bonarum*
must be supplied in the lacuna, as
Peerlkamp suggested. With the
idea cf. 61. 226 ff.

23b. Cf. Crit. App.

24. Cf. Theocr. I. 144 ὦ χαίρετε
πολλάκι Μοῖσαι, χαίρετ'· ἐγὼ δ'
ὕμμιν καὶ ἐς ὕστερον ἅδιον ᾀσῶ.

25. taedis aucte: cf. 66. 11
auctus hymenaeo.

26. Thessaliae columen: cf.
Ter. *Phor.* 287 *columen familiae;*
Hor. *Carm.* II. 17. 3 *mearum colu-
men rerum;* Sen. *Troad.* 128
columen patriae; Hom. *Il.* ἕρκος
Ἀχαιῶν.

27. amores: not of Thetis herself (cf. 6. 16 n.), but of the passion
of Zeus for her, — 'in whose favor
the father of the gods himself re-
signed his passion.' With the plural cf. 38. 6; 64. 334, 372; 68. 69;
96. 3 ; Plaut. *Merc.* 2 *et argumentum et meos amores eloquar;* Hor.
Carm. II. 9. 10 *nec tibi Vespero
surgente decedunt amores;* Verg.
Ecl. 9. 56 *nostros in longum ducis
amores.*

28. tenuit: *sc. complexu;* cf.
72. 2; but otherwise in 11. 18; 55.
17. — **Nereine**: Gr. Νηρηΐνη; but
elsewhere the Latins use either
Nereis (cf. v. 15) or *Nerine* (cf.
Verg. *Ecl.* 7. 37 *Nerine Galatea*).

29. Tethys: the daughter of
Uranus and Ge, and the wife of her
own brother Oceanus, by whom
she became the mother of the sea-
nymphs called Oceanides, of the
rivers of earth, and of Nereus.
From the marriage of Nereus with
his sister Doris, one of the Oceanides, sprang the sea-nymphs called
Nereides, of whom the most famous
were Thetis, Amphitrite, the wife
of Poseidon, and Galatea, the beloved of Polyphemus.

**30. totum amplectitur or-
bem**: cf. Hom. *Il.* XVIII. 399
ἀψορρόου Ὠκεανοῖο; Aesch. *Prom.*

Quae simul optatae finito tempore luces
Aduenere, domum conuentu tota frequentat
Thessalia, oppletur laetanti regia coetu :
Dona ferunt prae se, declarant gaudia uultu.
35 Deseritur Cieros, linquunt Phthiotica Tempe
Crannonisque domos ac moenia Larisaea,
Pharsalum coeunt, Pharsalia tecta frequentant.
Rura colit nemo, mollescunt colla iuuencis,
Non humilis curuis purgatur uinea rastris,

138 τοῦ περὶ πᾶσάν θ' εἰλισσομένου
χθόν' ἀκοιμήτῳ ῥεύματι . . . πατ-
ρὸς Ὠκεανοῦ ; Val. Flac. I. 195 terras salo complecteris omnes ; Pan.
Mess. (Tib. IV. 1) 147 Oceanus
ponto qua continet orbem ; Bryant
Thanatopsis 42 and, poured round
all, Old Ocean's gray and melan-
choly waste.

31–42. The introductory narra-
tive finished, the poet turns to the
main theme, and describes first the
gathering of the mortal wedding-
guests.

31. quae luces: with a general
reference to the fixing of the wedding-day in v. 29. — simul: sc.
atque; cf. 22. 15 n. — optatae: cf.
with the thought, 62. 30; 66. 79.

32. domum: sc. of Peleus.

34. dona: wedding-gifts, not pro-
pitiatory offerings to a superior. —
prae se: thus commonly of things
carried in the hands ; cf. Verg.
Aen. XI. 249 munera praeferimus.

35. Cieros: otherwise Cierium,
a town of Thessaliotis, according to
Strabo 435. — Phthiotica Tempe:
with a poet's license concerning
geography, Catullus calls the famous
vale of Tempe through which the
Peneus flows (cf. v. 285) Phthiotic,
as synonymous with Thessalian in
general, though in strictness the
district of Phthiotis was the south-
ernmost of the divisions of Thessaly,

extending not so far north even as
Pharsalus.

36. Crannon and Larisa were
both towns of Pelasgiotis near the
Peneus.

37. Pharsalum coeunt: the
commoner form of the legend
made Mt. Pelion the place of the
wedding, and Chiron the host.

38. mollescunt colla iuuencis:
since they no longer bore the yoke;
in this expression, as in the following verses, the absolute desertion of
the farm is pictured by representing
it as if it had lasted a long time.

39 f. Cf. Verg. Ecl. 4. 40, 41
non rastros patietur humus, non
uinea falcem ; robustus quoque iam
tauris iuga soluet arator. — humilis uinea: here, as, according to
Varro (R. R. I. 8), in Spain and
some parts of Asia, the vines were
not trained on trees, but either ran
along the ground or were so cut as
to be kept low. The latter plan
is followed to-day in the great vine-
yards of California, and to some
extent in Italy itself. — curuis: perhaps referring to the crescent-shaped
iron, the two points of which form
the teeth of the rastrum pictured
in Rich's Dict. Ant. s.v. — rastris:
the rastrum was a heavy sort of
rake of from two to four strong iron
teeth, used to break up clods and to
loosen the surface of the ground.

40 Non glaebam prono conuellit uomere taurus,
    Non falx attenuat frondatorum arboris umbram,
    Squalida desertis robigo infertur aratris.
    Ipsius at sedes, quacumque opulenta recessit
    Regia, fulgenti splendent auro atque argento.
45 Candet ebur soliis, conlucent pocula mensae,
    Tota domus gaudet regali splendida gaza.
    Puluinar uero diuae geniale locatur
    Sedibus in mediis, Indo quod dente politum
    Tincta tegit roseo conchyli purpura fuco.

40. prono: of the point of the share *down-pressed*, that it may cut a deep furrow; cf. Verg. *Geor*. I. 45 *depresso aratro;* II. 203 *presso sub uomere.*

41. attenuat arboris umbram: that the sun may reach and ripen the grapes. Attempts have been made by various critics to rearrange vv. 38–42 so as to produce a more consistent picture by bringing together details that concern the same objects ; but there seems to be no good reason for criticising the alternation of the description between the tasks which men performed alone and those in which cattle shared (after the general statement made in v. 38 that men and beasts ceased from toil).

43–266. The adornment of the palace of Peleus.

43. ipsius: *i.e.* Peleus ; such a remote reference of *ipse*, so that it is equivalent to some such word as *dominus*, is not uncommon ; cf. 114. 6; Ter. *Andr.* 360 *paululum obsoni ; ipsus tristis;* Verg. *Ecl.* 3. 3 *ipse Neaeram dum fouet ;* Juv. 1. 61 *lora tenebat ipse.* — **opulenta recessit regia**: the guest standing at the door looks through an imposing vista of room succeeding room ; cf. on the word Verg. *Aen.* II.

300 *Anchisae domus arboribus obtecta recessit ;* Plin. *Ep.* II. 17. 21 *contra parietem medium zotheca recedit;* and with the idea, the description of the first series of rooms in Pliny's villa (*Ep.* II. 17. 5).

44 ff. Cf. Vergil's description of Dido's palace in *Aen.* I. 637–641.

45. candet ebur soliis: the couches arranged about the tables have ivory legs; cf. v. 303 and 61. 115; like **mensae, soliis is a dative.**

46. gaudet: *i.e.* wears a festive appearance, as Sirmio was to do at the master's return (31. 12); cf. Hor. *Carm.* IV. 11. 6 *ridet argento domus.*

47. puluinar geniale: for *lectus genialis,* as a more formal and imposing term, and one especially connected with divinity.

48. sedibus in mediis: the poet is apparently thinking of a Roman house, where the *lectus genialis* stood in the *atrium*. — **Indo dente politum** = *ebore polito ;* cf. Ov. *Met.* VIII. 288 *dentes* [*apri*] *aequantur dentibus Indis.*

49. Observe the favorite contrast of color between the ivory of the couch and its crimson drapery ; cf. Hor. *Sat.* II. 6. 102 *rubro ubi cocco tincta super lectos canderet uestis eburnos.*

50 Haec uestis priscis hominum uariata figuris
　 Heroum mira uirtutes indicat arte.
　 Namque fluentisono prospectans litore Diae
　 Thesea cedentem celeri cum classe tuetur
　 Indomitos in corde gerens Ariadna furores,
55 Necdum etiam sese quae uisit uisere credit,
　 Vt pote fallaci quae tunc primum excita somno
　 Desertam in sola miseram se cernat harena.
　 Immemor at iuuenis fugiens pellit uada remis,
　 Irrita uentosae linquens promissa procellae.
60 Quem procul ex alga maestis Minois ocellis

50. With this verse begins the episode of Ariadne's Lament, which extends through v. 266, thus forming more than half of the entire poem, and setting in striking contrast the unhappy love of Ariadne with the happy love of Thetis. Episodic digressions of a similar character, depicting actions represented in graving or embroidery, are as old as the description of the shield of Achilles (Hom. *Il.* XVIII. 478 ff.), and are multiplied in later writers. With the episode of Catullus may be compared the story of Ariadne as told by Ovid in *Art. Am.* I. 527–564; *Her.* 10.

52. **fluentisono**: ἅπαξ λεγόμενον, though *fluctisonus* and *undisonus* are found in post-Augustan poets. The word has reference to the crash of breakers upon a rock-bound coast, perhaps here to point the impossibility of escape; cf. v. 121 *spumosa ad litora Diae*, and the more neutral epithet used by Homer in *Od.* XI. 325 Δίῃ ἐν ἀμφιρύτῃ. — **Diae**: asserted by several of the Greeks to be but an earlier name for Naxos. But Homer (*Od.* XI. 321 ff.) very probably thought of the island of Dia that lies very near the north coast of

Crete, whence the tradition may have been transferred to Naxos, the favorite haunt of Dionysus, as the later story of Ariadne's rescue by Dionysus gained ground. Catullus certainly must have followed the later tradition, if he had any definite tradition in mind.

53. A favorite subject in the Pompeian frescoes is Ariadne awaking from sleep and gazing after the departing ship of Theseus; cf. Roux *Herc. et Pompeii, passim.* — **classe**: cf. v. 212 n.

54. **indomitos furores**: of uncontrollable love; cf. 50. 11; 64. 94; 68. 129.

55. Cf. Ov. *Her.* 10. 31 *aut uidi, aut tanquam quae me uidisse putarem.*

56. **fallaci**: sleep is traitorous since he made the secret flight of Theseus possible; cf. Ov. *Her.* 10. 5 *in quo me somnusque meus male prodidit et tu.*

57. **desertam, miseram**: with this use of the adjective *miser*, instead of the adverb, with another adjective, cf. 65. 21 *miserae oblitae.*

58. **immemor**: used absolutely and with similar meaning in 30. 1.

59. Cf. 30. 10 n.

60. **ex alga**: *i.e.* from the beach;

Saxea ut effigies bacchantis prospicit, eheu,
Prospicit et magnis curarum fluctuat undis,
Non flauo retinens subtilem uertice mitram,
Non contecta leui uelatum pectus amictu,
65 Non tereti strophio lactentis uincta papillas,
Omnia quae toto delapsa e corpore passim
Ipsius ante pedes fluctus salis adludebant.
Sic neque tum mitrae neque tum fluitantis amictus
Illa uicem curans toto ex te pectore, Theseu,

v. 168 ; Mart. X. 16. 5 *quidquid Erythraea niger inuenit Indus in alga.*

61. The figure is that of a Bacchante speechless, motionless, and utterly forgetful of her own appearance through the very exaltation of her wild emotions ; cf. Hor. *Carm.* III. 25. 8 *non secus in iugis Edonis stupet Euhias Hebrum prospiciens;* Ov. *Her.* 10. 49 *mare prospiciens in saxo frigida sedi, quamque lapis sedes, tam lapis ipsa fui.* — **prospicit, eheu, prospicit** : she stands absorbed in long-continued, but alas, fruitless gazing.

62. **curarum** : cf. 2. 10 n. — **undis** : with the figure cf. Lucr. III. 298 *irarum fluctus ;* VI. 34 *uoluere curarum tristis in pectore fluctus ;* Verg. *Aen.* IV. 532 *saeuit amor, magnoque irarum fluctuat aestu;* VIII. 19 *magno curarum fluctuat aestu.*

63. **flauo**, etc. : cf. the apparent reminiscence in *Ciris* 511 *purpureas flauo retinentem uertice uittas.* Fair hair is traditionally a mark of beauty in the poets. — **subtilem mitram**: the finely-woven, variegated coif worn by Greek women, as by Orientals in general. In Greece it seems to have consisted of a sort of scarf arranged either as headdress or as girdle.

64. **non contecta**, etc.: her

breast unshielded by its veil of light drapery. With the reinforcement of the idea by the introduction of **uelatum** cf. v. 103 *ingrata . . . frustra* (but see Crit. App.). — **leui amictu**: doubtless the *chiton ;* cf. Ov. *Art. Am.* I. 529 *ut erat e somno tunica uelata recincta, nuda pedem, croceas inreligata comas.*

65. **strophio**: a girdle woven or wound like a cord (cf. **tereti**, and the mother's dress in the well-known Herculanean Toilet of the Bride), and worn by women over the inner tunic just below the breasts, to which it was apparently designed to furnish support. — **lactentis** : not of the color, but of the full development, of the breasts in the mature woman; cf. Verg. *Geor.* I. 315 *frumenta in uiridi stipula lactentia turgent ;* Ov. *Fast.* I. 351 *sata uere nouo teneris lactentia sucis ;* and especially Petron. 86 *impleui lactentibus papillis manus.*

67 f. **adludebant**: with the figure cf. Cic. *N. D.* II. 39. 100 *ipsum mare terram appetens litoribus adludit ;* Top. 7. 32 *solebat Aquilius quaerentibus iis quid esset litus ita definire, qua fluctus eluderet.*

69. **toto pectore, toto animo, tota mente**: cf. *Vulg. Luc.* 10. 27 *diliges dominum deum tuum ex toto corde tuo, et ex tota anima tua, . . . et ex omni mente tua.*

70 Toto animo, tota pendebat perdita mente.

Ah misera, adsiduis quam luctibus exsternauit

Spinosas Erycina serens in pectore curas

Illa tempestate, ferox quo ex tempore Theseus

Egressus curuis e litoribus Piraei

75 Attigit iniusti regis Gortynia tecta.

Nam perhibent olim crudeli peste coactam

Androgeoneae poenas exsoluere caedis

Electos iuuenes simul et decus innuptarum

Cecropiam solitam esse dapem dare Minotauro.

80 Quis angusta malis cum moenia uexarentur,

71. **exsternauit**: apparently the first appearance of this rare word; cf. also only v. 165; Ov. *Met.* I. 641; XI. 77; and much later Latin.

72. **Erycina**: Venus was so called by the Romans from her ancient and famous shrine on Mt. Eryx in western Sicily.

73. **illa tempestate quo ex tempore**: a variation of the ordinary prose pleonasm *illo die quo die.* For one simple ablative repeated by another with *ex* cf. 35. 13 *quo tempore . . . ex eo*, where, as here, the starting-point of a continued effect is indicated. — **ferox**: used absolutely, as in v. 247.

74. **curuis litoribus**: embracing the harbor.

75. **iniusti**: so called of course from the Athenian standpoint, since he required such a heavy penalty for the death of one man, his son; but cf. Ov. *Her.* 10. 69 *pater et tellus iusto regnata parenti*, and the references to Minos as appointed because of his justice to judge souls in the lower world, *e.g.* Hom. *Od.* XI. 568 Ἔνθ᾽ ἦ τοι Μίνωα ἴδον, Διὸς ἀγλαὸν υἱόν, χρύσεον σκῆπτρον ἔχοντα, θεμιστεύοντα νέκυσσιν; Hor. *Carm.* IV. 7. 21 *cum semel occideris et de te splendida Minos fecerit arbitria.*

— **Gortynia**: probably simply 'Cretan'; cf. v. 172 *Gnosia litora.*

76. **nam perhibent**: the poet drops the thread of his story for a moment to relate the circumstances that led to the present condition of Ariadne; cf. v. 2 n. *dicuntur.*

77. **Androgeoneae caedis**: Androgeos, son of Minos and Pasiphae, conquered all his competitors at wrestling in Athens, and was through jealousy assassinated while on his way to the games at Thebes. According to another story, King Aegeus himself caused his death by sending him against the fire-breathing Marathonian bull. Minos thereupon besieged the Athenians, who were compelled to yield to him by a pestilence sent by the gods, and to accept his hard conditions of peace.

78. **electos**: cf. v. 4 *lecti iuuenes.* The number is commonly given as seven of each sex (as also, perhaps, in Verg. *Aen.* VI. 20 ff.). — **innuptarum**: for *uirginum*, as in 62. 6.

79. **Cecropiam**: traditionally the ancient name of the city of King Cecrops, which was called *Athenae* after the goddess Athena became recognized as its patron.

80. **angusta**: of the small size of the young city, and not of the

Ipse suum Theseus pro caris corpus Athenis
Proicere optauit potius quam talia Cretam
Funera Cecropiae nec funera portarentur.
Atque ita naue leui nitens ac lenibus auris
85 Magnanimum ad Minoa uenit sedesque superbas.
Hunc simul ac cupido conspexit lumine uirgo
Regia, quam suauis exspirans castus odores
Lectulus in molli complexu matris alebat,
Quales Eurotae progignunt flumina myrtos
90 Auraue distinctos educit uerna colores,
Non prius ex illo flagrantia declinauit
Lumina quam cuncto concepit corpore flammam

straitening by the hardships of siege.

83. **funera nec funera** : with the oxymoron cf. 112. 1 *multus neque multus* (where, however, there is an ἀμφιβολία); Cic. *Phil.* I. 2. 5 *insepultam sepulturam;* Ov. *Art. Am.* II. 93 *pater nec iam pater* (repeated in *Met.* VIII. 231) ; and especially such favorite Greek expressions as πόλεμος ἀπόλεμος, τάφος ἄταφος, etc. The reference is doubtless to the life-in-death of the victims on their way to Crete, who were mourned as dead from the moment of their sailing.

84. **atque ita** : *i.e.* with the purpose mentioned in the preceding verses; cf. v. 315 *atque ita.* — **naue leui et lenibus auris** : the happy indications of a swift and prosperous voyage are contrasted with the shrinking horror and dread in the hearts of the passengers. — **nitens,** *pressing forward.*

85. **magnanimum** : the Homeric μεγάθυμος. — **sedes superbas,** *the abode of tyranny;* with reference to v. 75 *iniusti regis.*

86 ff. This account of the sudden love of Ariadne for Theseus closely

resembles that given by Apollonius (III. 275 ff.) in describing Medea's love for Jason. — **uirgo regia** : *i.e.* Ariadne; cf. Ov. *Met.* II. 570 *fueramque ego regia uirgo.*

87. **suauis exspirans odores lectulus** : cf. *Ciris* 3 *suaues exspirans hortulus auras.* The idea seems to have been suggested by the Homeric phrase θάλαμος θυώδης (*e.g. Od.* IV. 121).

88. **in molli complexu matris** : cf. 61. 58; 62. 21.

89. **quales**, etc.: cf. 61. 22 n.

90. **aura educit** : cf. v. 282; 62. 41 n. — **colores** : by metonymy for *flores;* cf. Val. Flac. *Arg.* VI. 492 *lilia per uarios lucent uelut alba colores.*

91. **non prius**, etc.: cf. 51. 6 (and note), and contrast the idea with the more complex treatment of Medea's first passion in Ov. *Met.* VII. 86 ff.

92. **cuncto**, etc.: cf., however, the commoner phrase in Verg. *Aen.* VII. 356 *necdum animus toto percepit pectore flammam ;* Ov. *Met.* VII. 17 *excute uirgineo conceptas pectore flammas;* Petron. 127 *Iuppiter et toto concepit pectore flammas.* On the figure see 2. 8 n.

Funditus atque imis exarsit tota medullis.

Heu misere exagitans immiti corde furores,

95 Sancte puer, curis hominum qui gaudia misces,

Quaeque regis Golgos quaeque Idalium frondosum,

Qualibus incensam iactastis mente puellam

Fluctibus in flauo saepe hospite suspirantem!

Quantos illa tulit languenti corde timores,

100 Quanto saepe magis fulgore expalluit auri,

Cum saeuum cupiens contra contendere monstrum

Aut mortem appeteret Theseus aut praemia laudis.

　　Non ingrata tamen frustra munuscula diuis

Promittens tacito succendit uota labello.

105 Nam uelut in summo quatientem bracchia Tauro

Quercum aut conigeram sudanti cortice pinum

Indomitus turbo contorquens flamine robur

Eruit (illa procul radicitus exturbata

Prona cadit, † lateque cum eius obuia frangens),

110 Sic domito saeuum prostrauit corpore Theseus

---

93. imis medullis: cf. 35. 15 n.

95. sancte: a general epithet of divinity; cf. 36. 3 n.; Tib. II. 1. 81 *sancte* [*Amor*], *ueni dapibus festis, sed pone sagittas.* — curis, etc.: cf. the similar phrase concerning Venus in 68. 18 *quae dulcem curis miscet amaritiem.*

96. Cf. 36. 12 ff.

98. flauo hospite: cf. v. 63 n.

100. quanto magis expalluit: with the construction cf. Cic. *Acad.* I. 3. 10 *quanto magis philosophi delectabunt;* with the figure, 81. 4. Dark-complexioned people, as the people of southern Europe usually are, turn yellow rather than white when pale.

103. ingrata, frustra: with the pleonasm cf. v. 64 *contecta, uelatum;* with ingrata in this passive sense,

'without due return,' cf. 73. 3; 76. 6; but in the active sense, 'ungrateful,' 76. 9.

104. tacito succendit uota labello: the beautiful figure of the incense of prayer is unique in Latin in this pure form, but is so simple that its authenticity is above reasonable suspicion. The connection of prayers with incense-offering is not infrequently noted; cf. Stat. *Theb.* XI. 236 *uota incepta tamen libataque tura ferebat.* Ariadne's prayer was offered silently, as became her maidenly feeling, and the necessary concealment of her love from her friends.

105 ff. uelut, etc.: with the figure cf. Verg. *Aen.* II. 626 ff.; Hor. *Carm.* IV. 6. 9 ff.; and often.

110. saeuum: apparently used

Nequiquam uanis iactantem cornua uentis.

Inde pedem sospes multa cum laude reflexit

Errabunda regens tenui uestigia filo,

Ne labyrintheis e flexibus egredientem

115 Tecti frustraretur inobseruabilis error.

  Sed quid ego a primo digressus carmine plura

Commemorem, ut linquens genitoris filia uultum,

Vt consanguineae complexum, ut denique matris,

Quae misera in gnata deperdita laetabatur,

120 Omnibus his Thesei dulcem praeoptarit amorem,

here, though perhaps here only, as a substantive, indicating the distinctive characteristic of this monster, as *ferus*, so often used substantively, (*e.g.* 63. 85), characterizes ordinary wild beasts.

111. nequiquam, etc.: cf. Cic. *Att.* VIII. 5. 1 πολλὰ μάτην κεράεσσιν ἐς ἠέρα θυμήναντα; cf. also Verg. *Aen.* XII. 105 [*taurus*] *uentos lacessit ictibus.* — uanis: *unsubstantial*, offering no resistance; cf. Val. Flac. I. 421 *saltem in uacuos ut bracchia uentos spargat;* but Shelley *Medusa of Da Vinci* 23 *to saw The solid air with many a ragged jaw.*

112. pedem reflexit: perhaps the verb is selected because it suggests the turnings (v. 114) of the labyrinth. — multa cum laude: cf. Hor. *Carm.* IV. 4. 66 *multa proruit integrum cum laude uictorem.*

113. Cf. of the same incident Verg. *Aen.* VI. 30 *caeca regens filo uestigia;* Prop. III. 14. 8 *Daedalium lino cum duce rexit iter ;* Ov. *Her.* 10. 103 *nec tibi quae reditus monstrarent fila dedissem.*

114. labyrintheis: ἅπαξ λεγόμενον.

115. inobseruabilis error: cf. Verg. *Aen.* V. 591 *irremeabilis*

error ; VI. 27 *inextricabilis error* (of the Labyrinth); Apoll. Sid. *Ep.* II. 5 *inextricabilem labyrinthum negotii multiplicis ;* Plin. *N. H.* XXXVI. 85 *itinerum ambages occursusque ac recursus inexplicabiles continet ;* Ov. *Met.* VIII. 160 *turbatque notas, et lumina flexum ducit in errorem uariarum ambage uiarum ;* Shelley *Medusa of Da Vinci* 35 *that inextricable error.*

118. consanguineae: for *sororis.* Apollodorus (III. 1. 2) speaks of three other daughters of Minos besides Ariadne, — Acale, Xenodice, and Phaedra, of whom Catullus probably had in mind Phaedra, who is the most prominent of them in mythology, and was later the wife of Theseus himself.

119. misera: contrasting the present wretched condition of Ariadne, betrayed by a false love, with the affection formerly lavished upon her by her family. — deperdita: of the limitless love of the mother, rather than of her present unhappiness; cf. 45. 3; 104. 3.

120. Thesei: dissyllabic, like v. 382 *Pelei*, and *Culex* 278 *Orphei* (cited on v. 139). — praeoptarit: with the synizesis cf. Plaut. *Trin.* 648 *praeóptauisti amórem tuom uti uirtuti praepóneres ;* Ter. *Hec.*

Aut ut uecta rati spumosa ad litora Diae
Venerit, aut ut eam deuinctam lumina somno
Liquerit immemori discedens pectore coniunx?
Saepe illam perhibent ardenti corde furentem
125 Clarisonas imo fudisse ex pectore uoces,
Ac tum praeruptos tristem conscendere montes
Vnde aciem in pelagi uastos protenderet aestus,
Tum tremuli salis aduersas procurrere in undas
Mollia nudatae tollentem tegmina surae,
130 Atque haec extremis maestam dixisse querelis,
Frigidulos udo singultus ore cientem:
      ' Sicine me patriis auectam, perfide, ab aris,
Perfide, deserto liquisti in litore, Theseu?
Sicine discedens neglecto numine diuum
135 Immemor ah deuota domum periuria portas?

---

532 *ddeon peruicdci esse animo ut*
puerum praeoptarés perire.

121. spumosa litora Diae: cf.
v. 52 n.

**122. deuinctam lumina som-
no**: cf. *Ciris* 206 *iamque adeo dulci
deuinctus lumina somno Nisus erat.*

124. perhibent: cf. v. 2 n. *dicuntur.* — **ardenti corde**: cf. v.
197 *ardens.*

125. clarisonas: a rare word,
occurring only here (of the shrill
cries of anguish), in v. 320 (of the
shrill voice of age), and in Cic.
Arat. 280 *a clarisonis auris Aqui-
lonis* (of the shrilling blast). — **imo
ex pectore**: *i.e.* after a long-drawn,
sighing inspiration; cf. Verg. *Aen.*
I. 371 *suspirans imoque trahens a
pectore uocem.*

126 f. Cf. Ov. *Her.* 10. 25–28.

128. tremuli, *rippling;* cf. Ov.
Her. 11. 75 *ut mare fit tremulum,
tenui cum stringitur aura.* — **procurrere**: with the vain impulse to
follow the fleeing vessel.

129. mollia, *soft;* cf. 65. 21 *molli
sub ueste.* — **nudatae**: proleptic.

130. extremis: for her grief so
far overcomes her that she supposes
herself to be dying; cf. Prop. IV. 7.
55 *flens tamen extremis dedit haec
mandata querelis.*

131. frigidulos singultus: carrying on the idea of **extremis**, indicating the last panting breaths as
chill death creeps on; cf. *Ciris* 347
*super morientis alumnae frigidulos
ocellos.*

132–201. With the complaint of
Ariadne cf. similar passages in
Verg. *Aen.* IV. 590 ff. (the complaint of Dido); Ov. *Met.* VIII.
108–142 (of Scylla).

132. patriis ab aris = *a domo;*
cf. Verg. *Aen.* XI. 269 *patriis red-
ditus aris,* and often; Charis. 33 K.
arae pro penatibus.

134. neglecto numine diuum:
the gods punish infidelity of all
sorts; cf. 30. 3–4.

135. deuota: *i.e.* under the

Nullane res potuit crudelis flectere mentis
Consilium? tibi nulla fuit clementia praesto
Immite ut nostri uellet miserescere pectus?
At non haec quondam blanda promissa dedisti
140 Voce mihi, non haec miserae sperare iubebas,
Sed conubia laeta, sed optatos hymenaeos:
Quae cuncta aerii discerpunt irrita uenti.
Nunc iam nulla uiro iuranti femina credat,
Nulla uiri speret sermones esse fideles:
145 Quis dum aliquid cupiens animus praegestit apisci,
Nil metuunt iurare, nihil promittere parcunt:
Sed simul ac cupidae mentis satiata libido est,
Dicta nihil meminere, nihil periuria curant.
Certe ego te in medio uersantem turbine leti
150 Eripui et potius germanum amittere creui
Quam tibi fallaci supremo in tempore deessem:

ban of Ariadne's curse; cf. v.
192 ff.

139. **blanda uoce**: after the
wont of persuasive lovers; cf. Enn.
Ann. 51 *blanda uoce uocabam; Cu-*
lex 278 *turba ferarum blanda uoce*
sequax regionem insederat Orphei;
Ov. *Art. Am.* I. 703 *quid blanda*
uoce moraris? III. 795 *nec blandae*
uoces cessent.

140. **miserae**: the dative with
dedisti seems to be continued into
the **iubebas**-clause, though a simple infinitive and dative is a rare
construction with that verb.

141. **sed**, etc.: cf. the close verbal
and metrical resemblance of Verg.
Aen. IV. 316 *per conubia nostra,*
per inceptos hymenaeos. The repetition of **sed** corresponds to that of
non haec in v. 139 f. — **conubia**:
plural with singular meaning, as in
v. 158; but singular in 62. 57. —
hymenaeos: cf. v. 20 n.

142. **uenti**, etc.: cf. 30. 10 n.

143. **nunc,** etc.: cf. Ov. *Fast.* III.
475 *nunc quoque ' nulla uiro' cla-*
mabo ' femina credat' (spoken by
Ariadne with reference to the infidelity of Bacchus).

145. **praegestit**: the word apparently occurs only here, in Cic.
Cael. 67 *praegestit animus iam*
uidere, and in Hor. *Carm.* II. 5. 9
iuuencae ludere cum uitulis prae-
gestientis.

149. **turbine leti**: cf. Val. Flac.
VI. 279 *doloris turbine.*

150. **germanum**: *i.e.* the Minotaur; cf. v. 181; Ov. *Her.* 10. 115
dextera crudelis quae me fratrem-
que necauit. — **creui**: archaic for
decreui; cf. Lucil. XIII. 1 *acribus*
inter se cum armis confligere cer-
nit; Plaut. *Cist.* 1 *mihi amicam*
esse creui matrem tuam.

151. **supremo in tempore**: *i.e.*
in extreme danger of life; cf. v. 169
extremo tempore; Hor. *Carm.* II.
7. 1 *tempus in ultimum.*

Pro quo dilaceranda feris dabor alitibusque
Praeda neque iniecta tumulabor mortua terra.
Quaenam te genuit sola sub rupe leaena,

155 Quod mare conceptum spumantibus exspuit undis,
Quae Syrtis, quae Scylla rapax, quae uasta Charybdis,
Talia qui reddis pro dulci praemia uita ?
Si tibi non cordi fuerant conubia nostra,
Saeua quod horrebas prisci praecepta parentis,

160 At tamen in uestras potuisti ducere sedes
Quae tibi iucundo famularer serua labore
Candida permulcens liquidis uestigia lymphis
Purpureaue tuum consternens ueste cubile.
Sed quid ego ignaris nequiquam conqueror auris

---

152. dilaceranda, etc.: cf. Hom.
Il. I. 4 αὐτοὺς δὲ ἐλώρια τεῦχε κύνεσσιν
οἰωνοῖσί τε πᾶσι; Verg. *Aen.* IX. 485
*canibus data praeda Latinis aliti-
busque iaces;* Ov. *Her.* 10. 96 *destit-
uor rapidis praeda cibusque feris.*

153. iniecta . . . **terra**: the passage of the soul across the Styx was
secured only by due burial under at
least three handfuls of earth ; cf.
Hor. *Carm.* I. 28. 36 *licebit iniecto
ter puluere curras.*

154 ff. Cf. *c.* 60.

155. mare, etc.: cf. Hom. *Il.*
XVI. 34 γλαυκὴ δέ σε τίκτε θάλασσα
πέτραι δ᾽ ἠλίβατοι, ὅτι τοι νόος ἐστὶν
ἀπηνής.

156. Scylla rapax: cf. Ap. Sid.
Carm. 9. 165 *Scyllae rabidum uo-
racis inguen.*

157. dulci uita: cf. Hom. *Od.*
V. 152 γλυκὺς αἰών.

158. tibi cordi conubia: cf. 44.
3 ; 81. 5 ; 95. 9 ; Ter. *Andr.* 328
tibi nuptiae haec sunt cordi.

159. prisci, *stern*, as the older
days were proverbially the stricter ;
cf. Hor. *Carm.* III. 21. 11 *narratur
et prisci Catonis saepe mero caluisse*

uirtus. — **parentis** : of course Aegeus, and not Minos, is meant, and
the commands that would shut
Ariadne, the rescuer of his son, out
of his home she justly calls **saeua**;
cf. Hyg. *Fab.* 43 *Theseus in insula
Dia cogitans, si Ariadnen in patriam portasset, sibi opprobrium
futurum,* etc.

160. uestras : *i.e.* of Theseus and
his family; cf. v. 176 *nostris.*

161. serua, etc.: cf. Shakspere
Tempest III. 1 *to be your fellow You
may deny me; but I'll be your servant, Whether you will or no.*

162. permulcens, etc.: a common duty of female slaves, and
Ariadne would especially delight in
performing personal service for her
hero ; cf. Hom. *Od.* XIX. 386 ὣς
ἄρ᾽ ἔφη, γρῆυς δὲ λέβηθ᾽ ἕλε παμφα-
νόωντα, τοῦ πόδας ἐξαπένιζεν, etc. —
uestigia : for *pedes,* an extremely
rare use; but cf. Sen. *Thy.* 1043
rupta fractis cruribus uestigia;
Oed. 833 *forata ferro uestigia.*

164. sed quid, etc.: with the
rhetorical question in self-address
cf. v. 116 ff.

165 Exsternata malo, quae nullis sensibus auctae
    Nec missas audire queunt nec reddere uoces?
    Ille autem prope iam mediis uersatur in undis,
    Nec quisquam adparet uacua mortalis in alga.
    Sic nimis insultans extremo tempore saeua
170 Fors etiam nostris inuidit questibus auris.
    Iuppiter omnipotens, utinam ne tempore primo
    Gnosia Cecropiae tetigissent litora puppes,
    Indomito nec dira ferens stipendia tauro
    Perfidus in Creta religasset nauita funem,
175 Nec malus hic celans dulci crudelia forma
    Consilia in nostris requiesset sedibus hospes!
    Nam quo me referam? quali spe perdita nitor?
    Idaeosne petam montes? ah, gurgite lato
    Discernens ponti truculentum ubi diuidit aequor?
180 An patris auxilium sperem, quemne ipsa reliqui

---

165. **exsternata**: cf. v. 71 n.
exsternauit. — **auctae**, *endowed;* cf.
Lucr. III. 628 *animas sensibus
auctas.*

168. **alga**: cf. v. 60 n.

169. **extremo tempore**, *at my
last hour;* cf. v. 151 n.

172. **Gnosia**: doubtless simply
'Cretan'; cf. v. 75 *Gortynia tecta.*

173. **tauro**: so the Minotaur is
called also in v. 230.

174. **religasset funem**: of moor-
ing to the shore; cf. Verg. *Aen.*
VII. 106 *gramineo ripae religauit
ab aggere classem;* Luc. *Phar.* VII.
860 *nullus ab Emathio religasset
litore funem nauita.*

175. **malus hic**: cf. 29. 21 n.

177 ff. Cf. Eurip. *Med.* 502 ff.;
Ov. *Met.* VIII. 113 ff. *nam quo deserta reuertar? in patriam? deserta iacet, . . . patris ad ora?
quem tibi donaui?* C. Gracchus
(Cic. *De. Or.* III. 214) *quo me miser*

*conferam? quo uertam? in Capi-
toliumne? at fratris sanguine madet.
an domum? matremne ut miseram
lamentantem uideam et abiectam?*

178 ff. Ariadne proposes to herself three courses, and rejects them
successively as impossible, the first,
because of her isolation from home,
the other two, because also of her
past deeds. — **Idaeos montes**: *i.e.*
Crete, the thought being simply
of returning home.

180. **sperem**: *sc.* even if I could
reach Crete. — **quemne** = *quippe
quem;* cf. v. 183; 68. 91. The interrogative particle *-ne* is not infrequently joined to relatives to point
the reason for controverting a previous assertion, or for answering in
the negative a previous question;
cf. Plaut. *Trin.* 360 *quin comedit
quod fuit, quod non fuit?* Ter.
Phor. 923 *quodne ego discripsi porro
illis quibus debui?* and Minton

Respersum iuuenem fraterna caede secuta?
Coniugis an fido consoler memet amore,
Quine fugit lentos incuruans gurgite remos?
Praeterea nullo litus, sola insula, tecto,

185 Nec patet egressus pelagi cingentibus undis:
Nulla fugae ratio, nulla spes : omnia muta,
Omnia sunt deserta, ostentant omnia letum.
Non tamen ante mihi languescent lumina morte,
Nec prius a fesso secedent corpore sensus

190 Quam iustam a diuis exposcam prodita multam
Caelestumque fidem postrema comprecer hora.
Quare, facta uirum multantes uindice poena
Eumenides, quibus anguino redimita capillo
Frons exspirantis praeportat pectoris iras,

195 Huc huc aduentate, meas audite querelas,
Quas ego, uae miserae, extremis proferre medullis
Cogor inops, ardens, amenti caeca furore.

Warren, *Amer. Jour. Phil.* Vol. II.
p. 50 ff.

181. **fraterna**: cf. v. 150 n.

183. **quine**, etc.: *i.e.* as if it were
not my husband who is now fleeing
from me.

184. **nullo**, etc.: the appositive
phrase **sola insula** is inserted between the subject and its modifying
ablative of characteristic **tecto** in a
somewhat unusual form of hyperbaton; cf. however Juv. 3. 48 *mancus
et exstinctae corpus non utile dextrae.*

186. **nulla spes**: on the lengthening of the final syllable see Intr.
86 *g.* — **omnia muta**: as no ear was
open to her grief (v. 170), so there
was no voice to speak sympathy; cf.
Prop. I. 18. 1 *haec certe deserta loca
et taciturna querenti.*

193. **anguino redimita capillo**:
cf. Aes. *Choeph.* 1049 πεπλεκτανημέ-
ναι πυκνοῖς δράκουσιν; Hor. *Carm.*

II. 13. 35 *intorti capillis Eumeni-
dum angues;* Verg. *Aen.* VI. 280
*discordia demens, uipereum crinem
uittis innexa cruentis.*

194. **exspirantis**: *i.e.* the angry,
hissing serpents but betoken the
anger that breathes forth from the
breasts of the furies. — **praeportat**:
of a thing prominently displayed;
cf. Lucr. II. 621 *tela praeportant,
uiolenti signa furoris.*

195. **huc huc aduentate**: cf.
61. 8 *huc huc ueni.*

196. **uae miserae**: cf. 8. 15 n.;
Ter. *Andr.* 743 *uae miserae mihi;*
Ov. *Her.* 3. 82 *hic mihi, uae miserae, concutit ossa metus.* — **extremis medullis**, *from my inmost
soul;* but this instance of the ablative alone with **proferre** is perhaps
unique. Cf. 35. 15 n.

197. **ardens**: like v. 124 *ardenti
corde.*

Quae quoniam uerae nascuntur pectore ab imo,
Vos nolite pati nostrum uanescere luctum,
200 Sed quali solam Theseus me mente reliquit,
Tali mente, deae, funestet seque suosque.'
  Has postquam maesto profudit pectore uoces
Supplicium saeuis exposcens anxia factis,
Adnuit inuicto caelestum numine rector,
205 Quo nutu tellus atque horrida contremuerunt
Aequora concussitque micantia sidera mundus.
Ipse autem caeca mentem caligine Theseus
Consitus oblito dimisit pectore cuncta
Quae mandata prius constanti mente tenebat,
210 Dulcia nec maesto sustollens signa parenti
Sospitem Erechtheum se ostendit uisere portum.
Namque ferunt olim, classi cum moenia diuae
Linquentem gnatum uentis concrederet Aegeus,
Talia complexum iuueni mandata dedisse:
215 'Gnate mihi longe iucundior unice uita,

200 f. **quali**, etc.: *i.e.* as Theseus
forgot his vows (v. 58 *immemor
iuuenis;* v. 123 *immemori pectore*),
let forgetfulness bring upon him the
fatal penalty (cf. vv. 247–248).

203. **anxia**: explained by v. 197;
cf. 68. 8.

204 ff. **adnuit**, etc.: cf. Hom. *Il.*
I. 528–530; Verg. *Aen.* IX. 106
*adnuit et totum nutu tremefecit
Olympum;* Stat. *Theb.* VII. 3 *concussitque caput, motu quo celsa
laborant sidera proclamatque adici
ceruicibus Atlas.*

206. **mundus**, *the firmament*, as
in 66. 1; but cf. 47. 2.

207. **caeca caligine**: cf. Cic.
Arat. 345 *adiment lucem caeca caligine nubes;* Lucr. III. 304 *caecae
caliginis umbra;* Verg. *Aen.* III.
203 *incertos caeca caligine soles.*

208. **consitus**, *beset;* very rare
in this figurative sense till post-
classical times; but cf. Plaut. *Men.*
756 *consitus sum senectute.*

209. Cf. the close verbal resemblance of v. 238; Lucr. II. 582
memori mandatum mente teneri.

211. **Erechtheum portum**: so
Homer calls the Athenians by the
name of their fabulous king in *Il.* II.
547 δῆμον Ἐρεχθῆος μεγαλήτορος.

212. **classi**: perhaps of a single
ship; cf. v. 53 with vv. 84 and 121.
— **diuae**: the use of the unmodified
noun to indicate Athena seems to
be made possible by the unmistak-
able reference to Athens in v. 211
Erechtheum portum.

215. **iucundior uita**: cf. 68. 106
uita dulcius atque anima; and on
similar expressions, 3. 5 n.

Gnate, ego quem in dubios cogor dimittere casus,
Reddite in extrema nuper mihi fine senectae,
Quandoquidem fortuna mea ac tua feruida uirtus
Eripit inuito mihi te, cui languida nondum
220 Lumina sunt gnati cara saturata figura,
Non ego te gaudens laetanti pectore mittam,
Nec te ferre sinam fortunae signa secundae,
Sed primum multas expromam mente querelas
Canitiem terra atque infuso puluere foedans,
225 Inde infecta uago suspendam lintea malo,
Nostros ut luctus nostraeque incendia mentis
Carbasus obscurata decet ferrugine Hibera.
Quod tibi si sancti concesserit incola Itoni,
Quae nostrum genus ac sedes defendere Erechthei

217. **extrema**, etc.: Theseus
passed his early life with his mother
Aethra in the home of her father
Pittheus, king of Troezene, and
when he finally came to Athens,
found Aegeus already an old man.
— **fine**: feminine, as regularly in
Lucretius, and not very infrequently
in other writers of all ages, in the
singular; but note the masculine
plural in 64. 3; 66. 12.

221. **gaudens laetanti pectore**:
cf. 67. 26 n.

222. **fortunae signa secundae**:
in this instance, white sails. On
white as the color proverbially connected with good fortune, cf. 68.
148 n.; Pers. I. 110 *per me equi-*
dem sint omnia protinus alba.

224. **terra**, etc.: a common
sign of extreme grief among the
ancients; cf. Vulg. *Iob* 2. 12 *plora-*
uerunt, scissisque uestibus sparse-
runt puluerem super caput suum
in caelum; Hom. *Il.* XVIII. 23
ἀμφοτέρῃσι δὲ χερσὶν ἑλὼν κόνιν
αἰθαλόεσσαν χεύατο κὰκ κεφαλῆς,
χαρίεν δ᾽ ᾔσχυνε πρόσωπον; Verg.

Aen. XII. 611 *canitiem immundo*
perfusam puluere turpans.

225. **uago**, *swaying;* cf. Enn.
trag. 151 R. *arbores uento uagant.*

227. **obscurata ferrugine Hi-**
bera: cf. Verg. *Aen.* IX. 582 *fer-*
rugine clarus Hibera; Geor. I. 467
caput obscura ferrugine texit; Ov.
Met. V. 404 *obscura tinctas ferru-*
gine habenas. The dye was apparently produced from a variety of
ochre, and its hue is described by
Plaut. *Mil.* 1181 *palliolum habeas*
ferrugineum (nam is colos thalasi-
cust), and by Servius on Verg. *ll. cc*
uicinus purpurae subnigrae; pur
pura nigrior. It was, therefore, a
sort of dull, dark violet.

228. **sancti incola Itoni**: the
shrine of Athena in the Boeotian
city (and mountain) of Itonus was
well known to the Romans; cf.
Liv. XXXVI. 20 *ibi statua regis*
Antiochi posita in templo Mineruae
Itoniae iram accendit.

229. **defendere**: the simple com-
plementary infinitive with *adnuere*
in this sense is very rare, but is

230 Adnuit, ut tauri respergas sanguine dextram,
    Tum uero facito ut memori tibi condita corde
    Haec uigeant mandata, nec ulla oblitteret aetas,
    Vt simul ac nostros inuisent lumina collis,
    Funestam antennae deponant undique uestem
235 Candidaque intorti sustollant uela rudentes,
    Quam primum cernens ut laeta gaudia mente
    Agnoscam, cum te reducem aetas prospera sistet.'
    Haec mandata prius constanti mente tenentem
    Thesea ceu pulsae uentorum flamine nubes
240 Aerium niuei montis liquere cacumen.
    At pater, ut summa prospectum ex arce petebat
    Anxia in adsiduos absumens lumina fletus,
    Cum primum inflati conspexit lintea ueli,
    Praecipitem sese scopulorum e uertice iecit
245 Amissum credens immiti Thesea fato.
    Sic funesta domus ingressus tecta paterna

justified by the similar construction with other verbs of promising. — Erechthei : genitive ; cf.
v. 120 *Thesei* (but v. 382 *Pelei*,
66. 94 *Hydrochoi*, dative).

230. tauri: cf. v. 173 n.

232. oblitteret aetas: cf. 68.
43; 64. 322. In these three places,
and in v. 237, aetas has the sense
of *tempus ;* elsewhere in Catullus,
of *uita.*

233. inuisent: cf. 31. 4 n.

234. funestam uestem, *the garb
of mourning ;* cf. Acc. *Trag.* 86 R.
*sed quaenam haec mulier est funesta
ueste, tonsu lugubri ?* — undique :
the word is probably used merely
to emphasize the urgency of the
bidding, — ' every stitch of mourning.'

237. te reducem sistet: cf. Liv.
XXIX. 27. 3 *domos reduces sistatis.*
— aetas : cf. v. 232 n.

238. Cf. v. 209.

239 f. ceu, etc.: cf. Hom. *Il.* V.
522 ff.

241. summa ex arce: *i.e.* from
the Acropolis, whence he would
have an unimpeded view over the
sea southward. This form of the
story is followed also by Diodorus
(IV. 61. 7) and Pausanias (I. 22.
5); but another form makes the
promontory of Sunium the place
whence Aegeus watched for the return of the ship, on descrying which
he threw himself into the thence-
named Aegean Sea; cf. Stat. *Theb.*
XII. 624 ff. *linquitur Eois longe
speculabile proris Sunion, unde
uagi casurum in nomina ponti
Cresia decepit falso ratis Aegea
uelo.*

243. inflati: the spread of can-
vas made the vessel the sooner visible to his straining eyes.

Morte ferox Theseus, qualem Minoidi luctum
Obtulerat mente immemori, talem ipse recepit.
 Quae tum prospectans cedentem maesta carinam
250 Multiplices animo uoluebat saucia curas.
 At parte ex alia florens uolitabat Iacchus
Cum thiaso satyrorum et Nysigenis silenis
Te quaerens, Ariadna, tuoque incensus amore.

. . . .

 Quae tum alacres passim lymphata mente furebant
255 Euhoe bacchantes, euhoe capita inflectentes.
 Harum pars tecta quatiebant cuspide thyrsos,

---

247. **ferox**: cf. with the absolute use of the adjective v. 73. — **Minoidi**: Gr. dative; cf. 66. 70 *Tethyï*.

247 f. **qualem Minoidi**, etc.: cf. v. 200 f.

249. **quae tum**, etc.: the poet has hastened on to describe the effect of Ariadne's curse, and now returns to tell her own fate.

250. **saucia**: of the wounds of love; cf. Verg. *Aen.* IV. 1 *regina graui iam dudum saucia cura*.

251. **at**, etc.: in immediate contrast with the absorbing grief of Ariadne is brought the joyous revelry of the Bacchic rout, the leader of which comes to fill the place of the fugitive lover. — **parte**: *sc.* of the coverlet. — **florens**: cf. 17. 14 n. — **Iacchus**: a mystical name of Bacchus especially used by the poets.

252. **thiaso**: cf. 63. 28 n. — **satyrorum, silenis**: of the male attendants upon Bacchus the poets usually designate the wanton younger as *satyri* and the drunken elder as *sileni*. — **Nysigenis**: Bacchus is apparently thought of as returning from his great journey to the far East; cf. Verg. *Aen.* VI. 804 *qui pampineis uictor iuga flectit*

habenis Liber, agens celso Nysae de uertice tigris, and Apollonius calls Dionysus the prince of Nysa, when speaking of his marriage with Ariadne (V. 431). Nysa is variously described by ancient authorities as a city (or mountain) in India (Plin.), Arabia (Diod.), or Thrace (Hom.; Strabo).

253. **tuo**: for the objective genitive, a not very common use; cf. 87. 4 *amore tuo;* Sall. *Iug.* 14. 8 *uos in mea iniuria despecti estis*.

254. **quae**: the following actions are those characteristic of the female followers of Bacchus (cf. also v. 256 *harum*), while only his male followers have thus far been referred to. Bergk is therefore correct in believing that a verse has been lost after v. 253. — **lymphata mente**: *i.e.* crazed with the mad enthusiasm inspired by the god; cf. Hor. *Carm.* I. 37. 14 *mentem lymphatam Mareotico*.

255. **capita inflectentes**: cf. 63. 23 n.

256. **tecta cuspide thyrsos**: *i.e.* the vine-rod, or spear, the traditional sceptre and weapon of Bacchus. Its stroke inspired madness; cf. Hor. *Carm.* II. 19. 7

Pars e diuulso iactabant membra iuuenco,
Pars sese tortis serpentibus incingebant,
Pars obscura cauis celebrabant orgia cistis,
260 Orgia quae frustra cupiunt audire profani,
Plangebant aliae proceris tympana palmis
Aut tereti tenuis tinnitus aere ciebant,
Multis raucisonos efflabant cornua bombos
Barbaraque horribili stridebat tibia cantu.
265 Talibus amplifice uestis decorata figuris
Puluinar complexa suo uelabat amictu.

*euhoe, parce, Liber, parce, graui
metuende thyrso.* It was also carried by his worshippers, as here,
and was tipped with a pine-cone or
with a bunch of vine-leaves (Verg.
Aen. VII. 396 *pampineas gerunt
hastas*), or ivy-leaves (Prop. IV. 3.
35 *haec hederas legit in thyrsos*).
All forms of the *thyrsus* are seen in
the frequent representations of Bacchic processions in ancient wall-
paintings and bas-reliefs (cf. Rich
Dict. Antiq. s. u.).

257. e diuulso, etc.: cf. Pers.
I. 100 *raptum uitulo caput ablatura
superbo Bassaris.* The action is
often represented in ancient monuments. So the frenzied Bacchantes
tore Pentheus in pieces (Ov. *Met.*
III. 701 ff.).

258. tortis, etc.: cf. Hor. *Carm.*
II. 19. 18 *tu separatis uuidus in
iugis nodo coerces uiperino Bistoni-
dum sine fraude crines; Ov. Met.*
IV. 483 [*Tisiphone*] *torto incingi-
tur angue.*

259. obscura, etc.: cf. Hor.
Carm. I. 18. 12 *nec uariis obsita
frondibus sub diuum rapiam* (addressing Bassareus). The *cista* was
either a cylindrical basket or a
box, in which the secret emblems
(orgia) of the worship of Bacchus,
or of Ceres, were concealed from

uninitiated eyes when carried in
procession (celebrabant).

261–264. plangebant, etc.: cf.
63. 21 n.; Lucr. II. 618 ff. *tympana
tenta tonant palmis et cymbala circum concaua, raucisonoque minan-
tur cornua cantu, et Phrygio stimulat numero caua tibia mentis.*
— proceris : perhaps with the
unusual meaning of *lifted high*
(see the monuments).

262. tereti aere: *i.e.* the hemispherical cymbals ; cf. 63. 21. —
tenuis tinnitus, *the sharp shrill*,
as contrasted with raucisonos
bombos of the horns. Note the
alliteration, and cf. Lucr. *l.c.*, and
the triple alliteration in v. 320.

263. raucisonos: cf. Lucr. *l.c.;*
IV. 544 *et reboat raucum regio cita
barbara bombum.*

264. barbara: *i.e.* Phrygian; cf.
63. 22. Catullus speaks from the
standpoint of a Greek; cf. Lucr.
l.c.; Hor. *Epod.* 9. 5 *sonante mix-
tum tibiis carmen lyra, hac Do-
rium, illis barbarum.*

265 f. talibus, etc.: the story of
Ariadne is left when happiness in
a divine marriage is just coming
to her; these verses, concluding
the description of the embroidered
spread, virtually repeat vv. 50–51,
with which it began.

Quae postquam cupide spectando Thessala pubes
Expleta est, sanctis coepit decedere diuis.
Hic, qualis flatu placidum mare matutino
270 Horrificans Zephyrus procliuas incitat undas
Aurora exoriente uagi sub limina solis,
Quae tarde primum clementi flamine pulsae
Procedunt, leuiterque sonant plangore cachinni,
Post uento crescente magis magis increbescunt
275 Purpureaque procul nantes ab luce refulgent,
Sic tum uestibuli linquentes regia tecta
Ad se quisque uago passim pede discedebant.
Quorum post abitum princeps e uertice Peli
Aduenit Chiron portans siluestria dona:
280 Nam quoscumque ferunt campi, quos Thessala magnis

267–277. The mortal guests give
place to the immortals, who come
also bringing gifts (278–302), and
sit down to the marriage-feast (303–
304), while the Parcae, still pursu-
ing their endless task of spinning
the thread of fate (305–322), sing
the prophetic marriage-song (323–
381).

267. **Thessala pubes**: cf. v. 32
tota Thessalia.

268. **sanctis**: cf. 36. 3 n.

269. **hic**: temporal, as in 68. 63.

270. **horrificans**: the word occurs only here in the sense of 'ruf-
fling,' but in later writers in that of
shudder-causing.' But cf. v. 205
horrida aequora; Acc. ap. Non.
422. 33 *mare cum horret fluctibus;*
Hor. *Epod.* 2. 6 *horret iratum mare.*

271. **uagi solis**, *the journeying
sun,* in distinction from the fixed
heavenly lights; cf. 61. 117 n.;
Tib. IV. 1. 76 *uagi pascua solis;*
Hor. *Sat.* I. 8. 21 *uaga luna.*

273. **leuiter sonant plangore**:
cf. Sen. *Ag.* 717 f. *licet alcyones
Cecya suum fluctu leuiter plangente*

sonent.— **cachinni**: genitive singular; for the figure cf. Aesch.
Prom. 89 ποντίων τε κυμάτων
ἀνήριθμον γέλασμα.

274. **magis magis**: cf. 38. 3 n.

275. **purpurea luce**: *i.e.* the
rosy light of dawn, reflecting which
the more distant surface of the sea
(**undae procul nantes**) loses in
the gleam its own color.

277. **ad se**, *to his own home;* cf.
Plaut. *Mil.* 121 *in aedis med ad se
adduxit domum;* and often. —
uago pede: corroborating **passim**,
with reference to the diverse directions in which the homes lay, and
not with the implication of 63. 86.

279. **Chiron**: the famous cen-
taur, a near neighbor and friend of
Peleus, and later the trainer of
Achilles. — **siluestria dona**: but
according to Homer one gift of
Chiron to Peleus was more warlike;
cf. *Il.* XVI. 143 Πηλιάδα μελίην τὴν
πατρὶ φίλῳ πόρε Χείρων Πηλίου ἐκ
κορυφῆς, φόνον ἔμμεναι ἡρώεσσιν.

280. **quoscumque**: continued
by the simple **quos** in the two fol-

Montibus ora creat, quos propter fluminis undas
Aura parit flores tepidi fecunda Fauoni,
Hos indistinctis plexos tulit ipse corollis,
Quo permulsa domus iucundo risit odore.

285 Confestim Penios adest, uiridantia Tempe,
Tempe quae siluae cingunt super impendentes,
Naiasin linquens Doris celebranda choreis,
Non uacuus: namque ille tulit radicitus altas

lowing clauses, in the latter of
which occurs the noun flores, which
the relatives modify. Chiron has
gathered the wealth of blossoms
from plain, mountain, and riverside
to deck the interior of the house,
while Peneus (v. 285) brings masses
of foliage to adorn the approaches
to it.

281. ora: *i.e.* the region; cf.
Cic. *N. D.* II. 164 *quacumque in
ora ac parte terrarum;* Mark 5. 17
to depart out of their coasts.

282. aura parit: cf. v. 90; 62.
41 n.

283. indistinctis: the great
number of the flowers precluded
their artistic assortment. — plexos
corollis: flowers were usually
woven into long cords for decora-
tive use at banquets, and were sold
among the Romans in that form ;
cf. the frescoes from Pompeii representing *Amoretti* in the business of
preparing such cords.

284. permulsa: often used of
the delightful effect of pleasing
sounds, but not often of odors; cf.,
however, Stat. *Silu.* I. 3. 11 *per-
mulsit crocis blandumque reliquit
odorem.* — risit odore: cf. Hom.
Hymn. Cer. 13 κηώδει δ' ὀδμῇ πᾶς
οὐρανὸς εὐρὺς ὕπερθεν γαῖά τε πᾶσ'
ἐγέλασσε καὶ ἀλμυρὸν οἶδμα θα-
λάσσης.

286. Tempe, etc.: cf. the description of the famous vale in Ov.

Met. I. 568 ff. ; Plin. *N. H.* IV. 8.
31; Anth. Lat. 315. 3 Mey. *fron-
dosis Tempe cinguntur Thessala
siluis.*

287. Naiasin: *i.e.* the nymphs
of the vale of Tempe ; cf. *Cul.* 18
*Pierii laticis decus, ite, sorores Nai-
des;* 115 ff. *hic etiam uiridi luden-
tes Panes in herba et Satyri Dryad-
esque choros egere puellae Naiadum
coetu.* This form of the Greek dative plural apparently occurs here
first in extant Latin ; but cf. citations from Varro in Charis. I. 15, p.
38 *schemasin,* and Non. p. 374 *ethe-
sin;* Prop. I. 20. 12 *Adryasin,* 32
Hamadryasin, 34 *Thyniasin;* Ov.
Her. 13. 137 *Troasin; Art. Am.*
III. 672 *Lemniasin,* etc. — linquens (= *relinquens,* as often in
Catullus): the nymphs who dance
with and in honor of the river-god
are this day left to dance alone. —
Doris: see Crit. App.

288. uacuus, *empty-handed;* the
word is rare in this meaning ; but
cf. Juv. 10. 22 *cantabit uacuus
coram latrone uiator;* Vulg. *Exod.*
23. 15 *non apparebis in conspectu
meo uacuus;* Hom. *Il.* II. 298
κενεὸν νέεσθαι. — ille: in contrast
with Chiron. — radicitus, *roots and
all;* cf. the figurative meaning in
Plaut. *Most.* 1092 *omnia malefacta
uostra repperi radicitus;* but in v.
108 the meaning is the more usual
one, 'from the roots.'

Fagos ac recto proceras stipite laurus,
290 Non sine nutanti platano lentaque sorore
Flammati Phaethontis et aeria cupressu.
Haec circum sedes late contexta locauit,
Vestibulum ut molli uelatum fronde uireret.
Post hunc consequitur sollerti corde Prometheus
295 Extenuata gerens ueteris uestigia poenae
Quam quondam silici restrictus membra catena
Persoluit pendens e uerticibus praeruptis.
Inde pater diuum sancta cum coniuge natisque
Aduenit, caelo te solum, Phoebe, relinquens
300 Vnigenamque simul cultricem montibus Idri :
Pelea nam tecum pariter soror adspernata est
Nec Thetidis taedas uoluit celebrare iugalis.

289. **fagos**, etc.: the wooded
banks of the Peneus (v. 286) made
trees his most natural gift.

290. **sorore flammati Phaethontis**: *i.e.* the poplar. On the
transformation of the Heliades into
poplar-trees see Ov. *Met.* II. 340 ff.;
Verg. *Aen.* X. 189 ff. *namque
ferunt luctu Cycnum Phaethontis
amati, populeas inter frondes um-
bramque sororum dum canit*, etc.;
Cul. 127 ff.

294. **sollerti corde**: cf. Aesch.
Prom. 506 πᾶσαι τέχναι βροτοῖσιν
ἐκ Προμηθέως. — **Prometheus**: according to the accounts of Hyginus
(*Astr.* II. 15) and Servius (on Verg.
Ecl. 6. 42), Prometheus warned
Zeus of the prophecy concerning
the son of Thetis (cf. v. 21 n.),
and was therefore released from
his confinement on Mt. Caucasus.
So Prometheus is here a chief
guest, as the promoter of the marriage.

295. **extenuata uestigia**, *the
fading scars*, not the bit of rock set
in a ring, mentioned by Servius

(*l.c.*) and Pliny (*N. H.* XXXVII.
2), which Zeus forced Prometheus
to wear as a reminder of his punishment.

296. **silici**: dative modifying **restrictus**.

298. **sancta**: cf. 36. 3 n. With
the hypermeter cf. 34. 22; 115. 5.

299. **caelo**: ablative of place.

300. **unigenam**: here *twin-sis-
ter;* but cf. 66. 53. — **montibus**:
dative modifying **cultricem**; cf.
66. 58 *Canopiis incola litoribus;*
and with the idea, 34. 9 · ff. n. —
Idri: if the reading be correct,
the name is perhaps that of the
district in Caria called Idrias by
Herodotus and Stephen of Byzan-
tium, where Artemis was worshipped
as Hecate.

301. **Pelea adspernata**: no
story accounting for this disdain is
known, and Homer (*Il.* XXIV. 62)
expressly speaks of the presence of
all the gods at the wedding, and of
a marriage-song sung by Phoebus
(cf. also Aesch. ap. Plat. *Rep.* II.
383).

Qui postquam niueis flexerunt sedibus artus,
Large multiplici constructae sunt dape mensae,
305 Cum interea infirmo quatientes corpora motu
Veridicos Parcae coeperunt edere cantus.
His corpus tremulum complectens undique uestis
Candida purpurea talos incinxerat ora,
At roseae niueo residebant uertice uittae,
310 Aeternumque manus carpebant rite laborem.
Laeua colum molli lana retinebat amictum,
Dextera tum leuiter deducens fila supinis
Formabat digitis, tum prono in pollice torquens
Libratum tereti uersabat turbine fusum,

303. **niueis**: being of ivory; cf.
v. 45.

305. **cum interea**: cf. 95. 3.—
infirmo, etc.: *i.e.* tremulous with
age; cf. v. 307; 61. 161.

306. **ueridicos cantus**: cf. Hor.
Carm. Saec. 25 ff. *uosque ueraces
cecinisse, Parcae, quod semel dic-
tum stabilis per aeuum terminus
seruat.*

309. **roseae**: the contrast between the white robe and its crimson border (v. 308) matches that
between the crimson fillets and the
snowy locks; cf. Prop. V. 9. 52
[*sacerdos*] *puniceo canas stamine
uincta comas.* — **niueo uertice**: cf.
Hor. *Carm.* IV. 13. 12 *capitis
niues.*

310. **aeternum**: the Fates never
cease from their task even to engage
in festivities, and the course of des-
tiny is never interrupted.

311 ff. The picture of the spinning is entirely realistic. A mass of
prepared wool but loosely fastened
together is attached to one end of the
distaff (*colus*), which is held in the
left hand. With the right hand
the spinner draws the filaments from
the mass and twists them between

thumb and finger into a thread, the
firmness of the twisting being assisted by attaching the end of the
thread to the spindle (*fusus*),
weighted by the *turbo*, which acts
as a fly-wheel.

312. **supinis**: the hand is turned
palm upward as the fingers draw the
filaments from the elevated distaff,
but palm downward (**prono pollice**) as they grasp the hanging
thread near the spindle and set it
twirling; cf. Tib. II. 1. 64 *fusus
apposito pollice uersat opus;* Ov.
Met. VI. 22 *leui teretem uersabat
pollice fusum.*

314. **tereti turbine**: a small circular plate of heavy material with a
hole through the centre somewhat
smaller than the thicker part of
the long, tapering *fusus.* Through
this the smaller end of the *fusus*
was passed as far as it would go,
and the symmetrically distributed
weight of the *turbo* thus gave additional momentum to the whirling
spindle. When the thread was
spun to a convenient length, its
lower part was wound around the
fusus, and the process continued
as before.

315 Atque ita decerpens aequabat semper opus dens,
     Laneaque aridulis haerebant morsa labellis
     Quae prius in leui fuerant exstantia filo.
     Ante pedes autem candentis mollia lanae
     Vellera uirgati custodibant calathisci.
320 Haec tum clarisona uellentes uellera uoce
     Talia diuino fuderunt carmine fata,
     Carmine perfidiae quod post nulla arguet aetas :
      ' O decus eximium magnis uirtutibus augens,
     Emathiae tutamen opis, clarissime nato,

315. atque ita : *i.e.* while the process thus described was going on; cf. v. 84 *atque ita*. — decerpens : while both hands were busy, the yarn was passed between the lips to strip off the outstanding fibres, or to smooth them down so that they might be included in the twist.

316. aridulis, morsa : both ἅπαξ λεγόμενα. On the diminutive of both noun and adjective in aridulis labellis see 3. 18 n.

317. fuerant exstantia (= *exstiterant*) : this periphrastic form is not very common, and where occurring is generally with the present tense of *esse*, as in 63. 57 *carens est*.

319. custodibant : older form, chiefly poetic or colloquial, except from *ire ;* cf. 68. 85; 84. 8.

320. haec : for *hac ;* so Varro, Lucretius, Vergil, etc., *passim.* — clarisona : cf. v. 125 n. *clarisonas.* — uellentes uellera : *i.e.* beginning their spinning by drawing from the mass of wool on the distaff the filaments to form the yarn ; cf. Ov. *Met.* XIV. 264 *quae uellera motis nulla trahunt digitis nec fila sequentia ducunt.* With the triple alliteration cf. v. 262.

322. aetas : cf. v. 232 n.

323–381. The marriage-song of Peleus and Thetis, arranged in twelve strophes, but without precise correspondence in the number of verses in each (cf. on this point *c.* 62). In theme and general treatment, and in certain details (*e.g.* the address in vv. 372 ff., with which cf. 61. 211 ff.), the song is a true *epithalamium*, such as might be sung outside the closed door of the marriage-chamber, and the conclusion of the description of the wedding with the song reinforces this impression of it. But it is represented as sur.g by the Fates while the other guests were feasting, and vv. 328 ff. suggest that the bride is yet to arrive. Evidently the poet is not attempting to reproduce the exact features of a marriage ceremonial, and precise interpretation from an archaeological standpoint is impossible.

323 f. Peleus boasts a glorious descent, and has made this glory greater by his own great deeds, but is to find his greatest glory in his son. — Emathiae : the name meant to the Greeks Macedonia, but with common poetic inexactness is here used of Thessaly; cf. Verg. *Geor.* I. 491 *nec fuit indignum superis sanguine nostro Emathiam pinguescere* (of the battle of Pharsalus).

325 Accipe quod laeta tibi pandunt luce sorores,
Veridicum oraclum.   Sed uos, quae fata secuntur,
Currite ducentes subtegmina, currite, fusi.

Adueniet tibi iam portans optata maritis
Hesperus, adueniet fausto cum sidere coniunx,
330 Quae tibi flexanimo mentem perfundat amore
Languidulosque paret tecum coniungere somnos
Leuia substernens robusto bracchia collo.
Currite ducentes subtegmina, currite, fusi.

Nulla domus tales unquam contexit amores,
335 Nullus amor tali coniunxit foedere amantes
Qualis adest Thetidi, qualis concordia Peleo.
Currite ducentes subtegmina, currite, fusi.

Nascetur uobis expers terroris Achilles,
Hostibus haud tergo, sed forti pectore notus,
340 Qui persaepe uago uictor certamine cursus
Flammea praeuertet celeris uestigia ceruae.

---

325. sorores: cf. Ov. *Trist.* V. 3. 17 *dominae fati quidquid cecinere sorores;* Mart. V. 1. 3 *ueridicae sorores.*

326. quae fata secuntur, *which the fates follow;* the clause modifies **subtegmina;** cf. Stat. *Theb.* I. 213 *uocem fata secuntur;* Anth. Lat. 227 Baehr. *consultum fata secuntur.*

327. subtegmina = *fila;* cf. Hor. *Epod.* 13. 15 *reditum certo subtegmine Parcae rupere.*

329. Hesperus: cf. *c.* 62 *passim* nn. — **adueniet coniunx**: see introductory note to vv. 323–381.

330. flexanimo, *heart-compelling;* cf. Pac. fr. 177 R. *o flexanima atque omnium regina rerum oratio;* Verg. *Geor.* IV. 516 *non ulli animum flexere hymenaei.*

331. languidulos somnos: cf. Verg. *Aen.* XII. 908 *languida quies;* Tib. IV. 1. 181 *languida otia.*

332. substernens, etc.: cf. Ov. *Am.* III. 7. 7 *illa quidem nostro subiecit eburnea collo bracchia.* — **leuia bracchia**: cf. 66. 10.

334. contexit, *sheltered,* doubtless with the notion of privacy usually connected with the verb.

336. adest concordia: with the arrangement cf. 30. 3 n. — **Peleo**: with synizesis, as in v. 382 *Pelei,* which is, however, the regular Greek dative.

339. haud tergo, etc.: cf. Hom. *Il.* XIII. 289–290 οὐκ ἂν ἐν αὐχέν᾽ ὄπισθε πέσοι βέλος οὐδ᾽ ἐνὶ νώτῳ, ἀλλά κεν ἢ στέρνων ἢ νηδύος ἀντιάσειε.

340. cursus: the commonest epithets of Achilles in the Iliad describe him as swift of foot.

341. Cf. Pind. *Nem.* 3. 90 [Ἀχιλεὺς] κτείνοντ᾽ ἐλάφους ἄνευ κυνῶν δολίων θ᾽ ἑρκέων· ποσσὶ γὰρ κρά-

Currite ducentes subtegmina, currite, fusi.

Non illi quisquam bello se conferet heros,

Cum Phrygii Teucro manabunt sanguine campi

345   Troicaque obsidens longinquo moenia bello

Periuri Pelopis uastabit tertius heres.

Currite ducentes subtegmina, currite, fusi.

Illius egregias uirtutes claraque facta

Saepe fatebuntur gnatorum in funere matres,

350   Cum incultum cano soluent a uertice crinem

Putridaque infirmis uariabunt pectora palmis.

Currite ducentes subtegmina, currite, fusi.

τεσκε; Stat. *Ach.* II. 111 (397) *uolucres praeuertere ceruos et Lapithas cogebat equos . . . Chiron.* — flammea, *fiery-fleet;* on the figure cf. Verg. *Aen.* XI. 718 *uirgo pernicibus ignea plantis;* Ov. *Met.* II. 392 *ignipedum uires expertus equorum.*

343. non illi, etc. : Achilles claims this pre-eminence for himself in Hom. *Il.* XVIII. 105 τοῖος ἐών, οἷος οὔ τις Ἀχαιῶν χαλκοχιτώνων, ἐν πολέμῳ.

344. campi: the vigorous emendation is supported by Stat. *Ach.* I. 86 *cum tuus Aeacides tepido modo sanguine Teucros undabit campos; Il. Lat.* 384 *sanguine Dardanii manabant undique campi.*

345. longinquo: of the length of the war, not of its distance from Greece.

346. periuri Pelopis: Pelops won the chariot-race, and so the hand of Hippodamia, from her father, Oenomaus, by offering half of his kingdom to the latter's charioteer, Myrtilus, if he would loosen the linch-pins of the chariot, or substitute pins of wax. Upon the success of the plot, Pelops refused to carry out his agreement, and threw

Myrtilus into the sea near Geraestus in Euboea. But the dying curse of Myrtilus followed the house of Pelops thereafter. Cf. Pind. *Ol.* 1. 114 ff. ; Apoll. Rh. I. 752 ; Hyg. *Fab.* 84. — tertius heres : *i.e.* Agamemnon, the succession being Pelops, Atreus, Thyestes, Agamemnon, as Homer shows in *Il.* II. 105 ff.

350 f. The traditional signs of grief on the part of women; cf. Hom. *Il.* XVIII. 30 χερσὶ δὲ πᾶσαι στήθεα πεπλήγοντο; Verg. *Aen.* I. 480 *crinibus Iliades passis suppliciter tristes et tunsae pectora palmis;* Ov. *Met.* XIII. 491 [*Hecuba*] *consueta pectora plangit.* Baehrens supports his emendation by citing Ov. *Her.* 9. 125 *nec uenit incultis captarum more capillis;* Stat. *Theb.* VI. 32 *incultam ferali puluere barbam.* — cano: here as elsewhere (cf. 17. 13; 61. 51; 68. 142) Catullus emphasizes the relations between parent and child, and appeals to our sympathy, by representing the former as in advanced age; cf. putrida (Hor. *Epod.* 8. 7 *pectus et mammae putres*) and infirmis. — uariabunt: of the discoloration produced by the blows, which, to mark the depth of

Namque uelut densas praecerpens messor aristas
Sole sub ardenti flauentia demetit arua,
355 Troiugenum infesto prosternet corpora ferro.
Currite ducentes subtegmina, currite, fusi.

Testis erit magnis uirtutibus unda Scamandri,
Quae passim rapido diffunditur Hellesponto,
Cuius iter caesis angustans corporum aceruis
360 Alta tepefaciet permixta flumina caede.
Currite ducentes subtegmina, currite, fusi.

Denique testis erit morti quoque reddita praeda,
Cum teres excelso coaceruatum aggere bustum

woe, were violent, though from weak
hands; observe the juxtaposition of
infirmis and **uariabunt**; cf. Plaut.
Poen. 26 *ne et hic uarientur uirgis
et loris domi.*

353 ff. **uelut**, etc.: the figure is
Homeric; cf. *Il.* XI. 67 ff. — **praecerpens**, *clipping down* (before
him as he advances); the word
apparently occurs only here in
this meaning, though the figurative meaning in Gell. II. 30. 11
*cuius rei causam, cum Aristotelis
libros problematorum praecerpere-
mus, notaui* seems to point in the
same direction; cf. Apoll. Rh. III.
1386 προτάμωνται ἀρούρας. — **messor aristas . . . demetit:** cf. *Il.
Lat.* 886 *maturasque metit robustus
messor aristas.*

354. **sole sub ardenti:** cf. Verg.
Ecl. 2. 13 *sole sub ardenti resonant
arbusta cicadis.* — **flauentia arua:**
cf. Verg. *Geor.* IV. 126 *qua niger
umectat flauentia culta Galaesus.*

357 ff. Referring to the great re-
pulse of the Trojans at the hands of
Achilles in Hom. *Il.* XXI.

358. **passim diffunditur:** of
the smaller stream losing itself in
the larger. — **rapido:** perhaps of
rushing waves rather than of swift

current; cf. 63. 16 *rapidum salum ;*
Hom. *Il.* II. 845 Ἑλλήσποντος
ἀγάρροος.

359. **caesis corporum aceruis:**
with hypallage of the adjective, as
not infrequently in poetry. — **angustans**, etc.: cf. Hom. *Il.* XXI.
218 ff. πλήθει γὰρ δή μοι νεκύων
ἐρατεινὰ ῥέεθρα, οὐδέ τί πη δύναμαι
προχέειν ῥόον εἰς ἅλα δῖαν στεινόμενος
νεκύεσσι, σὺ δὲ κτείνεις αἰδήλως (from
the address of the Scamander to
Achilles; Verg. *Aen.* V. 806 ff.
[*Achilles*] *milia multa daret leto,
gemerentque repleti amnes, nec re-
perire uiam atque euoluere posset
in mare se Xanthus.*

360. **tepēfaciet:** see Intr. 86 f.

362. **morti quoque reddita
praeda:** *i.e.* the power of Achilles
will be shown by the fact that he
continues even after death to make
the Trojans his prey.   Polyxena,
daughter of Priam, in the course of
the siege betrothed on pretence of
peace to Achilles, was at the capture of the city sacrificed to his
manes by Pyrrhus; cf. Ov. *Met.*
XIII. 439 ff.; Serv. on Verg. *Aen.*
III. 321; Hyg. *Fab.* 110; Eurip.
Hec. 37 ff.; 521 ff.

363. **teres**, *round, i.e.* circular;

Excipiet niueos percussae uirginis artus.
365 Currite ducentes subtegmina, currite, fusi.
    Nam simul ac fessis dederit fors copiam Achiuis
Vrbis Dardaniae Neptunia soluere uincla,
Alta Polyxenia madefient caede sepulcra,
Quae, uelut ancipiti succumbens uictima ferro,
370 Proiciet truncum submisso poplite corpus.
Currite ducentes subtegmina, currite, fusi.
    Quare agite optatos animi coniungite amores.
Accipiat coniunx felici foedere diuam,
Dedatur cupido iam dudum nupta marito.
375 Currite ducentes subtegmina, currite, fusi.
    Non illam nutrix orienti luce reuisens

cf. v. 314. — **bustum**: Servius and Hyginus apparently think of the tomb of Achilles as on the Sigean shore; Ovid, following Euripides, has in mind a cenotaph on the shore of Thrace.

366. **copiam**: with a dependent infinitive, **soluere**; cf. Sall. *Cat.* 17. 6 *molliter uiuere copia;* Verg. *Aen.* IX. 483 *te adfari data copia.*

367. **Neptunia**: *i.e.* built by Neptune. — **soluere uincla**: cf. Hom. *Il.* XVI. 100 ὄφρ' οἶοι Τροίης ἱερὰ κρήδεμνα λύωμεν; similarly according to Polybius (XVII. 11. 5) the fortresses of Chalcis, Corinth, and Demetrias were called πέδαι Ἑλληνικαί.

368. **madefient**: cf. v. 360 n. *tepefaciet.*

369. **quae**: referring to the adjective **Polyxenia** (= *Polyxenae*); cf. Liv. II. 53. 1 *Veiens bellum exortum, quibus Sabini arma coniunxerunt.* — **ancipiti**, *two-edged;* probably with reference to the *bipennis*, used both as a weapon of warfare and as a sacrificial axe; cf. Lucil. 751 Lachm. *uecte atque ancipiti ferro effringam cardines.*

370. **truncum,** *headless.* — **summisso poplite** : cf. Ov. *Met.* XIII. 477 *super terram defecto poplite labens* (of Polyxena).

372. **animi amores**: with this use of an apparently otiose genitive cf. 2. 10 *animi curas;* 68. 26 *delicias animi;* 102. 2 *fides animi.* On the plural see v. 27 n.

374. **iam dudum**, *forthwith,* modifying **dedatur**; the emphasis rests on **iam**, as the speaker looks from a distant beginning; cf. Verg. *Geor.* I. 213 *papauer tempus humo tegere et iam dudum incumbere aratris; Aen.* II. 103 *iam dudum sumite poenas.* But in Plautus the phrase generally means 'a long time ago,' the emphasis usually resting upon *dudum,* as the speaker looks backward from the present; though the play on Amphitruo's misunderstanding of the term as a synonym for *modo (Amph.* 692) points toward the beginning of the use here fairly inaugurated by Catullus.

376 f. The belief indicated by these verses was widespread in antiquity ; cf. Nem. *Ecl.* 2. 10 ff. —

Hesterno collum poterit circumdare filo
(Currite ducentes subtegmina, currite, fusi),
Anxia nec mater discordis maesta puellae
380 Secubitu caros mittet sperare nepotes.
  Currite ducentes subtegmina, currite, fusi.'
    Talia praefantes quondam felicia Pelei
Carmina diuino cecinerunt pectore Parcae.
Praesentes namque ante domos inuisere castas
385 Heroum et sese mortali ostendere coetu
Caelicolae nondum spreta pietate solebant.
Saepe pater diuum templo in fulgente, reuisens
Annua cum festis uenissent sacra diebus,
Conspexit terra centum procumbere tauros.
390 Saepe uagus Liber Parnasi uertice summo
Thyiadas effusis euantis crinibus egit,

nutrix : the nurse continued to be
the girl's confidential attendant
throughout her married life, as was
often the case in the times of slavery in the southern part of the
United States. — orienti luce, *with
the morning light ;* cf. Lucr. V. 664
orienti lumine ; Ov. *Fast.* IV. 832
oriens dies.

380. Cf. 66. 15–16.

382–408. Epilogue, commenting
upon the withdrawal of divine
presence from the ceremonies
of men after the heroic age, on
account of the impiety of the
race.

382. **Pelei** : with synizesis, as in
v. 336 *Peleo,* which is, however, the
pure Latin dative ; but cf. 66. 94
hydrochoi (dat.), and v. 120 *Thesei,*
v. 229 *Erechthei* (gen.).

384. Ellis quotes Hes. frag. 218
ξυναὶ γὰρ τότε δαῖτες ἔσαν ξυνοὶ
δὲ θόωκοι ἀθανάτοισι θεοῖσι κατα-
θνητοῖς τ' ἀνθρώποις. — **praesentes,**
in bodily presence ; cf. Hor. *Carm.*

III. 5. 2 *praesens diuus habebitur
Augustus.* — **namque** : cf. 66. 65 n.

385. **coetu** : dative, as in 66. 37.

386. **caelicolae** : cf. 30. 4 ; 68.
138.

387. **templo in fulgente** : modifying v. 389 *conspexit,* etc. Evidently the poet is thinking of the
splendid temples of a later date
rather than of the simple structures
of heroic times. — **reuisens** : if the
correct reading, probably used absolutely ; cf. the ordinary use of *re-
uisere* with *ad.*

388. **annua,** etc. : doubtless a
typical occasion only, rather than
a known festival.

390. **uagus** : often used of the
aimless, frenzied rushing to and
fro of the god's followers ; cf. 63.
13, 86. — **Parnasi** : this famous
mountain of Phocis, the haunt
of the gods, rose just behind
Delphi.

391. **effusis,** etc. : cf. the description of the Bacchic rout in vv.

Cum Delphi tota certatim ex urbe ruentes
Acciperent laeti diuum fumantibus aris.
Saepe in letifero belli certamine Mauors
395 Aut rapidi Tritonis era aut Rhamnusia uirgo
Armatas hominum est praesens hortata cateruas.
Sed postquam tellus scelere est imbuta nefando,
Iustitiamque omnes cupida de mente fugarunt,
Perfudere manus fraterno sanguine fratres,
400 Destitit exstinctos natus lugere parentes,
Optauit genitor primaeui funera nati
Liber ut innuptae poteretur flore nouercae,

254 ff.; Ov. *Fast.* VI. 514 *Thyiades,
effusis per sua colla comis.*

392. Delphi: *i.e.* the inhabitants
of the city; cf. Just. XXIV. 7. 8
*urbem suam Delphi aucti uiribus
sociorum permuniuere*, and Grk.
Δελφοί often. The city was early
connected with the worship of Bacchus as of Apollo; cf. Aesch. *Eum.*
25 ἐξ οὔτε [*i.e.* Δελφῶν] Βάκχαις
ἐστρατήγησεν θεός, λαγὼ δίκην Πεν-
θεῖ καταρράψας μόρον; Paus. X. 4. 3
αἱ δὲ Θυιάδες γυναῖκες μέν εἰσιν
Ἀττικαί, φοιτῶσαι δὲ ἐς τὸν Παρνα-
σὸν παρὰ ἔτος αὐταί τε καὶ αἱ
γυναῖκες Δελφῶν ἄγουσιν ὄργια
Διονύσῳ.

394. Mauors: antique and poetic form for *Mars.*

395. rapidi Tritonis hera: *i.e.*
Athena, called Τριτογένεια by
Homer (*Il.* VIII. 39, etc.), probably from the river Triton in Boeotia (Strab. IX. 407; Paus. IX. 33.
7), rather than from the lake, or
river, Triton in Libya (Herod. IV.
178; Plin. *N. H.* V. 28). — **Rhamnusia uirgo**: *i.e.* Nemesis, so called
from her famous temple at Rham-
nus in Attica; cf. 66. 71; 68. 77;
Ov. *Met.* III. 406 *adsensit precibus
Rhamnusia iustis;* Stat. *Silu.* III.

5. 5 *audiat infesto licet hoc Rhamnusia uultu.* Ares and Athena often encourage men to battle in the
Iliad, but this function on the part
of Nemesis is nowhere else mentioned. Perhaps it is from an unknown Alexandrian source, or else
the conjecture of Baehrens is right
(*Amarunsia uirgo* = Artemis of
Amarynthus in Euboea; cf. Strabo.
X. 448; Paus. I. 31. 4).

397 ff. With this description of
the iron age cf. Hes. *Op.* 182 ff.;
Ov. *Met.* I. 127 ff.; Verg. *Geor.* II.
sub fin.

398. iustitiam, etc.: cf. Ov. *Fast.*
I. 249 *nondum iustitiam facinus
mortale fugarat.*

399. perfudere, etc.: cf. Lucr.
III. 72 *crudeles gaudent in tristi
funere fratris;* Verg. *Geor.* II. 510
gaudent perfusi sanguine fratrum.

401 f. genitor, etc.: was the op-
timate Catullus thinking of Catiline
in his own day (cf. Sall. *Cat.* 15. 2),
or of the story of Hippolytus (to
which, however, v. 402 hardly applies)? Cf., however, v. 402 n.

402. innuptae, *virgin;* the idea
apparently is that the father con-
ceives a passion for his son's promised bride, has him put out of the

Ignaro mater substernens se impia nato
Impia non uerita est diuos scelerare parentes,
405 Omnia fanda nefanda malo permixta furore
Iustificam nobis mentem auertere deorum.
Quare nec talis dignantur uisere coetus
Nec se contingi patiuntur lumine claro.

65.

Etsi me adsiduo defectum cura dolore
Seuocat a doctis, Ortale, uirginibus,

way upon the eve of the marriage,
and proceeds to contract a practically incestuous union with her himself, uniting two unnatural crimes.
And as the father sins with the
daughter, so (v. 403) the mother
with the son. — **nouercae**: said
by a sort of anticipation, to emphasize the unnaturalness of the position
of the former wife and sister, now
become the stepmother.

403. **ignaro**, etc.: again, is the
story from the poet's own day, or
only that of Jocasta (though **impia**
hardly applies to the action of the
innocent mother, equally ignorant
with her son)?

404. **diuos parentes**: *i.e.* the
deified ancestors of the family, who
would be especially outraged by such
impiety in their descendants; cf.
Grk. θεοὶ πατρῷοι; Leg. Reg. *diuis
parentum sacer esto;* C. I. L. I.
1241 *deis inferum parentum sacrum.*

405. **fanda nefanda**: cf. similar
phrases in Ter. *Ad.* 990 *iusta iniusta;* Hor. *Ep.* I. 7. 72 *dicenda
tacenda;* Verg. *Aen.* XII. 811 *digna
indigna;* but without asyndeton in
Verg. *Aen.* I. 543 *fandi atque nefandi;* Ov. *Art. Am.* I. 739 *mix-
tum fas omne nefasque.*

406. **iustificam**, *justly-dealing;*
ἅπαξ λεγόμενον.

408. **lumine claro**: *i.e.* the open
light of day, as distinct from the
cloud in which the gods commonly
hide themselves.

65. An address to Ortalus accompanying a translation from Callimachus (which is quite possibly
c. 66), and explaining that it is
sent instead of an original poem
because the death of the poet's
brother has made all poetic composition impossible for him; cf. in
general *c.* 68ᵃ, and with the lament
68. 20 ff. and 92 ff. Date of composition, about 59 B.C. (see Intr.
22). Beginning with *c.* 65, all the
remaining poems of the *liber Catulli* are in the elegiac metre, which
is used in none of the previous
poems. See Intr. 48.

1. **defectum**: the word apparently occurs here first in this sense, and
even later is more common either in
the absolute use or with an ablative
of specification than with an ablative
of means; cf. Ov. *Ex Pont.* III. 4.
37 *his* [*incitamentis*] *ego defectus;*
Phaedr. I. 21. 3 *defectus annis et
desertus uiribus.*

2. **doctis uirginibus**: *i.e.* the
Muses; cf. Ov. *Art. Am.* III. 411
doctis Musis; Met. V. 255 *doctas
sorores.* — **Ortale**: Q. Hortensius
Ortalus (see Intr. 65).

Nec potis est dulcis Musarum expromere fetus
  Mens animi: tantis fluctuat ipsa malis, —
5 Namque mei nuper Lethaeo gurgite fratris
  Pallidulum manans adluit unda pedem,
Troia Rhoeteo quem subter litore tellus
  Ereptum nostris obterit ex oculis.

. . . . . .

10 Nunquam ego te uita frater amabilior
  Adspiciam posthac: at certe semper amabo,
  Semper maesta tua carmina morte canam,
  Qualia sub densis ramorum concinit umbris
  Daulias absumpti fata gemens Ityli, —

3. **Musarum fetus:** cf. Cic. *Tusc.* V. 24. 68 *animi fetus.*

4. **mens animi:** cf. Plaut. *Epid.* 530 *pauor territat mentem animi;* Lucr. IV. 755 *cum somnus membra profudit mens animi uigilat.* — **fluctuat malis:** for the same figure carried a little further see 64. 62 *curarum fluctuat undis;* 68. 3, 13.

5. **Lethaeo gurgite:** the river of forgetfulness is first mentioned by Plato *Rep.* 621 C. Riese cites the (earlier) phrase of Simonides 171 Λήθης δόμοι, where the reference, however, is only to the lower world in general (cf. Hor. *Carm.* IV. 7. 27 *Lethaea uincula*). Vergil (*Aen.* VI. 705) describes the river as far within the lower world, *Lethaeumque domos placidas qui praenatat amnem;* but in *Culex* 215 *Lethaeas transnare per undas* is clearly meant, as here, the boundary-stream of Orcus, from beyond which there is no return (elsewhere the Styx); cf. Prop. V. 7. 91; Tib. III. 3. 10 *nudus Lethaea cogerer ire rate;* III. 5. 24 *cognoscere Lethaeam ratem.*

6. **pallidulum:** the diminutive

of affection; the paleness is that of death. — **adluit unda pedem:** as a general expression for crossing a river, although it strictly refers only to fording, while Lethe was crossed by boat; cf. Prop. I. 20. 8 *siu Aniena tuos tinxerit unda pedes.*

7. **subter:** the idea is closely connected with that of v. 8 **obterit**, *crushes*, the utterance of the brotherly love that shudders at the grave; contrast the familiar *sit tibi terra leuis.*

10 ff. **te,** etc.: the fresh grief of the writer carries him away from his theme into an apostrophe to his dead brother.— **uita amabilior:** cf. 64. 215 n.

14. **Daulias:** so the transformed Philomela (Ov. *Met.* VI. 424 ff.) was called, according to Thuc. II. 29, from Daulis, the town of Phocis, where Tereus lived; Homer, however (*Od.* XIX. 518 ff.), represents Itylus as the only son of Zethus, king of Thebes, by Aedon, daughter of Pandareus, king of Crete, and slain unwittingly by his own mother, who was jealous of the motherhood of Niobe, and supposed herself to be killing Niobe's eldest son.

15 Sed tamen in tantis maeroribus, Ortale, mitto
  Haec expressa tibi carmina Battiadae,
 Ne tua dicta uagis nequiquam credita uentis
  Effluxisse meo forte putes animo,
 Vt missum sponsi furtiuo munere malum
20 Procurrit casto uirginis e gremio,
 Quod miserae oblitae molli sub ueste locatum,
  Dum aduentu matris prosilit, excutitur ;
 Atque illud prono praeceps agitur decursu,
  Huic manat tristi conscius ore rubor.

15. **sed tamen**: after the long parenthesis the poet returns to his theme, **sed**, as often, being resumptive.

16. **haec**: probably *c.* 66 is referred to. — **expressa**, *translated;* cf. Ter. *Ad.* 11 *uerbum de uerbo expressum extulit.* — **Battiadae**: Callimachus, the famous Alexandrian scholar and poet at the court of Ptolemy Philadelphus, was the son of a certain Battus of Cyrene, and claimed descent from the founder of that city; cf. 7. 4, 6 n.; 116. 2.

17. **credita uentis**: with the figure cf. 30. 10 n.

19. **ut**, etc.: the comparison is of the irrevocable swiftness with which the apple falls and the reminders vanish. — **missum munere**: cf. 101. 8 *tradita munere.* — **sponsi**: the secrecy of the gift, and the confusion of the maiden at its discovery, show that a secret lover is meant. — **malum**: apples were proverbially the gifts of lovers; cf. the Callimachean story of Cydippe; Theocr. 3. 10, *et al.;* Verg. *Ecl.* 3. 71 *aurea mala decem misi;* 64 *malo me Galatea petit;* Prop. I. 3. 24 *nunc furtiua cauis poma dabam manibus;* Petron. *Frag.* 33. 1 Büch. *aurea mala mihi, dulcis mea Marcia mittis.* Cf. also the story of

Atalanta, and the explanation of the *aureolum malum* (2. 12) by the quotations from Vergil and Petronius.

20. **procurrit**, etc.: Festus (p. 165) refers to a proverb based on such accidents. — **casto**: the girl is not of loose character, but a carefully trained daughter who has not learned how not to blush. — **gremio**: the girdle around the body just below the breasts made the upper part of the robe a convenient, if not safe, receptacle for small objects.

21. **miserae oblitae**: with this use of the adjective instead of the adverb *misere* with another adjective cf. 64. 57. — **molli** carries still further the general impression of gentle innocence conveyed by **casto**, and thus emphasizes the painful blush of her embarrassment.

22. **prosilit**: the girl rises respectfully as her mother enters, but hastily, because she is surprised while dreaming of her lover, and is at first oblivious of other matters; thus her sudden movement dislodges the apple.

23. The spondaic verse well expresses the girl's dismay, which makes even the swift fall of the apple seem to occupy a life-time.

24. **huic**: contrasted with v. 23

66.

Omnia qui magni dispexit lumina mundi,
     Qui stellarum ortus comperit atque obitus,
Flammeus ut rapidi solis nitor obscuretur,
     Vt cedant certis sidera temporibus,
5 Vt Triuiam furtim sub Latmia saxa relegans

illud; the eye turns from the tell-tale apple to the tell-tale face of the maiden.

66. This translation of the Βερενίκης Πλόκαμος of Callimachus, a few fragments of which are extant, is quite possibly the poem sent to Hortensius with *c.* 65. It is complex and artificial, and, indeed, if the translation was made when Catullus was burdened with grief for the loss of his brother, it is not strange that his native genius shows so little through it. Whether the obscurity of some passages in it is due to lack of care on the part of the translator, or to an excessive fidelity to the original, cannot be determined; but the general characteristics of Alexandrian poetry would lead us to refer the fault to Callimachus himself. The theme, a compound of court tradition and of astronomical knowledge, is as follows: Berenice, daughter of Magas, king of Cyrene, and wife of her cousin Ptolemy Euergetes (reigned 247–222 B.C.), king of Egypt, had for her husband's safety vowed to the gods a lock of her hair, when, shortly after his accession to the throne and marriage, the king was setting out on an expedition against Syria. Upon his safe return the vow was paid, and the tress deposited in the temple of the deified Arsinoe on the promontory of Zephyrion. Next morning, however, it had disappeared; but the anger of the king

was appeased by the court astronomer, Conon, who said that he had descried it among the stars, where it must have been placed by divine agency. To verify his words Conon pointed out the hitherto undistinguished minor constellation which is now known as *Coma Berenices.* Date, about 59 B.C. (cf. introductory note to *c.* 65).

1. **omnia qui**: the antecedent clause begins in v. 7. — **dispexit**, *descried;* as distinguishing in the darkness, or amid the multitude of other stars. — **mundi**, *the firmament;* as in 64. 206; but with a different meaning in 47. 2.

3. **rapidi**, *scorching,* as the words **flammeus nitor** clearly indicate; cf. Verg. *Geor.* I. 92 *rapidi potentia solis acrior;* IV. 425 *rapidus torrens sitientis Sirius Indos.* — **obscuretur**: *sc.* in an eclipse; cf. Plin. *N. H.* II. 47 *nullum aliud sidus eodem modo obscuretur.*

4. **ut cedant**, etc.: in v. 2 the reference is to the apparent daily motion of the stars, due to the revolution of the earth on its axis; in v. 4, to their yearly motion with reference to the apparent position of the sun, due to the revolution of the earth about the sun.

5. **Triuiam**: cf. 34. 15 n. — **Latmia saxa**: Selene was wont to meet secretly upon Mt. Latmus in Caria the beautiful shepherd Endymion, with whom she had fallen in love (cf. Paus. V. 1); **sub saxa** = *in antrum.*

Dulcis amor gyro deuocet aerio,
Idem me ille Conon caelesti in lumine uidit
   E Bereniceo uertice caesariem
Fulgentem clare, quam cunctis illa deorum
10   Leuia protendens bracchia pollicita est,
Qua rex tempestate nouo auctus hymenaeo
   Vastatum finis iuerat Assyrios,
Dulcia nocturnae portans uestigia rixae
   Quam de uirgineis gesserat exuuiis.
15 Estne nouis nuptis odio Venus, atque parentum
   Frustrantur falsis gaudia lacrimulis
Vbertim thalami quas intra limina fundunt?
   Non, ita me diui, uera gemunt, iuerint.
Id mea me multis docuit regina querelis
20   Inuisente nouo proelia torua uiro.

6. **aerio**: so Horace of the heavens, *Carm.* I. 28. 5 *aerias temptasse domos*.

7. **me**: the poem is a monologue spoken by the lock (v. 51) of Berenice's hair itself. — **ille**: *i.e.* the person referred to in v. 1 ff., **me ille Conon** corresponding to *omnia qui*. — **Conon**: the astronomer-royal of Ptolemy, a native of Samos, and friend of Archimedes. He wrote some astronomical treatises, which, however, have not been preserved; cf. Verg. *Ecl.* 3. 40 ff. *Conon et quis fuit alter descripsit radio totum qui gentibus orbem, tempora quae messor, quae curuus arator haberet?*

7–10. Cf. Callim. *Frag.* 34 ἦ με Κόνων ἔβλεψεν ἐν ἠέρι τὸν Βερενίκης βόστρυχον, ὃν κείνη πᾶσιν ἔθηκε θεοῖς.

9. **cunctis deorum**: cf. v. 33 *cunctis diuis*, and Call. *l.c.*

10. **leuia bracchia**: cf. 64. 332. — **protendens**: standing in the attitude of prayer, with arms outstretched and lifted, and palms turned upward.

11. **auctus hymenaeo**: cf. 64. 25 *taedis felicibus aucte*. On the hiatus **nouo auctus** in thesis and the lengthening of the short syllable before **hymenaeo** see Intr. 86 *d, g*.

12. **Assyrios**: for *Syrios;* cf. 68. 144; Verg. *Geor.* II. 465; Hor. *Carm.* II. 11. 16, etc. The war was to avenge the murder of Berenice, sister of Ptolemy Euergetes and widow of Antiochus Theos, by her step-son Seleucus Callinicus, who had in 246 B.C. succeeded his father on the throne of Syria.

15. **parentum gaudia**: *i.e.* in their hope of descendants; cf. 64. 379 f.

18. **ita me diui iuerint**: cf. 61. 196; 97. 1; and with the hyperbaton, 44. 9. With the syncopation of the consonant *u* in the verb cf. Enn. *Ann.* 339 Vahl. (ap. Cic. *De Sen. init.*) *adiuero*.

20. **inuisente**: apparently unique

At tu non orbum luxti deserta cubile,
　　Sed fratris cari flebile discidium?
Quam penitus maestas exedit cura medullas!
　　Vt tibi tunc toto pectore sollicitae
25 Sensibus ereptis mens excidit! at te ego certe
　　Cognoram a parua uirgine magnanimam.
Anne bonum oblita es facinus, quo regium adepta es
　　Coniugium, quod non fortior ausit alis?
Sed tum maesta uirum mittens quae uerba locuta es!
30　　Iuppiter, ut tristi lumina saepe manu!

in the sense of active participation in an affair.

21. **at**: introducing a possible protest of Berenice against the charge of inconsistency. — **luxti**: for *luxisti;* see 14. 14 n. *misti*.

22. **fratris**: Berenice was the first cousin of Ptolemy (III.) Euergetes, both being grandchildren on the father's side of Ptolemy I. But *frater* may be used here, like the Gr. ἀδελφός, of this relationship (cf. III. 4 n.); or, more likely, it represents the way in which Ptolemy and Berenice were usually spoken of; for the custom in the Egyptian royal house of marriage between brother and sister is well known; cf. the decree of Canopus l. 7 βασιλεὺς Πτολεμαῖος . . . καὶ βασίλισσα Βερενίκη ἡ ἀδελφὴ αὐτοῦ καὶ γυνή θεοὶ εὐεργέται.

23. **quam**, etc.: beginning the triumphant rejoinder to the protest in vv. 21 and 22; sisters show no such extremity of grief over separation from brothers. — **penitus exedit medullas**: cf. 35. 15 n.; Verg. *Aen.* IV. 66 *est mollis flamma medullas.*

25. **sensibus ereptis**: cf. 51. 5 *misere quod omnis eripit sensus mihi.*

27 f. Hyginus (*Poet. Astr.* II. 24), evidently referring to this passage,

says that Berenice (whom he calls the daughter of Ptolemy Philadelphus) once saved her father's life by mounting a horse and rallying his wavering troops. But this would not have won her husband. The reference is doubtless to the story told by Justin (XXVI. 3) that Berenice's mother was opposed to her betrothal to Ptolemy, and desired to marry her rather to Demetrius, brother of Antigonus, king of Macedonia. Demetrius, however, formed a criminal connection with the mother, and was assassinated by a band of conspirators, at whose head stood Berenice, who thereby was enabled to fulfil her former engagement.

28. **coniugium** = *maritum ;* cf. 68. 107; Tac. *Ann.* II. 13. 3 *matrimonia ac pecunias hostium praedae destinare.* — **quod . . . alis**: *i.e.* a deed which none other would dare, and prove himself thereby the braver. Ellis compares Hor. *Carm.* III. 23. 18 *non sumptuosa blandior hostia molliuit auersos Penates.* — **alis**: cf. 29. 15 n. *alid.*

29. **tum**: directing the thought once more to the later period and greater fear. — **mittens**: cf. 96. 4 n. *missas.*

30. **Iuppiter**: cf. 1. 7 n. —

Quis te mutauit tantus deus? an quod amantes
   Non longe a caro corpore abesse uolunt?
Atque ibi me cunctis pro dulci coniuge diuis
   Non sine taurino sanguine pollicita es,
35 Si reditum tetulisset. Is haud in tempore longo
   Captam Asiam Aegypti finibus addiderat.
Quis ego pro factis caelesti reddita coetu
   Pristina uota nouo munere dissoluo.
Inuita, o regina, tuo de uertice cessi,
40   Inuita: adiuro teque tuumque caput:
Digna ferat quod si quis inaniter adiurarit:
   Sed qui se ferro postulet esse parem?

---

tristi: cf. v. 21 *luxti;* 14. 14 n. *misti*. The action was, of course, that of dashing the tears away.

31. **an**, etc.: *i.e.* (*utrum deus te mutauit*) *an eo factum est quod*, etc.

33. **cunctis diuis**: but cf. v. 9 *cunctis deorum.*

34. **taurino sanguine**: the sacrifices of cattle may have been in acknowledgment of past favors, while the new vow was made for the future; or they may have been part of the vow to be paid in the future; cf. in either case the *uotorum nuncupatio* of the Roman consuls at their entry upon office, and Hannibal's offering (Liv. XXI. 21. 9).

35. **tetulisset**: see 34. 8 n.

36. **Asiam**: Ptolemy ravaged Asia Minor and the eastern districts, at least as far as the Euphrates; cf. Inscr. of Adule; Just. XXVII. 3.

37. **caelesti reddita coetu**: the lock speaks from its final resting-place among the stars, passing over the brief interval of deposit in the temple of Zephyritis. On the form **coetu** see 34. 8 n.

38. **pristina**, *of the past.* — **nouo**,

of the present; the lock has but lately reached its present seat, and is explaining to its mistress the cause of its mysterious disappearance. — **dissoluo**: on the diaeresis see Intr. 86 *b.*

39. **inuita**, etc.: cf. Verg. *Aen.* VI. 460 *inuitus, regina, tuo de litore cessi.*

40. **adiuro**, etc.: cf. Callim. *Frag.* 35[b] σήν τε καρὴν ὤμοσα σόν τε βίον; oaths are sworn by that which is dearest, especially, then, by the life or head of the person himself or of his nearest friend. So with especial fitness the lock swears by the head from which it was severed; cf. Verg. *Aen.* IV. 492 *testor te, germana, tuumque dulce caput;* IX. 300 *per caput hoc iuro per quod pater ante solebat;* Ov. *Trist.* V. 4. 45 *per caput ipse suum solitus iurare tuumque;* Plin. *Ep.* II. 20. 6 (of the perjury of Regulus by the head of his son). In direct imitation of Callimachus (*l. c.*) Catullus uses the accusative with **adiuro** in this sense, a construction which appears next in the Augustan age; cf. Verg. *Aen.* XII. 816 *adiuro Stygii caput implacabile fontis.*

Ille quoque euersus mons est quem maximum in oris
      Progenies Thiae clara superuehitur,
45 Cum Medi peperere nouum mare, cumque iuuentus
      Per medium classi barbara nauit Athon.
   Quid facient crines, cum ferro talia cedant?
      Iuppiter, ut Chalybon omne genus pereat,
   Et qui principio sub terra quaerere uenas
50   Institit ac ferri fingere duritiem!
   Abiunctae paulo ante comae mea fata sorores
      Lugebant, cum se Memnonis Aethiopis
   Vnigena impellens nutantibus aera pennis
      Obtulit Arsinoes † elocridicos ales equus,

---

43. maximum: cf. Strab. 331
fr. 33 ὑψηλότατον (of Mt. Athos).
— **in oris**: not restrictive of **maximum**, but modifying **quem** directly
(= *in litore stantem*), 'that most
mighty promontory-mountain.'
   44. progenies Thiae: *i.e.* the
sun; Hesiod (*Theog.* 371) says that
Thia bore Helios and Selene to
Hyperion; cf. Pind. *Isth.* 4. 1.
   45 f. The cutting by Xerxes of
a ship-canal through the isthmus of
Athos is described in Herod. VII. 24.
   **47. quid facient . . . cum . . .
cedant**: cf. the inverse construction
of moods in Verg. *Ecl.* 3. 16 *quid
domini faciant, audent cum talia
fures?*
   48. Chalybon, etc.: cf. Callim.
Frag. 35° Χαλύβων ὡς ἀπόλοιτο
γένος, γειόθεν ἀντέλλοντα κακὸν
φυτὸν οἵ μιν ἔφηναν; Hor. *Sat.* II.
1. 42 *o pater et rex Iuppiter, ut
pereat positum robigine telum.* The
Chalybes here referred to are undoubtedly not those of Spain, but
the tribe of iron-workers in Pontus;
cf. Xen. *Anab.* V. 5. 1 ἀφικνοῦνται
εἰς Χάλυβας. οὗτοι ὀλίγοι τε ἦσαν
καὶ ὁ βίος ἦν τοῖς πλείστοις αὐτῶν
ἀπὸ σιδηρείας.

50. fingere: the verb, usually
applied to easily worked substances
(such as wax and clay), is strongly
contrasted with **duritiem**; the
Chalybes worked against nature in
learning to dig iron from the con-
cealing earth, and to mould its
hardness so wonderfully into form.
   51. With this verse begins a passage of peculiar and probably un-
surmountable difficulty. — **abiunctae** (*sc. a me*), *bereaved;* modifying
comae. The lock had been severed
but a short time from its sister-locks
on the head of Berenice, and their
sorrow was still fresh (**lugebant**),
when it was snatched from the temple and carried to heaven.
   53. unigena: born of the same
parents, the brother (cf. 64. 300);
i.e. Emathion (cf. Apollod. III. 12.
4 Τιθωνὸν μὲν οὖν Ἠὼς ἁρπάσασα
δι' ἔρωτα εἰς Αἰθιοπίαν κομίζει, κἀκεῖ
συνελθοῦσα γεννᾷ παῖδας Ἡμαθίωνα
καὶ Μέμνονα), who was apparently
identified mythically with the ostrich
(cf. v. 54) as was Memnon himself
with a certain species of black hawk
(cf. Ov. *Met.* XIII. 600 ff.).
   54. Arsinoes: Arsinoe was the
sister-wife of Ptolemy Philadelphus,

55　Isque per aetherias me tollens auolat umbras
　　　Et Veneris casto conlocat in gremio.
　Ipsa suum Zephyritis eo famulum legarat,
　　　Graia Canopiis incola litoribus,
　† Hi dii uen ibi uario ne solum in lumine caeli
60　　Ex Ariadneis aurea temporibus
　Fixa corona foret, sed nos quoque fulgeremus
　　　Deuotae flaui uerticis exuuiae,
　Vuidulam a fletu cedentem ad templa deum me
　　　Sidus in antiquis diua nouum posuit :
65　Virginis et saeui contingens namque Leonis

and was worshiped under the attributes of Aphrodite in a temple
erected to her honor on the promontory of Zephyrion, between Alexandria and Canopus, whence she
was called Zephyritis. — No satisfac-
te ry emendation of **elocridicos** has
yet been proposed. — **ales equus**:
according to Pausanias Arsinoe was
represented riding upon an ostrich;
IX. 31. 1 τὴν δὲ Ἀρσινόην στρουθὸς
φέρει χαλκῆ τῶν ἀπτήνων.

55. aetherias umbras: it was
in the night that the lock disappeared. With **aetherias** in the
sense of *aerias* cf. Lucr. IV. 182
*clamor in aetheriis dispersus nubi-
bus austri;* Ov. *Fast.* I. 682 *aetheria
spargite semen aqua.* — **auolat**:
though the ostrich does not fly, yet
his exceedingly swift running when
aided by his wings was enough like
flight to satisfy the poet.

56. Veneris: *i.e. Arsinoes;* cf.
v. 54 n. *Arsinoes.*

57. famulum: as the ostrich is
called the *famulus* of Arsinoe, so
the hind is the *famula* of Diana in
Silius Italicus (XIII. 124 *numen
erat iam cerua loci, famulamque
Dianae credebant*), and the lion
the *famulus* of Cybele in Manilius
(IV. 760 *Idaeae matris famulus*).

58. Graia: as the daughter of
Ptolemy I., Arsinoe was of Greek
descent. — **Canopiis**: *i.e.* Egyptian;
cf. Luc. *Phar.* X. 64 *imbelli Canopo;*
Verg. *Geor.* IV. 287 *Pellaei gens
fortunata Canopi.* — **incola litoribus**: cf. 64. 300 *cultricem montibus.*

59. See Crit. App.

61. **corona**: the wedding-wreath
of Ariadne, given by Dionysus upon
her marriage with him, was placed
among the stars; cf. Ov. *Met.* VIII.
177 ff. *utque perenni sidere clara
foret, sumptam de fronte [Ariad-
nae] coronam immisit caelo;* Germ.
Phaen. 71 *clara Ariadnaeo sacrata
e crine corona.* — **nos**: perhaps
plural under the influence of *exuuiae* (v. 62).

62. **flaui**: so of Ariadne's hair
in 64. 63 *flauo uertice.* — **exuuiae**:
since the lock had yielded only to
force; cf. v. 39 ff.

63. **uuidulam a fletu**: the lock
does not cease to emphasize its own
unwillingness to leave its mistress;
the words refer to v. 51 f.

65. **uirginis**: according to the
older account she was Astraea, the
daughter of the Titan Astraeus,
who fought against the gods. She,
however, descended to earth and

Lumina, Callisto iuncta Lycaoniae,
Vertor in occasum, tardum dux ante Booten,
Qui uix sero alto mergitur Oceano.
Sed quamquam me nocte premunt uestigia diuum,
70   Lux autem canae Tethyi restituit,
(Pace tua fari hic liceat, Rhamnusia uirgo :
Namque ego non ullo uera timore tegam,
Nec si me infestis discerpent sidera dictis,
Condita quin ueri pectoris euoluam)

dwelt among men, and was the last of the immortals to leave earth when the brazen age came on; cf. Hyg. *Astrom.* II. 25; Ov. *Met.* I. 149 *uirgo caede madentes, ultima caelestum, terras Astraea reliquit.* According to another tradition Virgo was Erigone, who hanged herself through grief at the murder of her father, Icarius, by shepherds to whom he had for the first time in their lives given wine to drink, and who supposed themselves poisoned by him; cf. Apollod. III. 14. 7; Hyg. *Fab.* 130; *Astron.* II. 4. — **namque**: postpositive, as in 64. 384; but nowhere else before Vergil does it stand after so many words in its clause; cf. Draeger *Hist. Synt.* II.² p. 162. — **Leonis**: according to Hyg. *Astron.* II. 24 the Nemean lion slain by Heracles.

66. Callisto: dative; she was the daughter of the Arcadian Lycaon, and an attendant of the huntress Artemis; but being ravished by Zeus and banished from the presence of her mistress, she was changed by Hera into a bear, and later, on being slain by her own son Arcas, was placed among the stars as the constellation Ursa Major or Helice; cf. Ov. *Met.* II. 401 ff.; *Fast.* II. 153 ff.

67. Booten: said by some to be Icarius (cf. v. 65 n.); by others,

to be Arcas (v. 66 n.) or Lycaon; cf. Ov. *Fast.* VI. 235 f.

68. uix sero, etc.: this was a traditional characteristic of Bootes from the time of Homer (cf. *Od.* V. 272 ὀψὲ δύοντα Βοώτην) and is explained by Sir Geo. C. Lewis (*Astron. of the Anc.*, p. 59 ap. Ellis) as derived from the fact that Bootes rises in a horizontal, but sets in a vertical, attitude.

69 f. sed quamquam, etc.: *i.e.* although I am one of the stars, and keep company with the gods; cf. Arat. 339 θεῶν ὑπὸ ποσσὶ φορεῖται; Verg. *Ecl.* 5. 57 *sub pedibus uidet nubes et sidera Daphnis.*

70. lux, etc.: *i.e.* at the approach of dawn I set beneath the western wave. — **Tethyi** (= *mari*): cf. 88. 5, and with the Greek dative, 64. 247.

71. Rhamnusia uirgo: Nemesis (cf. 64. 395 n.; 68. 77) might punish the arrogance that exalted in estimation things human above things divine.

73. nec: apparently the first instance of the use of *nec* in the sense of *ne quidem*. — **discerpent**: perhaps the only instance of the figurative use of this word in the sense of *revile;* cf. however *carpo* and *concerpo.*

74. quin: depending on **non tegam**, v. 73 being parenthetical.

75 Non his tam laetor rebus quam me afore semper
       Afore me a dominae uertice discrucior,
   Quicum ego, dum uirgo quondam fuit, omnibus **expers**
       Vnguentis, una milia multa bibi.
   Nunc uos optato quom iunxit lumine taeda,
80   Non prius unanimis corpora coniugibus
   Tradite nudantes reiecta ueste papillas,
       Quam iucunda mihi munera libet onyx,
   Vester onyx, casto colitis quae iura cubili.
       Sed quae se impuro dedit adulterio,
85 Illius ah mala dona leuis bibat irrita puluis :
       Namque ego ab indignis praemia nulla peto.
   Sed magis, o nuptae, semper concordia uestras,
       Semper amor sedes incolat adsiduus.
   Tu uero, regina, tuens cum sidera diuam
90   Placabis festis luminibus Venerem,
   Vnguinis expertem non siris esse tuam me,

—**euoluam**: on the diaeresis see Intr. 86 *b*.

75 f. Observe the epanalepsis with inversion in **me afore . . . afore me**.

77 ff. The sense is, ‘I shared, to be sure, the simple life of my mistress before her marriage; but since that time have lived a life of indulgent luxury for which my present position is not a gratifying exchange. I miss my costly ointments; therefore do you, who, like her, are chaste and happy brides, offer me that gift upon your marriage.’ — **quicum**: feminine, as in 69. 8, but rare in this gender. — **expers** modifies **ego** and **una** goes with **quicum**.

79. **optato lumine**: cf. 64. 31 *optatae luces;* with **lumine** = *die* cf. v. 90.

80. **non**: instead of *ne*, as belonging more closely to **prius** than to

the clause as a whole. — **prius . . . quam mihi** (v. 82): cf. Callim. *Frag.* 35^d πρὶν ἀστέρι τῷ Βερενίκης. — **unanimis**: cf. 9. 4 n.; 30. 1.

82. **onyx**: *i.e.* the alabaster box in which ointment was kept; cf. Prop. III. 13. 30 *cum dabitur Syrio munere plenus onyx.*

83. **uester**: restrictive, as defined by the **quae**-clause. — **iura**: used absolutely as contrasted with *illicita* (*i.e. adulteria*).

85. **ah** : here expressing strong reprobation; cf. 60. 5; 64. 135. — **bibat puluis** : cf. Ov. *Fast.* III. 472 *en iterum lacrimas accipe, harena, meas;* Prop. V. 11. 6 *nempe tuas lacrimas litora surda bibent.*

87. **sed magis**: cf. 73. 4 *immo etiam magis;* 68. 30 n. *magis.*

90. **festis luminibus**: cf. 64. 388 *festis diebus.*

91. **unguinis**, etc.: *i.e.* do not

Sed potius largis adfice muneribus.
Sidera cur retinent? utinam coma regia fiam:
Proximus Hydrochoi fulgeret Oarion.

67.

O dulci iucunda uiro, iucunda parenti,
Salue, teque bona Iuppiter auctet ope,

suppose me happy beyond limit now, and so subject me to the same privations that I suffered before you became queen (v. 77). — **non**: not infrequent in poetry and post-Augustan prose instead of *ne* in prohibitions, in spite of Quintilian's censure; I. 5. 50 *qui tamen dicat pro illo* ne feceris, non feceris, *in idem incidat uitium* [*soloecismum*], *quia alterum negandi est, alterum uetandi.* — **tuam**: Hor. *Carm.* I. 25. 7 *me tuo pereunte;* Ov. *Her.* 10. 75 *uiuimus, et non sum, Theseu, tua;* Prop. I. 9. 22 *et nihil iratae posse negare tuae.*

94. **proximus**, etc.: the sense is, 'All I care for is to return to my former station; then the stars might do whatever they liked for all of me.' — **Hydrochoi**: dative, as from ὑδροχοεύς; cf. 64. 382 n. *Pelei.* The constellation, called by the Romans *Aquarius*, extends over a space from 90° to 140° distant from Orion. — **fulgeret**: from *fulgĕre*, an ante-classical and poetical variant for *fulgēre*. The imperfect subjunctive follows naturally upon an easily understood protasis like *si modo hoc fieret.* — **Oarion**: from the Greek Ὠαρίων.

67. This pasquinade, in the form of a conversation between the poet and the door of a certain house, abounds in difficulties of interpretation for us, though its directness of personal reference must have made it clear enough to the Veronese.

Its tone of familiarity with, and personal interest in, the tittle-tattle of the city seems to indicate that it was composed before Catullus left Verona to live at Rome, and not during one of his brief visits to his old home. The motive is apparently as follows (see also later notes): The Door is that of a house in Verona (v. 34), formerly owned by an aged (v. 4) bachelor or widower (v. 6) named Balbus, after whose death (v. 6) it came into the possession of his son (v. 1) Caecilius, who thereupon married (v. 6) and brought home a young and lively widow (v. 20) from Brixia (v. 32), who claimed to be also a maid (v. 19). Strange rumors about her life soon began to spread through Verona, and the poet inquires of the Door why it has betrayed its master's confidence (presumably by letting in lovers to corrupt the young wife). The Door defends itself by saying that it has not betrayed its trust, but the woman was a bad lot before she came to Verona, and the current gossip is true of the period of her former marriage; for though her husband was notoriously impotent, his father stepped in to fill the son's place in the household, and the woman moreover was too intimate with certain other people named and hinted at. The proof of this culpability is found not only in rumors that have followed her

Ianua, quam Balbo dicunt seruisse benigne
   Olim, cum sedes ipse senex tenuit,
5 Quamque ferunt rursus uoto seruisse maligne,
   Postquam es porrecto facta marita sene,
Dic agedum nobis quare mutata feraris
   In dominum ueterem deseruisse fidem.
'Non (ita Caecilio placeam, cui tradita nunc sum)
10   Culpa mea est, quamquam dicitur esse mea,
Nec peccatum a me quisquam pote dicere quicquam:
   † Verum istius populi ianua qui te facit!
Qui, quacumque aliquid reperitur non bene factum,

from Brixia, but in her own familiar talk with her maids in the presence of the Door, which she treated as if it could neither hear nor speak.— The conception of the door as a bar in the way of would-be lovers is familiar enough in ancient poetry (cf. 63. 65 and Plautus, Horace, Ovid, Propertius, etc. *passim*); Propertius (I. 16) also represents the door as speaking of its experiences.

1–8. The poet speaks: You have been the trusted servant of the newly-made husband (Caecilius), as you were of his father (Balbus); the latter you served faithfully (vv. 3, 4); now that he is dead (v. 6) you know well what he would wish you to do (v. 5 uoto), but you have wilfully disregarded it (seruisse maligne), and have entirely changed (v. 7 mutata) your character; why have you thus abandoned your former habit of fidelity to your master's interests (v. 8)?

1. dulci uiro: cf. 66. 33 *dulci coniuge.*

2. teque, etc.: cf. the formal expression in the invocation of Scipio, Liv. XXIX. 27 *ea uos omnia bene iuuetis, bonis auctibus auxitis.* — bona ope: cf. 34. 23 *bona ope.*

— auctet: the word apparently occurs only here and in Plaut. *Amph.* 6 *bono atque amplo auctare lucro,* and Lucr. I. 56 *unde omnis natura creet res, auctet, alatque.*

4. ipse senex: the aged master, in contrast to his son and heir.

5. rursus, *on the contrary;* cf. 22. 11.— uoto seruisse maligne: observe the emphatic contrast to v. 3 *Balbo seruisse benigne.*

6. porrecto: *sc.* in death; cf. Prop. II. 8. 33 *uiderat informem multa Patroclon harena porrectum.* — marita: *i.e.* you have come into the possession of a married couple (Balbus having been, therefore, a bachelor or a widower); cf. Liv. XXVII. 31. 5 *uagabatur per maritas domos;* and on the other hand such phrases as 68. 6 *in lecto caelibe.*

7. agedum: cf. 63. 78.

9. ita Caecilio placeam: the Door is sincere in its desire to be faithful to the husband, Caecilius, and to be acquitted in his sight, for it evidently views him as sinned against by a designing and criminal wife; cf. 20 ff. n.

11. pote: see 17. 24 n.

12. See Crit. App.

13. qui ... omnes: apparently referring to v. 12 † populi. — qua-

Ad me omnes clamant, "Ianua, culpa tua est."'
15 Non istuc satis est uno te dicere uerbo,
    Sed facere ut quiuis sentiat et uideat.
'Qui possum? nemo quaerit nec scire laborat.'
    Nos uolumus; nobis dicere ne dubita.
'Primum igitur, uirgo quod fertur tradita nobis,
20   Falsum est.   Non illam uir prior attigerit,
    Languidior tenera cui pendens sicula beta
    Nunquam se mediam sustulit ad tunicam:
    Sed pater illius gnati uiolasse cubile
    Dicitur et miseram conscelerasse domum,
25 Siue quod impia mens caeco flagrabat amore,
    Seu quod iners sterili semine natus erat
    Et quaerendus is unde foret neruosius illud
    Quod posset zonam soluere uirgineam.'
    Egregium narras mira pietate parentem,
30   Qui ipse sui gnati minxerit in gremium.
'Atqui non solum hoc se dicit cognitum habere
    Brixia † chinea suppositum specula,

cumque: *sc. ratione*, modifying
factum.

15. non satis, etc.: the poet suggests that a categorical denial is
not enough, but convincing proof
of innocence should be offered.

18. nos ... nobis: referring to
the speaker only, as in v. 7.

19 ff. uirgo, etc.: *i.e.* to be sure,
though a widow, she passed herself
off as a maid, and every one knew
that she might well be so as far as
her husband was concerned.

19. nobis: the Door unites interests with the injured husband
against the guilty wife.

20. uir prior: carefully to distinguish her weakling husband from
Caecilius. — attigerit: subjunctive
of concession.

21. tenera beta: so Augustus is
said (Suet. *Oct.* 87) to have used
betissare for *languere*. — sicula:
ἅπαξ λεγόμενον.

23. illius: elsewhere in Catullus
this and similar genitives have the
penult short.

24. conscelerasse domum: cf.
64. 404 *diuos scelerare parentes*,
also of unnatural crime.

26. iners sterili semine: on the
repetition of idea in the adjectives
cf. 64. 64, 103, 221; 90. 5; and
(with Ellis) v. 48.

28. zonam, etc.: cf. 2. 13 n.

32. Brixia; the modern Brescia,
the capital of the (Gallic) Cenom-
ani (Liv. XXXII. 30).   It is about
as far to the westward of Sirmio as
Verona is to the eastward (one half-

Flauus quam molli praecurrit flumine Mella,
    Brixia, Veronae mater amata meae,
35 Sed de Postumio et Corneli narrat amore,
    Cum quibus illa malum fecit adulterium.
Dixerit hic aliquis, "Quid? tu istaec, ianua, nosti,
    Cui nunquam domini limine abesse licet,
Nec populum auscultare, sed hic suffixa tigillo
40   Tantum operire soles aut aperire domum?"
Saepe illam audiui furtiua uoce loquentem
    Solam cum ancillis haec sua flagitia,
Nomine dicentem quos diximus, ut pote quae mi
    Speraret nec linguam esse nec auriculam.
45 Praeterea addebat quendam, quem dicere nolo
    Nomine ne tollat rubra supercilia.

hour by rail).—The remainder of the verse is involved in great difficulty; it might naturally be taken to refer to the situation of Brixia at the base of a hill, but suppositum is apparently not used elsewhere in the sense of 'lying at the foot of,' and no hill in the neighborhood of Brixia is called by a name resembling chinea till about A.D. 1500, when this passage from Catullus might have influenced local nomenclature (cf. the case of the Grampian Hills).

33. praecurrit Mella: the Mella (cf. Verg. *Geor.* IV. 278 *curua prope flumina Mellae*) flows about a mile to the westward of Brixia.

34. mater: Brixia is nowhere else called the mother-city of Verona, though some writers speak of Verona as a Gallic town; cf. Ptol. III. 1. 27; Just. XX. 5. 8; not so, perhaps, Livy (V. 35. 1), nor, certainly, Pliny (*N.H.* III. 130).

35. The two men, evidently inhabitants of Brixia, are otherwise unknown

37–40. A remark of the Door itself, which, having been fairly started on its story by v. 18, continues it to the end, preferring to anticipate rather than to await criticism. — dixerit aliquis: see Roby (*Lat. Gram.* vol. II. *Pref.*), who thinks the verb in this construction probably indicative.

39. tigillo: the lintel, not the jamb, as suffixa sufficiently indicates. The ancient door, like some heavier specimens of modern make, swung on two vertical pivots fitting into sockets near the extremity of lintel and sill respectively.

46. tollat supercilia: *sc.* in anger; cf. Schol. on Ar. *Vesp.* 655 τὰς ὀφρῦς αἴρειν ἔθος τοῖς ὀργιζομένοις. — rubra: perhaps not of the color of the brows, as a mark of identification, but of the flush of anger on the forehead: the hints toward identification follow later.

47. longus, *tall;* as in 86. 1 *longa.* — magnas cui, etc.: *i.e.* he had been sued on a charge of bastardy (though the expected birth

Longus homo est, magnas cui lites intulit olim
  Falsum mendaci uentre puerperium.'

68ª.

Quod mihi fortuna casuque oppressus acerbo
  Conscriptum hoc lacrimis mittis epistolium,

finally did not take place), and the case had been a noteworthy (**magnas**) one.

68ª. Over the question of the unity of *c.* 68 students of Catullus have long been at variance, some believing that vv. 1–40 have nothing to do with vv. 41–160, and others claiming that a more or less perfect union exists throughout the two, or perhaps three (cf. vv. 149–160), divisions of the poem. On the whole the weight of evidence seems to lie in favor of absolute division of vv. 1–40 from 41–160. (1) The absence of division indicated by the MSS. is paralleled by similar omission in the case of other poems: (2) the person addressed in 68ª is Malius (or Manlius; cf. v. 11 n.), in 68ᵇ, Allius, while the use of two *nomina* by one man was at this time unprecedented, and there is also no reason why one name should be consistently used in vv. 1–40 and the other in vv. 41–160: (3) Malius, in 68ª, is in extremest sorrow, which the expressions (see notes) show can be only over the death of his wife, while Allius, in 68ᵇ, is happy with either wife or mistress (cf. v. 155): (4) Malius asks for consolation in the shape of love-poems, and Catullus explains why he cannot send them; there is no reference to any request on the part of Allius, but he receives an apparently spontaneous expression of thanks for his services to Catullus in the affair with Lesbia, with

which is incorporated an account of the poet's happiness entirely incongruous in 68ª: (5) in 68ª the poet is so overcome with grief that he waives all reference to his relations with Lesbia (vv. 28, 29); in 68ᵇ he is happy with her, and is disposed to condone her frailties (vv. 135 ff.), while his grief is not ever-present, but is aroused only by a chance allusion to Troy, and is forthwith suppressed: (6) the repetition of vv. 20 ff. of 68ª in 68ᵇ (vv. 92 ff.) shows that the two poems were not far separated in time, but is more consistent with the theory of division than of unity (see also heading 5). 68ª was evidently written (at Verona or Sirmio) not long before 68ᵇ (see 5 above, and later notes), and both before Catullus had become thoroughly aware of Lesbia's real character, and had finally broken away from her. Perhaps her loose life during this period of separation finally opened his eyes. For convenience of general reference the continuous numbering of verses is retained throughout 68ª and 68ᵇ.

1. **quod**, etc.: the poetical epistle opens in pure prose form.

2. **conscriptum lacrimis**: a somewhat forced figure for 'tear-stained.' — **epistolium**: (Gr. ἐπι-στόλιον) a rare word, occurring elsewhere only in Apul. *Ap.* 6 and 79, and in glossaries.

3. **naufragum**, etc.: the figure is not infrequently used of great

Naufragum ut eiectum spumantibus aequoris undis
   Subleuem et a mortis limine restituam,
5 Quem neque sancta Venus molli requiescere somno
   Desertum in lecto caelibe perpetitur,
Nec ueterum dulci scriptorum carmine musae
   Oblectant, cum mens anxia peruigilat,
Id gratum est mihi, me quoniam tibi dicis amicum
10   Muneraque et Musarum hinc petis et Veneris.
Sed tibi ne mea sint ignota incommoda, Manli,
   Neu me odisse putes hospitis officium,

and overwhelming misfortune; cf.
v. 13; 64. 62; 65. 4.

4. a mortis limine restituam:
cf. Lucr. II. 960 *leti iam limine ab
ipso; Culex* 224 *te restitui superis
leti iam limine ab ipso.*

5. sancta Venus: cf. 36. 3 n.
— **molli somno**: cf. Hom. *Il.* X.
2 μαλακῷ δεδμημένοι ὕπνῳ; Verg.
Geor. III. 435 *mollis sub diuo carpere somnos;* Prop. I. 3. 7 *mollem
spirare quietem ;* Tib. I. 2. 74 *mollis
et inculta sit mihi somnus humo ;*
Ov. *Met.* I. 685 *ille tamen pugnat
molles euincere somnos.*

6. lecto caelibe: cf. 6. 6 *uiduas
noctes ;* Ov. *Her.* 13. 107 *aucupor
in lecto mendaces caelibe somnos.*
The great grief expressed in vv.
1–6 can hardly be attributed to
temporary estrangement or separation from wife or mistress, but only
to her death; cf. also v. 13 n.

7. ueterum scriptorum musae:
cf. Eur. *Med.* 421 μοῦσαι παλαι-
γενέων ἀοιδᾶν. The ancient poets
would be chiefly Greeks, and the
word with those following stands in
sharp contrast to v. 9 **me**, and the
following words. Manlius tries to
find distraction from his grief in the
books of the ancient (Greek) poets
(cf. Hor. *Sat.* II. 6. 61 *nunc ueterum
libris, nunc somno et inertibus*

horis) and fails; he therefore appeals to his friend for writings of
his, either new or old.

**10. munera Musarum et Vene-
ris**: *i.e.* love-poems; cf. Theog.
250 ἀγλαὰ μουσάων δῶρα ἰοστεφά-
νων; Anacr. 94ᵇ μουσέων τε καὶ
ἀγλαὰ δῶρ' 'Αφροδίτης συμμίσγων
ἐρατῆς μνήσκεται εὐφροσύνης.

11 ff. Manlius, who apparently has
not heard of the affliction of Catullus, had in the first part of his letter
begged for consolatory verses from
him, and in the second, urged his
return to Rome, supporting his
urgency by hints about the loose
life of Lesbia during the unexplained
absence of her lover. Catullus here
and in vv. 33 ff. replies to the first
part of the letter, and to the second
part in vv. 27 ff. — **Manli**: the reading of *V mali* can readily stand for
manli, as 61. 16 *mallio,* and 61. 222
maulio sufficiently show; and very
tempting is the conjecture of Muretus that the happy bridegroom of
61 is now the grief-stricken widower
of 68ᵃ who turns to his friend for
comfort in his sorrow as he had for
congratulation in his joy. Yet both
Malius and *Mallius* are *nomina*
supported by inscriptions of this age.

12. hospitis: apparently, like
ξένος, of one with whom a treaty of

Accipe quis merser fortunae fluctibus ipse,
    Ne amplius a misero dona beata petas.
15 Tempore quo primum uestis mihi tradita pura est,
    Iucundum cum aetas florida uer ageret,
Multa satis lusi; non est dea nescia nostri
    Quae dulcem curis miscet amaritiem:
Sed totum hoc studium luctu fraterna mihi mors
20   Abstulit.   O misero frater adempte mihi,
Tu mea tu moriens fregisti commoda, frater,
    Tecum una tota est nostra sepulta domus,
Omnia tecum una perierunt gaudia nostra,
    Quae tuus in uita dulcis alebat amor.
25 Cuius ego interitu tota de mente fugaui
    Haec studia atque omnes delicias animi.

friendship and hospitality has been made; cf. Cic. *Lael.* 37 *hospes familiae uestrae.*

13. The reason that leads Manlius to apply to Catullus for help, the death of one dearly loved, is the very reason why Catullus is unable to comply with the request, so reasonable from an *amicus et hospes.*— **merser fortunae fluctibus**: cf. v. 3 n.; Hor. *Ep.* I. 2. 22 *aduersis rerum immersabilis undis.*

15. **tempore quo,** *since the time when;* cf. 35. 13 n.— **uestis . . . pura**: the exchange of the crimson-bordered *toga praetexta* for the *toga uirilis* of pure white marked the legal coming of age at about 16 years.

17. **multa satis lusi**: *i.e.* I have written love-poems enough; cf. Hor. *Carm.* I. 32. 2 *lusimus tecum, barbite;* Ov. *Am.* III. I. 27 *quod tenerae cantent, lusit tua Musa, puellae.* — Apollinaris Sidonius (*Ep.* V. 21) says of himself *mihi quoque semper a paruo cura Musarum.*— **non est,** etc.: a repetitive

amplification of the preceding phrase; for love-poems with Catullus were closely connected with love-experiences.

18. **dulcem amaritiem:** cf. Sappho *Frag.* 40 γλυκύπικρον ἀμάχανον ὄρπετον (of love); Theog. 1353 πικρὸς καὶ γλυκύς ἐστι . . . ἔρως; Plaut. *Pseud.* 63 *dulce amarumque una nunc misces mihi;* Goethe *Egmont* III. 2. *freudvoll und leidvoll . . . die Seele die liebt;* Ellis quotes *Romaunt of the Rose,* p. 86 Bell *For ever of love the siknesse Is meinde with swete and bitternesse.*

19 ff. Cf. *c.* 65; 68. 92 ff.; 101. 6.

22. **tecum,** etc.: not so much, perhaps, that the bachelor Catullus looked to his brother's prospective children to keep alive the family name, as that brotherly love led him to ascribe to his brother all the qualities that honored the family, and to himself none.

26. **haec studia:** *i.e.* the writing of love-poems; corresponding to v. 17 *multa satis lusi* as **omnes delicias animi** does to *non est dea,*

Quare, quod scribis Veronae turpe Catullo
 Esse quod hic quisquis de meliore nota
Frigida deserto tepefactet membra cubili,
30 Id, Manli, non est turpe, magis miserum est.
Ignosces igitur, si, quae mihi luctus ademit,
 Haec tibi non tribuo munera, cum nequeo.
Nam quod scriptorum non magna est copia apud me,

etc. With **delicias** cf. 45. 24. n; 74.
2; with the otiose genitive **animi**,
2. 10 *animi curas;* 64. 372 *animi
amores;* 102. 2 *fides animi.*

27–30. The reference to love-
affairs in v. 26 leads Catullus to the
second part of the letter of Manlius,
wherein the writer, desiring the personal presence and sympathy of
Catullus, and not knowing any
reason for his long tarrying in
Verona, endeavored to draw him
thence by a warning (though using
no names) that his duty to himself
in the protection of his honor summoned him back to Rome; Catullus replies that his grief makes it
impossible for even such considerations to move him.

27. **Veronae turpe Catullo
esse**: apparently the predicate infinitive *esse* is (though contrary to
general usage) omitted here, or else
(and most improbably) the later **esse**
serves as both subject and predicate;
for in spite of v. 28 *hic* and the MS.
Catulle, a direct quotation in such
a setting would be extremely rare.
The meaning evidently is, 'to be
staying at Verona is dishonorable
for Catullus, when his place with
Lesbia is being filled by promiscu-
ous lovers.' The reply is, 'the matter is not one of dishonor but of
sorrow.' — **Catullo**: the poet likes
to refer to himself in the third person, and *V* not infrequently gives
e for *o*; hence the MS. reading is
no great argument for a direct
quotation.

28. **hic**: at the place where
Manlius was writing, the word being quoted directly from his letter:
there is no reason for believing the
place to be other than Rome. —
quisquis: apparently the masculine
is here used absolutely (without
est) after analogy of established use
of the neuter in that way. — **de
meliore nota**, *of the better sort;* cf.
Cic. *Fam.* VII. 29. 1 *Sulpicii succes-
sori nos de meliore nota commenda.*
Clodia's lovers were naturally not
from the lowest orders of society.

29. **frigida membra**: they had
been excluded while Catullus was
on hand. — **tepĕfactet**: on the
quantity cf. 64. 360 n. *tepefaciet;*
the word is ἅπαξ λεγόμενον.

30. **magis**: in a sense approaching that of the French *mais;* cf.
Sall. *Iug.* 85. 49 *neque quisquam
parens liberis uti aeterni forent,
optauit, magis uti boni honestique
uitam exigerent.* — **miserum**, *piti-
ful;* cf. 91. 2; 99. 15; Cic. *Fin.* V.
84 *bonum liberi, misera orbitas.*

33 ff. Catullus now returns to the
first part of the letter of Manlius
and explains why he cannot send
poems earlier composed, — he has
none with him, or none that would
be new and pleasing to Manlius.
The lack of logical order, with the
prosaic sentence-openings in vv. 1,
27, 33, and prosaic expression elsewhere, may be taken to indicate the
distracted state of the writer's mind.

33. **scriptorum copia**: the gene-
tive is neuter; cf. Hor. *Ep.* I. 18.

Hoc fit quod Romae uiuimus : illa domus,
35   Illa mihi sedes, illic mea carpitur aetas ;
Huc una ex multis capsula me sequitur.
Quod cum ita sit, nolim statuas nos mente maligna
Id facere aut animo non satis ingenuo
Quod tibi non utriusque petenti copia parta est :
40   Vltro ego deferrem, copia si qua foret.

68ᵇ.

Non possum reticere, deae, qua me Allius in re
Iuuerit aut quantis iuuerit officiis,
Ne fugiens saeclis obliuiscentibus aetas

109 *sit bona librorum copia;* Ov.
Trist. III. 14. 37 *non hic librorum
copia.*

36. **capsula** : *i.e. scrinium.*

37. **mente maligna**, etc., *in
grudging temper or ungracious
spirit.*

39. **non** : modifying the entire
expression, though placed before
the pronoun, as frequently in Catullus. Riese gives a full list of such
phrases. — **utriusque** : *i.e.* of verses
composed especially for you at this
time, and also of earlier verses.

40. **ultro ego deferrem**, etc.:
Catullus had apparently known of
the sorrow of Manlius before his
letter came, but because of his own
grief had taken no notice of it till
personally appealed to.

68ᵇ. A panegyric on Allius for
his assistance in furthering the
poet's affair with Lesbia, into characterization of whose love as like
that of Laodamia the poem straight-
way glides, to be recalled to Allius
once more only with v. 149. — The
Allius addressed is otherwise unknown, though the name is found
not infrequently in inscriptions; he
must, however, have been a man

of some position in Rome for
Clodia's visits to his house (v. 68)
not to arouse question. — The invo-
lution of theme, with the introduction of the Laodamia episode, itself
interrupted by the lament over the
death of the poet's brother, is
thoroughly Alexandrian. — See also
introductory note to *c.* 68ᵃ.

41. **non possum reticere** : the
earnestness of the poet's feeling is
well expressed by the abruptness of
the opening, carried out by the
emphatic repetition of **iuuerit**.—
deae : the poem opens, in epic style,
with an address to the Muses; cf.
Theocr. 17 (the panegyric upon
Ptolemy).

43. **ne**, etc.: it gives an easier
passage of thought to v. 45 **sed
dicam** to take vv. 43 and 44 as a
final clause directly dependent upon
non possum reticere, rather than
to read with the MSS. *nec* and understand the clause as a parenthetical
wish (for a potential subjunctive
here seems impossible). With MS.
nec for a genuine *ne* cf. v. 103; 21.
13; 62. 59; 99. 9. — **fugiens . . .
aetas**, *the flight of time through ages
of forgetfulness* ; cf. 64. 232.

Illius hoc caeca nocte tegat studium :
45 Sed dicam uobis, uos porro dicite multis   5
Milibus et facite haec charta loquatur anus

.   .   .   .

Notescatque magis mortuus atque magis,
Nec tenuem texens sublimis aranea telam
50 In deserto Alli nomine opus faciat.   10
Nam mihi quam dederit duplex Amathusia curam
Scitis, et in quo me corruerit genere,
Cum tantum arderem quantum Trinacria rupes
Lymphaque in Oetaeis Malia Thermopylis,
55 Maesta neque adsiduo tabescere lumina fletu   15
Cessarent tristique imbre madere genae,
Qualis in aerii perlucens uertice montis

45. **porro**, *in time to come;* cf. 45. 3.

46. **anus**: with the adjectival use of the word cf. 9. 4 n.; 78^b. 4; Mart. XII. 4. 4 [*hoc te*] *fama fuisse loquax chartaque dicet anus;* I. 39. 2 *famaque nouit anus.*

48. **magis atque magis**: a frequent and classical phrase; but cf. the asyndetic form in 38. 3 n.; 64. 274.

49 f. The figure is of a forgotten memorial inscription. The spider-web as a sign of human desertion is as old as Homer; cf. *Od.* XVI. 34 Ὀδυσσῆος δέ που εὐνὴ χήτει ἐνευναίων κάκ᾽ ἀράχνια κεῖται ἔχουσα; and the reminiscence in Prop. IV. 6. 33 *putris et in uacuo texetur aranea lecto;* also Ov. *Am.* I. 14. 7 *uel pede quod gracili deducit aranea filum, cum leue deserta sub trabe nectit opus.*

51. **duplex**: of the twofold character of Venus as causing grief as well as joy; cf. v. 18 n.; 64. 95; but the expression is sometimes understood to refer to the hermaphroditic

statue of the goddess at Amathus. — **Amathusia**: *i.e.* Venus; cf. 36. 14 n.

52. **in quo genere**, *after what manner.* — **corruerit**, *overwhelmed;* love's visit to him was with a vigorous assault that carried all defenses at once. With the active meaning of the verb cf. Lucr. V. 367 *quae possint forte coorta corruere hanc rerum summam.*

53. **quantum**, etc.: the comparison of figurative flames to the fires of Etna is not uncommon; cf. Hor. *Epod.* 17. 30 *ardeo quantum . . . nec Sicana feruida uirens in Aetna flamma;* Ov. *Epist. Sapph.* 12 *me calor Aetnaeo non minor igne tenet.* — **rupes**: for *mons*, as in 61. 28; cf. Grat. *Cyn.* 430 *in Trinacria rupe.*

54. **lympha**, etc.: the waters referred to are the hot springs that by their vicinity gave its name to the pass of Thermopylae.

57. **qualis**, etc.: *i.e.* the lover's tears ran as freely and constantly as an unfailing mountain-brook. The

Riuus muscoso prosilit e lapide,

Qui, cum de prona praeceps est ualle uolutus,

50   Per medium densi transit iter populi,   20

Dulce uiatori lasso in sudore leuamen

    Cum grauis exustos aestus hiulcat agros.

Hic, uelut in nigro iactatis turbine nautis

    Lenius adspirans aura secunda uenit

65 Iam prece Pollucis, iam Castoris implorata,   25

    Tale fuit nobis Allius auxilium.

Is clausum lato patefecit limite campum,

    Isque domum nobis isque dedit dominae,

Ad quam communes exerceremus amores.

development of the details of the figure is but a poetical embellishment. With the figure in general cf. Hom. *Il.* IX. 14 ἵστατο δάκρυ χέων ὥς τε κρήνη μελάνυδρος, etc.; XVI. 3; and a similar comparison of tears to melting snows in Sen. *Phaedr.* 389 ff. — **perlucens**: of the thread-like sheen of a stream seen afar off on a mountain-side.

59 ff. The stream rises among lofty mountains, finds its way down through a valley, and finally emerges from its solitudes upon the plains in the midst of the paths of a great people (v. 60), whom it furnishes with refreshment on their journeys.

63. **hic**: temporal, as in 64. 269. — **nigro turbine**: cf. Verg. *Aen.* X. 603 *torrentis aquae uel turbinis atri more furens.*

64. **lenius**, etc.: cf. Sil. Ital. XV. 162 *leuis inde secunda adspirans aura propellit carbasa flatus.*

65. **Pollucis**: objective genitive; cf. Verg. *Aen.* XI. 4 *uota deum uictor soluebat;* Liv. *Praef.* 13 *cum precationibus deorum dearumque;* and on the divinities appealed to, 4. 26 n. — **implorata**: probably a nominative modifying **aura** (cf.

Hor. *Ep.* II. 1. 135 *caelestes implorat aquas docta prece blandus*), though Nipperdey and Jordan believe it to be an ablative with **prece** absolute, after the analogy of Plaut. *Rud.* 258 *qui sunt, qui a patrona preces mea expetessunt?* Corn. Nep. *Ep. Corn. non pudet te deum preces expetere?*

66. **nobis**: for *mihi*, as in vv. 68 and 156, where Lesbia (*domina*) is mentioned separately.

67. **clausum**, etc.: *i.e.* he gave us free course, by allowing us to meet under the protection of his roof; with the figure cf. Sen. *De Ben.* I. 15. 2 *minus laxum limitem aperire.*

68. **domum dedit**: with the order cf. 30. 3 n. — **dominae**: *i.e.* Lesbia, as in v. 156 and elsewhere; the emendation appears certain for MSS. *dominam* (from *dominē;* cf. v. 73 MSS. *amorem* for *amore*).

69. **ad quam**: for *in qua* (*sc. domo*); cf. Cic. *Verr.* II. 4. 2 *ad aedem Felicitatis;* *Att.* XII. 36. 2 *ad uillam;* Liv. XXXIX. 4. 2 *ad aedem Apollinis in senatu;* and Draeger *Hist. Synt.* I.² p. 585. — **communes**: *i.e.* shared mutually

70 Quo mea se molli candida diua pede   30
    Intulit et trito fulgentem in limine plantam
    Innixa arguta constituit solea,
    Coniugis ut quondam flagrans aduenit amore
    Protesilaeam Laodamia domum
75 Inceptam frustra, nondum cum sanguine sacro   35
    Hostia caelestis pacificasset eros.
    Nil mihi tam ualde placeat, Rhamnusia uirgo,
    Quod temere inuitis suscipiatur eris.

by Catullus and Lesbia; cf. Lucr.
IV. 1200 *est communis uoluptas*
(*sc.* to two lovers); Ov. *Am.* II.
5. 31 *haec tibi sunt mecum, mihi
sunt communia tecum.*

70. **molli**: an almost formal epithet, as often. — **diua**: only here
as an appellation of a mistress,
though comparisons to particular
deities are not uncommon; cf. v. 133
where Lesbia is invested with the
attributes of Venus.

71. **trito**: a formal epithet of a
threshold, as worn smooth by use;
cf. the Homeric οὐδὸς ξεστός, and
v. 115 *tereretur*. — **fulgentem**: of
the smooth, luminous skin; cf.
Hom. λιπαροὶ πόδες.

72. **arguta**: apparently of sound
rather than of shape (cf. 6. 11), but
whether some omen was connected
with the creaking of the sandal, or
it was simply the happy presage of
her coming to the eagerly listening
lover, is doubtful.

73–130. The comparison of the
warmth of Lesbia's love to that of
Laodamia's. The episode is thoroughly Alexandrian in its length
and complexity. It seems unnecessary and unfitting after observation
of other similar mythological illustrations in Catullus to suppose the
comparison to extend to the details of the unrighteous beginning

(vv. 75, 76) and fatal effects (vv.
85, 86) of the passion, even if
Catullus could have admitted to
himself such an extension of the
resemblance. — Part of the story is
as old as Homer (cf. *Il.* II. 695 ff.),
though nothing is said there of the
final cause of the death of Protesilaus. Euripides in his *Protesilaus*
appears first to embody the tale of
the hero's return to earth for one
day in accordance with his wife's
prayer (cf. also Hyg. *Fab.* 103, and
Wordsworth *Laodamia*).   On the
subject cf. also Ov. *Her.* 13.

75. **inceptam frustra**: *i.e.* his
home-life was indeed begun, but
was not to last; cf. Hom. *Il.* II.
701 δόμος ἡμιτελής.

76. **hostia**: probably not with
reference to a special pre-nuptial
sacrifice, but to the sacrifices thought
necessary before entering upon any
new undertaking. — **caelestis eros**,
the lords of heaven; repeated, without distinguishing epithet, in v. 78.

77 f. Cf. Verg. *Aen.* II. 402
*heu nihil inuitis fas quemquam
fidere diuis.* — **Rhamnusia uirgo**:
cf. 64. 395 n.; 66. 71. — **inuitis
eris**: cf. 76. 12 *dis inuitis;* Hom.
Il. XII. 8 θεῶν ἀέκητι, where the
lack of divine favor was due solely,
as here, to the omission of preliminary sacrifice (XII. 6).

Quam ieiuna pium desideret ara cruorem

80   Docta est amisso Laodamia uiro,   40

Coniugis ante coacta noui dimittere collum

Quam ueniens una atque altera rursus hiems

Noctibus in longis auidum saturasset amorem,

Posset ut abrupto uiuere coniugio :

85 Quod scibant Parcae non longo tempore abesse,   45

Si miles muros isset ad Iliacos :

Nam tum Helenae raptu primores Argiuorum

Coeperat ad sese Troia ciere uiros,

Troia (nefas) commune sepulcrum Asiae Europaeque,

90   Troia uirum et uirtutum omnium acerba cinis :   50

Quaene etiam nostro letum miserabile fratri

---

79. quam ieiuna, *how thirstily ;*
with the adjective in this meaning
cf. Prop. IV. 15. 18 *uilem ieiunae
saepe negauit aquam.*

80. amisso : *i.e.* by his departure
for Troy, whither he was compelled
to go by the other Greeks.

82. una atque altera hiems :
i.e. winter after winter; cf. v. 152.

84. uiuere : *i.e.* to endure life;
cf. 5. 1 n.

85. quod, etc., *which* (*i.e.* the
final severing of the marriage bond
by death) *the Fates knew to be not
far distant.* — **scibant :** as if the
Fates were powerless to alter this
decree of Necessity, and could only
register it; with the form cf. 64.
319 *custodibant ;* 84. 8 *audibant.*
— **abesse :** the MSS. *abisse* can be
only the perfect for the future in a
definitely decided contingency, and
that effect is interfered with by the
occurrence of a phrase (**non longo
tempore**) pointing definitely to the
future. With the MSS. error cf.
Prop. III. 16. 32 where *V* reads
abire for *abesse.*

89. Troia : the word leads the
poet into a digression on his broth-

er's death, from which he returns to
the main digression with v. 101. —
nefas : a parenthetical exclamation,
as in Verg. *Aen.* VII. 73 *uisa
(nefas) longis comprendere crinibus
ignem.* — **commune sepulcrum :**
so of the earth itself in Lucr. V.
259 *omniparens eadem rerum commune sepulcrum ;* but of a public
burying-ground in Hor. *Sat.* I. 8.
10 *hoc miserae plebi stabat commune
sepulcrum.*

90. uirum et uirtutum : cf.
Verg. *Aen.* I. 566 *uirtutesque uiros-
que.* — **acerba :** of the 'untimely'
death of young warriors; cf. on this
meaning of the word Mayor on
Juv. 11. 44, who gives numerous citations. — **cinis,** *funeral-pyre ;* found
only here in this sense. The noun
is feminine also in the singular in
101. 4 (as in Lucr. IV. 926 and
not infrequently in late Latin), but
masculine in the plural in 68. 98;
cf. Non. 198 [*cinis*] *feminino apud
Caesarem et Catullum et Caluum
lectum est, quorum uacillat aucto-
ritas.*

91. quaene = *quippe quae :* cf.
64. 180 n.; 64. 183.

Attulit. Hei misero frater adempte mihi,

Hei misero fratri iucundum lumen ademptum,

Tecum una tota est nostra sepulta domus,

95 Omnia tecum una perierunt gaudia nostra,   55

Quae tuus in uita dulcis alebat amor.

Quem nunc tam longe non inter nota sepulcra

Nec prope cognatos compositum cineres,

Sed Troia obscena, Troia infelice sepultum

100 Detinet extremo terra aliena solo.   60

Ad quam tum properans fertur simul undique pubes

Graeca penetralis deseruisse focos,

Ne Paris abducta gauisus libera moecha

Otia pacato degeret in thalamo.

105 Quo tibi tum casu, pulcherrima Laodamia,   65

Ereptum est uita dulcius atque anima

Coniugium : tanto te absorbens uertice amoris

Aestus in abruptum detulerat barathrum,

92–96. **hei**, etc.: cf. vv. 20–24.

98. **compositum** : in the meaning of *buried* the word is poetical and post-Augustan only; its next appearance is in Hor. *Sat.* I. 9. 28 *omnes composui.*

99. **obscena**, *malign.* The word was originally applied to things of ill omen. — **infelice**, *baleful.* Elsewhere in Catullus the ablative in *-i* (of the simple adjective) occurs; cf. 62. 30; 64. 373.

100. **extremo**, *far distant;* cf. 11. 2 *in extremos Indos.*

102. **penetralis focos** : the sacred hearths that formed the centre of the home and its life.

103. **libera**, *unchallenged;* cf. 64. 402.

105. **quo casu** : *i.e.* by the sudden despatch of a Greek army against Troy.

106. **uita dulcius atque anima** : cf. 3. 5 n

107 ff. **tanto**, etc.: explaining *uita dulcius*, etc.; he was dearer to you than life; for your love was deeper than the abyss of Pheneus (vv. 109–118), and your joy in him greater (vv. 129, 130) than that of the aged grandfather in the birth of an heir (vv. 119–124), or of a dove in the endearments of her mate (vv. 125–128). And such was the joy with which Lesbia came to me (vv. 131–134).

107. **coniugium** : cf. 66. 28 n. — **absorbens**, etc.: cf. Verg. *Aen.* III. 421 [*Charybdis*] *imo barathri ter gurgite uastos sorbet in abruptum fluctus.*

108. **barathrum** : this name was sometimes applied by the Greeks to an artificial, in many cases subterranean, channel for the draining of a lake or overflowing river; cf. the *emissarium* of the Alban Lake.

Quale ferunt Grai Pheneum prope Cylleneum
110 Siccare emulsa pingue palude solum,   70
Quod quondam caesis montis fodisse medullis
Audit falsiparens Amphitryoniades,
Tempore quo certa Stymphalia monstra sagitta
Perculit imperio deterioris eri,
115 Pluribus ut caeli tereretur ianua diuis,   75
Hebe nec longa uirginitate foret.
Sed tuus altus amor barathro fuit altior illo,
Qui tunc indomitam ferre iugum docuit.
Nam nec tam carum confecto aetate parenti

---

109. Pheneum: Pheneus was a city in northwestern Arcadia, near Mt. Cyllene. Pausanias (VIII. 14) mentions the ascription to Heracles of an existing outlet for the swollen waters of the neighboring river Olbios.

111. montis medullis: cf. the more common figure in Verg. *Aen.* III. 575 *uiscera montis.*

112. audit = *dicitur ;* perhaps only here in this sense with an infinitive ; but cf. Grk. ἀκούειν, and Latin *cluere* (*e.g.* Lucr. IV. 46 *imago cuiuscumque cluet de corpore fusa uagari*). — **falsiparens**: ἅπαξ λεγόμενον, possibly suggested by Call. *Hymn. Cer.* 99 ψευδοπάτωρ (though in a different sense from that). Heracles was the reputed son of Amphitruo, but really the son of Zeus.

113. Stymphalia: the place lay just to the east of Pheneus, and the destruction of the ravenous birds congregating there was the fifth of the labors imposed upon Heracles by Eurystheus, the *deterioris eri* (v. 116). — **certa sagitta**: cf. Hor. *Carm.* I. 12. 23 *metuende certa Phoebe sagitta.*

114. deterioris eri: cf. the words of Heracles himself in Hom.

Od. XI. 621 μάλα γὰρ πολὺ χείρονι φωτὶ δεδμήμην, ὁ δέ μοι χαλεπούς ἐπετέλλετ' ἀέθλους.

115 f. The mighty deeds of Heracles were proving his fitness for a place among the gods and for the hand of Hebe.

116. Hebe: called *Iuuentas* by the earlier Romans; her marriage with Heracles is mentioned as early as Homer (*Od.* XI. 602).

118. qui: *sc. amor.* — **tunc**: *i.e.* at the time of v. 107 f. — **indo-mitam**: *sc. prius ;* cf. Hor. *Carm.* III. 3. 14 *tigres indocili iugum collo trahentes*: with the compari-son of the maiden to an untamed heifer cf. Hor. *Carm.* II. 5. 1 *nondum subacta ferre iugum ualet ceruice :* on the yoke of love, Hor. *Carm.* III. 9. 17 *Venus diductos iugo cogit aeneo ;* I. 33. 11 *formas atque animos sub iuga aenea saeuo mittere cum ioco ;* Stat. *Silu.* I. 2. 138 *thalami quamuis iuga ferre secundi saepe neget maerens.*

119 ff. Cf. Hom. *Il.* IX. 481 καί μ' ἐφίλησ' ὡς εἴ τε πατὴρ ὃν παῖδα φιλήσῃ μοῦνον τηλύγετον. — **con-fecto aetate parenti**: cf. Verg. *Aen.* IV. 599 *confectum aetate pa-rentem.*

120   Vna caput seri nata nepotis alit,   80
        Qui, cum diuitiis uix tandem inuentus auitis
        Nomen testatas intulit in tabulas,
        Impia derisi gentilis gaudia tollens
        Suscitat a cano uulturium capiti :
125   Nec tantum niueo gauisa est ulla columbo   85
        Compar, quae multo dicitur improbius
        Oscula mordenti semper decerpere rostro
        Quam quae praecipue multiuola est mulier :
        Sed tu horum magnos uicisti sola furores,
130   Vt semel es flauo conciliata uiro.   90

120. **caput**: cf. 15. 16 n.

121 ff. The birth of an heir finally
sets at naught the joy of the next-
of-kin at the prospect of his own
succession to the old man's wealth.
By the Voconian Law (B.C. 169)
no woman, not even an only daughter, could be the heir; cf. Gaius II.
274; Aug. *Ciu. Dei* III. 21. 5 *lata
est etiam illa lex Voconia, ne quis
heredem feminam faceret, nec uni-
cam filiam.*

121. **qui** : *sc. nepos.* — **inuentus** :
sc. heres.

122. **testatas tabulas** : *i.e.* the
will, as duly signed and sealed in
the presence of witnesses. After
the completion of this legal form
in favor of the grandson, the old
man for the first time feels safe
from the greedy expectations of the
gentilis.

123. **impia** : because his joy was
over the childlessness (save for a
daughter) or a relative. — **derisi** : as
the *gentilis* has rejoiced over the
disappointed hopes of the old man,
so his own disappointment now becomes the object of mockery; for a
similar example see Hor. *Sat.* II. 5.
55. — **gentilis** : the next-of-kin was
not even one of the nearest relatives, the order of legal heirs estab-

lished in the Twelve Tables being
sui heredes, agnati, gentiles.

124. **uulturium** : *i.e.* the pre-
sumptive heir, awaiting the old
man's death as a vulture circles
above his expected prey; cf. Sen.
Epist 95. 43 *at hoc hereditatis causa
facit : uultur est, cadauer exspectat ;*
Mart. VI. 62. 1 and 4 *amisit pater
unicum Salanus ... cuius uulturis
hoc erit cadauer ?* and (probably in
the same sense) the reference to
the *coruus* in Hor. *Sat.* II. 5. 56.
— **capiti** : a very rare form of the
ablative; see Neue *Formenlehre* I²
p. 238.

125 ff. Doves were patterns of
conjugal affection and fidelity; cf.
Prop. III. 15. 27, 28 *extemplo iunctae tibi sint in amore columbae,
masculus et totum femina coniugium ;* Plin. *N. H.* X. 104 *columbae
coniugi fidem non uiolant commu-
nemque seruant domum ;* Porph.
on Hor. *Epod.* 16. 32 *dicitur
columba nulli alii concumbere quam
cui se semel iunxit.*

126. **improbius**, *more wantonly.*

128. **multiuola** : from the comparison to the dove, apparently with
the meaning of *multa oscula uolens,*
rather than of *multos amatores
uolens* like v. 140 *omniuoli.* The

Aut nihil aut paulo cui tum concedere digna
 Lux mea se nostrum contulit in gremium,
Quam circumcursans hinc illinc saepe Cupido
 Fulgebat crocina candidus in tunica.
135 Quae tamenetsi uno non est contenta Catullo,   95
 Rara uerecundae furta feremus erae,
Ne nimium simus stultorum more molesti :
 Saepe etiam Iuno, maxima caelicolum,
Coniugis in culpa flagrantem concoquit iram
140 Noscens omniuoli plurima furta Iouis.   100
 Atqui nec diuis homines componier aequum est

. . . .

. . . .

Ingratum tremuli tolle parentis onus.

word occurs elsewhere only in the Vulgate (*Sir.* 9. 3).

131. **aut nihil**, etc.: the theme now turns back to Lesbia, whom it left with v. 72.

132. **lux mea**: cf. the same pet-name in v. 160; Tib. IV. 3. 15; (Sulp.) IV. 12. 1; Ov. *Am.* I. 8. 23.

133. The lover ascribes to Lesbia the attributes of Venus; cf. Hor. *Carm.* I. 2. 33 *Erycina ridens, quam Iocus circum uolat et Cupido.* — **hinc illinc**: cf. 3. 9 n.

134. **crocina in tunica**: on the less common representation of a draped Eros see Sappho *Frag.* 64 [Ἔρωτα] ἐλθόντ' ἐξ ὀράνω πορφυρίαν περθέμενον χλάμυν; and illustrations in Baumeister *Denkmäler* I. p. 498. The saffron color is chosen perhaps because it was the color of Hymen's garb also ; cf. 61. 8 and 10.

135 ff. Catullus has apparently been informed (perhaps by Manlius; 68. 27) of the other infidelities of Lesbia, but now at first is trying to compromise with his love for her

by pleading that they are but few (**rara**), and do not indicate a settled defection from his love, since they are so carefully concealed (**uerecundae erae**); that even Queen Juno puts up with the multitudinous wanderings of her husband, and that after all Lesbia is not his wife, and, therefore, he ought rather to be grateful for the favors he does receive than to be overjealous of others.

136. **furta**: the word occurs first here in the erotic sense, but is found often in this sense in Vergil and the elegiasts ; cf. however v. 145 *furtiua munuscula ;* 7. 8 *furtiuos amores.* — **erae** : cf. v. 68 *dominae ;* v. 156 *domina.*

140. **omniuoli**: *i.e. omnes puellas uolens ;* ἅπαξ λεγόμενον. — **plurima furta**: see the list in Hom *Il.* XIV. 317 ff.

141. **componier**: cf. 61. 42 n. *citarier.* The very evident loss of at least two vv. between vv. 141 and 142 makes the point of v. 141 unintelligible.

Nec tamen illa mihi dextra deducta paterna
Fragrantem Assyrio uenit odore domum,
145 Sed furtiua dedit mira munuscula nocte   105
Ipsius ex ipso dempta uiri gremio.
Quare illud satis est, si nobis is datur unis
Quem lapide illa diem candidiore notat.

Hoc tibi quod potui confectum carmine munus
150   Pro multis, Alli, redditur officiis,   110
Ne uestrum scabra tangat robigine nomen
Haec atque illa dies atque alia atque alia.
Huc addent diui quam plurima, quae Themis olim
Antiquis solita est munera ferre piis :
155 Sitis felices et tu simul et tua uita   115
Et domus, in qua nos lusimus et domina,

143. tamen, *after all.* — dextra deducta paterna : not literally that the father conducted the bride in the marriage procession to the bridegroom's house, but figuratively only, in that marriages were arranged with the consent of the head of the family; cf. 62. 60.

144. Assyrio odore : cf. 6. 8 n.

148. lapide candidiore : cf. 64. 222 n.; 107. 6; Hor. *Carm.* I. 36. 10 *Cressa ne careat pulchra dies nota,* which Porphyrio explains by saying that the Cretans were accustomed to drop a white pebble into their quivers as a memorial of a day of happiness, and a black pebble to mark a day of sorrow. Bentley on the same passage gives further citations.

149–160. The panegyric concludes with a direct address to Allius, which some critics have taken as a distinct poem, or as a strongly marked division of *c.* 68 as a threefold, though single, poem.

151. uestrum : as the name belonged, not to Allius alone, but to his family; cf. 64. 160 *uestras sedes.*

152. haec atque illa dies : apparently a unique expression for 'to-day and to-morrow' (*i.e.* the course of time). Cf. with the entire verse v. 82. — alia atque alia : cf. Plin. *Ep.* I. 3. 4 *reliqua rerum tuarum post te alium atque alium dominum sortientur.*

153. huc : *i.e.* to this small tribute of mine. — Themis : the goddess of justice, often identified with Astraea, on whom see 66. 65 n. *uirginis.*

155. sitis felices : so also with reference to a love affair in 100. 8 *sis felix.* — uita : see 45. 13 n., and cf. 104. 1 ; 109. 1.

156. lusimus : cf. 17. 17 *ludere.* — domina : *i.e.* Lesbia; together with nos the word is the subject of lusimus; not together with tu, etc., of sitis, since the wish for Lesbia's prosperity is expressed in v. 159 f.

Et qui principio nobis † terram dedit aufert,
　　A quo sunt primo omnia nata bona,
Et longe ante omnes mihi quae me carior ipso est,
160　　Lux mea, qua uiua uiuere dulce mihi est.　　₁20

69.

Noli admirari quare tibi femina nulla,
　　Rufe, uelit tenerum supposuisse femur,
Non si illam rarae labefactes munere uestis
　　Aut perluciduli deliciis lapidis.
5 Laedit te quaedam mala fabula, qua tibi fertur
　　Valle sub alarum trux habitare caper.
Hunc metuunt omnes.　Neque mirum : nam mala
　　　ualde est
Bestia, nec quicum bella puella cubet.

157. The verse apparently refers to some person whose assistance antedated that of Allius, perhaps in that he introduced Catullus to Lesbia or to Allius.

158. primo: on the hiatus following see Intr. 86 *d*. — omnia bona: the love of Lesbia was all in all to Catullus; cf. 77. 4.

159. longe ante omnes: *sc. sit felix*. — me carior ipso: cf. *Culex* 211 *tua dum mihi carior ipsa uita fuit uita;* Ov. *Ex. Pont.* II. 8. 27 *per patriae nomen, quae te tibi carior ipso est;* and for similar comparisons in Catullus, 3. 5 n.

160. lux mea: *i.e.* Lesbia; cf. v. 132 n. — qua uiua, etc.: cf. Hor. *Epod.* I. 5 *nos quibus te uita si superstite iucunda, si contra, grauis.*

69. A bit of personal satire directed probably against M. Caelius Rufus; see Intr. 59. Caelius is generally known as an exquisite and a lady-killer, — a reputation

probably better deserved than that indicated in this satire.

3. non si: following a preceding negation (*nulla*), as in 48. 5; 70. 2; 88. 8. — rarae uestis: *i.e.* the delicate and translucent Coan robes; cf. Ov. *Am.* I. 5. 13 *deripui tunicam : nec multum rara nocebat;* Hor. *Sat.* I. 2. 101 *Cois tibi paene uidere est ut nudam.* — labefactes, *corrupt;* cf. Cic. *Clu.* 194 *fidem pretio labefactare conata sit.*

4. perluciduli: ἅπαξ λεγόμενον as diminutive; but cf. Sen. *Epist.* 90. 45 *non aurum nec argentum nec perlucidos lapides.* — deliciis: cf. 2. 1 n.; Hor. *Carm.* IV. 8. 10 *animus deliciarum egens.*

6. caper: a common figure for this particular odor; cf. 37. 5; 71. 1; Hor. *Ep.* I. 5. 29 *nimis arta premunt olidae conuiuia caprae.*

7. neque mirum: cf. 23. 7 n.

8. quicum: feminine, as in 66. 77, but rare in this gender.

Quare aut crudelem nasorum interfice pestem,
10 Aut admirari desine cur fugiunt.

70.

Nulli se dicit mulier mea nubere malle
    Quam mihi, non si se Iuppiter ipse petat.
Dicit : sed mulier cupido quod dicit amanti
    In uento et rapida scribere oportet aqua.

71.

Si cui iure bono sacer alarum obstitit hircus,
    Aut si quem merito tarda podagra secat,

9. **interfice**: carrying on the figure in **bestia**.

10. **fugiunt**: on the indicative instead of subjunctive in indirect questions in archaic and colloquial Latin see Draeger *Hist. Synt.* II. § 463. 1 e.

70. A jesting epigram addressed to Lesbia, and written while the *amour* with her was as yet undisturbed. The precise date cannot be more accurately determined. It is unnecessary to suppose that Metellus was actually dead and Lesbia considering a new marriage as a practical problem.

1. **mulier mea**: cf. Hor. *Epod.* 12. 23 *magis quem diligeret mulier sua quam te* (of lovers); and *mea puella* of Lesbia in 2. 1 and often.

2. **non si**: see 69. 3 n.—**Iuppiter ipse petat**: cf. 72. 2; Plaut. *Cas.* 302 *negaui enim ipsi me [Casinam uxorem] concessurum Ioui;* Ov. *Met.* VII. 801 *nec Iouis illa meo thalamos praeferret amori.*

3 f. Cf. Soph. *Frag.* 741 n. ὅρκους ἐγὼ γυναικὸς εἰς ὕδωρ γράφω; Plat. *Phaedr.* 276 οὐκ ἄρα σπουδῇ αὐτὰ ἐν ὕδατι γράψει, and frequent examples in the Greek; Aug. *Ciu.*

Dei XIX. 23 *magis poteris in aqua impressis litteris scribere . . . quam pollutae reuoces impiae uxoris sensum;* also 30. 10 n., and the epitaph of Keats, *Here lies one whose name was writ in water.*

71. A puzzling bit of coarseness addressed, perhaps in a satirical tone (cf. v. 4 n. *a te*), to an unnamed and unknown man (cf. in this respect *cc.* 78^b and 104). Perhaps, however, the *aemulus* (v. 3) is Caelius Rufus (cf. *c.* 69).

1. **iure bono**, *justly;* apparently with the meaning of the familiar *iure optimo*, though not found elsewhere. The conjunction of *iure* with *merito*, as here (v. 2), was common; cf. Plaut. *Most.* 713 *te ipse iure optumo merito incuses licet;* Cic. *Cat.* III. 6. 14 *merito ac iure laudantur;* Juv. 2. 34 *iure ac merito uitia ultima fictos contemnunt Scauros.* — **sacer**, *cursed;* cf. 14. 12.—**alarum hircus**: cf. 69. 6 n.—**obstitit**: *i.e.* hindered him from being an attractive lover, while the gout hindered him from being a happy one.

2. **tarda podagra**, *the limping gout,* the adjective being used in

Aemulus iste tuus, qui uestrum exercet amorem,
    Mirifice est a te nactus utrumque malum.
5 Nam quotiens futuit totiens ulciscitur ambos :
    Illam adfligit odore, ipse perit podagra.

72.

Dicebas quondam solum te nosse Catullum,
    Lesbia, nec prae me uelle tenere Iouem.
Dilexi tum te non tantum ut uulgus amicam,
    Sed pater ut gnatos diligit et generos.
5 Nunc te cognoui : quare etsi impensius uror,

the factitive sense; cf. Hor. *Sat.*
I. 9. 32 *tardo podagra.* — seca̍t, *torments;* cf. Mart. IX. 92. 9 *tortorem
metuis? podagra cheragraque seca-
tur Gaius.*

3. qui uestrum exercet amo-
rem : if it be true that there are no
cases so early as this period of *uester*
for *tuus,* the meaning must be somewhat as follows : 'your rival has
usurped your place entirely, and now
himself enjoys all that love shared
mutually by you and your mistress
(uestrum).' But the passage is at
best unsatisfactory. With exercet
amorem cf. 61. 235 *exercete iuuentam;* 68. 66 *exerceremus amores.*

4. a te nactus : *i.e.* in succeeding
to your place in the affections of
your mistress he has also succeeded
to your diseases, and thereby brings
upon himself and her the punishment due to false friend and faithless mistress. In the character of
the consolation administered there
seems to be a back-handed slap for
the person addressed, in implying
that he was himself thus afflicted
with diseases arising from habits of
dissipation.

6. podăgra : but v. 2 *podāgra;*
with the variation in quantity of the

syllable containing a short vowel
before a mute and a liquid cf. Lucr.
IV. 1222 *quae pătribus pātres tra-
dunt ab stirpe profecta;* Verg. Aen.
II. 663 *gnatum ante ora pătris,
pātrem qui obtruncat ad aras;* Hor.
Carm. I. 32. 11, 12 *et Lycum nigris
oculis nigroqve | crine decorum;*
Ov. *Met.* XIII. 607 *et primo similis
uolŭcri, mox uera uolŭcris.*

72. An address to Lesbia written after the poet had become convinced of her unworthiness, and
showing more, perhaps, than any
other one poem the pure sentiment
of his passion for her (in vv. 3 and
4). With the theme cf. *cc.* 75 and
85.

1 f. A reminiscence of 70. 1 f. —
nosse : *sensu uenerio.*

2. tenere : *sc. complexu;* cf. 64. 28.

3. dilexi : doubtless chosen here
to indicate pure sentiment as distinguished from physical passion,
though *diligere* sometimes has the
same meaning as *amare,* as in 6. 5;
81. 2.

4. generos : *i.e. generum et nu-
rum,* as gnatos is equivalent to
filium filiamque, and 63. 59 *genitoribus* to *patre et matre.*

5. impensius uror : in spite of
his better knowledge of her char-

Multo mi tamen es uilior et leuior.
Qui potis est? inquis.   Quod amantem iniuria talis
Cogit amare magis, sed bene uelle minus.

73.

Desine de quoquam quicquam bene uelle mereri
  Aut aliquem fieri posse putare pium.
Omnia sunt ingrata, nihil fecisse benigne :
  Immo etiam taedet, taedet obestque magis :
5 Vt mihi, quem nemo grauius nec acerbius urget
  Quam modo qui me unum atque unicum amicum
    habuit.

acter, his passion continues to grow, and overmasters his judgment. But the fact that he recognizes this shows at least a possibility of recovery. Cf. *c.* 85; Ter. *Eun.* 70 ff. *nunc ego et illam scelestam esse et me miserum sentio et taedet; et amore ardeo.*

7. **potis est:** *sc. fieri,* as in 42. 16; 76. 16, 24. **potis** stands here before a vowel for *pote,* as in 76. 24.

8. **bene uelle,** *to respect;* cf. 75. 3.

73. A disheartened complaint concerning the ingratitude and faithlessness of some friend, perhaps of Caelius Rufus, whose rivalry with Catullus in the affections of Lesbia is referred to in *c.* 77. Cf. also Intr. 21.

1. **quicquam** modifies **bene mereri,** while **uelle** depends upon **desine.**

2. **aliquem** : instead of *quemquam,* as if repeated from the form

of direct discourse *aliquis fieri pius possit.* — **fieri** = *esse;* cf. 80. 2 *fiant.* — **pium,** *grateful;* cf. Ov. *Trist.* V. 4. 43 *pro quibus adfirmat fore se memoremque piumque;* Cic. *Fam.* I. 9. 1 *cum illud ipsum grauissimum et sanctissimum nomen pietatis leuius mihi meritis erga me tuis esse uideatur.*

3. **omnia sunt ingrata** : cf. Plaut. *Asin.* 136 f. *ingrata atque irrita esse omnia intellego quae dedi et quod bene feci.* With **ingrata** in this sense cf. 64. 103 n. — **nihil** (*sc. est*), *'tis of no avail to have done deeds of kindness;* cf. Ter. *And.* 314 *id 'aliquid' nil est;* Cic. *Fam.* VII. 33. 1 *nos enim plane nihil sumus.*

5. **ut mihi:** *sc. obest.*

6. **unum atque unicum** : cf. Gell. XVIII. 4. 2 *se unum et unicum lectorem esse;* Apul. *Met.* IV. 31 *idque unum et pro omnibus unicum.* The succession of elisions in this verse is noteworthy; cf. Intr. 86 *a*

74.

Gellius audierat patruum obiurgare solere,
  Si quis delicias diceret aut faceret.
Hoc ne ipsi accideret, patrui perdepsuit ipsam
  Vxorem et patruum reddidit Harpocratem.
5 Quod uoluit fecit : nam, quamuis irrumet ipsum
  Nunc patruum, uerbum non faciet patruus.

75.

Huc est mens deducta tua, mea Lesbia, culpa,
  Atque ita se officio perdidit ipsa suo,

74. The first in arrangement,
though apparently not in time of
composition, of seven virulent in-
vectives directed against a rival (cf.
c. 91) named Gellius. The other six
poems are *cc.* 80, 88, 89, 90, 91, 116.
See Intr. 72.

1. **patruum**: proverbially among
the Romans the stern and rigorous
relative; cf. Cic. *Cael.* 11. 25 *fuit
in hac causa pertristis quidam
patruus, censor, magister;* Hor.
Carm. III. 12. 3 *metuentes patruae
uerbera linguae;* Sat. II. 3. 87 *siue
ego praue seu recte hoc uolui, ne sis
patruus mihi.*

2. **delicias**: cf. 45. 24; 68. 26;
2. 1 n. *deliciae.*

3. **perdepsuit**: ἅπαξ λεγόμενον.

4. **patruum reddidit Harpocratem**: *i.e.* made him the very picture of silence; for the Egyptian
deity Horus, the rising sun, is called
in the Osiris myths Harpocrates
(*i.e.* the child Har), and is often
represented with the left forefinger
laid upon the lips, as if to enjoin
silence; cf. the cut in Rawlinson's
Anc. Egypt, vol. I., chap. 10; also
Varr. *L. L.* V. 57 *etsi Harpocrates*

digito significat ut taceam. The
phrase is parodied in *Anth. Lat.*
159. 6 Riese, 346. 6 Baehrens.

75. Another address to Lesbia,
resembling in tone, and agreeing in
time with *cc.* 72 and 85. There is
no good reason for believing, with
Scaliger and some later critics, that
these verses are the conclusion of
c. 87, from which they were acci-
dently severed in the life of the
archetype. The poem is complete
and satisfactory in itself, while a
union with *c.* 87 would necessitate
the substitution of *nunc* for *huc*
(with Scaliger and one interpolated
MS.) and of *diducta* for *deducta* (with
Lachmann), contrary to the MSS.

1. **mea Lesbia**: the use even
here of the earlier affectionate address is in accord with the declara-
tion that love for her still dominates
him; cf. 87. 2.

2. **se perdidit**: *i.e.* by devotion
to her (suo officio) through good
and ill his reason has so far suffered
that he is no longer in a normal
mental condition, and cannot be
consistent, and cease to love when
he has ceased to respect.

Vt iam nec bene uelle queat tibi, si optuma fias,
　　Nec desistere amare, omnia si facias.

76.

Si qua recordanti benefacta priora uoluptas
　　Est homini, cum se cogitat esse pium,
Nec sanctam uiolasse fidem, nec foedere in ullo
　　Diuum ad fallendos numine abusum homines,
5 Multa parata manent in longa aetate, Catulle,
　　Ex hoc ingrato gaudia amore tibi.
Nam quaecumque homines bene cuiquam aut dicere possunt
　　Aut facere, haec a te dictaque factaque sunt :
Omnia quae ingratae perierunt credita menti.
10　　Quare cur tu te iam amplius excrucies ?

3 f. Cf. 72. 7, 8. — si **optuma
fias** : all confidence in her has been
irrevocably lost, so that no change
in her character could make him
believe her true.

4. **omnia** : for *quidlubet;* cf.
Hor. *Carm.* I. 3. 25 *audax omnia
perpeti.*

76. A prayer to be cured of love
for the unworthy Lesbia. On its
chronological position in the cycle
of Lesbia poems see Intr. 41.

1. **priora** : as man with increasing age (v. 5 **in longa aetate**) is
more inclined to review the course
of his past life.

2. **pium** : explained by v. 3 f.

3 f. **nec sanctam uiolasse
fidem** : of fidelity in all relations
with one's fellow-men. — **nec foedere . . . homines** : of practical
reverence for the gods, toward
whom, as witnesses to an oath,
obligation exists.

5. **parata manent tibi** : *i.e.* are
from now on yours to enjoy; on

manere with the dative cf. 8. 15 n.
tibi manet. In his despair Catullus
speaks as if the chapter of his active
life were closed, and nothing were
left him but the reminiscent period
of old age.

6. **ingrato** : in the passive sense;
i.e. his love and faithfulness had
won no return; cf. 64. 103 n. *ingrata munuscula ;* but in the active
sense in v. 9.

7. **cuiquam** : one of the less frequent cases where *quisquam* occurs
when no negative is either used or
implied; but perhaps here the preceding **quaecumque** suggesting an
idea of contingency (= *si qua*) is
sufficient to prompt the use of **cuiquam.**

9. **ingratae . . . menti** : cf. 65.
16 f.; the adjective is here active,
and not passive as in v. 6.

10. **tu** : the conjecture of Schoell
in adding this word is more satisfactory than the awkward transposi-
tion to *iam te cur.* The omission

Quin tu animo offirmas atque istinc teque reducis
　　Et dis inuitis desinis esse miser ?
Difficile est longum subito deponere amorem ;
　　Difficile est, uerum hoc qua libet efficias.
15 Vna salus haec est, hoc est tibi peruincendum ;
　　Hoc facias, siue id non pote siue pote.
O di, si uestrum est misereri, aut si quibus unquam
　　Extremam iam ipsa in morte tulistis opem,
Me miserum adspicite et, si uitam puriter egi,
20 　　Eripite hanc pestem perniciemque mihi !
Hei mihi subrepens imos ut torpor in artus
　　Expulit ex omni pectore laetitias.
Non iam illud quaero, contra ut me diligat illa,

of *tu* by the copyist was of course
due to **te** standing next.

11. **animo offirmas**: a phrase
apparently not occurring elsewhere,
though approximated by, *e.g.*, Plaut.
Merc. 82 *animum offirmo meum;*
Ter. *Eun.* 217 *censen posse me
offirmare perpeti;* Ov. *Met.* IX.
745 *quin animum firmas teque ipsa
recolligis;* Plin. *Ep.* VII. 27. 8 *offirmare animum.* — -**que**: correlative
with v. 12 **et**; the recovered soul-
courage is to be shown by aban-
doning once for all his unworthy
passion, and, as a consequence, by
regaining his peace of mind. With
-*que* appended to the second word
of its clause cf. 57. 2. — **te reducis**:
expressions of the same meaning
are 8. 9 *tu quoque noli;* 30. 9 *retrahis te.*

12. **dis inuitis**: *i.e.* it is his own
choice and not the will of the gods
that keeps him in his present state
of wretchedness; cf. the appeal in
vv. 17 ff. — **desinis esse miser**:
cf. 8. 1 *desinas ineptire;* 8. 10 *nec
miser uiue.*

13. **longum amorem**: the con-

nection with Lesbia had extended
over four or five years.

14. **qua libet**, *no matter how;*
cf. 40. 6.

16. **pote**: *sc. est fieri;* cf. 17.
24 n.; 42. 16.

17. **si**: not as intimating a possible doubt, but, as in the following
clause si unquam, suggesting *nunc
potissimum;* cf. 96. 1; 102. 1.

18. **extremam**, etc. : cf. Verg.
Aen. II. 447; XI. 846 *extrema iam
in morte.*

19. **puriter**: explained by v. 3 f.
On the form see 39. 14 n.

20. **pestem perniciemque**: *i.e.*
the deadly disease of v. 25 (cf. 75.
2). The union of the two allit-
erated words is common; cf. Cic.
Cat. I. 13. 33 *cum tua peste ac
pernicie.*

21. **hei**: with MS. *seu* for *hei* cf.
77. 4 *si* for *hei.* — **subrepens ut
torpor**, *like a creeping palsy.* —
imos artus: cf. 64. 93 *imis medullis;* 35. 15 *interiorem medullam.*

23. **contra diligat**, *love in return;* cf. Plaut. *Mil.* 101 *is amabat
meretricem, et illa illum contra.*

Aut, quod non potis est, esse pudica uelit :
25 Ipse ualere opto et taetrum hunc deponere morbum.
O di, reddite mi hoc pro pietate mea.

77.

Rufe mihi frustra ac nequiquam credite amice
  (Frustra ? immo magno cum pretio atque malo),
Sicine subrepsti mi atque intestina perurens
  Hei misero eripuisti omnia nostra bona ?
5 Eripuisti, eheu nostrae crudele uenenum
  Vitae, eheu nostrae pestis amicitiae.

78.

Gallus habet fratres, quorum est lepidissima coniunx
  Alterius, lepidus filius alterius.
Gallus homo est bellus : nam dulces iungit amores,
  Cum puero ut bello bella puella cubet.

24. **potis** : before a vowel for *pote*, as in 72. 7.

77. Like *c.* 73, addressed probably to M. Caelius Rufus. Cf. Intr. 59.

1. **frustra** : often of a finally unproductive investment ; **nequiquam**, of one hopeless from the very beginning. — **credite**, *believed ;* cf. Verg. *Aen.* II. 247 [*Cassandra*] *non unquam credita Teucris.*

2. With the rhetorical figure (*epanorthosis*) in **frustra . . . frustra? immo**, etc., cf. Cic. *Cat.* I. 1. 2 *hic tamen uiuit. uiuit? immo*, etc. — **magno cum pretio** : cf. 40. 8 *cum longa poena.*

4. **hei misero** : cf. 68. 92, 93. — **omnia nostra bona** : *i.e.* Lesbia's love ; cf. 68. 158 *omnia bona ;* **nostra** is for *mea*, with a change from the singular personal pronoun

in the preceding verse like that in 91. 1, 2 ; 116. 5, 6.

6. **nostrae** : *i.e.* the mutual friendship of Catullus and Rufus. With the change from the singular meaning in the preceding verse cf. 68. 94, 95.

78. A finely-pointed epigram directed against a man otherwise unknown.

1. **lepidissima** : like v. 2 **lepidus**, of physical rather than of mental characteristics ; cf. 1. 1 *lepidum libellum ;* Ter. *Heaut.* 1060 *tibi dabo illam lepidam quam tu facile ames.*

3. **bellus** : here of the charming politeness of a man of society training and discrimination ; cf. 22. 9 n.

4. **bello bella** : synonymous with *lepidissima . . . lepidus* above, as the similar conjunction shows. —

5 Gallus homo est stultus nec se uidet esse maritum,
  Qui patruus patrui monstret adulterium.

78ᵇ.

.   .   .   .

.   .   .   .

Sed nunc id doleo quod purae pura puellae
Sauia comminxit spurca saliua tua.

5 Verum id non impune feres : nam te omnia saecla
  Noscent et qui sis fama loquetur anus.

puella: of a youthful matron; cf. the frequent application of the same word to Lesbia.

5. Gallus . . . stultus: an abrupt correction of the commendation in v. 3; instead of having a fine sense of the fitness of things, Gallus has no sense at all.

6. qui, etc.: *i.e.* in helping his nephew to dishonor another uncle he prompts him to practice upon his teacher. The clause modifies **se** and not **maritum**.

78ᵇ. It is evident that these verses lack an introduction, but quite as clear that (as Statius decided) they cannot be the ending of *c.* 78, which is admirably complete in itself. Scaliger would add them to *c.* 77; but (1) the tone of that reproachful hexastich is entirely different from the coarse bitterness of these verses; (2) Catullus would hardly think of Lesbia as an innocent girl, as in vv. 1, 2; (3) vv. 5, 6 seem to indicate that the person addressed is not named in the poem (cf. *cc.* 71 and 104), while in *c.* 77 and the group to which it belongs Rufus is expressly named Nor does either *c.* 80, as

Bergk thought, or *c.* 91, as was the opinion of Corradius de Allio, need any completion at all, still less such a completion as these verses would afford. It seems best to regard them as a fragment of an independent poem, from the beginning of which certain verses are lost. These, which need not be more than two, apparently contained a conditional sentence embodying some sentiment like ' if you were a man of cleanly life, I would not object to your *amour*' (cf. 21. 9, 10 *si faceres satur, tacerem: nunc ipsum id doleo, quod*, etc.).

3. puellae: apparently not Lesbia (see note above).

4. sauia: here, as sometimes *oscula*, of the lips; cf. Plaut. *Mil.* 94 *maiorem partem uideas ualgis sauiis;* Gell. XIX. 11. 4 *dum semihiulco sauio meo puellum sauior.* — **comminxit**, etc.: cf. 99. 10.

5. id non impune feres : of stealing and carrying off something without challenge; cf. 99. 3; 14. 16.

6. fama loquetur anus: cf. 68. 46 n. *charta loquatur anus.*

79.

Lesbius est pulcher : quid ni ? quem Lesbia malit
　　Quam te cum tota gente, Catulle, tua.
Sed tamen hic pulcher uendat cum gente Catullum,
　　Si tria notorum sauia reppererit.

80.

Quid dicam, Gelli, quare rosea ista labella
　　Hiberna fiant candidiora niue,

79. Against his rival Lesbius; written after the final rupture with Lesbia.

I. **Lesbius**: surely P. Clodius Pulcher, the brother of Clodia 'Quadrantaria,' if Lesbia is this Clodia (cf. Intr. 28). The allusion in vv. 1, 2 must, therefore, be to that incestuous connection of which Cicero speaks (*e.g. Pis.* 28; *Sest.* 16; *Har. Resp.* 42, 59). — **pulcher** : Cicero plays on this well-known cognomen of P. Clodius in *Att.* I. 16. 10 *surgit pulchellus puer ;* and similarly in II. 1. 4 and II. 22. 1. — **quid ni**, etc.: *i.e.* to be sure, since Lesbia's preference is proof sufficient of it. The play is on **pulcher** as a true descriptive adjective, and as also the *cognomen* of Lesbia's brother; the intimation being that the very fact that he is her brother gives him added attraction in her eyes as a paramour; cf. the ascription of a similar taste for enormities to Gellius in 91. 5, 6.

2. **quam te**: since he is *pulcher* (*i.e.* a beauty), and you are not. — **cum tota gente tua**: since he is Pulcher (*i.e.* an eminent Claudian), and you are a nobody.

3. **tamen hic pulcher**: *i.e.* in spite of his being beautiful and of high birth. — **uendat**: apparently a colloquial expression of superior worth, like our 'he can buy and sell me.' The phrase comes from the sale of the goods of an insolvent debtor. — **Catullum**: for *bona Catulli ;* cf. Juv. 3. 33 *praebere caput domina uenale sub hasta.*

4. **si tria**, etc.: *i.e.* if peradventure he can find even so few as three acquaintances who will accept the common friendly greeting from his lips. The allusion is doubtless to the defilement of his lips by unnatural lust; cf. Cicero *ll. cc.* — **tria** : of an indefinitely small number; cf. Plaut. *Trin.* 963 *te tribus uerbis uolo,* and often. — **notorum,** *acquaintances ;* cf. Caes. *B. C.* I. 74. 5 *hi suos notos hospitesque quaerebant ;* Hor. *Sat.* I. 1. 85 *uicini oderunt, noti, pueri atque puellae.* Others, reading with *G, natorum,* understand the reference to be to the *ius trium liberorum* of so much importance later (the implication being that Clodius was impotent). But there is no indication that at this time the lack of three children was a political disadvantage, and Clodius had a son and a daughter (Drumann *Gesch. Roms* II. p. 385 f.), both young at the time of his death.

80. See introductory note to *c.* 74.

I. **rosea**: Gellius is apparently youthful; cf. 45. 12 n. *purpureo ore.*

2. **fiant**: for *sint ;* cf. 73. 2 *fieri.*

Mane domo cum exis et cum te octaua quiete
    E molli longo suscitat hora die?
5 Nescio quid certe est: an uere fama susurrat
    Grandia te medii tenta uorare uiri?
Sic certe est: clamant Victoris rupta miselli
    Ilia, et emulso labra notata sero.

81.

Nemone in tanto potuit populo esse, Iuuenti,
    Bellus homo quem tu diligere inciperes
Praeterquam iste tuus moribunda ab sede Pisauri
    Hospes inaurata pallidior statua?

— candidiora niue: cf. Hom. *Il.*
X. 437 [ἵπποι] λευκότεροι χιόνος;
Verg. *Aen.* XII. 84 [*equi*] *qui can-
dore niues anteirent;* Ov. *Pont.* II.
5. 37 [*pectora*] *lacte et non calcata
candidiora niue.*

3. quiete: *i.e.* the midday siesta;
cf. 32. 3; 61. 118.

4. longo die, *well along in the
day;* contrasted with v. 3 mane.

7. sic certe est: cf. 62. 8 n. —
clamant: cf. 6. 7 n. — Victoris:
otherwise unknown. — rupta ilia:
cf. 11. 20.

81. A poem of the Juventian cycle (cf. introductory note to *c.* 15),
and, like *c.* 24, a remonstrance addressed to Juventius for his intimacy,
this time with a certain Pisaurian
who was his host. This last circumstance would seem to point to Aurelius (*c.* 15), and the supposition is
further strengthened by the facts
that Aurelius and Furius were inti-
mately associated in the mind of
Catullus; that he broke friendship
with both; that the cause of the
break with at least Furius was his
intimacy with Juventius; that Aurelius was at least an object of sus-

picion and warning on the same
score. Bruner finds this idea confirmed by a possible play upon the
name of Aurelius in v. 4 *inaurata.*

2. bellus homo: such a lover
Juventius also found in Furius;
cf. 24. 7 f.

3. Pisauri: Pisaurum (now
Pesaro) was an Umbrian town on
the Adriatic planted as a Roman
colony B.C. 184 (cf. Liv. XXXIX.
44). Plutarch (*Ant.* 60) reports that
the town was swallowed up by an
earthquake just before the battle of
Actium. The previous settlement
there of a number of military colonists by Antony (Plut. *l.c.*) may
have been an attempt to check the
decay (moribunda sede) noted
by Catullus.

4. inaurata statua: gilded statues were common in Rome at a
later date, the second supplement
to the *Notitia* (written in the first
half of the fourth century A.D.)
mentioning eighty of gods alone.
This number is understood to be
exclusive of statues in temples and
other shrines. With the comparison
cf. 64. 100 n.

5 Qui tibi nunc cordi est, quem tu praeponere nobis
    Audes et nescis quod facinus facias.

82.

Quinti, si tibi uis oculos debere Catullum
    Aut aliud si quid carius est oculis,
Eripere ei noli multo quod carius illi
    Est oculis seu quid carius est oculis.

83.

Lesbia mi praesente uiro mala plurima dicit:
    Haec illi fatuo maxima laetitia est.
Mule, nihil sentis.   Si nostri oblita taceret,
    Sana esset: nunc quod gannit et obloquitur,

5. **cordi est**: cf. 44. 3 n.

6. **nescis**, etc.: perhaps the idea is that Nemesis will avenge the slighted love of Catullus (cf. 50. 20 n.), or simply that Catullus by great and continued kind services has a strong claim upon the gratitude and affection of Juventius. But the offense of slighting love was often exaggerated by the poets. With **facinus facias** cf. 110. 4 n.

82. An appeal to Quintius not to rob the poet of Lesbia. This Quintius is probably the lover of Aufilena in *c.* 100, and now, like his friend Caelius Rufus, has joined the ranks of Lesbia's lovers, and thus aroused the indignation of Catullus.

2. **si quid est**, etc.: cf. 13. 10 n. — **carius oculis**: cf. 3. 5 n.

3. **ei**: here monosyllabic.

4. **seu**: for *uel si*, as in 13. 10.

83. On the evidence of Lesbia's love for him. Written at least before 59 B.C. (when Q. Metellus Celer, the husband of Clodia, died) and probably to be placed among the earliest of the poems concerning Lesbia (see Intr. 16). With the theme cf. *c.* 92; Prop. IV. 8 *passim;* Ov. *Rem. Am.* 647 f.

1. **mi praesente uiro**: it does not follow, however, that Catullus was himself present; but the epigram may have been sent to Lesbia on hearing of the incident from others, and may date from the period when he was first paying court to her. — **mala dicit**: cf. Plaut. *Men.* 717 *omnia mala ingerebat, quemquem aspexerat;* Tib. I. 2. 11 *mala siqua tibi dixit.*

2. **fatuo**: cf. 98. 2 n. *fatuis.*

3. **mule**: not common as a synonym for a fellow of persistent dullness; but cf. Juv. 16. 23 *mulino corde Vagelli.*

4. **sana**: *i.e.* free from the passion of love; cf. Verg. *Aen.* IV. 8 [*Dido*] *adloquitur male sana sororem;* Tib. IV. 6. 18 *uritur nec sana fuisse uelit.* — **gannit**: strictly of

5 Non solum meminit, sed, quae multo acrior est res,
    Irata est : hoc est, uritur et loquitur.

84.

Chommoda dicebat, si quando commoda uellet
    Dicere, et insidias Arrius hinsidias,
Et tum mirifice sperabat se esse locutum
    Cum quantum poterat dixerat hinsidias.
5 Credo, sic mater, sic liber auunculus eius,
    Sic maternus auus dixerat atque auia.

the snarling of a dog; cf. Non. 450. 11 *gannire cum sit proprie canum;* Ter. *Ad.* 556 *quid ille gannit? quid uolt?* Juv. 6. 64 *Appula gannit.*

5. **acrior**, *more to the point.*

6. **uritur**: of the passion of love; cf. Hor. *Carm.* I. 13. 8 *quam lentis penitus macerer ignibus; uror,* etc.; 2. 8 n. *ardor.* — **et**, *and therefore;* introducing a result of the preceding fact; cf. Plaut. *Asin.* 447 *audio et quiesco.*

84. A jest at the tendency to aspiration in pronunciation of a certain Arrius, perhaps the Quintus Arrius mentioned by Cicero (*Brut.* 242) as an orator of low birth and poor parts, who by time-serving had won some success. He was especially a follower of M. Crassus, but his career as an orator was wrecked by the time-limit imposed upon pleas by the Pompeian law of 52 B.C. — The tendency of the age toward excessive aspiration is noticed by Cicero in his *Orat.* 160, and was discussed by Caesar in his (lost) *De Analogia;* see also Quint. I. 5. 20, who cites this poem of Catullus. The skit was perhaps written in 55 B.C. (cf. v. 7 n.).

1. **uellet**: the subjunctive imperfect in the protasis of a general con-

dition with the imperfect indicative in the apodosis is a construction rarely found in writers of the republican period, though it is not infrequent in Livy and later writers.

3. **sperabat**, *used to flatter himself.*

4. **quantum poterat**: *i.e.* with so great an effort after distinctness and precision that he fairly shouted the words out at the top of his voice.

5 f. The point of these two parenthetical verses (cf. the verse introduced by *credo* in 2. 8) seems to be that this super-aspiration was considered to be a characteristic of low-born and uneducated people (Gell. XIII. 6. 3); and as the relations cited are all on the mother's side, it looks as though the ancestry of Arrius in the female line had already been the subject of jest among his acquaintances (cf. Cicero's remark concerning him in *Brut.* 243 *infimo loco natus*). The point of **liber** as an adjective and not a proper name is then clear, if *infimo loco* be understood of the condition of slavery: his maternal uncle (perhaps only one of his uncles on that side) was a *libertus,* and the social standing of the entire family is thus indicated.

Hoc misso in Syriam requierant omnibus aures :
    Audibant eadem haec leniter et leuiter,
Nec sibi postilla metuebant talia uerba,
10   Cum subito adfertur nuntius horribilis
Ionios fluctus, postquam illuc Arrius isset,
    Iam non Ionios esse, sed Hionios.

85.

Odi et amo.   Quare id faciam fortasse requiris.
Nescio, sed fieri sentio et excrucior.

86.

Quintia formosa est multis, mihi candida, longa,
    Recta est.   Haec ego sic singula confiteor,

7. **misso** : *sc.* on some public service; perhaps with his friend Crassus, who assumed the governorship of Syria in 55 B.C.

8. **audibant** : with the form cf. 64. 319 n. *custodibant.* — **leniter et leuiter** : *i.e.* though the people left behind misused aspirates, they did not at any rate bellow out so horribly their mispronunciations.

9. **postilla** : a word of older Latin for the later *postea*, perhaps, however, still used colloquially in the time of Catullus.

11. **Ionios fluctus** : that part of the Mediterranean Sea lying west and northwest of Greece, and hence the first sea encountered by Arrius on his journey. The report of its fate was, then, but a foretaste of what was to come to the Romans who had hoped for relief on the departure of Arrius.

85. An epigram on his own feeling for Lesbia; written at about the same time with *cc.* 72 and 75.

1. **odi et amo** : cf. Ov. *Am.* II. 4. 5 *odi nec possum cupiens non esse quod odi.*

2. **nescio**, etc.: cf. Mart. I. 32 *Non amo te, Sabidi, nec possum dicere quare : hoc tantum possum dicere, non amo te ;* and its imitation by Tom Brown, *I do not love thee, Dr. Fell*, etc.

86. On the inferiority of Quintia to Lesbia. Cf. also *c.* 43. Quintia is evidently not the sister of the Quintius of *cc.* 82 and 100; for this poem dates from the time of the faith of Catullus in Lesbia, at which time Quintius was his friend (cf. *c.* 100). With the sentiment cf. Petron. ap. *Poet. Lat. Min.* IV. 89 Baehrens *non est forma satis*, etc.

1. **candida, longa, recta** : these being characteristics of typical female beauty, as of that of the goddesses; cf. Ov. *Am.* II. 4. 33 *tu, quia tam longa es, ueteres heroidas aequas ;* Hor. *Sat.* I. 2. 123 f. *candida rectaque sit, munda hactenus, ut neque longa nec magis alba uelit,*

Totum illud 'formosa' nego : nam nulla uenustas,
  Nulla in tam magno est corpore mica salis.
5 Lesbia formosa est, quae cum pulcherrima tota est,
  Tum omnibus una omnis subripuit Veneres.

87.

Nulla potest mulier tantum se dicere amatam
  Vere, quantum a me Lesbia amata mea es :
Nulla fides ullo fuit unquam in foedere tanta
  Quanta in amore tuo ex parte reperta mea est.

88.

Quid facit is, Gelli, qui cum matre atque sorore
  Prurit et abiectis peruigilat tunicis ?
Quid facit is patruum qui non sinit esse maritum ?
  Ecquid scis quantum suscipiat sceleris ?
5 Suscipit, o Gelli, quantum non ultima Tethys
  Nec genitor nympharum abluit Oceanus :

quam dat natura, uideri; Tennyson *Princess, A daughter of the gods, divinely tall, and most divinely fair.*

3. **uenustas**: cf. 3. 1 n. *Veneres.*

4. **mica salis**: cf. Mart. VII. 25 *nullaque mica salis nec amari fellis in illis* [*uersibus*] *gutta sit.*

6. **Veneres**: cf. Plaut. *Stich.* 278 *amoenitates omnium Venerum et uenustatum adfero;* Quint. X. 1. 79 *Isocrates omnes dicendi Veneres sectatus est.*

87. A fragment, written on losing faith in Lesbia, and resembling in tone 75. 3–4. Scaliger sought vainly to complete it by affixing *c.* 75 (*q.u.*).

1 f. Cf. 8. 5; 37. 12 *amata tantum quantum amabitur nulla.*

4. **tuo**: cf. 64. 253 n. *tuo amore.*

— **ex parte mea** : not as contrasted with Lesbia in her faithlessness, — the phrase **in amore tuo** precludes that, — but as contrasted with the mere wanton passion of Lesbia's new lovers.

88. On the crimes of Gellius; cf. *c.* 74.

1. **matre** : perhaps his stepmother only; cf. Intr. 72.

5. **ultima** : *i.e.* to her farthest bounds. — **Tethys** : cf. 64. 29 n.; 66. 70.

6. **nec abluit** : cf. Lucr. VI. 1077 *non, mare si totum uelit eluere omnibus undis;* Sen. *Phaedr.* 723 ff. *quis eluet me Tanais? aut quae barbaris Maeotis undis Pontico incumbens mari? non ipse toto magnus oceano pater tantum expiarit sce-*

Nam nihil est quicquam sceleris quo prodeat ultra,
    Non si demisso se ipse uoret capite.

89.

Gellius est tenuis : quid ni ? cui tam bona mater
    Tamque ualens uiuat tamque uenusta soror
Tamque bonus patruus tamque omnia plena puellis
    Cognatis, quare is desinat esse macer ?
5 Qui ut nihil attingat, nisi quod fas tangere non est,
    Quantumuis quare sit macer inuenies.

90.

Nascatur magus ex Gelli matrisque nefando
    Coniugio et discat Persicum haruspicium :
Nam magus ex matre et gnato gignatur oportet,
    Si uera est Persarum impia religio,
5 Gratus ut accepto ueneretur carmine diuos
    Omentum in flamma pingue liquefaciens.

leris. — Oceanus : with this conjunction of *Oceanus* with *Tethys* cf. Hom. *Il.* XIV. 201 Ὠκεανόν τε, θεῶν γένεσιν, καὶ μητέρα Τηθύν.

7. nihil quicquam : a not infrequent expression in the comedians; cf. Plaut. *Bacch.* 1036 *nihil ego tibi hodie consili quicquam dabo;* Ter. *Andr.* 90 *comperiebam nil ad Pamphilum quicquam attinere.*

8. non si : see 48. 5 n.

89. On the same theme as *c.* 88.

1. bona, *obliging;* cf. 110. 1 *bonae amicae.*

3. bonus patruus : the expression finds an explanation in *c.* 74. — omnia plena : cf. Cic. *Att.* II. 24. 4 *ita sunt omnia omnium miseriarum plenissima;* Verg. *Geor.* II. 4 *tuis hic omnia plena muneribus;*

Tib. I. 8. 54 *lacrimis omnia plena madent.*

90. On the same theme as the preceding.

4. Persarum : the practice of incestuous marriages among the Persian Magi is mentioned by Strabo XV. p. 735 τούτοις δὲ καὶ μητράσι συνέρχεσθαι πάτριον νενόμισται; cf. also Eurip. *Androm.* 173 ff. and scholia; Tert. *Apol.* p. 10 *Persas cum suis matribus misceri Ctesias refert.*

5. gratus accepto carmine : cf. 67. 26 n. — carmine : the litanies of these priests are also mentioned in Strabo XV. p. 733.

6. omentum, etc.: cf. Pers. 2. 47 *in flammas iunicum omenta liquescant.* — liquēfaciens : cf. Intr. 86 *f.*

91.

Non ideo, Gelli, sperabam te mihi fidum
    In misero hoc nostro, hoc perdito amore fore
Quod te cognossem bene constantemue putarem
    Aut posse a turpi mentem inhibere probro,
5 Sed neque quod matrem nec germanam esse uidebam
    Hanc tibi cuius me magnus edebat amor ;
Et quamuis tecum multo coniungerer usu,
    Non satis id causae credideram esse tibi.
Tu satis id duxti : tantum tibi gaudium in omni
10   Culpa est in quacumque est aliquid sceleris.

92.

Lesbia mi dicit semper male nec tacet unquam
    De me : Lesbia me dispeream nisi amat.
Quo signo ? quia sunt totidem mea : deprecor illam
    Adsidue, uerum dispeream nisi amo.

91. On the same theme as the preceding, but making clear the original grievance of Catullus against Gellius, that he was one of Lesbia's numerous lovers.

2. **misero**: cf. 68. 30 n. — **nostro**: for *meo ;* with the change in the same sentence from **mihi** to **nostro** cf. 77. 3, 4; 116. 5, 6.

3. **cognossem bene**: cf. 61. 187 n. *cognitae bene :* the subjunctive indicates a possible reason, but marks it as contrary to fact; the indicative, in v. 5, states the real reason.

5 f. A bitter turn of irony, explained by *cc.* 88–90. — **edebat :** cf. 35. 15 *edunt.*

7 ff. **quamuis,** etc.: *i.e.* any misdoing (**culpa**) which has a spice of wickedness (**sceleris**) in it has a charm for Gellius, and if a chance

to violate the most sacred ties of kindred is not at hand, the ties of friendship will do.

92. On the same theme as *c.* 83, and written about the same time.

1. **dicit nec tacet**: cf. 6. 3.

2. **dispeream nisi** : cf. Hor. *Sat.* I. 9. 47 *dispeream ni summosses omnes ;* Verg. *Cat.* 9. 2 *dispeream nisi me perdidit iste putus ;* Mart. XI. 90. 8 *dispeream ni scis* (where the expression is labeled as an antique).

3. **totidem mea** : Ellis takes these words to mean 'I have scored the same number of points' (*i.e.* my case is exactly the same), referring to the game of *duodecim scripta* described by Ovid in *Art. Am.* III. 363 ff. : but though the general meaning of the clause is clear, the precise interpretation is doubtful.

93.

Nil nimium studeo, Caesar, tibi uelle placere,
   Nec scire utrum sis albus an ater homo.

94.

Mentula moechatur.   Moechatur mentula certe.
   Hoc est quod dicunt, ipsa olera olla legit.

95.

Zmyrna mei Cinnae nonam post denique messem
   Quam coepta est nonamque edita post hiemem,

— **deprecor**, *exsecrate;* see the discussion of this use of the word by
Catullus in Gell. VII. (VI.) 16.

93. Apparently a rude answer to
some approaches by, or on behalf
of, Julius Caesar. The date of its
composition, even with reference to
cc. 29 and 57, is doubtful; see Intr.
38. Cf. the remark of Quintilian
XI. 1. 38 *negat se magni facere
aliquis poetarum 'utrum Caesar
ater an albus homo sit,' insania ;
uerte, ut idem Caesar de illo dixerit,
adrogantia est.*

1. **nimium :** cf. 43. 4 n. — **studeo uelle :** with the pleonasm cf.
Nep. *Att.* 4. 2 *noli aduersum eos
me uelle ducere;* Cic. *Dom.* 146
nolite eum uelle esse priuatum (and
Markland's note); Petron. 98 *si
Gitona tuum amas, incipe uelle
seruare;* Sen. *Apoc.* 14 *incipit
patronus uelle respondere.*

2. **nec scire**, etc. : *i.e.* I have no
interest in you whatever. — **albus
an ater :** the expression is proverbial ; cf. Cic. *Phil.* II. 41
*uide quam te amarit is qui albus
aterne fuerit ignoras;* Phaedr. III.
15. 10 *unde illa sciuit niger an*

albus nascerer? Apul. *Apol.* 16
*etiam libenter te nuper usque albus
an ater esses ignoraui.*

94. A play on the name of a
certain dissolute person called here,
and in *cc.* 105, 114, and 115, Mentula. On his identification with the
Mamurra mentioned in *cc.* 29, 41,
43, and 57, cf. 29. 13 n. and Intr. 73.
The point of the epigram is, 'You say
that Mentula is an adulterer. Why,
of course. How could he be otherwise with such a name as his. 'Tis
as natural as for a pot to gather in
potherbs.'

2. **hoc est quod dicunt :** of a
proverbial expression; cf. 100. 3.

95. On the enduring fame of the
Zmyrna of C. Helvius Cinna, who
was mentioned in 10. 29 f.; see also
Intr. 63.

1. **nonam**, etc. : so also Quint.
X. 4. 4 *Cinnae Smyrnam nouem
annis accepimus scriptam ;* Serv. on
Verg. *Ecl.* 9. 35 *quem libellum
[Smyrnam] decem annis elimauit ;*
cf. Hor. *A. P.* 388 *nonum prematur
in annum, membranis intus positis.*

2. **edita :** *sc. est*, suggested from
the preceding *est*.

Milia cum interea quingenta Hortensius uno

. . . .

5 Zmyrna cauas Satrachi penitus mittetur ad undas,

Zmyrnam cana diu saecula peruoluent.

At Volusi annales Paduam morientur ad ipsam

Et laxas scombris saepe dabunt tunicas.

Parua mei mihi sint cordi monumenta sodalis:

10   At populus tumido gaudeat Antimacho.

---

3. **cum interea**: cf. 64. 305.—
milia quingenta: cf. 9. 2 n.—
Hortensius: perhaps Q. Hortensius Ortalus, the poet and man of
letters, to whom *c.* 65 is addressed;
cf. Intr. 65. But the genuineness of
the reading has often been doubted.
— **uno**, etc.: *sc. anno*, or perhaps,
as Haupt suggests, *die* (cf. Plut. *Cic.*
40). The simplest guess at the
gist of the lost verse is that it contrasted the careless literary fecun-
dity of Hortensius with Cinna's
careful elaboration of merely a short
poem. But others, troubled by
the speedy introduction of Volusius, see in v. 4 a reference to him
as the facile author of the myriads
of verses, and to Hortensius only
as his patron (cf. Crit. App.).

5. **cauas**, *deep;* cf. 17. 4 *caua
in palude.* — **Satrachi**: a river of
Cyprus, a favorite haunt of Aphrodite and Adonis, the son of Myrrha,
or Zmyrna. The idea is that the
poem of Cinna will be read in
the depths of the distant island
where its scene was laid. — **penitus**: *i.e.* far into the interior.

6. **cana saecula**, *the hoary ages;*
so Martial of the distant past in
VIII. 80. 2. — **peruoluent**: with
diæresis; cf. Intr. 86 *b.*

7. **Volusi annales**: cf. *c.* 36.
Why Catullus turns suddenly from
Hortensius to Volusius it is im-
possible to say, in the lack of

knowledge concerning the latter,
between whom and Hortensius
there may have been some definite
connection. — **Paduam**: with the
river Satrachus is here contrasted
the branch of the Po called by
Polybius (II. 16) Παδόα. Near
this stream lay the birthplace of the
Annals (as **ipsam** shows), and
doubtless of Volusius himself.

8. **laxas**: as both fish and wrap-
ping-paper were cheap, the parcel
was not wrapped as neatly as it
might have been. — **scombris dabunt tunicas**: cf. the reminiscence in Mart. IV. 86. 8 *nec scombris tunicas dabis* [*libelle*] *molestas*
(also III. 2. 3; III. 50. 9); and
on a similar fate for bad verses,
Hor. *Ep.* II. 1. 269, *et al.* — **saepe**:
for the Annals covered many pages,
and would serve the fish-mongers
a long time.

9. **parua**: of the length of the
Zmyrna. — **sodalis**: cf. 10. 29.

10. **populus**: *i.e.* the οἱ πολλοί,
who have no critical sense. — **Antimacho**: an epic poet of Colophon,
who flourished about 400 B.C. He
was proverbial among the ancients
for wordiness; for a famous story
about him see Cic. *Brut.* 191.
Quintilian (X. 1. 53) remarks that
he is generally accorded the second place among epic writers, but
criticises his looseness and carelessness of style, which would be

96.

Si quicquam mutis gratum acceptumue sepulcris
  Accidere a nostro, Calue, dolore potest,
Quo desiderio ueteres renouamus amores
  Atque olim missas flemus amicitias,
5 Certe non tanto mors immatura dolori est
  Quintiliae, quantum gaudet amore tuo.

97.

Non (ita me di ament) quicquam referre putaui
  Vtrumne os an culum olfacerem Aemilio.
Nilo mundius hoc, nihiloque immundius illud,
  Verum etiam culus mundior et melior :
5 Nam sine dentibus est.   Hoc dentis sesquipedalis.

unpardonable sins in the eyes of an Alexandrian like Catullus. But the comparison of Volusius to him here is plainly in respect of his voluminousness.

96. To Calvus on the death of his wife, Quintilia ; cf. Intr. 60. From Propertius (III. 34. 89 f.) we learn that Calvus himself wrote a threnody on his loss.

1. si quicquam, etc. : the phrase is probably not intended as an expression of skepticism which might destroy the effect of the consolation, but to emphasize the apodosis following in v. 5 f.; cf. 76. 17 n. 102. 1. For more definite echoes of the prevailing agnosticism among the Romans regarding immortality cf. Sulpicius ap. Cic. *Fam.* IV. 5. 6; Tac. *Agr.* 46. — **mutis sepulcris** : cf. 101. 4 *mutam cinerem*. — **gratum acceptumue** : the conjunction of these adjectives is common; cf. also 90. 5 *gratus ut accepto*.

2. nostro : of men in general, —

though Catullus had himself felt the need of similar consolation.

3 f. desiderio, etc. : in apposition with **dolore**, carrying on the idea with specification; cf. 2. 8 and note.

4. missas : not here, as frequently, of a thing voluntarily surrendered, but of one given up in obedience to a greater power; cf. 66. 29. — **amicitias** : of the sentiment rather than the passion of love; cf. 109. 6.

97. An exceedingly coarse epigram on a certain Aemilius, of whom nothing further is known.

1. ita me di ament : a colloquial form of asseveration; cf. Ter. *Andr.* 947 *ita me di ament, credo;* and similar phrases with *iuuare* in 61. 196; 66. 18. On the hiatus in arsis see Intr. 86 *d*.

3. hoc . . . illud : with this reference of *hic* to the former and *illt* to the latter of two items cf. 100. 3.

5. hoc : referring to os, as in v. 3.

Gingiuas uero ploxeni habet ueteris,
Praeterea rictum qualem diffissus in aestu
   Meientis mulae cunnus habere solet.
Hic futuit multas et se facit esse uenustum,
10   Et non pistrino traditur atque asino ?
Quem si qua attingit, non illam posse putemus
   Aegroti culum lingere carnificis ?

98.

In te, si in quemquam, dici pote, putide Victi,
   Id quod uerbosis dicitur et fatuis :
Ista cum lingua, si usus ueniat tibi, possis
   Culos et crepidas lingere carpatinas.
5 Si nos omnino uis omnes perdere, Victi,
   Hiscas : omnino quod cupis efficies.

---

6. ploxeni: explained by Festus to mean a wagon-box (*capsum in cisio capsaue*), and said by Quintilian to be circumpadane (Gallic?) in origin; I. 5. 8 *Catullus 'ploxenum' circa Padum inuenit.* The comparison here may be of the wrinkled and fissured look of diseased gums to some peculiarity in shape of the *ploxenum*, or to its wrinkled and split rawhide covering.

10. pistrino, etc.: *i.e.* relegated to the occupation of the rudest slaves, that of driving the ass that turns the mill.

98. Against an unknown Victius, or Vittius (Haupt and a single interpolated MS.), or Vettius (Statius and many others). The man referred to may be L. Vettius, the Titus Oates of his time, who in B.C. 62 charged Julius Caesar with complicity in the conspiracy of Catiline (Suet. *Iul.* 17), and three years later trumped up against a

number of leading senators a charge of conspiracy to assassinate Pompey. He was himself accused of forging his evidence, and was cast into prison, and died there. But though Vettius is a much more common name than either of the others, some mere loud-mouthed nonentity may be meant instead of the notorious Lucius Vettius.

2. fatuis : especially used of silly speakers, and distinguished from *insulsus* by Donatus (ad Ter. *Eun.* 1079 *fatui sunt qui uerbis et dictis fatui sunt ; insulsi uero corde et animo*); cf. Serv. ad Verg. *Aen.* VII. 47 *fatuos dicimus inconsiderate loquentes.*

4. carpatinas : a rude shoe made from a single piece of hide and apparently worn only by the lowest classes.

5 f. si nos, etc.: *i.e.* such is our just fear of being addressed by your foul tongue that you have only to

99.

Subripui tibi, dum ludis, mellite Iuuenti,
  Sauiolum dulci dulcius ambrosia.
Verum id non impune tuli : namque amplius horam
  Suffixum in summa me memini esse cruce,
5 Dum tibi me purgo nec possum fletibus ullis
  Tantillum uestrae demere saeuitiae.
Nam simul id factum est, multis diluta labella
  Guttis abstersisti omnibus articulis,
Ne quicquam nostro contractum ex ore maneret,
10   Tanquam commictae spurca saliua lupae.
Praeterea infesto miserum me tradere Amori
  Non cessasti omnique excruciare modo,
Vt mi ex ambrosia mutatum iam foret illud

open your mouth to see us immediately drop dead. — **omnino**, *out-*
and-out ; modifying not **omnes**,
but **perdere**; cf. v. 6 *omnino effi-*
cies (but Cic. *Inuent.* 86 *omnino*
omnis argumentatio).

99. On the cruelty of Juventius
in shunning the poet's kisses. On
Juventius cf. *c.* 15 and Intr. 37. This
poem antedates *c.* 15 and the rest of
the cycle immediately connected
therewith.

2. **dulci dulcius**: cf. 22. 14 n.
infaceto infacetior.

3. **non impune tuli**: cf. 78^b. 5
non impune feres.

4. **suffixum in cruce,** *kept upon*
the rack. The reference is perhaps
to the punishment by impalement,
rarer and more dreaded than the
ordinary forms of crucifixion; cf.
Sen. *Cons. ad Marc.* 20. 3 *uideo*
istic cruces non unius quidem gene-
ris, sed aliter ab aliis fabricatas . . .
alii per obscoena stipitem egerunt ;
Ep. 101. 12 *suffigas licet et acutam*
sessuro crucem subdas. — **summa** :

of the intensity of the torture; cf.
Colum. I. 7. 2 *summum ius antiqui*
summam putabant crucem.

6. **tantillum,** *an atom.* — **ues-**
trae saeuitiae : *i.e.* the cruelty that
is peculiar to you and your like.

7. **simul**: *sc. atque;* cf. 22. 15 n.
— **id**: with reference to the theft
of the kiss.

8. **guttis** : *sc.* of water; cf. Lucr.
VI. 942 *saxa superne guttis manan-*
tibus stillent. — **articulis,** *fingers,*
as occasionally in the elegiasts and
later.

9. **contractum** : a technical word
connected with contagious and in-
fectious diseases.

10. Cf. 78^b. 4. — **lupae** : a nickname for a prostitute; cf. Liv. I. 4.
7 *sunt qui Larentiam uulgato cor-*
pore lupam inter pastores uocatam
putent.

11. **infesto tradere Amori**: *i.e*
to hand me over as a captive to a
merciless jailer, — the idea being
that the boy's petulant anger made
him more attractive than ever, and

Sauiolum tristi tristius elleboro.

15 Quam quoniam poenam misero proponis amori,
   Nunquam iam posthac basia subripiam.

100.

Caelius Aufilenum et Quintius Aufilenam
   Flos Veronensum depereunt iuuenum,
Hic fratrem, ille sororem.   Hoc est quod dicitur illud
   Fraternum uere dulce sodalicium.
5 Cui faueam potius ?   Caeli, tibi : nam tua nobis
   Per facta exhibita est unica amicitia
Cum uesana meas torreret flamma medullas.
   Sis felix, Caeli, sis in amore potens.

quickened, instead of quenching, the poet's passion.

14. tristi, *bitter ;* cf. Anth. *Pal.* V. 29. 2 πικρότερον γίγνεται ἑλλε-βόρου. On the collocation tristi tristius cf. 22. 14 n.

15 f. The poem concludes with a mock simplicity that allows the sportive character of the preceding complaints to be seen. — misero : cf. 91. 2 n.

16. basia : cf. 5. 7 n.

100. On the love of two friends for a certain brother and sister respectively. On Caelius see Intr. 59; Quintius is probably the Quintius of *c.* 82, but apparently not the brother of the Quintia of *c.* 86 (see introductory note to *c.* 86). Aufilenus is otherwise unknown, though to Aufilena are addressed *cc.* 110 and 111, in which she is accused of faithlessness as a mistress and of incest with an uncle. The lack of any apparent feeling against Aufilena in *c.* 100 leads to the supposition that it was written before *cc.* 110 and 111 ; but it is not necessary to suppose that its scene is laid at

Verona, for v. 2 *Veronensum* indicates merely origin and not residence.

2. flos iuuenum : cf. 24. 1. — depereunt : see 35. 12 n.

3. hic : referring to the first-mentioned person, Caelius, while ille refers to Quintius ; cf. the similar use of *hoc* and *illud* in 97. 3. — hoc est quod dicitur : cf. 94. 2.

5. cui faueam potius : *i.e.* in whose success shall I feel the most lively interest? With the question and answer cf. 1. 1 ff. cui is for *utri,* as occasionally in writers of this and the following periods.

6. per facta exhibita : the friendship may have been proved by withdrawing from rivalry with Catullus in his affair with Lesbia; but if Caelius be Caelius Rufus, we must suppose the withdrawal was but feigned, as Catullus afterward discovered; see Intr. *l.c.*

7. uesana flamma : of the love of the poet for Lesbia; cf. 7. 10 *uesano Catullo.* — torreret medullas : cf. 35. 15 n.

8. potens, *successful ;* cf. Prop.

101.

Multas per gentes et multa per aequora uectus
    Aduenio has miseras, frater, ad inferias,
Vt te postremo donarem munere mortis
    Et mutam nequiquam adloquerer cinerem,
5 Quandoquidem fortuna mihi tete abstulit ipsum,
    Heu miser indigne frater adempte mihi.
Nunc tamen interea haec, prisco quae more parentum
    Tradita sunt tristi munere ad inferias,
Accipe fraterno multum manantia fletu
10   Atque in perpetuum, frater, aue atque uale.

III. 26. 21 *quod tam mihi pulchra puella seruiat et tota dicar in urbe potens;* and the fuller form in Ov. *Met.* VIII. 409 *uoti potente.*

101. An invocation accompanying offerings made at the tomb of the poet's brother in the Troad (cf. 65. 5 ff.; 68. 19 ff. 89 ff.). See Intr. 22.

1. **multas**, etc. : the exaggeration of the expression marks the intensity of the poet's grief over the distance that separated him from his brother's deathbed and tomb.

2. **miseras** : cf. 68. 30 n. — **inferias** : defined by Servius on Verg. *Aen.* X. 519 *inferiae sunt sacra mortuorum, quod inferis soluuntur.* Perhaps Catullus is now offering the *cena nouemdialis,* omitted perforce up to this time, since none of the family were present at the burial. In this case the offerings would be especially dishes of eggs, lentils, and salt, and the phrase in v. 9 *multum manantia fletu* would be quite in point, as it would not be if libations only were offered.

4. **mutam cinerem** : cf. 96. 1 *mutis sepulcris.* — **adloquerer** : cf. v. 10 n.

5. **quandoquidem**, etc. : cf. 64. 218 f. — **tete** : cf. 30. 7 *tute.*

6. Cf. 68. 20 and 92.

7. **interea** : with an imperative, indicating the relinquishment of the previous line of thought, at least for a season; cf. 14. 21; 36. 18; *Ciris* 44 ff. *haec tamen interea . . . accipe dona meo multum uigilata labore.* — **haec** : *i.e.* the offerings he came to bring; cf. v. 2 n.

8. **tradita**, *offered;* cf. with the collocation 65. 19 *missum furtiuo munere;* Tac. *Ann.* I. 62. 2 *caespitem Caesar posuit gratissimo munere in defunctos.* — **ad inferias**, *as funeral offerings.*

9. **accipe**, etc.: cf. Mart. VI. 85.
11 f. *accipe cum fletu maesti breue carmen amici,* atque haec absentis tura fuisse puta.

10. **aue atque uale** : the offerings are concluded with the final farewell that should have been spoken at the burial. The fullest form of this *conclamatio* was *salue, uale, aue,* but other forms are mentioned; cf. Verg. *Aen.* XI. 97 *salue aeternum mihi, maxime Palla, aeternumque uale;* Servius on Verg. *Aen.* II. 644; and the selection of forms occurring in inscriptions in the index to Wilmann's *Exempla Inscr. Lat.* II. p. 692.

102.

Si quicquam tacito commissum est fido ab amico
    Cuius sit penitus nota fides animi,
Meque esse inuenies illorum iure sacratum,
    Corneli, et factum me esse puta Harpocratem.

103.

Aut sodes mihi redde decem sestertia, Silo,
    Deinde esto quamuis saeuus et indomitus:
Aut, si te nummi delectant, desine quaeso
    Leno esse atque idem saeuus et indomitus.

104.

Credis me potuisse meae maledicere uitae,
    Ambobus mihi quae carior est oculis?
Non potui, nec, si possem, tam perdite amarem:
    Sed tu cum Tappone omnia monstra facis.

102. A pledge of secrecy to Cornelius, otherwise unknown: for he apparently was not Cornelius Nepos (cf. 1. 3), if we may judge anything from the tone of equality rather than of inferiority that prevails here; nor is it likely that he was the Brixian Cornelius (cf. 67. 35), for whom Catullus had no regard.

1. **tacito**: dative.

2. **cuius**: referring to **tacito**. — **fides animi**: on the pleonastic genitive cf. 2. 10 n. *animi curas.*

3. **meque**: for *me quoque* or *et me.* — **illorum**: *i.e. tacitorum*, apparently with a reference to initiation into the mysteries. — **iure sacratum**: *i.e. initiatum.*

4. **Harpocratem**: cf. 74. 4 n.

103. To an arrogant pander who had received a large sum for his services. Apparently the epigram

is prompted by the manner of Silo's reception of some complaint on the part of Catullus.

1. **sodes**, *pray;* colloquial, and almost always with imperatives (from *si audes* for *si audies*). — **decem sestertia**: cf. 41. 2 n.

2. **esto**: cf. Juv. 5. 112 *hoc fac et esto, esto diues tibi, pauper amicis.* 4. **idem**: cf. 22. 3 n.

104. On the impossibility of his maligning Lesbia. Apparently written when he was beginning to hear of Lesbia's depravity; cf. 68. 135 ff., 159 ff. See Intr. 21.

1. **meae uitae**: cf. 109. 1; 45. 13; 68. 155.

2. **carior oculis**: cf. 3. 5 n.

3. **non potui**, etc.: however true this statement at the time of writing (cf. Intr. 24), Catullus found it possible later to love and hate

105.

Mentula conatur Pipleum scandere montem:
Musae furcillis praecipitem eiciunt.

106.

Cum puero bello praeconem qui uidet esse,
Quid credat, nisi se uendere discupere ?

107.

Si cui quid cupido optantique obtigit unquam
Insperanti, hoc est gratum animo proprie.

(*c.* 85), and to speak bitter enough
words of Lesbia.—**perdite amarem**: cf. 45. 3.

4. **Tappone** : otherwise unknown, though the name is not rare
in inscriptions. B. Schmidt, however, suggests that as Tappo was
shown by Mommsen (*Arch. Zeit.*
vol. XL. col. 176) to be a stock
comic figure at Roman feasts, Catullus may here mean to reprove jestingly his unnamed friend for taking
in earnest words of the poet about
Lesbia let fall *in ioco atque uino.*
—**omnia monstra facis**: *i.e.* you
and Tappo are given to that scanda-
lous gossip that makes mountains
out of mole-hills, and delights in
fanning enmities between friends.

105. On the attempt of Mentula
to become a poet. Concerning him
cf. *cc.* 94, 114, 115, and Intr. 73, 74.
He is sneered at as *eruditulus* also
in 57. 7.

1. **Pipleum montem**: Pimpla
(Pipla) was a region (with a hill
and fountain) in the Macedonian
district of Pieria, and was sacred to
the Muses. — **scandere**: cf. Enn.
Ann. 223 Vahl. *neque Musarum
scopulos quisquam superarat.*

2. **furcillis eiciunt**: a proverbial
expression for expulsion with violence and ignominy; cf. Hor. *Ep.*
I. 10. 24 *naturam expelles furca,
tamen usque recurret;* Cic. *Att.*
XVI. 2. 4 *sed, quoniam furcilla
extrudimur, Brundisium cogito;*
Arist. *Pax* 637 τήνδε μὲν δικροῖς
ἐώθουν τὴν θεὸν κεκράγμασιν.

106. On a boy walking with an
auctioneer. Some critics, comparing
21. 5, have thought of Juventius
and Furius; others, of Clodius; but
the epigram may well be suggested
by an accidental encounter on the
street.

2. **se** : *i.e. puerum,* the implied
subject of **discupere.** — **discupere** :
of eager desire that searches for satisfaction in every direction (*dis-*);
cf. Plaut. *Trin.* 932 *quin discupio
dicere;* Cic. *Fam.* VIII. 15. 2 *te
uidere discupio.*

107. On a visit of reconciliation
from Lesbia. Apparently written
after the period of temporary estrangement marked by *c.* 8. Cf.
Intr. 19.

1. **cupido** : on the hiatus see
Intr. 86 *d.*

2. **proprie,** *genuinely;* cf. Quint.

Quare hoc est gratum nobis quoque, carius auro,
    Quod te restituis, Lesbia, mi cupido :
5 Restituis cupido atque insperanti, ipsa refers te
    Nobis.   O lucem candidiore nota !
Quis me uno uiuit felicior, aut magis hac res
    Optandas uita dicere quis poterit ?

108.

Si, Comini, populi arbitrio tua cana senectus
    Spurcata impuris moribus intereat,
Non equidem dubito quin primum inimica bonorum
    Lingua exsecta auido sit data uulturio,
5 Effossos oculos uoret atro gutture coruus,
    Intestina canes, cetera membra lupi.

X. 1. 114 *mira sermonis, cuius proprie studiosus fuit, elegantia.*

3. **carius auro**: for similar expressions of estimated value cf. 3. 5 n.

6. **lucem candidiore nota**: cf. 68. 148 n.

7. **quis**, etc. : cf. 9. 10 n.

108. On a certain unpopular Cominius, perhaps one of two brothers from Spoletium, P. and C. or L. Cominius, who are mentioned by Cicero (*Cluent.* 100) as prosecutors. In the year 66 B.C. a popular tumult terrified them into giving up their prosecution of C. Cornelius, though one of them, in spite of general unpopularity, resumed it the following year, on which occasion Cornelius was defended by Cicero.

1. **cana senectus**: cf. 61. 162 *cana anilitas.*

2. **spurcata impuris moribus**: the hoary head that should be a crown of glory is to him but a mark of confirmed infamy.

3. **bonorum** : perhaps in the sense of *optimatium* (as often in Cicero), if this Cominius was one of the prosecutors.

4. **lingua exsecta**: cf. Cic. *Cluent.* 187 *Stratonem in crucem esse actum exsecta scitote lingua.* — **sit data** : perfect, followed by the present **uoret**, since the loss of the tongue, as a punishment for his perjuries, would be inflicted upon him before his execution and the throwing of his body to the crows and their associates. — **uulturio**: cf. 68. 124 n.

5. **effossos oculos**, etc. : cf. Vulg. *Prouerb.* 30. 17 *oculum . . . effodiant eum corui de torrentibus, et comedant eum filii aquilae*, Hor. *Ep.* I. 16. 48 *non pasces in cruce coruos.* With vv. 5 and 6 Statius compares Ov. *Ib.* 167 ff.

6. **canes**: cf. Hor. *Epod.* 17. 11 *addictum feris alitibus atque canibus.* — **lupi**: cf. Hor. *Epod.* 5. 99, 100 *post insepulta membra different lupi et Esquilinae alites.*

109.

Iucundum, mea uita, mihi proponis amorem
  Hunc nostrum inter nos perpetuumque fore.
Di magni, facite ut uere promittere possit
  Atque id sincere dicat et ex animo,
5 Vt liceat nobis tota perducere uita
  Aeternum hoc sanctae foedus amicitiae.

110.

Aufilena, bonae semper laudantur amicae :
  Accipiunt pretium quod facere instituunt.
Tu, quod promisti mihi, quod mentita, inimica es ;

109. On Lesbia's wish for un-broken harmony between herself and Catullus. Apparently following *c.* 107 by a brief interval that has allowed the first joy of reconcilia-tion to subside and give place to a less passionate feeling : for the tone of vv. 3 and 4 seems to indicate that the voyage has been not without some storms.

1. **mea uita** : cf. 104. 1 ; 45. 13 ; 68. 155.— **proponis**, *proclaim*, but with a suggestion of pledge rather than of mere prophecy ; cf. Caes. *B. G.* V. 58. 5 *magna proponit iis qui occiderint praemia ;* Cic. *Tusc.* V. 20 *praemium proposuit qui in-uenisset nouam uoluptatem.*

3. **di magni** : here a true invo-cation, and not, as in 14. 12 and 53. 5, a mere expletive. Ellis compares Cic. *Att.* XVI. 1. 6 *di faxint ut fa-ciat ea quae promittit, — commune enim gaudium, — sed ego,* etc.

5. **perducere** : Lachmann, fol-lowing the early Italian editors, would read *producere,* on the ground that *perducere* occurs only when a limit is definitely set. But the MSS. of Prop. I. 3. 39 *o utinam tales per-*ducas, improbe, noctes* seem to sup-port this reading, and the omitted limit is easily supplied from **tota uita.**

6. **sanctae amicitiae** : of the pure sentiment rather than the pas-sion of love ; cf. 96. 4.

110. On the faithlessness of the courtesan, Aufilena, mentioned in *c.* 100 as the mistress of Quintius.

1. **bonae,** *obliging ;* cf. 89. 1. So Tibullus (II. 4. 45) praises the courtesan *bona quae nec auara fuit,* and Horace's Cinara was *bona* (*Carm.* IV. 1. 3).

2. **accipiunt,** etc. : *i.e.* the price they set is willingly paid.— **quod** : see Crit. App.— **facere,** *to set ;* cf. Plaut. *Pers.* 582 '*Indica ; fac pre-tium.*' '*Tua merx est ; tua in-dicatio est.*'

3 ff. **quod . . . quod** : the first *quod* is probably a conjunction and the second a relative. In promising what she has not performed Aufi-lena has played the part of an **in-imica** instead of an *amica.* (With **quod** as direct object of **mentita** cf. Prop. III. 17. 1 *mentiri noctem.*) Thus vv. 3 and 4 correspond verb

Quod nec das et fers saepe, facis facinus.
5 Aut facere ingenuae est, aut non promisse pudicae,
    Aufilena, fuit : sed data corripere
Fraudando † efficit plus quam meretricis auarae,
    Quae sese toto corpore prostituit.

III.

Aufilena, uiro contentam uiuere solo
    Nuptarum laus e laudibus eximiis :
Sed cuiuis quamuis potius succumbere par est
    Quam matrem fratres ex patruo parere.

112.

Multus homo est, Naso, neque tecum multus homo
    est qui
    Descendit : Naso, multus es et pathicus.

for verb, — **promisti . . . nec das,**
she promises but does not perform,
mentita . . . fers, she breaks her
appointment but pockets the price.
— **promisti:** cf. v. 5 *promisse ;* 14.
14 n. *misti.*

4. **saepe :** for she had often received money from him, and hence
ought to treat him better now. —
facis facinus : cf. 81. 6; Propertius also (*l.c.*) thought such a breach
of faith an awful crime.

5. **ingenuae,** *honest.*

6. **fuit :** strictly related in time to
v. 5 *est :* the time to profess virtue
was before she made the promise;
now honesty requires her to keep it.
— **data corripere fraudando,** etc. :
to secure the reward by fraud is to
exceed the wicked greed of the
most abandoned of prostitutes. But
none of the emendations yet offered
for the corrupt **efficit** are at all
satisfactory.

111. On the incest of the same
Aufilena with her uncle.

1. Riese compares Afran. 117 R.
*proba et pudica quod sum . . . com-
paratum est, uno ut simus contentae
uiro.* — uiro, *husband,* as frequently.

2. **nuptarum :** Aufilena was evidently married.

4. The swift succession of **matrem, fratres, patruo** indicates the
jumble of relationship involved.
The point lies in the fact that Aufilena's children by her uncle would
be her own cousins. — **fratres :** *sc.
patrueles ;* cf. Cic. *Att.* I. 5. 1 *Lucii
fratris nostri morte.* — **parere :** see
Crit. App.

112. On an unknown Naso, who
is apparently a candidate for office.
The text is unusually corrupt, and
the interpretation extremely uncertain.

1. **multus,** *wordy ;* cf. Afran.
202 R. *multa ac molesta ;* Plaut.

113.

Consule Pompeio primum duo, Cinna, solebant
  Maeciliam : facto consule nunc iterum
Manserunt duo, sed creuerunt milia in unum
  Singula.   Fecundum semen adulterio.

Men. 316 *hominem multum et odio-sum ;* Cic. *N. D.* II. 46. 119 *nolo in stellarum ratione multus uobis uideri.* — neque multus : the apparent contradiction (cf. 64. 83) involves an untranslatable play upon the word *multus*, which is, perhaps, as has been suggested, a colloquial form for *molitus*, from *molere (sensu obscoeno)* ; cf. *colere cultus, adolere adultus,* etc. — tecum qui descendit, *your competitor ; sc. in campum,* perhaps omitted colloquially ; but cf. Hor. *Carm.* III. 1. 10 *hic generosior descendat in campum petitor ; Ep.* I. 20. 5 *fuge quo descendere gestis.*

2. multus et pathicus : contrasted with multus neque multus, the emphasis lying especially upon the conjunctions, while the ambiguous second multus of v. 1 is unveiled by the substitution for it of the brutally plain pathicus ; *i.e.* your competitor is *multus* (' wordy ') and yet not *multus (sens. obsc.)* ; but you, Naso, are *multus* (' wordy ') and *multus,* for you are *pathicus ;* in other words, your competitor is foul-mouthed but not foul-lived, while you, Naso, are foul-mouthed and foul-lived.

113. On the profligacy of a Maecilia. Pleitner emends in v. 2 to *Mucillam,* as a diminutive of Mucia, understanding the reference to be to the daughter of Q. Mucius Scaevola, married to Pompey soon after the death of Aemilia, his second wife, and divorced by him upon his return from the conquest of Mithradates, on the charge of adultery, especially with Julius Caesar. The mention of Pompey's consulships gives some color to this view, but as Maecilia is a well-known Roman name, and this epigram was written in 55 B.C. (cf. v. 2), seven years after the divorce of Mucia and several years after her marriage to M. Aemilius Scaurus, it is needless to emend the MSS. in order to bring in a special reason for the reference to Pompey.

1. consule Pompeio : in the year 70 B.C., with M. Licinius Crassus. — Cinna : doubtless the poet C. Helvius Cinna mentioned in 10. 29 and 95. 1 ; cf. Intr. 63.

2. Maeciliam : dependent upon an infinitive euphemistically omitted with solebant ; cf. such constructions as Plaut. *Cist.* 37 *uiris cum suis praedicant nos solere ;* Mart. III. 76. 4 *cum possis Hecuben, non potes Andromachen.* — consule iterum : in the year 55 B.C., with the same colleague as before.

3. manserunt, etc. : *i.e.* there are still two, but it is two thousand. If the reading be correct, the numeral unum, which is not infrequently joined with distributive pronouns, is here used instead of the distributive *utrumque,* because of the contrast with the numeral milia ; ' to each one has accrued a thousand.' But the expression of such an idea by *crescere* with an accusative with *in* is unprecedented, the meaning apparently demanding *increscere* with the dative.

114.

Firmanus saltu non falso Mentula diues
    Fertur, qui tot res in se habet egregias,
Aucupium omne genus, piscis, prata, arua, ferasque,
    Nequiquam : fructus sumptibus exsuperat.
5 Quare concedo sit diues, dum omnia desint ;
    Saltum laudemus, dum domo ipse egeat.

115.

Mentula habet iuxta triginta iugera prati,
    Quadraginta arui : cetera sunt maria.
Cur non diuitiis Croesum superare potis sit

114. On Mentula as a 'land-
poor' property owner. On the
identity of Mentula with Mamurra
see Intr. 73. The next poem speaks
of the same estate as this.

1. **Firmanus** : Firmum, now
Fermo, was a town in Picenum,
about forty miles south of Ancona.
— **saltu** : the word denoted first
uncultivated land (cf. Fest. p. 302
*saltus est ubi siluae et pastiones sunt,
quarum causa casae quoque*), and
then a measure of 800 *iugera* as a
single grant of such land by the
land-commissions (Varr. *R. R.* I.
10. 2), and then the grant in general, an 'estate,' even though comprising, as here, some arable land
(cf. Fest. *l.c. si qua particula in eo
saltu pastorum aut custodum causa
aratur, ea res non peremit nomen
saltui*).

2. **tot res egregias** : spoken
ironically, like *non falso* in v. 1, for
c. 115 shows that the fine things
specified in 114. 3 are but supposed attractions of the estate,
which is really a small and worthless affair.

3. **omne genus** : accusative of
specification.

4. **exsuperat** : *sc.* probably *saltus* as subject; the estate is good
for nothing, and its necessary ex-
penses more than eat up the income
from it.

5. **concedo**, etc. : *i.e.* I grant,
then, that he is rich, if a man can be
rich who hasn't a cent to his name.

6. **laudemus**, etc. : *i.e.* let us
praise the estate, if praise can mean
anything when the owner hasn't a
roof over his head. — **domo** : with
hiatus; see Intr. 86 *d.* — **ipse**, *the
owner ;* cf. 64. 43 n.

115. On Mentula, reputed great
in riches, but great only in profligacy.

1, 2. These verses give the plain
facts about the size of Mentula's
estate, while in vv. 3–6 are ironically rehearsed the exaggerated
rumors about it.

1. **iuxta**, *all in one lot* (ironically); with *iuxta* of the proximity
of several objects to one another
cf. Plin. *N. H.* XXXVI. 117.

2. **maria** : *i.e.* swamps; cf. v. 5.

3. **Croesum** : cf. 24. 4 n. *Midae.*

Vno qui in saltu tot bona possideat,
5 Prata, arua, ingentis siluas saltusque paludesque
Vsque ad Hyperboreos et mare ad Oceanum ?
Omnia magna haec sunt, tamen ipse est maximus ultro,
Non homo, sed uero mentula magna minax.

116.

Saepe tibi studioso animo uenante requirens
Carmina uti possem mittere Battiadae
Qui te lenirem nobis, neu conarere
Tela infesta mihi mittere in usque caput,
5 Hunc uideo mihi nunc frustra sumptum esse laborem,
Gelli, nec nostras hic ualuisse preces.

5. **paludes**: apparently common report had bestowed extensive and well stocked fish-ponds upon Mentula, but it is only marsh-land that he owns (cf. v. 2 *maria*). — **-que**: hypermetric: see Intr. 76.

6. **Hyperboreos**: the fabulous dwellers in the extreme north by the streams of ocean. — **mare ad Oceanum**: cf. Caes. *B. G.* III. 7. 2 *proximus mare Oceanum ;* Tac. *Ann.* I. 9 *mari Oceano aut amnibus longinquis saeptum imperium.*

7. **ultro**: emphasizing **ipse**; cf. Plaut. *Men.* 831 *hei mihi, insanire me aiunt, ultro quom ipsi insaniunt ;* Varr. *R. R.* III. 17. 6 *nisi etiam ipse eos pasceret ultro.*

8. **mentula**: a similar play to that in *c.* 94. The triple alliteration is noteworthy.

116. On his rejected advances toward a reconciliation with Gellius, concerning whom see Intr. 72.

1. **studioso**: the adjective probably modifies **tibi**, indicating that Gellius was a man of literary tastes, and perhaps an especial admirer of

Callimachus; for the modification of **animo** by two words of similar meaning would be extremely awkward, and is not supported by such phrases as Verg. *Geor.* IV. 370 *saxosus sonans Hypanis*, where the adjectives differ in meaning. Perhaps, after all, the conjecture of Guarinus (*studiose*) was right.

2. **carmina**: *i.e.* translations, like *c.* 66. — **Battiadae**: *i.e.* Callimachus; cf. 65. 16 n.

3. **qui**, *whereby;* the use of *qui* for *quibus* is not uncommon in other writers (cf. Munro's Lucr. V. 233). — **nobis**: for *mihi;* especially noteworthy because immediately following a verb in the first person singular. On the metre of the verse see Intr. 76.

4. **usque**: this addition to **in** seems to imply that the aim was effectual, and pain was inflicted; cf. 4. 24 *ad usque* .

6. **hic**, *in this matter.* — **nostras**: for *meas ;* with the change in the same sentence from **mihi** to **nostras** cf. 77. 3, 4; 91. 1, 2.

Contra nos tela ista tua euitamus amictu :
At fixus nostris tu dabis supplicium.

7. **contra**, *instead of this ; i.e.* instead of my former policy of depre-
cating your anger, I am now armed
for defense (v. 7) and offense (v. 8).
— **amictu** : *i.e.* the toga is wrapped
about the left arm to serve as a
shield; cf. Pacuvius 186 R. *chlamyde
contorta astu clipeat bracchium ;*
Sen. *De Const.* 7. 4 *non minus latro*
*est cuius telum opposita ueste elusum
est ;* Petron. 80 *intorto circa bracchium pallio composui ad proelian-
dum gradum.*

8. **dabis** : the elision of final *s*
occurs only here in Catullus, though
often found in Cicero's juvenile
verses and in Lucretius, as well as in
the earlier writers (see Cic. *Or.* 161).

CRITICAL APPENDIX.

———◦✦◦———

THE sources chiefly used in constituting the text of this edition (cf. Intr. 53, 54) are as follows : —

Codex Oxoniensis (*O*), preserved in the Bodleian Library at Oxford, numbered 30 in the official catalogue of Latin MSS. formerly in the possession of the abbot Canonici of Venice. It is without date, but was apparently written in the latter part of the 14th century, and is therefore of about equal age with *codex G*. The book, which is in a beautiful state of preservation, contains only the poems of Catullus. It consists of 37 leaves of parchment, each 27 centimeters long and 19.5 centimeters wide. The rectangular space on each page reserved for writing is carefully indicated by ruling, and averages 20 centimeters long and 10.5 centimeters wide. Each page of the first four fascicles (of 8 leaves each) is ruled to contain 31 lines of writing, from 5.5 to 6.5 millimeters apart. Beginning with fol. 33 r., each page is ruled to contain 32 lines. The initial letter of each verse is a capital, and is somewhat separated from the rest of the text, being placed to the left of the vertical boundary line. Illuminated initials are found at the beginning of *cc*. 1 (very elaborate), 2 (with considerable tracery), 65, 68, 69, 72, 77, 80, and 89. In some other instances space was left in the text at the beginning of a poem for a large illuminated letter, and the proper letter indicated in the margin by the scribe, but never filled in. In other instances yet, the initial letter of a poem was omitted from the text and indicated in the margin as a guide to the illuminator, but no space was left for it in the text. Poems are occasionally separated by an interval of one verse, but often are written continuously (cf. also *c*. 60 *fin*. n.). In many instances the beginning of a poem (whether divided from the preceding poem by an interval, or not) is indicated by a paragraph mark consisting of two slight, inclined, parallel strokes of the scribe's pen just before the initial letter; but this mark, too, is often lacking. In a single instance (before *c*. 31) it is accompanied by a paragraph mark of more formal shape, illuminated in greenish blue. A few scholia are found on the first and second pages, and again on fol. 21 r., on the opening verses of *c.* 64.

In a pocket inside the back cover of the book are five sheets of note-paper of four pages each containing variant readings, and headed *Varie lectiones cod- ms- catulli memb- in f² sec- XIV- apud Ab- Canonici cum edit- Aldina 1502 collati.* Just below and to the right on the same page is written, apparently by the same hand, but at a later date, *coeperam in gratiam Laurentii Santenii, sed non absolui, neque ei misi quicquam.* The first of these readings is *arido modo* . . (1. 2), and the last (apparently) *sanna esset nunc quod gannit* . . (83. 4).

A facsimile of fol. 26 u.(64. 336–366) by the collotype process is given in the edition of Catullus by Robinson Ellis (Oxford, 1878²); facsimiles of fol. 13 r. (50. 3–51. 12) and fol. 20 u. (63. 57–87) were published by Mr. Ellis in his *XII. Facsimiles from Latin MSS. in the Bodleian Library* (1885); a reduced facsimile of fol. 21 r. follows the preface to this volume, and since it has passed through the press a facsimile of the same page by the heliographic process has come to hand as plate XV.A in the *Paléographie des Classiques Latins* of M. Chatelain (Paris, 1892).

Codex Sangermanensis (*G*), now No. 14,137 of the Latin MSS. in the National Library in Paris, formerly No. 1,165 in the library of the abbey of St.-Germain-des-Prés. Its subscription shows it to have been written in the year 1375; and even if the words *et cetera* there occurring are taken as an indication that its scribe was but copying from a longer subscription of the year 1375, the style of the writing shows that this copy could not have been made much later than that date. The book contains the works of Catullus only, and is described by Schwabe as consisting of 36 leaves of parchment, each 24.3 centimeters long and 16.9 centimeters wide, with 33 lines of writing on a page. The last page, however, contains 34 lines. The text presents many erasures and corrections, the very large majority of which, at any rate, were made either by the original copyist, or by another not far removed from him in time. The copyist of *G* seems to have been somewhat more sophisticated than the copyist of *O,* and (as the subscription also intimates) to have been more worried about the condition of the text he was reproducing. The result is that the more ignorant blunders committed or perpetuated in *O* are often the better guide to the readings of the common original of the two MSS. A heliographic facsimile of two adjoining pages of *G,* fol. 35 u. and 36 r. (110. 7–116. 8), forms plate XV. in the *Paléographie des Classiques Latins* of M. Chatelain, and the entire MS. has recently been reproduced in excellent facsimile by a photolithographic process (Paris, Leroux, 1890).

Codex Thuaneus (*T*), which is of great importance for the text of *c.* 62, is now No. 8,071 of the Latin MSS. in the National Library in Paris. It is a book of 61 leaves, each measuring 29 by 20.5 centimeters, and is written in a Carolingian hand of the ninth century. It contains the writings of Juvenal, and of Eugenius of Toledo, together with extracts from Martial, the 62nd poem of Catullus, and a Latin Anthology. A heliographic facsimile of fol. 51, containing some epigrams of Martial and 62. 1–22 of Catullus, forms plate XIV. of the *Paléographie des Classiques Latins* of M. Chatelain, and a less accurate reproduction of the same verses of Catullus was published by Mr. Ellis in his second edition.

Orthographical peculiarities, as such, are noted in this Appendix only when they occur in proper names, or are otherwise of especial interest.

Italics are used in the variant readings to designate all letters that are written in the MSS. in abbreviation or ligature. Where variant readings are given in the MSS. themselves, not written as a part of the text, but either between the verses or in the margin, they are enclosed in parentheses.

O denotes *codex Oxoniensis.*

G denotes *codex Sangermanensis.*

T denotes *codex Thuaneus.*

V (*codex Veronensis*) denotes the common reading of *O* and *G*. Where the reading of but one of these MSS. is given, the reading of the other is that adopted in the text.

The letter ω is often used to designate such readings as occur in at least several of the interpolated MSS. or of the earliest (Italian) editions of Catullus. Where the source of a reading adopted in the text is not otherwise noted, it is understood to be due to ω. In ascribing emendations to individual sources the names of scholars of the present century are usually given in the vernacular; those of scholars of preceding centuries, with a few more familiar exceptions, in the Latin form.

Catulli Veronensis liber Incipit. *G* (*as if first line of text, but in red ink, to which* ad Corneliu*m is appended in a different style of letter, resembling that in the titles to following poems and in most of the glosses*) Catullus Ve*ronensis poeta *O* (*in upper margin of first page, and apparently in a more recent hand*) [Q. Catuli Veronensis liber incipit ad Cornelium I *D* Q. Valeri Catulli ueronens. ad Corn. Nepotem liber carm. I *C Other MSS. give neither praenomen nor nomen*].

1. 1 cui *V* ω *the ancients who quote the verse and Riese* (*There is not the slightest reason to doubt that in both G and O the elaborately illuminated initial is* C *and not* Q) qui *Pastrengicus Ellis* quoi ω *and almost all recent* *editors* (*It should be noted that nowhere does* quoi *actually occur in V, the form of the dative singular being in all cases either* qui, *as in 2. 3, or* cui, *as in 23. 1.   On the other hand* cui *is sometimes found for* qui, *as in 11. 22*). — **2** arido *the ancients who quote the verse* arida ω *Pastrengicus* (*Cf. Serv. on Verg. Aen. XII. 587* 'in pumice' autem iste masculino genere posuit, et hunc sequimur : nam et Plautus ita dixit, licet Catullus dixerit feminino). — **5** tame*n* O tamen G ‖ est V. — **7** iupite*r* O Iupiter G *and so usually elsewhere, though the spelling* iuppite*r* *occurs in* O *in 66. 30, 48, but is nowhere found in* G. — **8** tibi habe V ‖ libelli al' mei G libelli est ω. — **9** o *omitted in V, added by* ω ‖ quod] quidem ω quidem, patrone, per te *Hand* quidem est, patroni ut ergo *Bergk*. — **10** periere O.

2. *Interval of one verse in V, filled in G with title* Fletus passeris lesbie. — **3** qui V ‖ at petenti V (al' pate*n*ti *or* parenti G). — **4** ea O. — **6** karum V. — **7** et] ut *or* in ω est *Hand* es *Jacobs* (*Spengel conjectures a lacuna after v.* 7). — **8** cum O cu*m* G ‖ acquiescet O adquiescet (*corrected from* acquiescet) G. — **9** ludere V (*corrected from* ludere*m* O, al' ludere*m* G). — **11** *No interval between this and preceding verse in V.   Pleitner, Klotz, and Baehrens subjoin vv. 11–13 to c. 14[b], and consider the whole to be a complete poem, which Pleitner and Klotz place before, and Baehrens after, c. 2.   Others add vv. 11–13 to c. 38, and still others (striking out* est) *insert them in c. 3 after v. 15.* — **13** negatam V (al' ligatam G) ligatam ω (*Cf. Prisc. Inst. I. 22* similiter Catullus Veronensis 'quod zonam soluit diu ligatam').

3. *No interval in V.* — **2** q*u*am tu*m* O. — **7** ipsam O ipsam G ipsa ω Issa *Bergk*. — **9** silens (al' siliens) O. — **10** piplabat V pipilabat ω pipiabat *Voss*. — **11** tenebrosu*m* V. — **12** illud V (al' illuc O). — **14** orciq*u*e V (al' q*u*ae G) ‖ bella (· i · pulcra) V. — **16** bonum factum · male bon*us* ille passer O bonu*m* factu*m* · male bonus ille passer G o factum male o (proh *Guarinus* io *Lachmann and others*) miselle passer ω uae f. m. uae m. p. *Ellis Postgate*.

4. *Interval of one verse in V, filled in G with title* De phaselo (*corrected from* phasello). — **1** hasellus O (*with space left for illuminated initial, and a minute* p *in outer margin to guide illuminator*) phaselus G (*corrected from* phasellus). — **2** aiu*n*t O aiunt G ‖ celerimu*m* O celerimum (*corrected to* celerrimum) G. — **3** illi*us* O illius G ‖ tardis V. — **4** neq*u*e esse O neque esse G ‖ sine V. — **5** sine V. — **6** h*aec* O ‖ mina ei V. — **7** insula uegeladas O insulas ue cicladas G. — **8** tractam O tractam G. — **9** sinia*m* O. — **10** ubuste O ‖ phaselus G (*corrected from* phasellus). — **11** silua *omitted in* O, *but added later in margin with caret* ‖ citeono O citeorio G. — **13** citheri V. — **14** cognotissi*m*a O cognotissima G, — **15** phaselus (*corrected from* phasellus) *G.* — **17** tuas *G.* — **20** uocare cura *V* uocaret (uagaret *Lachmann*) aura ω. — **23** amaret *V* a marei *Lachmann.* — **24** nouissime *V.* — **25** h*aec O* hoc *G* ‖ recomdita *O.* — **27** castru*m V* (al' casto*rum G*).

5. *Interval of one verse in V, filled in G with title* ad lesbia*m.* — **1** iuamus *O* (*with space left for illuminated initial, and a minute* v *in outer margin to guide illuminator*). — **3** estinemus *O* extimemus *G.* — **4** ocidere *O.* — **8** deind*e* mille · altera d*e*ind*e O* deinde mi (*corrected from* mille) altera da (*corrected from* deinde). — **11** conturbauimus *V* ‖ nesciamus *V.* — **13** tantus *V* ‖ sciet *Buecheler cf. Priap. 52. 12* cum tantum sciet esse mentularum.

6. *No interval in O, but two parallel strokes for paragraph mark opposite first verse in margin. Interval of one verse in G, filled with title* ad Flauium, *with first part of proper name written over erasure.* — **1** catulo *O.* — **2** ne *V* ni ω nei *Lachmann.* — **5** h*i*c *O.* — **8** asirio *V* ‖ flagrans *V Ellis* (*perhaps rightly; cf. note and excursus in edition of Ellis*). — **9** h*aec O* hec (al' hic) *G* ‖ illo *V* (al' ille *G*). — **12** nam inista pra*e*ualet *O* nam ni ista preualet *G* nam nil stupra ualet *Haupt* iam nil stupra uales *Schwabe.* — **13** et futura panda *V* ec fututa *Lachmann.* — **14** nec *V* nei *Marcilius.* — **15** babes *O* ‖ bonique *O.* — **17** u*e*r*s*um *O* uersu (*corrected from* uersum) *G.*

7. *Interval of one verse in V, filled in G with title* ad lesbiam. — **1** q*u*od *V.* — **3** libisse *O* lybisse *G.* — **4** lasarpici fecis iaces tyrenis *O* lasarpici feris (al' fretis) iacet ty*renis al' cyrenis *G.* — **5** oradum *O* ora dum *G.* — **6** beati *V* (al' beari *G*). — **7** sydera *V.* — **9** basiei *V* (al' basia *G*). — **10** catulo *O.* — **11** euriosi *V.*

8. *Interval of one verse in V, filled in G with title* ad se ipsum. — **1** iser *O* (*with space left for illuminated initial, and minute* m *in margin to guide illuminator*) ‖ catule *O.* — **4** quod *O* quo (*corrected from* quod) *G* ‖ dicebat *Dousa iunior.* — **5** nobis] tantum *Schoell* (*cf. 37. 12*). — **6** cu*m O* tum *G* (*corrected from* cum). — **8** candid*i G.* — **9** inpote *O* impote *G* ‖ noli *omitted in V* impotens noli *Auantius* impotens ne sis *Scaliger* impete insano *Heyse.* — **15** ne teq*u*e tibi *O* ne te q*u*a*e* tibi *G* uae te *Balthazar Venator* tene ω rere *Scaliger* nosce *Heyse* quae te, uae tibi, *Froehlich.* — **16** teadhibit *O.* — **18** cui] cu*m O.*

9. *Interval of one verse in V, filled in G with title* Ad Verannium. — **1** ueranni *V* Verani *Ramler* ‖ e *omitted in O* o *Baehrens.* — **2** antistas *V* ‖ millib*us G.* — **4** uno a*n*imo sanamq*u*e *O* uno animo sua*m*q*u*e (al' sana*m*) *G* anumque *Faernus.* — **9** suabior *V.*

10. *No interval in V.* — **1** uarius *V* ‖ mens *O* meus *G* (*corrected from* mens, *and with* meus *written above it*). — **3** tunc *O* tu*m* *G.* — **4** ille-pidu*m* *G* (*corrected from* nlepidu*m*). — **7** iarbithinia *O* iam bithinia *G* ‖ se] posse *V.* — **8** et quonia*m* (al' quona*m* *G*) *V* ecquonam *Statius* ‖ here *V.* — **9** n*i*hil ne*que* n*e*c in ip*s*is *O* nihil (*corrected from* nichil, *the usual spelling*) ne*que* in* ip*s*is (al' ne*que* ip*s*is · n*e*c) *G.* — **13** non (al' n*e*c) *G.* — **16** letica*m* *O* letic*am *G* ‖ homis *O* hominis *G.* — **21** n*e*c h*i*c *O* n*e*c h*i*c *G.* — **22** fractu*m*que *V.* — **24** docuit *V* ‖ sinediore*m* *O* cinediorem *G.* — **25** inq*u*id *O.* — **26** comoda*m* *O* istos commoda : enim *Burmann* istos : commodum enim *Hand* istos : nam uolo commode *Statius* ‖ serapini *O* sarapim (al'e *above first* a) *G.* — **27** de*s*erti mane me inq*u*id *O* deserti (al' deferri) mane me inquit *G* minime *Pontanus* meminei *Munro* mi anime *Bergk.* — **30** cuma *V* ‖ grauis *V* Gauius *Ribbeck* erat grauis *Heyse.* — **31** ad me] a me *V.* — **32** paratis *Statius.* — **33** s*e*d tulsa *O* sed tu insula *G* ‖ male *corrected in G from some word ending differently* ‖ niuis *O*.

11. *No interval in V, but two parallel strokes for paragraph mark in outer margin opposite first verse in O, and paragraph mark in G with title in inner margin* Ad furiu*m* *et* Aureliu*m.* — **2** penetra*u*it *O* penetrauit *G.* — **3** coa *O.* — **5** hircanos *O* ‖ arabaes q*u*e *G.* — **6** siue sagax *V.* — **8** epra *O.* — **9** sui *O.* — **11** renu*m* horribilesq*u*e *O* Rhenu*m* horribiles-q*u*e *G* ‖ ulti *omitted in O* (*but cf. next verse*), *omitted at first in G, but added later.* — **12** uitimosq*u*e *O* mosque (*apparently corrected from* ultimosque) *G.* — **13** fere *V.* — **14** tentare *G.* — **15** nunciare *O.* — **17** me-chis *V.* — **22** cui *V.* — **24** *continued with v. 23 in O, and also at first in G, where, however, it was later erased, and written on the next line, the first words of the title of c. 12 being erased to make room for it.*

12. *Interval of one verse in V, filled in G with 11. 24* (*see note above*), *leaving of the title that earlier stood there only the last word* Asinium. — **1** matrucine *V* (*above which word in G stands in minute letters* al' [*not* ad] *followed by* matr . . . . , *of which the last few letters are mere scratches and illegible. As it appears in the photolithographic facsimile the word* matrucine *of the text may have been written over an erasure*). — **2** loco *O* ioco (al' loco) *G.* — **4** falsu*m* al' salsu*m* *O* salsum (al' falsu*m*) *G.* — **7** frater *O* (*cf. 68. 91*). — **8** uoluit *O.* — **9** dissert*us* *O* differtus *Passera-tius.* — **12** monet *O* ‖ extimatio*ne* *O* extimatione *G.* — **13** ueru*m* nemo es*t* sinu*m* *O* ueru*m* est nemo sinu*m* *G.* — **14** s*e*d*t*aba exhibere *O* sethaba exhibere *G.* — **15** miserunt (*corrected from* misserunt) *G* ‖ num*e*ri *O* numeri (al' muneri) *G.* — **16** ameni *V*.

13. *Interval of one verse in V, filled in G with title* Ad Caluum Poe-tam. — **1** enabis *O* (*with no space left for initial, but with* minute c *in*

margin to guide illuminator). — **2** dii *V.* — **6** imq*uam O* unq*uam G.* —
9 meos *O.* — **10** qui *V* (al' q*uid G*).

14. *Interval of one verse in V, filled in G with title* Ad Caluum Poe·
tam. — **1** e *O* (*with no space left for initial, but with minute* n *in margin
to guide illuminator*) ne *G.* — **3** uaciniano *G.* — **5** mal' (*i.e.* mal*e; cf. 5.
7* d'ind', *17. 4* palud', *etc.*) *O* malis *G.* — **6** dii *V* ‖ da*n*t *O* dant *G.* —
9 si illa *V.* — **10** $\frac{i}{m}$ *O* (*i.e.* mi, *as in 31. 5, 51. 1, 76. 26, and 99. 13. But
elsewhere in O* mi *is written in full, or* me *stands for it, while* $\frac{i}{m}$ *is almost
always for the dissyllabic dative form, which is occasionally written in full
as* michi, *though never as* mihi) michi *G.* — **12** dii *V.* — **14** misisti *V.* —
15 oppinio *O* opimo (al' optimo) *G.* — **16** h' (*i.e.* h*aec*) *O* hec (*i.e.* haec)
G ‖ false fit adhibit *O* salse (al' false) sit abibit (*corrected from* adbibit)
G. — **17** luserit (al' x *above the* s) *G.* — **18** curam *O* cur tam *G* ‖ scrinia
O scrine*am* (*corrected from* scrinia) *G.* — **19** suffena*m V.* — **20** hac *V* ‖
tibi hiis supplit*us O.* — **23** seculi *V.*

14[b]. *No interval in V. Avantius inserted these three verses after
16. 13 ; Froehlich prefixed them to c. 16 ; cf. also note on 2. 11-13, and
commentary on 14*[b]. — **3** āmouere *O.*

15. *Interval of one verse in V, filled in G with title* Ad Aurelium. —
1 omendo *O* (*with no space left for initial, but with minute* c *in margin to
guide illuminator*). — **2** pudentem *O* pudentem peto *G* (*but with signs to
indicate that the order is wrong*) pudenter *Maehlius cf. v. 13.* — **5** pudicum
Baehrens. — **6** ueremur *G* (*but with* i *later inserted after* m). — **8** re
(*corrected from* te) *G* ‖ occupa*r*i *O.* — **10** bonisq*ue V.* — **11** qualibe*t* ut
al' iubet moneto *O* qualubet (*corrected from* qualibet) ut iubet moueto *G.*
— **13** huc *G* ‖ prudenter (al' puden*ter*) *G.* — **16** nos*t*roru*m O.* — **17** ha
tame*n O* ah (*corrected from* ha) tame*n* (al' tu*m*) *G.* — **18** atractis *O.* —
19 percurrent (*corrected from* percurret) *G.*

16. *No interval in V.* — **1** dedicabo *V.* — **3** mi *V* (*corrected to* me *G*).
— **4** q*u*od (*corrected to* q*u*ot) *G* ‖ moliculli (*corrected to* molliculi) *G.* —
6 recesse *O.* — **7** tame*n O* tame*n* (al' tu*m*) *G* tunc *MSS. of Plin. Ep.
IV. 14. 5.* — **8** sint *V.* — **10** hiis *O.* — **12** hosq*ue O* uosq*ue G* uos quei
Rossbach uos quom *L. Müller* ‖ basiōrum *G.* — **14** dedicabo *V.*

17. *No interval, but paragraph mark, in V.* — **1** oculo inaq*ue O*
oculo in aque *G* ‖ led*ere O* ledere *G* loedere *Scaliger.* — **3** ac sulcis tantis
i*n*reduiuis *O* ac sulcis tantis in rediuiuis *G* assulis stantis *Statius* axulis
Hand axuleis *Schwabe* acsuleis *Ellis.* — **4** canaq*ue O.* — **6** sali s*u*bsili *O*
sali subsili *G* Salisubsilis *Statius* Salisubsali *Bergk* ‖ suspia*n*t *O* suspia**nt**
G. — **7** maximi *omitted at first, but added in margin in G.* — **8** queda*m O.* —

10 pudice*que* paludes *V* punicaeque *Heyse.* — **12** insulsi simus *O.* —
13 himuli *O.* — **14** cui iocu*m* *O* cui iocum *G.* — **15** ut *V* est *Lachmann.*
— **18** se] me *V* ‖ aluus *O.* — **19** superata *V cf. Festus s. u.* suppernati,
Catu[llus ad Coloniam ‘In] fossa Ligari ia[cet suppernata se]curi. —
21 merus *Passeratius* ‖ ni*hil* uidet n*ihil O* nichil uidet nichil *G.* —
22 qu*id* (*altered from* qui) *G.* — **23** nunc uolo uolo *O* nu*n*c cu*m* uolo
G hunc meum *Froehlich.* — **24** pot*est* olidu*m O* potest olidum *G* ‖ exi-
tare *O* exita*re G.* — **25** delinquere *G.*

21. *Interval of one verse in V, filled in G with title* Ad Aurelium. —
1 *Westphal prefixes a conjectural verse* O qui pessimus es mali sodalis ‖
exuricionu*m O* exuricionum *G* essuritionum *Bergk.* — **3** aut posthac aliis
Hand. — **4** dedicare *V.* — **5** nam *omitted, but inserted later, in G* ‖ simul
exiocaris *V.* — **6** haeres *Voss* ‖ exp*e*ribis *O* experib*us* (al’ bis) *G.* —
7 struentem *Ribbeck.* — **8** irruminati*one O* irruminatione *G.* — **9** ip*s*i *V.* —
10 esuriere *O* (*but with secon*d *e cancelled by dot below it*) exurire *G* essurire
Bergk. — **11** ah *omitted in V, added by Scaliger* meus mi *Meleager* mi
meus *Rossbach* uae meus *Faernus* a temet *Froehlich* a te mei *Munro* a te
mi *Schmidt* ieiunus *Huschke* mellitus *Hand* tenellus *Baehrens.* — **12** desi-
nat *V.* — **13** nec facias fine*m* s*ed* irruminatu*s* su*m O* (*but with signs to
indicate that the order of* facias finem *should be reversed*) nec finem facias
sed irruminatus sum *G* nei *Baehrens.*

22. *No interval, but paragraph mark in margin in V, and in G
marginal title* Ad Varum. — **3** idemque (al’ itemq*ue*) *G.* — **4** ad decem
Baehrens. — **5** sit ut *V* ‖ palmisepto *V.* — **6** noue *V* nouei *Lachmann*
nouae *Birt.* — **7** membrane *V* membrana *Avantius.* — **8** detecta *V* derecta
Statius. — **10** capri mulg*us O* capri · mulgus *G.* — **11** aberrat *Ellis.* —
13 ac retristi*us O* hac re tristius *G* scitius *L. Mueller* tersius *or* tertius
Munro hoc retritius *Scaliger.* — **14** infaceto rure *V.* — **15** attigit ul’ n*e*que
nec *O.* — **16** ac] ha *V.* — **17** tamq*uam V.* — **18** n*ec O.* — **20** siuis *O.* —
21 maritice *O.*

23. *No interval, but paragraph mark in margin in V, and in G
marginal title* Ad Furium. — **1** furei *V* ‖ seruo *V* (al’ seruus *G*) seruos
Statius. — **2** cimex al’ n*e*qu*e O* cimex a*n*imal (*perhaps cancelled later*)
n*e*que *G.* — **7** ne *O* nec *corrected to* ni *G.* — **9** minas *O.* — **10** facta *O*
faç*t*a *G* furta *Haupt cf. 68. 140.* — **12** aut qui *V.* — **13** aridu*m* mag*is O*
aridu*m* magis *G.* — **14** essuritione *Bergk.* — **15** si *G.* — **16** sudor abest
· saluia *O* (*in G the second* abest *is written over an erasure*). — **17** muc-
tus ue *O* muccusue *G* ‖ piç*t*uita *G.* — **19** cuius *O* cul*us altered from* cui*us*
(al’ cui*us*) *G* ‖ sal illo *V* (*but the words were afterward connected in G*).
— **23** posses *V* pos*s*eis *Baehrens.* — **24** tua *V.* — **26** sextercia *G.*

27 satis beat*us* *O* satis beatus *G Heyse* satis beatu's *Bergk* sat is beatus *Passeratius* sat es beatus *Calpurnius.*

24. *No interval in V.* — **1** *est O* est *G* ‖ uiue*n*cioru*m O* iuuenciorum *G.* — **2** q*uod V.* — **4** mi dededisses *O* mi didisses *G* Midae dedisses *Voss.* — **5** qui *V* (al' cui *G*) ‖ n*ec* ser*uus O* neq*ue* (al' nec) seruus *G.* — **7** qui *G.* — **9** hec tu qua lubet *G.*

25. *No interval, but paragraph mark in margin in V, with marginal title* Ad Tallum *in G.* — **1** talle *V.* — **2** medulla *G* ‖ imulla *O* ‖ moricula *O* moricilla *G* oricilla *Scaliger.* — **3** aurracoroso *or* a*r*racoroso *O* ara*n*coroso (al' araneoso) *G.* — **4** tale *O* talle *G.* — **5** m*u*lieraries *(afterward corrected to read* mu*li*er aries) ostendet ossita*n*tes *O* mulier alios *(altered from* alies) (al' aues ul' aries) ostendet *(corrected to* ostendit) os*citantes *(with* c *written over erasure) G* munerarios *Lachmann* mulierarios *Haupt* luna mulierarios *Heyse* balnearios *Riese. Many others have applied more vigorous methods of emendation, and yet others think the verse spurious.* — **7** śathabu*m* cathag*r*aphosq*ue* thinos *O* saethabu*m* cathagraphosque thinos *G.* — **8** ineptoq*ue O.* — **9** remite *O.* — **10** manusque] natisque *Scaliger.* — **11** insula *V.* — **12** inimica *V.* — **13** de*p*rensa *O* deprehensa *G.*

26. *No interval, but paragraph mark in margin in V, and in G marginal title* Ad Furium. — **1** u*e*stra *O ed. 1473 Heinsius Baehrens Schmidt* nostra *G Lachmann and many others* uostra *Muretus Lipsius Klotz Schwabe Postgate.* — **2** *omitted in O* ‖ fauonii *G.* — **3** apheliotae *V.* — **5** horribilem *(with dot under* h) *G.*

27. *No interval, but paragraph mark in margin in V, and in G marginal title* Ad pincerna*m* suu*m.* — **1** falerui *O.* — **2** ingeremi *O* ingere mi *G.* — **3** posthumie *G.* — **4** ebriose *V cf. Gell. VI. 20. 6* Catullus quoque elegantissimus poetarum in hisce uersibus ' Minister . . . ebriosioris ' cum dicere ' ebrio ' posset, et, quod erat usitatius, ' acinum ' in neutro genere appellare, amans tamen hiatus illius Homerici suauitatem, ' ebriam' dixit propter insequentis ' a ' litterae concentum. Qui ' ebriosa' autem Catullum dixisse putant, aut ' ebrioso', nam id quoque temere scriptum inuenitur, in libros scilicet de corruptis exemplaribus factos inciderunt. — **5** ad uos q*uod* iubet *O* q*uo*d iubet *G* ‖ limphe *V.* — **7** thionianus *V.*

28. *No interval, but paragraph mark in margin in V, and in G marginal title* Ad Verannium *(apparently corrected from* Veraniu*m) et* Fabullu*m.* — **2** artis *Schwabe.* — **3** uerā *O.* — **4** satis ue *O.* — **6** et quid na*m O* et quid nam *G* ‖ p*a*tet *O* patet *G.* — **8** in lucello *Heinsius.* — **9** o mē mi *O* omne*m* mi *G.* — **10** trahe *V* ‖ tentus *Voss* ‖ yrruinasti *O.* — **11** paru*m* (al' pari) *G* ‖ fuisti *V.* — **12** urpa *O* uerba *G.* — **14** nob*is C* uobis (al' nobis) *G* ‖ dii *V.* — **15** romule *O* romulei *G.*

29. *No interval, but paragraph mark in margin in V, and in G marginal title* In Romulu*m* cathamitu*m.* — **3** na*m* murra*m* O nam murra*m* G ‖ comota O. — **4** cu*m* te V ante *Statius Lachmann and others* uncti *Faernus* unctum *Scaliger* umquam Schwabe *cf. Licinius Caluus ap. Suet. Iul. 49* ‖ brittania O. — **5** hoc *Heinsius.* — **7** p*er*ambulauit O perambulauit G. — **8** aut ydoneus V aut Adoneus *Statius* haut idoneus *Sillig* aut Aedonis *W. Everett.* — **13** nos*t*ra O nostra G ‖ diffutura V defututa *Lachmann.* — **14** comerset O comeset G. — **15** alit V alid *Avantius.* — **16** partu*m* O. — **17** p*r*imu*m* O primu*m* G prima *Auantius.* — **19** libera O hybera G (*corrected from* hibera, *and apparently with the* h *written over an erasure*) ‖ sit G ‖ amni V ‖ thagus V. — **20** hu*n*c gallie timet *et* brittanie (britannie G) V nunc Galliae timetur (tenentur *Ribbeck* minatur *Peiper*) et Britanniae *Froelich Schwabe Westphal* hunc Galliae timetis et Britanniae *Faernus* nunc Galliae timent, timent Britanniae *Puccius* et uncta Gallia ultima et Britannia *Bergk. Many other emendations have also been proposed by various critics.* — **21–24** *Mommsen would place these verses* (*Schwabe only vv. 23–24*) *after v. 10.* — **21** hinc V. — **23** orbis *Haupt* ‖ o piissime *Lachmann* o piissimei *Haupt* o potissimei *L. Mueller* orbis o probissimei *or* putissimei *Schwabe* urbis o pudet meae *Ellis.*

30. *No interval, but paragraph mark in V, and in G marginal title* Ad Alphenu*m.* — **1** alphene V ‖ salse V. — **3** no*n* me dubitas V. — **4, 5** *Lachmann placed these verses after v. 12; Ellis conjectures a lacuna after v. 3.* — **4** nec] nunc *Baehrens* num *Schwabe* ‖ falla cu*m* O. — **5** quod *L. Mueller* ‖ negligis V. — **6** o heu V ‖ dico V dice *Ellis cf. Charis. 349 K.* ‖ cui ne O. — **7** tu te G ‖ me *omitted in* V iniquius *Schwabe.* — **8** tuta *omitted in* O om*n*ia tuta G. — **9** inde G. — **10** uento V ‖ finis O. — **11** ut dii V.

31. *No interval, but paragraph mark in margin in V, and in G marginal title* Ad Sirmiu*m* Insula*m.* — **1** sirinio O sirmio (*corrected from* sirinio) G. — **3** neptunu*s* O neptũnus G. — **4** libente V. — **5** $\frac{i}{m}$ O (*cf. 14. 10 n.*) michi G ‖ crederis (al' credens) G ‖ thimia*m* O thimiam G ‖ bithinios O bithinos (*corrected from* bithinios) G. — **8** meus O. — **10** acquiesimu*s* O acquieximus G. — **13** gaude uos quoq*ue* lidie O gaudete uos quoq*ue* lydie G Lydii *Scaliger* Libuae *Lachmann* limpidae *Auantius* lucidae *Guarinus* liquidae *Postgate* uiuidae *Munro* uos quoque, incitae *Heyse.* — **14** ridere O.

32. *No interval, but paragraph mark in margin in V, and in G marginal title* Ad Ipsicillam. — **1** meas O mea (*with erasure of one letter following*) G ‖ ipsi illa O ipsi thila G Ipsitilla *or* Ipsicilla ω Hypsithilla *Scaliger* Ipsimilla *Baehrens.* — **5** luminis O. — **6** lube foras habire O.

33. *No interval, and no paragraph mark in V, but in O a long hori-zontal line is drawn from the left hand margin just above the first verse of the poem (which begins a new page) and extending as far as the second word.* — **4** uoratiore *V* (al' uolantiore *G*). — **5** horas *V*. — **8** pōt (= po-test) ase *V*.

34. *No interval in V, and no paragraph mark in O, but in G para-graph mark in left margin, and in right* Carmen Diane. — **1** dyane *G*. — **3** *omitted in V*. — **5** latonnia *O*. — **8** deposuit *V*. — **11** saltumque recun-ditorum *O*. — **12** omniumque sonancium *O* omnium sonantium *G*. — **15** (al' et noto es) *G*. — **17** menstrua *O* menstrua *G*. — **18** mentiens *O* ∥ animum *O*. — **21** quaecumque (*same abbreviation as in 11. 13*) *O* scis quecumque tibi placet *G* (*with the last two letters of* placet *apparently written over an erasure, and* al' sis quocumque tibi placet *in margin*). — **23** Ancique *Merula and others*.

35. *No interval, but paragraph mark in V (the poem begins a new page in O), and in G marginal title* Ad Cecilium iubet libello loqui. — **2** occilio *O* ∥ papire *V*. — **4** ueniam *O* menia (*corrected from* meniam) *G*. — **5** quasdam (*corrected from* quosdam) uolō *G*. — **10** inities *O*. — **12** impotentem amorem *O* impotentem amore (*corrected from* amorem) *G*. — **13** eligit indotatam *O* elegit indotatam *G*. — **14** dindimi *V*. — **16** saphica *O* saphyca *G*. — **17** docior *O*. — **18** cecilia *V* ∥ inchoata *G*.

36. *No interval in V, and no paragraph mark in O; but in G para-graph mark and marginal title* Ad lusi cacatam. — **1** anuale (annuale *G*) suo lusi *V*. — **5** dedissemque *O* dedissemque *G* ∥ yambos *G*. — **6** se lec-tissima *Peiper* se electissima *Maehly*. — **9** haec (*apparently so rather than* hoc) *O* ω ∥ me *Bursian*. — **10** ioco se lepido *Bursian* ∥ uouere se diuis *V*. — **11** o *omitted in O* ∥ poncto *O* punto *G*. — **12** adalium *O* adalium (al' ydalium) *G* ∥ utriosque (al' uriosque) *G* Surosque apertos *Voss* Vrios-que portus *Heinsius*. — **13** gnidumque *O* gnidumque *G*. — **14** colisque *O* colis que *G* ∥ amathuntam *O* ∥ alcos *V*. — **15** durachium *O* durachium *G* ∥ hadrie *V*. — **18** intereo *O*. — **19** turis *V*. — **20** anuale (annuale *G*) suo lusi *V*.

37. *No interval, but paragraph mark in V, and in G marginal title* Ad contubernales. — **1** uoxque *O*. — **2** pileatis (*corrected from* pilleatis) *G Haupt* ∥ non (non *G*) afratribus *V*. — **3** mentualas *O*. — **5** confutere *V* ∥ hyrcos *V* hinnos *Bonnet*. — **10** scipionibus *or* scorpionibus ω ropi onibus *Peiper* (*cf. Sacerd. Art. Gram. I. 461 K.*). — **11** me *V* mi *Heinsius* mei *Schwabe* namque *Avantius*. — **13** q̄ (= qua, *as in 39. 15*) *O*. — **14** comsedit *O*. — **16** semitani *O* semitarii (*with* -rii *over* *erasure*) *G* ‖ mechi *G*. — **17** *Paragraph mark in V, and in G marginal title* Ad Egnatiu*m* ‖ une (al' uno) *G*. — **18** Celtiberosae *Priscianus V. 77; VII. 22.* — **20** edens *O.*

38. *No interval in V, but paragraph mark in O, though not in G.* — **1** *est* (est *G*) si carnifici *V.* — **2** male sime hercule *et* laboriose *V* ei et *Lachmann* et est *Sillig.* — **3** ei *Birt.* — **7** iuuet *Heinsius.* — **8** symonideis *G.* — *Some critics conjecture a lacuna after v. 8. Froehlich transposes hither 2. 11–13.*

39. *No interval and no paragraph mark in V.* — **1** candides *O.* — **2** sei *O* seu *G.* — **3** subscellum *O* subsellum *G* ‖ excitat orator *V.* — **4** adimpii regu*m* filii *O* ad pii (al' impii) regum filii *G.* — **5** ingetur orbicu*m O.* — **9** te *omitted in V* monendus es ω te est *Spengel* est te *Maehly.* — **11** fartus *Venator* pastus *Voss* pinguis *Gloss. Vat.* (*in Mai VII. 574*). *The MS. reading has been impugned because (1) no other instance of* parcus *as descriptive of the Umbrians can be cited, and (2) a Vatican glossary quotes this passage with* pinguis *instead of* parcus (*cf. Pers. 3. 74* pinguibus Vmbris): *but (1) the Vatican glossary makes other blunders in this and other quotations, and (2) its reading may have been affected by that of Persius, while (3) the Umbrians appear from Martial XII. 81 to have been proverbial for poverty or frugality.* ‖ *et* trusc*us O* etruscus (*corrected from* ettruscus) *G.* — **12** lamiuin*us O* lamiuinus *G.* — **13** au*t* (aut *G*) meos *V.* — **16** risti *O.* — **17** es *omitted in V, added by Conradius de Allio.* — **18** quiq*ue* nuxit *O* mixit *Ellis* ‖ inane *O.* — **20** nos*ter O* ‖ expolitor *O* expolitior (*corrected from* expolitor) *G* ‖ deus *O.* — **21** lot*us O* lotus *G.*

40. *No interval, but paragraph mark in V, and in G marginal title* Ad Rauidu*m.* — **3** dens *O* deus (*corrected from* dens) *G* ‖ auocat*us O* aduocatus (*corrected from* auocatus) *G.* — **5** p*er*ueniamus *V* ‖ inhora *O.* — **6** nis *O.* — **7** ens *O.* — **8** pena *O* poema (al' p*oe*na) *G.*

41. *No interval and no paragraph mark in V.* — **1** a me an · a · puella *O* a me an apuella *G* Ameana *Statius* Ametina *Haupt* Arretina *Peiper* Anniana *Schwabe* anne sana *Conr. de Allio* amens illa *Pleitner* ‖ diffututa *Guarinus.* — **2** popossit *O.* — **4** forniani *O* formiani (*corrected from* forniani) *G.* — **5** puelle *V.* — **6** *con*uocare *O* conuocare *G.* — **7** rogate ω *Schwabe.* — **8** solet · *et V* ‖ ymaginosu*m O* ymaginosum *G* haec imaginosum ω esse imaginosa *Schwabe* solide est imaginosa *Haupt* solet: en imaginosam *Doering* rogare q. s. solet aes imaginosum *Froehlich.*

42. *No interval and no paragraph mark in V.* — **1** endecha sillabi *V.* — **3** locum (al' Iocum *G*) *V* ‖ meca *O* mecha *G.* — **7** illam *G.* — **8** mirmice *V* mimice *Turnebus.* — **9** catulli *V.* — **11** meca *O* mecha *G.*

— **12** moeca *O* mecha *G.* — **13** o lupanar *Statius.* — **14** potest *ω and many editors.* — **16** al*iud *G.* — **17** ferre ocanis *O* ferre|o|canis *G Westphal placed vv. 16 and 17 after v. 23, writing* quo si non; *Pleitner, after v. 21, writing* pote ut *for* potest, *which emendation was adopted by Munro, but without transposition.* — **19** meca *O* mecha *G.* — **20** meca *O* mecha *G.* — **21** s*ed* nichi*l O* sed nichil *G* ‖ nihil] nil (*corrected from* nichil) *G.* — **22** uobis *ω Lachmann.* — **23** putatis *Schwabe* uoletis *Maehly.*

43. *No interval and no paragraph mark in V.* — **1** nimio *ω Scaliger.* — **7** compara*n*tur *O.* — **8** sedum *O* seclum (*corrected from* sedum) *G* ‖ et] atqu*e* (*corrected from* et) *G.*

44. *No interval and no paragraph mark in V.* — **2** cum qu*i*bus (*with* cum *afterward crossed out*) *G.* — **4** pignoris *V* ‖ *con*tedu*n*t *O.* — **7** alia*m*qu*e O* aliamqu*e G* ‖ expuls*u*s si*m O* expulsus sim *G* expuli tussim *Avantius* expui tussim *Scaliger.* — **8** men*s* u*e*rtur *O* mens uertur *G* meus uenter *Faernus.* — **10** festianus *O.* — **11** oratione minantiu*m O* oratione*m* minantium *G* orationem in Antium *Statius* ‖ petitorum (*corrected from* petitorem) *G.* — **12** pestilen*te O.* — **13** h*o*c *O.* — **17** ulte *Faernus* ultu' *Muretus* ultus erratum *Baehrens.* — **19** sestire cepso *V* ‖ qu*i O* qui *G.* — **20** sectio *V* ‖ ferant *Schwabe.* — **21** tunc (*but with* t *over erasure*) *G* tum *Haupt* ‖ legi*t O* legit *G* legi *Lachmann* fecit *Baehrens* legit librum *ω.*

45. *No interval and no paragraph mark in V.* — **1** ac men *V* ‖ septimios *O* septimos *G.* — **2** inqu*i*d *O* ‖ ac me *V.* — **3** perditi *V.* — **4** o mens *O.* — **5** pot*e*st *O* potest *G.* — **6** inlibia *V* ‖ Indiaue *L. Mueller.* — **8** sinistra, ut ante, (9) dextram *or* sinistram ut ante (9) dextram *ω* sinister ante, (9) dextram *Voss.* — **9** appro*b*ati*o*ne *O* approbatione *G.* — **10** ad hac (ha*n*c *G*) me *V.* — **12** saniata *V.* — **13** inqu*i*d *O* ‖ septinulle *V.* — **17** sinistrauit an*te* (ante *G*) *V.* — **18** dextra*m O* dextram *G* ‖ approbacione*m O* approbationem *G.* — **21** septumiu*s O* septumius *G* ‖ agm*e*n *O* agmen (*apparently corrected from* acmen) *G.* — **22** siriasqu*e* britaniasqu*e O* syriasque *G.* — **23** ac me *V.* — **24** libidinisqu*e V.*

46. *No interval and no paragraph mark in V.* — **1** uere gelidos *V.* — **3** cephiri *O* cephyri *G* ‖ silesit *O* ‖ aureis *V.* — **4** liqua*n*tur *O* ‖ frigii *V* ‖ catule *O.* — **5** ruber estuore *V.* — **6** asye *G.* — **7** pra*e*tepida*n*s *O.* — **8** laeto *Schwabe.* — **9** cetus *O* coetus *G.* — **10** quo simul *V.* — **11** diuerse uarie uie *V* diuerse uariae *Scaliger* diuersae uarie *Guarinus* diuersae uariae *Victorius Lachmann.*

47. *No interval and no paragraph mark in V.* — **2** mundae *Buecheler* nummi *Baehrens.* — **4** proposuit *O* proposuit *G.*

48. *No interval and no paragraph mark in V.* — **1** inuenti *O* inuenti
G. — **4** numq*uam* ind*e* corsater *O* numq*uam* inde corsater *G* mi unquam
Statius uidear satur *Guarinus.* — **6** sint *O* sit (*corrected from* sint) *G.*

49. *Interval of one verse in V, filled in G with title* Ad Ciceronem, *of
which the second word is written over an erasure. In O there is a paragraph mark.* — **2** · ⌒ · tulli *O* m̊arce Tulli *G.* — **5** pessumus *O.* — **6** pessimus *V.*

50. *Interval of one verse in V, filled in G with title* Ad lucinium. *In
O there is a paragraph mark.* — **2** inuicem *Sabellicus* in tueis *Schwabe.* —
5 h*aec O* ‖ illos *O.* — **7** abiit *V.* — **8** lacini faceti tuiq*ue V.* — **10** somnos
O somnos *G.* — **12** u*e*rsaret*ur O* uersaretur *G.* — **13** simuliq*ue O* ‖ omnem (al' essem) *G.* — **14** ad *V.* — **16, 17** *Cf. note after 54. 1.* —
18 caueris *V* ‖ praecepsq*ue O.* — **19** ocello *V.* — **20** penas *V* ‖ ne
messis *O* n*e*messis *G* ‖ resposcat *O.* — **21** uemens *Statius Haupt* (*cf.
Lachmann on Lucr. II. 1024*).

51. *Interval of one verse in V, filled in G with title* Ad lesbiam. *In
O there is a paragraph mark.* — **1** m*i*hi (*cf. 14. 10 n.*) impar *O* mi* impar
G. — **3** te *omitted here, but prefixed to v.* **4** *in V ; but in G it was later
inserted in its proper place here, and* te spectat *at the beginning of v.* **4**
altered to read spe ctat. — **5** miseroque *O* miseroquod (*corrected from*
-q*ue*) *G.* — **7** aspexi *V.* — **8** *omitted in V* quod loquar amens *Parthenius*
in fauce loquellae *Ezra van Ieuer* uocis in ore *Ritter* gutture uocis *Westphal* in pectore uocis *Pleitner.* — **10** flamina *V.* — **11** tintia*n*t *O* ‖
geminae *Schrader Lachmann* gemina et *Spengel* gelida *Baehrens* gemina
obteguntur *Schwabe.* — **12** limina *G.* — **13** catuli *O* catulli *G.* — **14** ex-
ultas *V.*

52. *Interval of one verse in V, filled in G with title* In Nouium. *In
O there is a paragraph mark.* — **1** mori *V.* — **2** incurulu *O* ‖ noui*us O*
nouius *G Nonius ancients who quote the verse* (*cf. especially Plin. N. H.
XXXVII. 81*). — **3** Vacinius *G.* — **4** mori *V.*

53. *No interval and no paragraph mark in V.* — **1** nisi *O* ‖ e] *et V*
ec *Baehrens.* — **2** uaciniana *G.* — **3** meos *V* ‖ crimina (al'. carmina) *G* ‖
caluos *V* ‖ explicaset *O.* — **4** amirans *O Between vv. 4 and 5 there is no
interval, but a paragraph mark in V, and in G marginal title* de Octonis
capite. — **5** dii *V* ‖ salapantiu*m* d*e*sertu*m O* salapantium desertum *G* salaputtium *Sen. Contr. VII. 4. 7.*

54. *No interval and no paragraph mark in V. But cf. 53. 4 n.* —
1 otonis cap*u*d apido *est* pussillu*m O* otonis caput o*pido est pu*sillum *G*

After v. 1 are repeated in V 50. 16, 17 (but in O with haec *for* hoc*), just one page removed in G from their true position.* — **2** heri (*corrected from* eri) *G* ‖ rustice *V* ‖ cruta *O*. — **5** sufficio seniore cocto *V* (*but with* al' · p · *above* cocto *in G*) Fuficio *Haupt. Between vv.* **5** *and* **6** *there is no interval, but a paragraph mark in V, and in G marginal title* In camerium.

55. *No interval and no paragraph mark in V. But cf. 54. 5 n.* — **1** molestus es *O* molestus es *G*. — **3** in campo *Sillig* ‖ inminore *O* in minore *G* te quaes. in minore campo *ω*. — **4** id (al' in *G*) circo *V*. — **7** prehendi *G*. — **8** serena *V*. — **9** ah uel te *or* Auli. te *ω* Aulum, te *Heyse* auens te *or* has uellens *Schwabe* auellent (sic ipse flagitabam) (10) . . . puellae? *Ellis.* — **11** quendam *G* ‖ inquid *O* ‖ nudum sinum reducens *Avantius* (recludens *Riese*) nudum reducta pectus *Ellis* nudum reduc amicum *Baehrens* (puellum *Schwabe*). — **12** em (*corrected from* hem *G*) *V* ‖ haec *O* hec (*corrected from* hic?) *G* heic *Schwabe.* — **13** herculei *V*. — **14** te infastu *V* ten *Muretus.* — **16** audaciter hoc *O* audacter · hoc *G* (15) ede hoc (16) audacter *Voss* ‖ crede (al' crude) *G* ‖ lucet *V* lucei *Scaliger.* — **17** nunc] non *Baehrens.* — **18** tenens *O* tenens *G*. — **19** prohicies *O* proiicies *G*. — **20** loquella *G*. — **22** uestri *O* uestri (al' no *over letters* ue) *G* nostri sis *ω* (fis *Heyse*) uestri sim ego *Avantius* dum ueri sis *Rossberg.*

56. *Interval of one verse in V, filled in G with title* Ad Catonem. *In O there is a paragraph mark.* — **3** nide *O*. — **5** populum *O* populum *G*. — **6** crisantem *ω* crusantem *Baehrens* ‖ dyone *G* Dianae *Westphal.* — **7** rigida (*corrected from* ridida) *G*.

57. *No interval and no paragraph mark in V.* — **3** paris *V*. — **5** impraese (= imprese) *O* ‖ nece luentur *V*. — **6** tenelli *Haupt.* — **7** lecticulo *O Baehrens* lectulo *G* lectululo *Avantius* lectulo et *Froehlich.* — **9** niuales *O* ‖ socii *et V* sociei *Scaliger.*

58. *No interval and no paragraph mark in V.* — **1** uestra *O* uestra *G*. — **2** catulus *V*. — **4** quadruuiis *G* ‖ angi portis *O*. — **5** magna amiremini *O* magna admiremini *G* magnanimos *ω*.

58[b]. *No interval and no paragraph mark in V. Many critics consider this a part of c.* **55,** *adding it to the end of that poem, or inserting it after v.* **5,** *or v.* **12,** *or v.* **13.** — **2, 3** *Muretus and others reverse the order of these verses.* — **3** primipes ue *O* primipes (al' pinnipes) ue *G*. — **4** thesi uinee *O* niueis citisque bigis *Muretus* niuea citaque biga *Hand.* — **5** plumipedas *O* plūmipedas *G*. — **7** uictos *O* iunctos (*corrected from* uictos) *G* uinctos *ω* cunctos *Schrader.* — **9** praesens *O*. — **10** esse *O* ‖ $\frac{i}{m}$ *O* michi *G* mi *ω* ‖ amiceque ritando *O*.

59. *No interval, but paragraph mark in V, and in G marginal title*
In Rufum. — **1** rufu*m* *O* rufum *G* Rufulum *Pleitner* Rufum egens *West-*
phal Rufum edax *Rossberg* ‖ fallat *G.* — **5** abse miraso *O.*

60. *No interval and no paragraph mark in V.* — **1** libissinis *O* libi-
sinis *G* Libystinis *Scaliger.* — **2** silla *V.* — **3** mente*m* *O.* — **4** suplic*us* *O*
suppliciis (*corrected from* supplicus) *G.* — **5** contenta*m* (*corrected later to*
read contenptam) *O* conteptam (*corrected from* contentam) *G* ‖ animis *V.*
There is an interval of five verses in O, extending to the bottom of the page.

61. *Interval of one verse in V* (*at top of page in O*), *filled in G with*
title Epythalamius Iunie et Mallii. *No interval between stanzas in V.* —
1 obellicon iei *O* o eliconei *G.* — **4** ohȳmenee (*omitting* hymen) *O.* —
5 hymen · ohymenee hym*en* *O* o hymenee hymen *G.* — **7** amaraci (*cor-*
rected from amarici) *O* amarici *G.* — **11** hylari *V.* — **12** *con*tinen*s* *O* con-
tinens *G.* — **13** tinnuula *O* tinnula (*corrected from* tinnuula) *G.* —
16 iunia *O* Iunia (*corrected from* uinia) *G* ‖ mallio *V.* — **17** id aliu*m* *O*
idalium (*corrected from* ad alium) *G.* — **18** adfrigiu*m* *O* ad frigium *G.* —
21 uult *O.* — **22** mirtus *V* ‖ asya *G.* — **23** amadriades *V.* — **24** ludri-
cu*m* *O* ludricum *G.* — **25** nutriunt in honore *or* odore ω nutriuntur honore
Maehly. — **27** tespie *V.* — **28** aouios *O.* — **29** nimpha *O* nympha (*cor-*
rected from nimpha) *G.* — **33** reuincens *V.* — **38** innodu*m* *O* in nodum
G. — **40** o himenee (hymenee *G*) hymenee hime*n* (hymen *G*) *V.* —
42 citaries *O.* — **46** amatis *V* magis ac magis *Guarinus* magis ah magis
Scaliger magis aemulis *Hermann* magis ancxiis *Haupt* mage mutueis
Pleitner magis est ama-(**47**) tis petendus *Bergk.* — *After v.* **49** *follows in*
V compar*a*ries (compar*a*rier *G*) ausit (*cf. vv.* **65, 70, 75**). — **50** o hime*n*
(hymen *G*) hymenee hym*en* (hymen *G*) *V.* — **51** te sui si remulus *O* te
sui siremulus (al' remus) *G.* — **54** nitens *Schenkl* tumens *Dousa iun.* te
te Hymen *Voss* ‖ nouos *V.* — **55** maritos *V.* — **56** fer oiùueni *O* fer o
iuueni *G.* — **58–60** dedis agremio sue mat*ris* | o hymenee hime*n* hymenee
O dedis agremio sue matris | o hymenee hymen o (*inserted above with*
caret) hymenee *G.* — **61** nich*il* *O* nil (*corrected from* nichil) *G.* —
66 quit (*corrected from* quid) *G.* — **68** uities *O* (*the first* i *is underscored,*
but apparently by a recent hand) uicier *G* uincier ADLP *Lachmann*
Baehrens iungier *Scaliger* nitier *Avantius Schwabe Schmidt Ellis Postgate*
cingier *Schrader Haupt.* — **70** compararies *O.* — **73** at potest *Peiper.* —
75 comparier *O* compararier (*corrected from* comparirier*) *G.* — **77** ades
Schrader. — *Several critics conjecture a lacuna after v.* **78**; *others, after*
v. **83**. *In older editions the order is here much disturbed by interpolation of*
other verses. — **79–82** *omitted in V without interval.* — **84** *This verse was*
judged spurious by Rossbach, and by Lachmann and others was placed after

v. **110.** — **86** Au- *omitted here in* V, *but prefixed to v.* **87**, *whence it was transferred by Turnebus.* — **87** aurunculeia *O* arunculeia *G.* — **92** ortullo (*corrected to* ortulo *G*) *V.* — **93** iactintin*u*s *O* iacintinus *G.* — **94** abiit *V.* — **95** *omitted in* V. — **98** uideri ut *O* uiden ut *G.* — **102** ad ultera *G.* — **103** procatur · pia *V* prona *Heyse.* — **106** quin] s*e*d *O Baehrens* q*u*e *G* quin *or* qui ω quei *Scaliger* *Most editors read* quin. ‖ uult *O.* — **109** abiit *V.* — **112–114** *omitted in* V *without interval.* — **119** abiit *V.* — **121** o *omitted in* V. — **122** flammineu*m* uido *O* flamineu*m* uideo *G.* — **123–125** io himen himenee io · | ite co*n*cinete in modu*m O* io hymen hymenee io | io hymen hymenee io | ite concinite in modum *G.* — **126** taceatis *V.* — **127** fosceninna locacio *O* lotatio (al' locutio) *G* iocatio *Heinsius.* — **129** uidens *Schwabe.* — **132** diu] domini *O* (*as if from* dñi). — **133** iubet *Schrader.* — **134** nam *O.* — **136** iulice *O* uillice *G.* — **139** misera miser *O.* — **141** diceres *V* ‖ malle (*corrected from* male *G*) *V.* — **142** unguenta te *V.* — **144** io hym*e*n (hymen *G*) hymenee io *V.* — **145** *omitted in* V, *as are also in O vv.* **150, 155, 160, 165,** *and* **170,** *while in G v.* **155** *was omitted, but inserted later in margin.* — **146** simus *O* ‖ tibiq*u*e (*corrected to* tibi q*u*ae *G*) *V.* — **149** io him*e*n (hymen *G*) hymenee io *V.* — **150** *omitted in O* io hymen hymenee io *G.* — **151** tuis *G.* — **153** ni *V.* — **154** io hym*e*n (hymen *G*) hymenee io *V.* — **155** *omitted in* V, *but in G* io hymen hymenee io *inserted in margin.* — **158** ser*u*it *O* seruit *G* sine fine seruit ω sine fine erit *Avantius Lachmann Rossbach Haupt L. Mueller* sine seruiat *Pisanus Sillig Heyse Pleitner Schwabe Baehrens Ellis Schmidt Postgate* quo tibicina fert uiam *Ellis and Ferruci.* — **159** io himen (hymen *G*) hymenee io *V.* — **160** *omitted in O* io hymen hymenee io *G.* — **162** anilis etas *O* annilis etas *G.* — **164** io himen (hymen *G*) hymenee io *V.* — **165** *omitted in O* io hymen hymenee io *G.* — **166** tranffer *O.* — **168** nassilem*qu*e sibi *O* rasilem*qu*e (*corrected from* rassilem*qu*e) sibi *G.* — **169** io hym*e*n (hymen *G*) hymenee io *V.* — **170** *omitted in O* io hymen hymenee io *G.* — **171** aspice *V* ‖ intus *Statius* unctus *Barthius* imus *Fruterius.* — **172** inthoro *O* in thoro *G.* — **174, 175** io hym*e*n (hymen *G*) hymenee io | io him*e*n (hymen *G*) himenee (hymenee *G*) io *V.* — **176** hac *V.* — **177** uritur (al' urimur) *G.* — **179, 180** *like* **174, 175.** — **181** mite *O.* — **182** pr*a*etextare *O* ‖ puelle *V.* — **183** cubibe *O* ‖ adea*n*t *G.* — **184, 185** io hymen hymenee io | io him*e*n (hymen *G*) hymenee io *V.* — **186** o *omitted in* V, *added by Baehrens* uos ω iam *Pleitner* ‖ unis *V* uiris *Statius* bonis *Passeratius* uos unis senibus bonae *Avantius.* — **187** berue *V* breue ω *Scaliger Lachmann.* — **188** puella*m O* puellam *G.* — **189, 190** *like* **174, 175.** — **192** est t*i*bi *O* est tibi *G.* — **194** ue*l*ut *O* uultu (*with final* u *added later*) (al' uult) *G.* — **196–200** *standing in* V *after v.* **205**; *placed here by Scaliger, perhaps*

wrongly. — **196** admaritu*m* tam*e*n iuuenem *O* ad **maritum tamen iuuenem**
G corrected by Scaliger. — **197** nich*i*l ominus *O* nich̥ilominus *G.* —
198 pulcre res nec *V* pulcer es *Robortello.* — **199** abiit *V.* — **200** re-
memorare *G.* — **201** remota es *O* remorata es *G.* — **203** inuen*e*rit *O*
inuenerit *G.* — **204** cupis capis *G* (*but Schwabe thinks the original reading
in G was* cupis cupis). — **205** abscondas *V.* — **206** pulu*e*ris (pulueris *G*)
ericei *V* Africi *Heinsius* Africei *Lachmann* aridi *Broukhusius Schrader.*
— **209** n*o*stri *O* nostri *G* ‖ uolu*n*t *O* uolunt *G.* — **210** ludere *V* ludei
Scaliger. — **211** et ludite et *V.* — **214** nidide*m* *O.* — **215** ingenerati *O.* —
216 torcutus *O.* — **217** et *O.* — **220** s*e*d m*i*chi (*cf. 14. 10 n.*) ante *O* sed
michi ante *G* semihiante *Scaliger* semhiante *L. Mueller.* — **222** maulio *O*
‖ facie *Burmann* ‖ insci*e*ns *O* insci*e*ns *G* inscieis *Lachmann.* — **223** nos-
cite *O* ‖ obuieis *Pleitner* omnibus noscitetur ab insciis *Dawes Haupt* (*cf.
Haupt Opusc. I. p. 18 ff.*). — **224** sua*m* *O* suam *G.* — **225** iudicet *O.* —
226 matr*e* (matre *G*) *added in V to this verse from the following.* —
227 matre *omitted in V* ‖ egenus *O.* — **228** ab *omitted in O.* — **229** the-
lamacho *O* theleamacho *G.* — **230** pene lopeo *O* penolopeo *G.* —
231 hostia *V.* — **232** adbonlei *O* ad bolnei (al' bonei) *G.* — **233** bone
uite *V* ‖ et *transposed by L. Mueller after* adsiduo. — **234** assidue *V.* —
235 exercere *O.*

    62. *Interval of one verse in V, filled in O with the words* explicit
epithalamiu*m, to which a paragraph mark is prefixed, and in G with the
title* Exametru*m* carmen nuptiale. *In O there is also a paragraph mark
before v.* **1.** — *For the text of this poem the Thuanean Anthology* (*cf. introductory note to Crit. App.*) *is of great value, and its readings, wherever
they differ from the text of this edition, are given with the signature* T, *but
without the indication of ligatures and of mere orthographical peculiarities.
In it occurs the title* Epithalamium Catulli (*cf. Quint. IX. 3. 16*). —
1 turba uiro*rum in margin G.* — **3** pinguis *OT* pingues *G* ‖ linqu*e*re *O*
(*the same stroke answering for the abbreviation in both syllables, as occasionally elsewhere*) linquere *G.* — **4** imene*us O.* — **6** *Paragraph mark, and
in margin* Puelle *G* consurgi eretera *T.* — **7** h*o*c eos ostendit *O* hoc eos
ostendit *G* oeta eos *T* ‖ imb*e*r *O* imber *G* imbres *T* ignes *Victorius* (*Ellis
compares similar confusion between* ignis *and* imber *in Val. Flac. V. 415;
Lucr. I. 784, 785; Tib. I. 1. 48*) Oetaeas obtendit n. umbras *Statius*
Oetaeos (*nominative*) se ostendit n. umbreis *Bergk.* — **8** c*e*rte si *O* certe
* *G* siccer tes · i · *T* certe est *Statius.* — **9** qu*o* uisere (uisere *G*) par*e*nt
V quod uisere par est *T* uincere *Avantius.* — **10** hymeno (*corrected from*
hymene) hymeneae hymeneae ades · o · hymenee *T.* — **11** *Paragraph
mark, and in margin* Puelle *G* ‖ nobilis *T* ‖ equal*i*s *O* equalis *G* **aequalis**

T. — **12** aspice *O* aspicite *G* ‖ quaerunt *at first written after* innupte *in O, but later the letters* runt *cancelled by dots below them* innupte que *G* innupte *T* ‖ meditare quaerunt *O* meditare querunt *G.* — **13** habent] hūc (= hunc) *O* hn̄t (= habent) *G* ‖ memora psile *T.* — **14** *omitted in V, given in T* ‖ neimirum *Baehrens* ‖ laborent *Voss.* — **15** non *T* ‖ diuisimus (al' diuidamus) *G* dimisimus ω. — **17** nunc *T* non *V* ‖ committite *O* committite *G* conuértite *T.* — **18** incipiaent *T.* — **20** *Paragraph mark, and in margin* Puelle *G* ‖ ignis *O.* — **21** amatris *O.* — **22** auelle *T* ‖ natae . . . matrem *Gronovius.* — **25** Kymeno hymeneae Kymenades · o · Kymeneae *T.* — **26** *Paragraph mark, and in margin* Iuuenes *G* ‖ quis *T.* — **27** fines *T.* — **28** quo *V* ‖ uir *T.* — **29** uinxere *O* ‖ prius · quam *O.* — **30** a *omitted in T.* — **31** Kymeno Kymeneae Kymenades o Kymeneae *T.* — **32** *Paragraph mark, and in margin* Puelle *G* ‖ equales (*with dot under* s *and* m *above it*) *G* aequalis *T.* — *After v.* **32** *no interval in V.* — **34** saepe] mane *Froehlich.* — **35** comprendis (*corrected from* comprehendis) *G* deprendis *Baehrens* ‖ eospem *T* Eous *Schrader.* — **36** adlucet *T.* — **37** quod tamen *O* quod (al' quid) tamen *G* quittum *T* ‖ carpiunt *T* ‖ quam *V* quema *T.* — **38** Kymeno Kymeneae Kymenales Kymeno Kymeneae *T.* — **39** *Paragraph mark, and in margin* Puelle *G* ‖ flos qui in *Spengel* flos si in *Baehrens.* — **40** conclusus *O* contusus (*apparently corrected from* conclusus) *G* conuolsus *T.* — **41** quaemulcens aure firma *T* ‖ ymber *G.* — *After v.* **41.** *Spengel and others conjecture a lacuna of one verse.* — **43, 44** *omitted in O and T.* — **45** tum cara sui · sed (sed *G*) *V* tum cara *T.* — **48** Kymeneo Kymeneae Kymenades Kymeneae *T.* — **49** *Paragraph mark, and in margin* Iuuenes *G* ‖ et *T.* — **50** extollit quam muniteamducatuuam *T* ‖ uitem *O.* — **51** per flectens *T.* — **52** flacellum *T.* — **53** coluere *O* coluere (*corrected from* colluere) *G* multi acoluere *T* ‖ iuuenci (iuuenci *G*) *with* c *corrected from* t *V* iuuenci *T* bubulci *Riese.* — **54** apsi *T* ‖ marita *T* maritae *Heinsius.* — **55** accoluere *V* acoluere *T* multei coluere *Haupt* ‖ iuuenci (iuuenci *G*) *with* c *corrected from* t *V* bubulci *Riese.* — **56** tum inculta *T.* — **58** cura *VT* ‖ uiro] suis *Baehrens After v.* **58** *Muretus added* Hymen o Hymenaee, Hymen ades o Hymenaee. *And many critics conjecture a lacuna in the strophe vv.* **59–66.** — **59** at ω ‖ tua *T* ‖ nec *VT* nei *Baehrens.* — **60** equo *V* equom *T.* — **62** *omitted in T.* — **63** pars *after* patri *omitted in O, added by Avantius* tercia pars patri data pars data tercia matri *G* tertia patris pars · est · data tertia matri *T* patri] patris est *Muretus* patrist *Haupt; Schoell expunges the verse.* — **64** solit tu est noli tuignare *T* tuast *Schwabe.* — **66** Kymeno Kymeneae Kymenades · o · Kymeneae *T* ades ohymene *G.*

63. *No interval, but paragraph mark in O; in G interval of one verse filled with title* De Berecinthia et Athi. — **1** uetus *O* ‖ actis celere *V* celerei *Baehrens.* — **2** frigium *V.* — **3** Rheae *L. Mueller.* — **4** ubi *O* ubi *G* ‖ amnis *O* amnis *G.* — **5** iletas *V* illa *Scaliger and many others* ile *Lachmann* ilei *Bergk* icta *Statius* ‖ pondere (pondere *G*) silices *V* pondera silice *Avantius* pondere silicis *Passeratius and many others* deuolsit ile acuto sibi rodere silicis *Haupt.* — **7** et iam *O* et iam *G* ‖ maculas *V.* — **8** timpanum *O* tympanum *G* typanum *Scaliger.* — **9** timpanum *O* tympanum (*corrected from* timpanum) *G* typanum *Scaliger* ‖ tuom *Lachmann* ac typum *Munro* ‖ cibeles tu *V   Here and elsewhere in c. 63 where the name of the goddess occurs with a long penult, many have followed Lachmann in adopting the spelling* Cybebe, *according to the norm of Bentley, on which see Commentary* ‖ matri *O.* — **10** -que] quod *V* ‖ tauri *et V* taurei *Lachmann.* — **11** hoc *O* (*the mark above the* h *is uncertain, but seems to be a period rather than an apostrophe*) hec *G* ‖ fremebunda *Muretus.* — **12** cibelles *O* cibeles *G.* — **13** dindimene *O* dindimenee (*corrected from* dindimene) *G* ‖ pectora *V* uaga pectora dominae *Ahlwardt* ad dominae uaga pecora *Ramler.* — **14** loca celeri *V, corrected by Guarinus.* — **15** secutae *Bergk.* — **16** rabidum *Bergk* ‖ pelage *Victorius.* — **17** euitastis *O.* — **18** hilarate erocitatis *O* hylarate crocitatis *G* erae citatis *Avantius* aere citatis ω io citatis *Baehrens* ‖ an animum *O* an animum *G.* — **19** cedat (al' cedit) *G* ‖ te *O.* — **20** frigiam *V* ‖ cibelles (cibeles *G*) phrigia *V* ‖ Rheae *L. Mueller.* — **21** cimbalum *O* ‖ timpana *O.* — **22** tybicen (*corrected from* tibicen) *G* ‖ phrix *V.* — **23** menade sui iaciurt (iaciunt *G*) ei derigere (derigere *G*) *V.* — **27** atris *V* ‖ mulies notha ʊ (*but with marks to indicate that the order should be inverted*) nota mulier *G.* — **28** thiasis *O* thyasiis (*corrected from* thysiis) *G.* — **29** timpanum *O* ‖ cimbala *O.* — **30** ydam *G.* — **31** animagens *O* anima gens *G* (*but apparently corrected from* aïagẽs) animam agens *Lachmann* animo egens *Avantius* animi egens *Statius* animae egens *Baehrens.* — **32** timpano *O* ‖ actis *V.* — **33** iugi] luci *V.* — **34** rabidae *Bentley* ‖ secuntur *O* sequntur *G* ‖ propere pedem *O* propere pedem *G* properipedem *Venator.* — **35** pedomum (*with* pe *cancelled by dots*) *G* ‖ cibelles *O* cibeles *G* ‖ lasulle *O.* — **37** hiis *O* ‖ labante (*corrected from* labente) *G.* — **38** abiit *G* ‖ mollis *V.* — **39** horis aureis *V.* — **40** sol adura *V.* — **42** sonus *O* somnus (*corrected from* sonus) *G* ‖ excitum *O* excitum *G* excitam *Lachmann.* — **43** eum] cum *V* quem *Bentley* ‖ pasitheo *V.* — **45** ipse *V* ‖ atris *O.* — **46** sineque is *O* sineque his *G* queis ω. — **47** estuanter (estuanter *G*) usum *V* aestuante rusum *Victorius* ‖ retulit *V.* — **49** allocuta est ita · uoce miseritus magestates *O* allocuta (*corrected from* alocuta) est ita · uoce miseritus (al' miseriter) maiestas *G corrected by Avantius* (miseritus *Schwabe*). —

50 genitrix *O.* — **51** misera *Froehlich* ‖ herifuge (*corrected from* uerıfuge)
G. — **52** yde retuli *G* ‖ memor*a O.* — **53** ut caput *V* ‖ stabilia *O* stabilla
(*corrected from* stabilia) *G.* — **54** omnia] amica *Muretus* omissa *Heyse*
opaca *L. Mueller* ad omnia irem *Avantius.* — **55** patriam *O* (*not corrected
to read* patria, *as Schwabe thinks*). — **56** popula atte *V* ‖ dirigere *O* dirigere *G.* — *On the page in O beginning with v.* **57** *four erasures have been
made, apparently of blots of considerable size, and the writing continued
over them.* — **58** ferar (*corrected from* ferat) *G.* — **60** gŭmasiis *O* gymnasiis (*corrected perhaps from* gimnasiis, *or, as Schwabe thinks, from* gynnas-
tis) *G* guminasiis *Ellis Baehrens Schwabe L. Mueller Riese Postgate.* —
61 ha *O.* — **62** figura est *V* ‖ q*u*id abier*i*m *O* quid abierim *G* quod habu-
erim *Scaliger* nunc quod obierim *Hand.* — **63** mulie*n*s *O* puber *Scaliger*
iuue*n*is *Rossberg* ‖ adolesce*n*s *O* adolescens *G.* — **64** gimnasti *V* ‖ sui *G* ‖
oleii *O* oley *G.* — **66** circul*i*s *O* circulis *G.* — **67** liquendu*m O* liquendu*m*
G ‖ solo *V.* — **68** nec *V* nunc *Santenius* ‖ de*um *G* deae *Riese* Rheae
L. Mueller ‖ ministr*e*t *et* (*for* ministra et, *the second* et *being a dittograph*)
cibello*s O* cibeles *G* ‖ ferar*um O* ferarum *G.* — **70** idenene (ydenene *G*)
amic*t*a *V.* — **71** frigie *O* phrigie *G* ‖ colŭnib*us O* colŭnibus *G.* —
72 apex *O.* — **74** hinc *O* hinc *G* hic *or* huic ω ‖ citus *omitted in V, added
by Bentley* ‖ adiit *V* palam sonitus abiit ω sonitus abiit celer *Lachmann* sonitus celer abiit *Heyse* sonus editus adiit *Froehlich.* — **75** geminas] matris
Ahlwardt ‖ deorum] matris *Lachmann* ‖ adauris *O.* — **76** ubi *V* ‖ cibelle
O ceible *G.* — **77** lenu*m*que *O* ‖ pectoris *V* ‖ hostem stimula*n*s (*but corrected from some indeterminable earlier reading*) *G. The erasure in O
noted by Schwabe is one that runs diagonally to the right downward into
the next line, and is only one of a number of erasures on this page, apparently of large blots.* — **78** inquid *O* ‖ i *omitted in V, added by Scaliger* fac
Schwabe ‖ face ω ‖ agitet *omitted in V, added in Cambridge edition of
1702* ut icat hunc furo*r Froehlich.* — **79** face ω ‖ ut *V* uti *Lachmann* ‖
ictu*m O* ictum *G* ictu ω ui furoris ictus *Baehrens.* — **81** a cede (al' age
cede) tergo *G* ‖ tua ue*rum* uera pat*e*re (patere *G*) *V.* — **82** face ω ‖
cunta *G.* — **84** cibelle *O* cibele *G* ‖ regligatq*ue O.* — **85** adortal*i*s rapidu*m O* adhortalis rapidu*m* (*last syllable written over erasure*) *G* rabidum
Schwabe. — **86** abit infremit *Scaliger.* — **87** bumida *O* humida *G* ‖ litio-
ris *O.* — **88** teneramque *Lachmann* ‖ marmorea (marmorea *G*) pelago *V.*
— **89** ficit *O* fecit *G* ‖ illa *Lachmann.* — **90** omne] esse *O* ‖ famula (*corrected from* famulla) *G.* — **91** cibelle *O* cibele *G* ‖ dindimei *O* dindimenei
G Didymi dea domina *Scaliger* dea Dindyma domina *Ahlwardt.* — **92** tuo
V. — **93** rapido*s V.*

64. *Interval of one verse in V, filled in G with title* Argonautia. *In O there is merely a paragraph mark before v.* **1.** *For the glosses on this page of O see the reduced facsimile following preface of this book.* — **1** pelliaco *V.* — **2** neptu*n*ni *G.* — **3** fasidicos *O* fascidicos (al' phasidos) *G* ‖ ceticos (al' tetidicos) *O* oeticos *G* Aeeteos *Haupt* (*from* Αἰητέιους) Aetaeos ω Aeetios *Schwabe.* — **4** iuuenes (*corrected from* iuuines) *O* ‖ pupis *O* puppis *G.* — **5** cholchis *O.* — **6** ualda (*but cancelled by dots below, and* uada *written in above* salsa) *O.* — **7** uerrentes (*corrected from* uerentes) abiegnis (*corrected from* abregnis) *G.* — **9** uolitā́tē (*corrected from apparently* uolū́tātē) *O* ‖ currum (*written over erasure*) *G.* — **10** testa *G.* — **11** posteam (*with marginal gloss* proram) *O* primam *G* ‖ aphitrite *O* (*some mark over the final letter was erased before the interlineal gloss was inserted*) *O* amphitritem *G* rudi . . . primam *Statius* proram . . . Amphitrite *Ellis Baehrens.* — **12** pro*ci*dit *O* proscidit (*corrected from* procidit) *G.* — **13** totaq*ue* *V.* — **14** feri *V* freti *Schrader* ‖ canenti ω fero candentis gurgite *Baehrens.* — **15** equore mo*n*stru*m* (al' monstro*rum*) *O* ‖ ammirante*s* *O.* — **16** si qua *omitted in* *O* atq*ue* *G* ‖ uidere *O* uidere *G* illa atque (*or* illaque) haud alia ω illac atque alia *Statius* illa si qua alia *Lachmann* illac hautque alia *Schwabe* illa, nulla alia *Schmidt* illac (quaque alia?) *Munro* (illa *Postgate*) illa felici *Riese* atque illa uidere beata *Baehrens* atque illic alma *L. Mueller.* — **17** oculi ω. — **19** cu*m* *O.* — **20** cu*m* *O* cum *G* ‖ himeneos *O.* — **21** cu*m* *O* cum *G* ‖ sanxit ω. — **22** seculo*rum* *O* seculoru*m* *G.* — **23** mat*er* *O* mater (al' matre) *G* marte *Baehrens* (*Cf. scholiast. Veron. on Verg. Aen. V. 80* Catullus ' saluete deum genus o bona matrum progenies saluete iter . . .'). — **23**[b] *omitted in V.* *The fragment from the scholiast is completed with* saluete precanti *Haupt* saluete bonarum *Peerlkamp* mihi terrenarum *Maehly* placidique fauete *L. Mueller.* *Others retain the MS. reading* o bona mater! *without supplement, understanding* mater *to refer either to the earth or to the Argo; cf. Apoll. Rh. IV. 1370.* — **24** uos] *post Bergk.* — **25** tedis *O* thetis *G.* — **26** thesalie *O* thessalie (*corrected from* te salie) *G.* — **28** nectine (al' neptine *G*) *V* Neptunine ω Nereine *Haupt.* — **29** thetis *V.* — **30** occeanusq*ue* *V.* — **31** queis *L. Mueller* ‖ optato *V* ‖ finite *O* optato finitae *Ellis.* — **32** adlenire *V.* — **33** Thesalia *O* Tessalia (*corrected from* Tesalia) *G* ‖ opplḗtur *O* ‖ cetu *O* coetu (*corrected from* cetu) *G.* — **35** siros *O* syros *G* Scyros ω Ciero*s* *Meineke* ‖ linqu*n*t ptiotica *O* linquu*n*t (*corrected from* linqunt) pthyotica *G.* — **36** grauinonisq*ue* *O* graiunonisque *G* Crannonisque *Victorius* ‖ ac nicenis alacr*i*ssea (alacrisea *G*) *V.* — **37** farsalia*m* *O* farsaliam *G* Pharsalum *Pontanus.* — **38–42** *variously transposed by various critics.* — **40** perno *O.* — **42** rubigo *V.* — **43** adsedes *O* ad sedes *G.* — **47** pluuinar *O.* — **48** aedibus *Guarinus.* — **49** conchili *O* conchili *G.* — **50** hec *V* (*but in*

G with mark below to make e *into* oe). — **52** fluentinoso (*with last four letters cancelled by dots, and* sono *following immediately*) *G* e fluctisono *Maehly* ‖ dia *O* dya *G*. — **53** tesea *O*. — **54** indomites *O* ‖ adriana *V*. — **55** seseq*ue* sui tui se credit *V corrected by Voss*. — **56** tum *G* ‖ sompno *O*. — **60** acta *Heinsius* (*cf. v. 168*). — **61** saxa *O* saxea (*corrected from* saxa) *G* ‖ heue *V* eu(h)oe ω eheu *Bergk*. — **62** con (*by confusion of sign*) *O* et (*with space following, and perhaps over erasure*) *G*. — **64** con*tenta O* ‖ nudatum *Schwabe* niueum per *Maehly*. — **65** strophyo *G* ‖ luctantes *Muretus*. — **66** delapse corpor*e O* delapso corpore *G*. — **68** sineq*ue* tam*en* (tum *G*) mitre neq*ue* tam*en* (tum *G*) *V* sed neque ω set neque *Lachmann*. — **69** te *omitted in O*. — **71** ha *O*. — **72** ericina *V* ‖ impectore *O*. — **73** feroxq*ue et V* ferox quo (ex) tempore ω ferox qua (quom *Ritschl*) robore *Froehlich* ferox qua pectore *Peiper*. — **75** inuisi *Heinsius* ‖ cortinia *V* ‖ tempta *O* tempta *G*. — **77** cu*m* androgeane penas *O* cum androgeanee penas *G*. — **79** minothaur*o O*. — **80** augusta ω ‖ *in*cenia *O* inoenia (*with dot under* o) *G*. — **82** p*r*ohicer*e O* proiicere *G*. — **83** nec funere *Statius* sine funere *Lange*. — **86** *con*pexi*t O*. — **89** europe *V* ‖ pergignu*nt O* pergignunt *G* praecingunt *Baehrens* ‖ mirtos *O* mirtus *G*. — **93** unis *O* imis (*corrected from* unis) *G*. — **94** corda furore *Ramler*. — **96** q*uod* neq*ue* regis cholcos q*uae*que *O* quique regis colchos queq*ue* ydaliu*m G*. — **100** quam tum *Faernus* quantum ω ‖ fuluore *Ritschl*. — **102** oppeteret *G*. — **104** succepit *Statius* succendit tura *Froehlich*. — **105** uult *O*. — **106** cornigera*m V* ‖ fund*anti O* sudanti (*corrected from* fundanti) *G* nutanti uortice ω. — **107** indomitum turben *Spengel* (*cf. Serv. on Verg. Aen. VII. 378* Catullus ' hoc turben ' dicit ut ' hoc carmen, fulmen.' *But others emend Servius by reading* Tibullus *for* Catullus, *citing Tib. I. 5. 3 on authority of Charisius*) indomitus turben *Bergk*. — **108** emit *O* ‖ radicibus extirpata ω. — **109** omnia (al' obuia) *G* lateque et cominus ω late quaecumuis *Voss* late qua est impetus *Lachmann* lateque ruineis *Schwabe Birt Riese* lateque et funditus *Schwabe* lateque furit uis *Madvig* lateque tumultibus *Bergk* frangit *Riese*. — **110** saeuum] taurum ω. — **111** naius *O* uacuis *Baehrens*. — **113** ereabu*n*da *O*. — **114** laberinthis *O* laberintheis *G*. — **116** cu*m V* a ω ‖ degressus *Baehrens*. — **119** leta *V* in gnata fieret deperdita, laeta ω (tabet *Baehrens*) laetabatur *Lachmann* luctabatur *Rossbach* lamentata est *Conington* lamentatur *Buecheler*. — **120** hiis *O* ‖ portaret *O* po*r*taret *G* praeoptarit *Statius*. — **121** aut necta ratis *O* aut ut uecta (*corrected from* necta) ratis *G* rati *Passeratius*. — **122** uenerit *omitted in V, added by Lachmann* fugerit *Froehlich* ‖ deuincta *O* deuincta *G* aut ut eam dulci *or* tristi *or* placito (molli *Baehrens*) deuinctam ω. — **123** immemori (al' nemori) *G*. — **125** epectore *G*. — **126** actu*m* praeruptes *O* ‖ tristes *V* ‖ *con*fend*e*re

O. — **127** in *omitted in V* ‖ pra*e*tenderet *O* pretenderet *G* pertenderet *Baehrens*. — **128** salus *O.* — **130** estremis *O* ‖ dixisse mestam (*with marks to indicate that the order should be inverted*) *G.* — **132** patris *O* ‖ au*e*rtam *O* auectam (*corrected from* auertam) *G* ‖ ab (*corrected from* ad) *G* ‖ oris *ω.* — **133** in *omitted in O.* — **134** discenden*s G* ‖ negleto *O.* — **135** ha *O.* — **136** nulla ueres *O* nullaue res *G* ‖ crudeles ... *me*ntes *O* crudelis ... mentis (*corrected from* crudeles ... mentes) *G.* — **138** mi-res*cere O* mitescere *G* mostri uellet mitescere *Scaliger.* — **139** blanda *O* nobis *G* non haec *Statius.* — **140** nec ha*e*c *O* nec hec *G Critics since the Italians have varied between* hoc *and* haec, *and between* miserae, miseram, *and* misera. — **141** himeneos *O.* — **142** desser*p*un*t O* disser-pun*t G.* — **143** tu*m O* tum *G* nunc *Guarinus* iam iam *ω.* — **144** uiris *Passeratius* ‖ sermones (*corrected from* sermonee) *O* ‖ fid*e*lis *O.* — **145** adipisci (*with the letters* di *cancelled by dots, and pro* adipisci *inserted above*) *O* pregestit (*corrected from* pergestit ?) apisci (*corrected from* adipisci) *G.* — **148** metu*e*re *O* metuere *G perhaps rightly* meminere *Czwa-lina.* — **149** lecti *O.* — **152** alitib*u*sque (*corrected from* altib*u*sque) *G.* — **153** post (*by mistake of sign*) ea *O* ‖ intacta *O i*n tacta *G.* — **156** sir-tix *O* ‖ scilla *O* silla *G* ‖ caribdis *V.* — **157** taliaq*u*e redis *O.* — **159** per-emtis *O.* — **160** inr̄as (= i*n* nos*t*ras) *O.* — **162** limphis *O.* — **163** *following v.* 160 *in O* ‖ cubile (*corrected from* cubille) *O.* — **164** siqu*i*d *O* sed quid (*corrected from* si quid) *G* ‖ nec quicqu*am conque*rar aures *O* nec quicqu*am conque*rar auris (*corrected from* aures) *G.* — **165** extenuata *G* ‖ maloq*u*e *O* ‖ aucte (al' to) *G.* — **168** acta *Heinsius* (*as in v.* 60). — **170** fers *et* iam *O.* — **174** increta *O* incretam *G.* — **175** h*a*ec *O.* — **176** co*n*silium requisiss*et O* consiliu*m no*st*r*is requisisset (*with* r *written above first* s) *G.* — **177** nunc *Spengel* iam *Peiper.* — **178** idoneos ne *O* ydoneos (al' Idmoneos) ne *G* Idaeosne *Guarinus* Idomeneosne *De Allio* Idomeneusne *Lachmann* (*cf. Hom. Il. XIII. 424*) Idomeneine *Buecheler* ‖ agurgite *V.* — **179** discedens *ω* ‖ pontu*m G* patriam *Avantius* ‖ ubi *omitted by ω.* — **180** impatris *O* an patris (*corrected from* in patris) *G* ac patris *Sillig* ‖ q*u*em (*with unusual ligature*) *O* quem (*with* que *over eras-ure*) *G.* — **182** co*n*soles me man' *O.* — **183** qui ne *O* qui ue *G* ‖ uentos *G.* — **184** nullo (litus solum) insula *Voss* litus solum, nullo insula *Scaliger* nullo litus, nullo insula *Froehlich.* — **189** affesso *O.* — **190** iusta *O* ‖ muleta*m O* mulctam *G.* — **192** mulcta*n*tes *O* mulctantes *G* ‖ pena *V.* — **193** eumenydes *G.* — **194** post*p*ortat (*by mistake of sign*) *O.* — **195** *In O there is a period before* meas, *in G, an erasure.* — **196** ue misera (mis*e*ra *G*) *V* ‖ ex imis *Vulpius.* — **198** u*e*re *O* uere *G.* — **200** qual*i*s sola *O* qualis sola *G* ‖ reliq*ui*d *O.* — **201** funestet (*corrected from* fimestet) *G.* — **204** inuito *V.* — **205** quō t*u*nc *O* quō tu*n*c *G* quo

nutu *Fea* quo modo tunc *or* quo tunc et ω quo motu *Heyse* quo tonuit *Riese*.
— **206** sydera *G*. — **207** m*e*nte *O* mente *G*. — **208** cunta *G*. — **210** lu-
cida *Wakefield*. — **211** ereptu*m* V Erechtheum *Voss* || uisere (*corrected
from* uiscere) *G*. — **212** classicu*m* (classi cu*m* *G*) moenico *V* castae cum
moenia ω. — **213** cu*m* crederet *V* || egen*s* *O* egens *G*. — **215** gnati *O* ||
longa *V* longe *Hoeufftius*. — **216** *placed by Baehrens after v.* **217** || quem]
q*u*onia*m* *O* (*by mistake of sign*). — **217** reddite (*corrected from* rediite)
G || extremae *Avantius*. — **219** que*m* (al' cui) *G*. — **221** lectanti *O*. —
224 infulso *O* || fedan*s* *O* fedans *G*. — **227** dicet *V* decet *Lachmann*
obscura dicet *or* decet ω obscura deceat *or* doceat *Statius* || hybera *G*. —
228 ithomi *O* ythomi *G*. — **229** ac] has *V* || secles *O* || freti *V* Erech-
thei *Voss*. — **231** tum *O* tu *G*. — **232** oblis**eret (*apparently, then corrected roughly to* oblit**eret *and* al' obliteret *inserted above*) *G*. — **233** simul h*ae*c *O* *Sillig* simul hec *G*. — **234** antennene ne *O* antenne ne (*but
last* ne *crossed out*) *G*. — **235** sustolant *O* substollant (*corrected from*
substolant) *G*. — **237** aetas *V* sors ω fors *Avantius* freta . . . sistent
Froehlich || sistent (*corrected from* sistens) *G*. — **239** seu *O* ceu (*corrected
from* seu) *G*. — **240** aereu*m* *O*. — **242** anxia (*perhaps corrected from*
ansia) *G*. — **243** infecti ω infausti *Heyse* || lintea s (*cancelled by dots*) ueli
G. — **244** e (*corrected from* et) *G*. — **245** inmiti (*corrected from* in-
mitti) *G* || fcō (= facto) *O*. — **246** paternae ω. — **247** Marte *Marcilius*
|| minoida *V*. — **249** que ta*m*en *O* que (*corrected from* quem) tamen
aspectans (*corrected from* prospectans) *G* || credente*m* *O*. — **251** at pat*e*r
O at pater *G* || iachus *V*. — **252** cum] tum *O* || thyaso (*corrected from*
thiiaso) *G* || sathiroru*m* *O* || nisi genis *O* nisigenis *G*. — **253** *inserted by
Koeler before v.* **252**; *Bergk conjectured a lacuna of one verse after v.* **253**
|| te] et *O* te (*corrected from* et) *G* || querenus *G* || adriana *V*. — **254** qui
V quae *Bergk* quam *Schwabe* quicum *Baehrens* || linphata *O*. — **255** euche
bachantes euche *O, in G with* euche *corrected to* euohe. — **256** horum ω
|| thirsos *O* tirsos *G*. — **257** ediuolso *V*. — **259** canis *O* || celabant
Broukhusius. — **260** prophani *O*. — **261** alii ω aliei *Lachmann* || pro
cer*i*s timpana *O*. — **262** tenais *O* || tinnitus (*corrected from* tintinitus) *G*.
— **263** multi *V* multis *Pisanus* multaque *Guarinus* multi (multae *Scal-
iger*) raucisonis . . . bombis ω || effleban*t* *O* efflebant *G*. — **267** thesala *O*
thessala (*corrected from* thesalla) *G*. — **268** cepit *O* coepit (*corrected
from* cepit) *G*. — **269** hec *O* heic *Baehrens* || quali *Voss*. — **270** cephi-
rus *O* || procliuit (*with dot under* t *and* s *above*) *O* procliuis *Baehrens*
procuruas *Schwabe*. — **271** sublimia *V* sub lumina ω. — **273** que *omitted
in G* leuiter resonant ω lenique sonant *Froehlich*. — **275** nascente ab
Baehrens || refulgen*s* *V*. — **276** ta*m*en *O* tamen (al' tibi) *G* ibi *Haupt* ||
uestibulo *or* uestibulis *Schrader* festini *Baehrens* || linqu*e*ntis *V*. — **277** at

V. — **278** abitum (*corrected from* habitum) *G* ‖ peley *O* pelei *G.* —
279 Chyron *G.* — **280** q*uo*dcumqu*e* *O* quodcumqu*e* *G* quoscumque
Aldus quotcumque ω ‖ campis *V* ‖ quot ω ‖ thesalia *O* thesala *G* ‖ mag*n*is
O magnis (*final letters over erasure*) *G.* — **282** aurea *O* ‖ p*er*it *O* parit
(*middle letters over erasure*) *G* ‖ secunda *O.* — **283** coru*l*is *O* curulis
(*corrected from* corulis) (al' corollis) *G* ‖ interstinctis *Heinsius.* —
284 qu*o*d *O* quot *G.* — **285** penies (al' os *G*) *V* ‖ adest ut *V.* —
287 minosi*m* *O* minosim *G* Naiasin *Haupt* Haemonisin *Heinsius* Mne-
monisin *Koeler* Meliasin *Madvig* ‖ Doris] claris ω doctis *Statius* crebris
Lachmann duris *Madvig* diuis (*or* diuis linquens) *Schwabe* solis *Schulze*
solitis *Magnus* uariis *Riese* caris *Schmidt.* — **288** non accuos *O* non acuos
(al' nonacrias) *G* uacuus *Guarinus* ‖ actas *Heinsius.* — **289** fages *O.* —
290 mutanti *O* nutanti (*corrected from* mutanti) *G* ‖ soro*rum* *O* sororum
G. — **291** flamanti *G* ‖ phetontis *V.* — **292** *con*testa *O* contesta *G.* —
293 uellatu*m* *O* uelatu*m* (*corrected from* uellatu*m*) *G* uallatum *Baehrens.*
— **295** pena *O* pene (*corrected from* pena) *G.* — **296** qua *V* ‖ silici]
Scythicis *Heinsius* Scythica *Riese* in Scythia *Schwabe* triplici *Baehrens* ‖
resittu*s* *O* ‖ cathe*n*a *O* chatena *G.* — **298** diui *V* ‖ gnatisqu*e* (al' gratis
G) *V.* — **299** aduenit caelo, te *Lachmann* ‖ phebe *V.* — **300** ydri *V*
Hydri ω. — **301** palea *O.* — **303** niueos ω. — **306** teperu*n*t *O* c*o*eperunt
(*corrected from* ce-) *G* ‖ eclere *O.* — **307** his (al' hic) *G* ‖ qu*es*tus *O*
questus *G.* — **308** tuos *V* talos ω ‖ intin*er*at *O.* — **309** roseo uinee *O*
roseo niuee *G* roseae niueo *Guarinus* ambrosio niueae *Vulpius* annoso
Schulze atro sed *Birt* ‖ uicte (*corrected from* uitte) *G.* — **311** collum *O*
colu*m* (*corrected from* collu*m*) *G* ‖ amictam *Guarinus.* — **312** filia *O.* —
315 ep*us* *O* ‖ dens (*last letters over erasure*) *G.* — **319** custodiebant *G.*
— **320** hae ω ‖ pellentes *V* uellentes *Fruterius* pectentes *Statius* polientes
Heinsius. — **322** arguit *Lachmann.* — **323** *Paragraph mark in G, and
marginal title* Epythalamiu*m* thetidis *et* pelei. *Many critics have attempted
to equalize the number of verses in the following strophes.* — **324** tutu*m*
opus (al' tu tame*n* opis *G*) carissime (carissime *G*) *V* clarissime natu
Dousa (Peleu *Froehlich*) carissime fato *Schwabe.* — **326** oraculum *G* ‖
uosqu*e* fac*t*a *O* uos quos *Schwabe.* — **328** aptata *O* optata (*corrected from*
aptata) *G.* — **329** hesp*er*eus *O* ‖ c*o*nsid*er*e *O* cu*m* sydere *G.* —
330 *omitted in O* ‖ flexo animo me*n*tis *G* ‖ amore*m* *G* te flexanimo mentis
perfundat amore *Lachmann.* — **331** sonos *V.* — **332** uenia *O* leuia *G.* —
334–337 *omitted in many minor MSS.* — **334** umq*uam* tales *O* unq*uam*
tales *G* ‖ conexit *Lachmann* conspexit *Lenz.* — **335** federe *O* federe *G.*
— **336** thetidi (*corrected from* tetidi) *O.* — **341** peruertet *O* preuertit *G.*
— **344** frigii *O* phrigii *G* ‖ teucto *O* teucro (*but* cr *over erasure*) *G* ‖
manebunt *O* ‖ teuen *O* tenen *G* campi *or* riui ω cliuei *Haupt* mari *or*

Phrygiae . . . terrae *Statius.* — **345** menia *V.* — **347** sub tegmina (*corrected from* tegmine) *G.* — **350** inciuu*m* (*corrected from* inciuos) *O* inciuium *G* in cinerem ω ‖ canos *V* ‖ soleu*n*t *O* ‖ *crimen O* crines *G* incuruo incanos uertice *Statius* incultum cano . . . crinem *Baehrens* incuruo canos . . . crines *Ellis.* — **353–356** *placed by Peiper after v.* **347.** — **353** dempsas *O* ‖ praecerne*n*s *O* praecernens (*corrected from* praeterriens) *G* praecerpens *Statius* prosternens ω ‖ messor *O* cultor *G.* — **355** tronigenu*m O* troiu genu*m* (*corrected from* tronigenu*m ?*) *G* ‖ prosterne*n*s (*corrected from* prosternet) *G* ‖ ferru*m O.* — **358** elesponto *O* elesponto *G.* — **359** cessis *O.* — **360** lumina (al' flumine) *G* ‖ cecle *O.* — **363** terrae ω ‖ ex celso *Martini-Laguna.* — **364** perculse *O* perculse *G.* — **366** simul hanc *V* ‖ fons *O.* — **368** polixenia *O* polisenia *G* ‖ madescen*t O* madescent *G* mutescent *Rossbach* ‖ cecle *O.* — **369** subecubens (*with dot under first* b) *G.* — **370** proiiciet *G* ‖ sumisso *O* su*m*misso *G.* — **372** animi (*with* n *over erasure*) *G.* — **373** fed*e*re *O* federe *G.* — **377** esterno *O* externo *G.* — **378** *expunged by* ω. — **379–381** *omitted in O.* — **381** ducite fusi *G.* — **382** peley *O.* — **383** c*e*rnere *O* cecinere *G* cecinere e *Baehrens.* — **385** *n*ereus sese *V* heroum et *Sigicellus* ‖ cetu *O* coetu (*corrected from* cetu) *G.* — **386** *After this verse V inserts* languidio*r* (languidior *G*) tenera cui pedens sicula beta (67. 21; *apparently just five pages removed in the archetype*). — **387** residens *Baehrens* renidens *Schwabe.* — **388** du*m O* dum *G* ‖ ueniss*et O* uenisset *G* ‖ facra *O* ‖ die*bus* (*corrected from* duobus) *O.* — **389** t*e*rra*m O* Creta *Wakefield* ‖ tauros] currus *V.* — **390** sumo *O.* — **391** thiadas *O* thyadas *G* ‖ euantis (*with* o *over* e) *G* ‖ esit *O.* — **392, 393** *Some critics expunge these verses as spurious. Others believe a lacuna to exist after v.* **391,** *in which the coming of Apollo to his Delphic shrine was mentioned.* — **393** acciperet *O* acciperet *G* ‖ lacti *O* laeti diuum] Latonigenam *Heinsius* diuum] Phoebum *Schmidt.* — **394** mauros *G.* — **395** ram*n*usia *O* ranusia *G* Amarunsia *Baehrens.* — **397** scelus tellus scel*e*re *O* ‖ nephando *O.* — **400** natos *G.* — **401** patrauit *Baehrens.* — **402** uti nuptae *Maehly* ut innupto *Schwabe* ut hinc nuptae . . . nouellae *Baehrens* ‖ potiretu*r V.* — **404** penates ω. — **406** m*e*nte adu*e*rtere *O.* — **407** cetus *O* coetus (*corrected from* cetus) *G.*

65. *Interval of one verse in V, filled in G with title* Ad Ortalem. — **1** defectu *O* confectu*m G.* — **2** sed uacat *V.* — **3** dulcissimus hauu*m* (ha*rum G) V* dulcis simul harum *Baehrens* ‖ fret*us O.* — **4** icta *Heinsius.* — **5** loethi *O* lethei *G* lethaeo in *Parthenius* ‖ factis (*cf.* **66. 22**) *O.* — **7** tidia retheo *O* lydia (al' troya) rhetheo *G* ‖ subter (*corrected from* sup-ter) *G.* — **8** obruit *Statius* obtegit *Morsbach.* — **9** *omitted in V without interval* alloquar a*u*diero numquam tua facta (*or* uerba) loquentem ω

Statius, however, and many others since his day judge the verse spurious.
Others think vv. **10–14** *also spurious, or at least, misplaced here.   Weise*
would insert vv. **9–14** *after* **101**. **6**, *while others believe them* (*either with*
or without certain verses of c. **68**) *to be a fragment of a separate poem on*
the death of the poet's brother.—**11** aut *V.*—**12** carmine *V* ‖ tegam *V*
canam *or* legam ω.—**14** bauilla *O* bauilas (*corrected from* bauila) *G* ‖
assumpta *O* assumpti (*corrected from* asumpti) *G* ‖ facta gemes ithilei *O*
ythilei *G.*—**16** Battiadae] actiade *O* acciade *G.*—**18** efluxisse *O* effluxisse (*corrected from* effuxisse *and that from* efuxisse) *G.*—**20** proccurit
(*with first* c *cancelled by dot below*) *O.*—**21** locataum (*with second* a *cancelled by dot below*) *O.*—**23** illic prono preces *O.*

66. *No interval and no paragraph mark in V.*—**1** despexit *V.*—
2 ha*b*itus *O* habitus *G.*—**3** obsculet*ur O.*—**4** ceter*i*s *O* ‖ sydera *G.*—
5 s*u*blamina *O* sublimia *G* ‖ religans *V.*—**6** guioclero *V* gyro *or* cliuo *or*
curru ω ‖ aetherio *Meineke.*—**7** celesti numine (numine *G*) *V* in lumine
Voss limine *Heinsius* limite *Doering* culmine *Maehly.*—**8** ebore niceo *V* ‖
*u*ertite cesar*i*e *O.*—**9** multis *V* cunctis *Haupt* ‖ dear*um O* dearum *G.*—
11 quare extempestate *V* ‖ mactus *Anna Fabri* abductus *Froehlich* auec-
tus *Peiper* functus *Riese* ‖ himeneo *O.*—**12** uast*um O* uastum *G* ‖ ierat
assirios *V.*—**13** nocturne (*corrected from* noctume) *G.*—**14** exiuius *O.*
—**16** salsis *Heyse.*—**17** uberum *O* ‖ lumi*n*a *O* lumina *G.*—**18** diu *V* ‖
geniu*n*t iuueri*n*t *O* iuuerint *G.*—**20** pr*a*elia *O* proelia (*corrected from*
prelia) *G.*—**21** et *O* et (al' at) *G* an ω ‖ tu u*e*ro *O.*—**22** sctis (= s*a*nctis; *cf. v.* **37**) *O* fratris *G* ‖ dissidium *G.*—**23** cu*m O* cum *G* quam
Bentley tum *Lachmann* ut *Baehrens.*—**24** ut ibi nu*n*c (al' t*u*nc) *G* ‖
solicitet *V.*—**25** e rectis *Voss* e trepidis *Maehly* ‖ te *omitted in V added*
by Avantius.—**26** magnanima *V.*—**27** q*u*am *V* ‖ adeptos *O* adeptus
G adepta's *Lachmann.*—**28** fortius *Muretus* ‖ aut sit *V.*—**29** sed cu*m*
O.—**31** tantum *Schrader.*—**32** adesse *G.*—**33** procunctis *O* pro
cuntis *G* me *Colotius and Perreius.*—**34** taurino *omitted in O.*—**35** s*e*d
O sed (al' si) *G* sei *Schwabe* ‖ reddit*um* te tulis*et O* te tulisset *G* ‖ aut *V.*
—**36** asyam *G* ‖ egipti *O.*—**37** sctis (= s*a*nctis; *cf. v.* **22**) *O* factis *G*
‖ coelesti (*corrected from* celesti) *G* ‖ cetu *O* coetu (*corrected from* cetu)
G. —**40** capud *O.*—**41** ferat*que O* ‖ adiuraret *V.*—**42** quis *Statius.*
—**43** q*u*ae maxi*m*a *O* que*m* maxima *G* maximum *Guarinus.*—**44** phitie
O phytie *G* Thiae *Voss* ‖ super uehit*ur O* (*between the two words* l *or* t
was written but at once cancelled).—**45** tu*m O* cum (*corrected from* tum)
G ‖ pr*o*pere *O* propere *G* peperere *or* rupere ω pepulere *Statius* fodere
Bergk ‖ cu*m*que *O* atq*ue G.*—**48** celerum *O* celitum *G* Chalybon *Politi-*
anus Lachmann's first edition.—**49** uenas (*but* ue *over erasure*) *G.*—

50 ferris fingere *O* ferris fringere *G* ferri infringere *Santenius* ferri uincere *Markland* ferri stringere *Heyse.* — **51** facta *O.* — **52** memnonis *O* menonis ethiiopis *G.* — **54** asineos (arsinoes) *G* ‖ claridos ω Locridos *Bentley* Cypridos *Berkg* ‖ alis equos *V.* — **55** isque (al' q2 *G*) *V* ‖ ethereas *G* aerias *Riese* ‖ aduolat *G* abuolat *Ellis.* — **56** aduolat (al' collocat) *G.* — **57** cyphiritis *O* zyphiritis (*corrected from* cyphiritis) *G* ‖ legerat (al' legarat) *G.* — **58** gracia *O* gratia *G* grata *Calpurnius* Graia *Lachmann* Graiia *Baehrens* ‖ conopicis *O* canopieis *G* Canopieis *Avantius.* — **59** numen ibi *Ritschl* lumine ibi . . . in limite '*H. R.*' *and Peiper* arduei ibi *Haupt* siderei *Bergk* hic niueei *Baehrens* hic etenim *Froehlich* hic iuueni Ismario *Ellis* inde Venus uario *Postgate* ‖ numine celi *O* numine coeli (*corrected from* celi) *G.* — **60** exadrianeis *O* exadrianeis *G* ‖ aurea (*but* re *over erasure*) *G.* — **61** uos *O.* — **62** eximie *O* exuuie (*corrected from* eximie) *G.* — **63** uindulum afluctu *O* uiridulum (*corrected from* uindulum) a fluctu *G* umidulam *Ellis* luctu *Baehrens* ‖ decumme *O* decumme *G.* — **65** uirgis *O.* — **66** calixto iuxta licaonia *V* Calisto *Baehrens* Lycaonida ω Lycaoniam *Rossbach.* — **67** boothem (*corrected from* boothen) *G.* — **69** quicquam *O.* — **70** aut *V* ‖ theti *V* ‖ restituem *O* restituem *G* luce . . . restituor ω lux . . . restituit *Lachmann.* — **71** parce *V* ‖ ranūsia *O* ranusia *G.* — **72** ullo *O* nullo *G.* — **73** si me] sine *V* ‖ diserpent *O* diserpent *G* ‖ ṣydera *G* ‖ doctis *O* dextris *Bentley, and L. Mueller thinks* dictis = digitis. — **74** candita *G* ‖ qui uere (uere *G*) *V* uerei *Lachmann* ‖ euolue *V.* — **77** quondam] curis *L. Mueller* ‖ ominis expers *Auratus* Hymenis expers *Eschenburg* adspersa *Marcilius* expersa *Heinsius Others divide* omnibus expers *from the rest of the text by commas.* — **78** una] murrae *Voss* unguenti Surii *Passeratius.* — **79** quem *V* quum *De Allio* quas *or* quam ω queis *Statius* quo *Lachmann* quom *Haupt.* — **80** post *O* post *G* prius ω ‖ uno animus *O* uno animus *G* unanimeis *Baehrens.* — **81** retecta *V.* — **82, 83** onix *V.* — **85** amala leuis bibat dona *V* ‖ inita *G.* — **86** abindignatis *O* ab indigetis *G.* — **87** sic ω ‖ nostras *O* nostras *G.* — **89** sydera *G.* — **91** sanguinis *V* unguinis *Bentley* ‖ ne *Scaliger* ‖ uestris V siueris *Scaliger* siris *Lachmann* ‖ tuum *V.* — **92** effice *V.* — **93** sydera *G* ‖ iterent *O* iterent *G* ‖ utina *O* cur retinent? utinam ω (iterum *Markland* ut iam *Baehrens*) cur inter? *Marcilius* corruerint utinam! *Lachmann* (corruerent *Ellis*) corruerint, iterum ut *Hertzberg.* — **94** id rochoi *O* idrochoi *G* ‖ fulgoret *Baehrens.*

67. *No interval in V, but paragraph mark in G.* — **4** secles *O* ‖ senes *O* — **5** quamquam *O* ‖ maligno *G* nato . . . maligne *Froehlich* (natae *Baehrens*) seruire *Riese.* — **6** est *O* est *G* ‖ marite *V.* — **7** age de *O* age de *G* ‖ uobis *O* uobis *G.* — **8** uenerem *G.* — **9** pateam *Statius* ‖

traditam *O.* — **10** quaquam *O.* — **11** qdquam (*by omission of sign*) *O.* —
12 isti populo ianua quidque (quanta *Schwabe*) facit ω (quid faciat *Voss*)
isti populi naenia, Quinte, facit *Scaliger* istud populi fabula, Quinte, facit
Lachmann. est uox populi : ianua cuncta facit *Baehrens* est os populi
' ianua,' Quinte, ' facit ' *Ellis* istud populi uana querela facit *Heyse* (loquella *Schmidt*) uerum, is mos populi, ianua quippe facit *Postgate* (*following Munro in* quippe). — **17** quid *V.* — **18** uobis *O* uobis *G* nobis *Muretus* ‖ ue *O* ne *G.* — **20** non] namque ω non qui *Scaliger* ‖ attigerat ω. —
21 *omitted here in O, but inserted after* **64. 386.** — **22** ad] hanc *O* hanc
G. — **23** ipsius *Muretus* ille sui *Scaliger* illusi *Baehrens.* — **27** is *omitted
in V, added by Lachmann* et (ut *Bergk*) quaerendum unde unde *Statius*
ne quaerendum aliunde ω ‖ ile *Rossberg.* — **29** parentum *O.* — **30** sui]
sunt *O.* — **31** at qui *V* ‖ hoc dicit se *O* se dicit (*omitting* hoc) *G.* —
32 Cycnea supposita in specula *Zanchius* Cycneae supposita speculae
Voss (Chinaeae *Haupt*) Cycnea suppositum specula *De Allio.* — **33,
34** *judged spurious by some critics.* — **33** percurrit *O* percurrit *G* praecurrit *Avantius* ‖ melo *O* mello *G.* — **34** tuae *Scaliger.* — **35** posthumio
V ‖ amat *G.* — **37** dixit haec *O* ‖ iste *V.* — **38** deum lumine *O.* —
39 ascultare *O* ‖ haec *O* hec *G* heic *Schwabe.* — **42** sola *V* ‖ concillis *O*
conciliis *G* ancillis *Robortellus.* — **43** pete *O.* — **44** sperent *O* sperent
(*with dot below* n) *G and many critics have read* speret. — **45** addebant
O. — **46** ne] te *V.* — **47** qui *O* qui *G.*

68ᵃ. *Interval of one verse in V, filled in G with title* Ad Mallium. —
1 quo *O.* — **2** conspersum *Schrader* ‖ haec *O* ‖ epystolium *G.* — **3** nau-
fragium *V.* — **6** disertum *G.* — **8** ansia *O.* — **9** ducis ω. — **10** petit *G.*
— **11** commoda mali *O* commoda mali (*with* o *written above*) *G* Mani
Lachmann. — **12** seu *G* ‖ sospitis *Schrader.* — **16** *omitted here in O, but
inserted after* **68ᵇ. 49.** — **18** amaritionem *O* amariritiem (*with first* ri
underlined) *G.* — **20** o] ei *Baehrens.* — **21-24** *judged spurious by
Froehlich.* — **21** tu nia tu *O* ‖ fratri *O* (*apparently, as in v.* **91**; *otherwise in vv.* **20** *and* **92**). — **26** omnem *O.* — **27** catulle *V.* — **28** quiuis
Lachmann ‖ nota est ω. — **29** tepefacit *V* tepefecit *or* tepefactat ω tepefactet *Bergk* tepefaxit *Lachmann.* — **30** mali *V* Mani *Lachmann* mi,
Alli *Schoell.* — **31** ignoscens *O.* — **32** cum] tum *O.* — **34** hec *O.* —
36 ima *O.* — **37** noli *O.* — **38** ingenio *V.* — **39** petiti ω ‖ posta est (est
G) *V* facta ω parta *Schwabe* praesto *Froehlich* porcta *Ribbeck* prompta
Baehrens. — **40** differrem *O* differem *G.*

68ᵇ. *No interval in V. First distinguished from* **68ᵃ** *by Ramler.* —
41 quam (quam *G*) fallius ire (ire *G*) *V* qua *or* quam Manlius ω qua me
Allius *Scaliger.* — **42** inuenit *O* ‖ et *Schwabe* ‖ uiuerit *O* auxerit *Usener.* —

43 nec *V* nei *Baehrens* ‖ sedis *V.*—**45** porto *O.*—**46** carta *O* certa *G.*
—**47** *omitted in* V, *with no interval in* O, *with interval of one verse in*
G *and* deficit *in margin.*—**48** *judged spurious by Hand* ‖ notescamque
G.—**49** *After this verse is inserted in* V iocundum (-dum *G*) cometas
florida ū (ut *G*) ageret (= **68. 16**, *just one page removed in the archetype*).
—**50** ali *G* Alli *Scaliger* (*without knowledge of* O) deserto in Manli ω
Auli *Westphal.*—**51** nam *O* non *G.*—**52** in me quo *Doering* torruerit
ω in qua me torruerit uenere *Schrader.*—**54** limphaque incetheis maulia
termopolis *O* in oetheis (*corrected from* eetheis) maulia termophilis *G.*—
55 nummula *O* numula *G* pupula *Ellis.*—**56** cessare ne tristique (tristique *G*) *V* neque tristi *Muretus* ‖ ymbre *G.*—**59** ualde *O* ualde *G* colle
Santenius ‖ uoluptus (*with* p *cancelled by dots*) *O.*—**60** densi] sensim
Haupt.—**61** duce *V* ‖ uiatorum *O* ‖ basso *V* salso *Baehrens* ‖ leuamus
(*but with unusual ligature*) *O* leuamus *G.*—**63** haec *O* ‖ ueluti nigro ω.
—**64** leuius *O* leuius *G.*—**65** iam face *Dorvillius* ‖ implorate *V* implo-
rati *Heyse* imploratu *Lachmann.*—**66** allius (l' manllius) *O* manlius *G*
Manius *Lachmann.*—**67** classum *G* laxum *Scaliger* clussum *Schwabe.*—
68 dominam *O* dominam *G Munro Ellis Postgate.*—**69** ut clam *Schoell.*
—**73** amorem *O* amorem *G.*—**74** protesileam *O* prothesileam *G* ‖ laudomia *V* Laudamia *Usener* (*and in vv.* **80** *and* **105**).—**75** incepta *V*
inceptam *Turnebus* incepto *Froehlich.*—**77** rāmusia *O* ranusia *G.*—
79 deficeret *V.*—**80** laudomia uirgo (uiro *in margin G*) *V* Laudamia
Usener.—**81** nouit *V* noui *Avantius* nouei *Schwabe* ‖ collum (*with dot
under first* l) *G.*—**82** hyemps *O* hyēms *G.*—**84** abinnupto *O* absumpto
Baehrens.—**85** scibat *Lachmann* scirant *L. Mueller* quem scirant *Peiper*
‖ abisse *V* adesse *Santenius* obisse *Baehrens* non longe tempus abesse
Schrader.—**86** similles (*with dot under first* l) *G* ‖ adyliacos *O* ad yliacos
G.—**87** tum] cum *O.*—**88** ceperat *O* ceperat *G.*—**89** asiie *O.*—
91 que uetet id nostro *V* quaene etiam *Heinsius* quae, uae, etiam ω quae
(uae te) *Scaliger* quin etiam id *Huschke* quae uel sic *Bergk* quae uitae
nostrae *Ribbeck* qualiter id *Ellis* ‖ frater *O* (*apparently, as in v.* **21**; *cf.*
12. 7) frater *G.*—**92** ei *O* ‖ frater *O* frateter (*with first* te *underlined*)
G.—**93–96** *judged spurious by Froehlich.*—**93** iocundumque limine *O*
‖ adeptum *V.*—**97** que *V* ‖ sepulcrea (*perhaps corrected to* sepulcra) *G.*
—**98** cineris *V.*—**101** tuum *G* ‖ simul *omitted in* V, *added by* ω cuncta
Froehlich ‖ pupes *O.*—**102** Graia *L. Mueller.*—**103** nec *O* nei *Baehrens* ‖ pars *O* paris *G* ‖ mecha *V.*—**104** octia *O.*—**105** quod tibi tum
O quod tibi cum *G* ‖ laudomia *V* Laudamia *Usener.*—**108** abruptum
(*corrected from* arruptum) *G* ‖ depulerat *Heinsius.*—**109** fuerunt (*with
first* u *underlined*) *G* ‖ peneum *V* ‖ cilleneum *V.*—**110** sicari *O* siccari
G siccare *Schrader.*—**112** audet *V* audit *Palmer* gaudet *Weise* ‖ amphi-

*tri*oniadis *O* **a**mphytrioniadis *G.* — **113** stimphalia *O.* — **114** p*e*rtulit *O*
pertullit *G.* — **115** t*e*rreretur (*or perhaps only* tereretur) *O* treerretur
(*with first* re *underlined*) *G.* — **116** heb'r *O.* — **118** tuu*m* (tuum *G*)
domitu*m* *V* diuum domitum ω tunc indomitam *De Allio* (indomitum
Santenius) tum te indomitam *Riese* tamen indomitam *Heyse* durum domi-
tam *Lachmann* toruum (*Voss*) dominum (ω) *Baehrens* dominum domitum
Ellis, and many conjectures by other critics. — **119** tam] causa *G.* —
122 ceratas *Schrader.* — **124** scuscitata cano uolta*rium O* scusoita*t*a cano
uoltarium *G.* — **125** nec t*a*m*en O* ‖ gauisa (*with dot under final* a) *G.* —
128 quam*quam V.* — **129** tuo*rum V.* — **130** efflauo *O* eflauo *G.* —
131 paulum *Colocius* ‖ tum] tu *V.* — **135** t*a*m*e*n *et*si *O* tam*e*n *et* si *G* ‖
cote*m*pta *O* ‖ catullo (*corrected from* catulo *O*) *V.* — **139** cotidiana *O*
quotidiana *G* concoquit iram *Lachmann* continet iram *Santenius* condidit
iram *Pohlius* contudit iram *Hertzberg* concitat iram *Pleitner* concipit iram
Baehrens. — **140** fac*t*a *O* facta *G.* — **141** atqu*e V* atquei *Schwabe* at
quia *or* atqui ω ‖ compone*re O* componere *G* ‖ equ*m O No interval
after v.* **141** *in V; Marcilius first conjectured a lacuna here.* — **142** tre-
mulist illa *Lachmann.* — **143** tandem *Baehrens* non etenim *Froehlich* ‖
deastra *O* de astra *G* dexstra *Schwabe* decstra *Ellis* claustris . . . paternis
Schoell. — **144** flagrante*m* assirio *O* flagrantem *G.* — **145** nigra ω muta
Heyse rara *Haupt.* — **147** hiis *O* his *G* ‖ unus ω. — **148** dies *V* ‖ can-
diore *O* notat candidiore, dies *Baehrens.* — **149** ha*e*c *O* ‖ quo *Muretus.*
— **150** aliis *V* Alli *Scaliger* Manli ω. — **151** rubigine *O* rubigine *G.* —
155 satis *V* seitis *Baehrens* ‖ uite *V.* — **156** nos *omitted in V, added by*
ω ipsi in qua *Pantagathus* (ipsa ω ipse *Scaliger*). — **157, 158** *judged
spurious by Doering and doubtful by Sillig; inserted elsewhere by some
others.* — **157** nobis te trandedit *Scaliger* (transdedit *or* tradidit *others*)
nobis dominam *or* teneram *or* caram *others* ‖ aufert] auctor ω Oufens *Scaliger* Anser *Heyse* Afer *Munro* auspex *Lipsius* a quo (**158**) Primo sunt
nobis ω. — **158** primo mi *Haupt* ‖ bono *V* omnia nostra bona *Schoell.* —
160 m*i*chi dulce es*t O* michi dulce est *G.*

69. *Interval of one verse in V, filled in G with title* In Rufum. —
2 Ruffe *V.* — **3** nos illa mare *V* non si illam rarae *Avantius* (Coae
Baehrens carae *Ellis*). — **5** q*u*e *O* qua (*corrected from* que) *G.* — **6** uale
O. — **8** cui cu*m* (cum *G*) *V.* — **10** cum *Froehlich* ‖ frigiu*n*t *O.*

70. *No interval in V.* — **1** male *O.*

71. *No interval in V.* — **1** siqua uiro bono sacratoru*m* (sacro*rum
G*) *V* si qua *Munro* iure bono *Palladius* Virro *Parthenius* sacratorum
Baehrens si quoi iure Bonae sacratorum *Froehlich*•‖ hyrcus *G.* — **2** siqu*am*

O siqua*m G* si qua *Munro* ‖ podraga secum *G* secu*n*t *O.*— **3** nostr*um G* iste putus qui nostrum *Schoell.*— **4** atei *Heyse* apte *Schoell* certe *Peiper* mirifico est fato *Hermannus* (astu *Muretus*).— **6** podraga *G*.

72. *Interval of one verse in V, filled in G with title* Ad lesbiam. — **2** nec prime *O* nec per me *G.*— **6** multo ita me nec uilior *V.*— **7** q*uam V* quod ω quia *Statius.* — *To c.* **72** *Guarinus appended c.* **85**, *Statius, both c.* **75** *and c.* **85**.

73. *No interval in V.*— **1** quisq*uam V.*— **4** immo (imo *G*) *etiam* (ecia*m G*) tedet obestqu*e* magisqu*e* mag*is* (magis *G*) *V* prodest *prefixed to v.* **4** *by Avantius,* iuuerit, *by Baehrens,* iam iuuat *by Munro* ‖ taedet *omitted in V after first* taedet, *restored by Avantius.* — **5** ut] uae ω ‖ m*ic*hiqu*e O* michi qu*e G.* — **6** habet *G*.

74. *No interval in V.*— **1** gellius (*corrected from* gelius) *O* lelius *G* ‖ flere *V.*— **3** h*ae*c *O* ‖ p*er*despuit *V* perdepsuit *Scaliger.* — **4** reddit *O* ‖ harpocrathem *G*.

75. *No interval in V. Scaliger (reading, with some interpolated MSS.,* nunc *for* huc) *first appended c.* **75** *to c.* **87**. *Lachmann followed him, but, believing two pages had become transposed in the archetype, also transferred c.* **76** *to a position after the compound c.* **87–75.**— **1** diducta *Lachmann.*— **3** uelleque tot t*i*bi (tibi *G*) *V*.

76. *No interval in V.*— **1** sique *O.*— **3** federe (federe *G*) nullo *V.* — **5** manentu*m* in *O* manenti in *G* manent cum *Baehrens* manent iam in *Munro.*— **6** h*ae*c *O* ‖ auicere *O.*— **8** sint *O.*— **9** ingrata (*final* a *over erasure*) *G.* — **10** tu *omitted in V, restored by Schoell* iam te cur o*r* te iam cur ω cur te iam iam *Baehrens* cur te, cur iam *Schmidt.*— **11** qui tui *V* ‖ affirmas ω tu animum offirmas *Statius* ‖ itaque *Scaliger* ‖ instincteque *O* instinctoque *G* istinc teque *Heinsius* tete *Baehrens* te ipse *Ellis.*— **12** des *V.*— **14** h*ae*c *O* ‖ q*uam* lubet *V* ‖ officias *O.*— **15** hoc] h*ae*c *O* hec *G.* — **16** h*ae*c *O* hec *G* ‖ sine id *O.*— **17** miseri *O.*— **18** extremo *V Schmidt* ‖ ips*am* (ipsam *G*) morte *V* ipsa *or* ipsa in ω.— **21** seu *V* hei *Lachmann* heu *or* quae ω haec *Statius* sei *Ellis* ‖ torpor] cor*pore O* corpore *G.*— **23** me ut me *V* ut me *or* me ut ω. — **26** dei *V* ‖ ṃ (*cf.* **14**. **10** *n.*) h*ae*c p*ro*prietate *O* michi hoc proprietate *G*.

77. *Interval of one verse in V, filled in G with title* Ad Rufum. — **1** Ruffe *V* ‖ amico *G.*— **3** subrepti mei *O* subrecti mei *G.*— **4** si *V* mi *or* sic ω ei *Lachmann.* — **5** heripuisti *G* ‖ heu *O* he heu *G* heu *or* heu heu ω eheu *Baehrens.*— **6** heu *O* he heu *G* heu heu ω eheu *Baehrens* ‖ nos*t*ro pectus *G* pect*us O.*— *To c.* **77** *Scaliger appended c.* **78**[b].

78. *No interval in V.* — **4** cubit *O*.

78^b. *No interval in V. This fragment was first separated by Statius from c.* **78**, *appended by Scaliger to c.* **77**, *by De Allio to c.* **91**, *by Bergk to c.* **80.** — **1, 2** *omitted without interval in V.* — **4** sania *V* || connuxit *O* coniunxit *G* conminxit *Scaliger.* — **5** non id *G* || seda *O*. — **6** quis scis *G* || famulo*que* tanus (canus *G*) *V* fama loquetur anus *Calpurnius*.

79. *No interval in V.* — **1** lesbius (*corrected from* lebius) *O* || qu*i*d (quid *G*) inqu*am* lesbia *V*. — **3** catullum (*corrected from* catulum) *G.* — **4** noto*rum O Avantius Scaliger* natorum *G* amatorum ω aratorum *Peiper* nostrorum *Schoell* || sania *O*.

80. *Interval of one verse in V, filled in G with title* Ad Gellium. — **2** ruberna *O* hyberna *G.* — **3** exiss*et* cu*m O* exisset cu*m G.* — **6** tn̄ta (= tanta *or* tenta) *O* tanta *G.* — **8** ille te mulso *V* ilia et emulso *Valerianus and Faernus* ilia te emulso . . . notare *Avantius* ilia ab emulso *Baehrens*.

81. *No interval in V.* — **1** uiuenti *O* uiuenti *G.* — **2** q*u*am *O.* — **3** pisanu*m O.* — **5** quid tibi *V* || nuc *G.* — **6** et] a *or* at ω en *Baehrens* || quid *V.*

82. *No interval in V.* — **2** aud *O.* — **4** si *Avantius* sei *Bergk.*

83. *No interval in V.* — **4** samia *G.* — **6** h*aec O* || oritur *O* || loquitur *V* coquitur *Lipsius.*

84. *No interval in V.* — **1** chommoda] commoda *V.* — **2** arrius (*corrected from* arius) *G* || hinsidias] insidias hee (he *G*) *V.* — **3, 4** *following v.* **10** *in V.* — **5** Liber ω Cimber *Heinsius* Umber *Riese* || eius est *O* eius est *G.* — **7** h*aec O* hic *G* || insiria *O* in syria *G.* — **8** audieba*nt O* audiebant *G.* — **10** nuncius *O* mincius *G.* — **11** illuc (*corrected from* illic) *O* || arcius *O* artius *G* || esset *G.* — **12** ess*et O* || Hionios] ionios *V.*

85. *No interval in V.* — **1** nequiris *O.* — **2** sed] si *O.*

86. *No interval in V.* — **1** quincia *O* || loga *O.* — **6** omnes *G.*

87. *No interval in V.* — **1** pot*est O* pone *G.* — **2** *est O* est *G* es *Scaliger.* — **3** nullo ω || in *omitted in V, added by Doering* || federe tanto *V.* — **4** quant*am O* || meo *Froehlich* illo *Baehrens.* — *To c.* **87** *Scaliger appended c.* **75.**

88. *No interval in V.* — **2** prorurit *O* proruit *G.* — **3** facis *O.* — **4** et quid *V* ecqui *Lachmann* || sis *O.* — **5** thetis *V.* — **6** nimpha*rum O* lympharum *L. Mueller.*

89. *Interval of one verse in V, filled in G with title* In Gellium. —
1 tellius *O.* — **4** mat*er O* mater *G.* — **5** attingit ω. — **6** qua*ntum* ius *O*
‖ fit *V.*

90. *No interval in V.* — **1** magnus *V.* — **3** magn*us O* magnus *G.* —
5 gnat*us O* gnatus *G* gratus *L. Mueller.* — **6** quïtū *O* omnetu*m G.*

91. *No interval in V.* — **3** te non nossem *Avantius.* — **4** a] aut *V* ‖
me*n*te *O* mente *G.* — **9** satis induxti *O* satis in duxti *G.*

92. *No interval in V, but paragraph mark in G and marginal title*
In Cesare*m.* — **1** esbia *O (but with minute* L *in very extreme margin to
guide illuminator; and, contrary to the usual custom in* O, *the letters* sbia
are written close to the capital E) ‖ mala ω *Westphal.* — **2** amo *G.* —
3, 4 *omitted in G.* — **3** totidem] eadem *Riese* quia sentio idem: nam
Froehlich ‖ mea] ea *O.*

93. *No interval in V.* — **1** belle *Usener.* — **2** nec si ore utru*m*
(utrum *G*) si saluus an alt*er* ho*m*o (alter homo *G*) *V.*

94. *No interval in V.* — **1** mentula *(corrected from* mentulla) *G* ‖
mechatur mechat*ur* metula (me*n*tula *G*) *V.*

95. *No interval in V.* — **1** zinirna *V* ‖ crine *O* ‖ me*n*sem *O.* —
2 cepta *V* ‖ hyemem *G.* — **3** in terrea *G* ‖ ortensius *O.* — **4** *omitted without
interval in V* ‖ miretur Volusi carmina facta die *Peiper* Tanusius uno |
uersiculorum anno quolibet ediderit *Froehlich.* — **5** zinirna canas *V.* —
6 zinirna*m V* ‖ p*er*uoluit *O* peruoluit *G.* — **7** Capuam *Passeratius*
Aduam *Voss.* — **9, 10** *judged by Statius to be a fragment of another poem.*
— **9** sodalis *omitted in V, restored by Aldus*[1] laboris ω poetae *Guarinus*
Philetae *Bergk* Phanoclis *Rossbach* Phalaeci *Munro* sint Cinnae cordi
monumenta *Baehrens.* — **10** populus u*e*l tu timido *O* ‖ eutimacho *V.*

96. *No interval in V.* — **1** mutis *et V* muteis *Schwabe.* — **3** que *O*
quei *Baehrens* quom *Guarinus* ‖ reuocamus *Peiper.* — **4** amissas ω Orco
missas *Haupt* scissas *Schwabe* obitu scissas *Pleitner* et quei discissas *Baehrens* et quo dimissas *Kiessling.* — **5** dolor est *V* dolorist *Haupt* doloreist
Ellis. — **6**᾿quintile *O* quintilie *(corrected from* quintile) *G.*

97. *No interval in V.* — **1** quicqu*id O* qu*i*cquid *G.* — **2** utru*m* os
anculu ol facere*m O* utrum os an culum olfacerem *G* utrumne *Avantius*
utrum culum anne os *Peiper.* — **3** nil omundi*us O* nilommundius *G* ‖
nihil*o*que *O* nobisqu*e G* ‖ inmundior ille *Lachmann And many other
critics have emended the verse in various ways.* — **5** hic *O* hic *G* os *Froehlich* dentibus hic: os dentis *Rossbach* ‖ seseq*ue* dedal*is* (dedal*is G*) *V.* —

6 ploxnio *O* ploxonio *G.* — **7** deffessus *O* defessus *G* diffissus *Statius* ‖ estu*m O* estum *G.* — **8** megentis *V* ‖ mulle *G* ‖ co*m*mis *O* connus *Ellis.* — **9-12** *judged by Lachmann to form a separate poem.* — **9** h*aec O* ‖ fecit *G.* — **10** pri*s*trino *O Baehrens.*

98. *No interval in V.* — **1** inte si inq*uam* q*uam V* ‖ pote *omitted in O* ‖ uicti *V perhaps falsely* Vetti *Statius* Vitti *Haupt (and so in v.* **5**). — **4** carpa*n*tinas *O.* — **5** uos *O* nos *G* ‖ Victi] *cf. v.* **1** *n.* — **6** discas *V* hiscas *Voss.*

99. *No interval in V.* — **1** s*ū*mpuit *O* surripuit *G* ‖ uiuenti *O* iuuenti *G.* — **2** suauiolu*m V* ‖ amb*r*osio *O* amrosio *G.* — **7** id] ad *G.* — **8** ab-stersti *O* astersi *G* abstersisti *Avantius* abstersti guttis *Aldus.* — **9** nec *V* nei *Baehrens* ‖ manaret *O.* — **10** comitte *O* ‖ saliuia *O* saliua (*corrected from* saliue) *G.* — **13** $\overset{i}{m}$ *O (cf.* **14. 10** *n.*) michi *G* ‖ ambrosio *V.* — **15** pena*m V.*

100. *No interval in V, but in G paragraph mark and marginal title* In Celiu*m et* Quintium. — **1** ellius *O (but with minute* G *in margin to guide illuminator, and with the letters* ellius *written close to the capital* G; *cf.* **92. 1** *n.*) ‖ Aufilenam et Quintius Aufilenum *Schoell.* — **2** trerone*n*su*m O* ‖ depere*n*t *O* depereret *G.* — **3** hoc] h*aec O.* — **6** *p*erfecta e*st igitur est* unica *O* perfecta e*st* exigitur est unica *G* perspecta exigit hoc ω per facta exhibita est *Lachmann* perspecta egregie est *Baehrens* (est igni tum *Palmer* eximie est *Koch*). — **7** correret *G* ‖ medulla*m O.*

101. *No interval in V, but in G paragraph mark and marginal title* Fletus de morte fratris. — **1** ultas *O (but with minute* M *in extreme margin to guide illuminator, and with the letters* ltas *written close to the capital* V; *cf.* **92. 1** *n.*). — **2** adueni *Avantius* adueni, has, miser a frater, *Baehrens* has seras *Markland.* — **3** mortis] amoris *Maehly.* — **6** hei misero *Avantius After this verse some critics have conjectured a lacuna ; Haase inserted here* **65. 9-14.** — **7** hoc *G* in terra hac *Rossbach.* — **8** tristis munera ω. — **10** ualle *O.*

102. *No interval in V.* — **1** i *O (but with minute* S *in margin to guide illuminator*) ‖ quoiquam tacitum *and* quidquid taciti *Statius* quoi quid *Maehly* quid quoi *Baehrens* tacite ω taciti *Heinsius* ‖ abantiq*uo O* ab antiquo *G.* — **3** me aeque *Voss.* — **4** putum *Schwabe* ar (*perhaps corrected from* at *or* ac) pocra*tem O* arpocratem *G.*

103. *No interval in V.* — **1** sextercia *O* sextercia *G.* — **2** est q*uam*-uis *O* est oq*uam* uis *G.* — **3** mimi *O* mimi *G* ‖ delectauit *O.*

104. *No interval in V.* — **3** si *omitted in O* ‖ perdita amare *O* perdite amare *G.* — **4** cum caupone ω.

105. *No interval in V, but paragraph mark in G.* — **1** pipileium *O* pipileium *G* Pimpleum ω ‖ scindere *O* scindere *G.*

106. *No interval in V.* — **1** obelio *O* obellio (*corrected from* obelio) *G* Obelli *Ellis* ‖ esse] ipse ω isse *Meleager* ire *Schwabe* uidet, ipsum *Vulpius.*

107. *No interval in V.* — **1** siquid quid *O* si quicquid *G* quicquam ω quoi quid *Ribbeck* quid quoi *Baehrens* ‖ optigit *O.* — **2** insperati *Heinsius* (*cf. v.* **5**) ‖ haec *O.* — **3** haec *O* ‖ nobis quoque] nobisque hoc *Statius* nobis, hoc *Froehlich* nobisque est *Haupt.* — **5** inspiranti *O* insperati *Heinsius* (*cf. v.* **2**). — **6** oluce *V.* — **7, 8** hac est | optandus uita *O* me est | optandus uita *G* hac res | optanda uita *Lachmann* hace | optandam uita dicere *Ribbeck* (degere *Baehrens*) horas | optandas uita *Schwabe* ab dis | optandum in uita *Ellis* hac re | optandam uitam *Riese* hac rem | optandam in uita *Postgate.*

108. *No interval in V.* — **1** sic homini populari *O* sic homini populari *G* Comini *Guarinus* populi *Statius.* — **2** in puris *O.* — **4** exercta *O* exerta *G.*

109. *No interval in V.* — **1** amore *V.* — **2** hunc (*corrected from* hinc) *G.* — **6** eterne *O* alterum ω ‖ fedus *V.*

110. *No interval in V.* — **1** auffilena *V.* — **2** q2 *O* que *G* quod *is perhaps right; cf.* quae *for* quod *in* **51. 5**; **66. 41.** — **3** promisisti *V.* — **4** nec *V* et *Guarinus.* — **5** promissa *V.* — **6** aut fillena *O* auffilena *G.* — **7** officium *Marcilius* officiis *Bergk* officio *Riese* est ficti *Schwabe* effectis *Ellis* nimio *Vahlen* est furis *Munro.* — **8** tota *V* totam ω.

111. *No interval in V, but the initial A of v.* **1** *in O is embellished with flourishes, as if to mark the beginning of a new poem.* — **1** aut fillenam *O* auffilenam *G* ‖ contemptam *O* contentas *Scaliger.* — **2** est *O* est *G* e *or* ex *Scaliger* laus est laudibus ex nimiis *Baehrens.* — **3** pars *O* pars *G.* — **4** parere *omitted in V* efficere ex patruo ω (concipere *Rossbach* suscipere *Heyse*) *The fitness of the swift succession of* matrem, fratres, patruo *to indicate the jumble of relationship involved is an indication in favor of supplying the needed infinitive at the end of the verse rather than in the middle, while a similar loss from the end of* **112. 1** (*which succeeds without an interval*) *is decisive in favor of this position. This bit of the leaf in the archetype was either torn off, or defaced so as to make it illegible.*

112. *No interval in V.* — **1** neque] nam ω ‖ est qui *omitted in V*
homost quin *Schwabe.* — **2** te escendit *Meleager* te scindit *Haupt* te scan-
dat *Peiper* te scindat *Schwabe* ‖ es *O* est *G* ‖ et] at *Schwabe.*

113. *No interval in V.* — **1** molebant *Maehly.* — **2** mecilia *G*
moechi : illo *Statius* moechari *Doering* Maeciliam *Lachmann* Moecillam
L. Mueller Mucillam *Pleitner* Mucilla *Riese* cum Moecilla. Atque hoc
consule *Baehrens.* — **3** mansuerunt *(with dot under first* u) *O.* — **4** singulum *O* singulum *G.*

114. *No interval in V.* — **1** saluis *V* Firmano *or* Formiano saltu ω
Firmanus saltu *Palladius* Formianus saltu *Heyse* ‖ mensula *V.* — **3** an
cupiam *O* aucupiam *G* ‖ aura *G* ‖ ferasque *(apparently corrected from*
feraque) *O.* — **4** exuperas *Scaliger.* — **5** sis *Froehlich.* — **6** saltem *G* ‖
modo *O* modo *G* domo *Lachmann* ‖ egeas *Avantius* tu ipse egeas *Froeh-*
lich te ipso egeat *Baehrens* eo ipse egeat *L. Mueller.*

115. *No interval in V.* — **1** istar *O* instar *G* iuxta *Scaliger* Mentula,
habes instar *Lachmann* noster *Avantius* uester *Postgate* iusti *Statius* habet,
Caesar, *Schwabe.* — **2** paria *Froehlich* uaria *Baehrens.* — **3** cresum *O*
cresum *G* ‖ potuisset *O* potuisset *G.* — **4** moda *V* bona *Avantius* ‖ possi-
derat *O.* — **5** plaudesque *O* altasque paludes ω (salsasque *Bergk* latasque
Rossbach uastasque *Pleitner*) tractusque paludesque *Baehrens.* — **6** hiper-
boreos *O.* — **7** est] si *V* es ω ipsest *Froehlich* ‖ ultor *V* horum *Avantius*
alter *Schwabe.*

116. *No interval in V.* — **1** studiose *Guarinus* ‖ requires *O* requires
G. — **2** batriade *O* batriade *G.* — **3** quis ω. — **4** celis *O* telis *G* ‖ mihi
omitted in V ‖ mitteremusque *O* mitteremusque *G* tela infesta meum
mittere in usque *Muretus* (mihi *Baehrens*) telis infestis *Froehlich* icere mi
usque ω mi icere in usque *Rossberg.* — **6** hinc *V* huc *Muretus.* — **7** euitabimus amitha (amicta *G*) *V* euitabimus icta *Rossberg.* — **8** affixus *O*
affixus *G.*

In O the text ends three lines from the bottom of the page, and on the last
line stands Finito libro referamus gracia χρο Am. *In G the last page is*
full, containing 34 lines instead of the usual 33, and on the next page
stands the following subscription :

Explicit Catulli Veronensis libellus.

Versus domini Beneuenuti de Campexanis de Vicencia de resurectione
Catulli poete Veronensis. : —

> Ad patriam uenio longis afinibus exul
> Causa mei reditus compatriota fuit.

Scilicet acalamis tribuit cui francia nomen
Quique notat turbe pretereuntis iter.
Quo licet ingenio uestrum celebrate Catullum
Cuius sub modio clausa papirus erat.

Tu lector quicumque ad cuius manus hic libellus ob uenerit Scriptori da
ueniam si tibi coruptus uidebitur . Quoniam a corruptissimo exemplari
transcripsit . non enim quodpiam aliud extabat unde posset libelli huius
habere copiam exemplandi   Et ut exipso salebroso aliquid tantum sugge-
ret decreuit pocius tamen coruptum habere quam omnino carere.   Sperans
adhuc ab alli quo alio fortuite emergente hunc posse corigere . Valebis si
ei in precatus non fueris.

. 1375. mense octobr. 19°.   qñ casignorius laborabat in extremis . et c
(= cetera) : —

Lesbia damnose bibens interpretatur. : —

(*This subscription is entirely wanting in O, and in several of the better
class of later and interpolated MSS.   Many other of these MSS., however,
contain the epigram of Campesani, either with or without the title given to
it here, though in some it stands at the beginning instead of the end of the
book.   The other concluding formulae of the later MSS. are of no critical
interest.*)

INDEX OF PROPER NAMES.

Rhamnusia: 64. 395; 66. 71; 68.
77; cf. Nemesis.
Rhenus: 11. 11.
Rhesus: 58b. 4.
Rhodus: 4. 8; Intr. 36.
Rhoeteus: 65. 7.
Roma: 68. 34.
Romulus: 28. 15; 29. 5, 9; 34.
22; 49. 1.
Rufa: 59. 1.
Rufulus: 59. 1.
Rufus: 69. 2; 77. 1; cf. Caelius.

Sabinus: 39. 10; 44. 1, 4, 5;
Intr. 10, 14.
Saces: 11. 6.
Saetabus: 12. 14; 25. 7.
Salisubsilus: 17. 6.
Sapphicus: 35. 16.
Sarapis: 10. 26.
Satrachus: 95. 5.
Saturnalia: 14. 15.
Satyrus: 64. 252.
Scamander: 64. 357.
Scylla: 60. 2; 64. 156.
Septimillus: 45. 13.
Septimius: 45. 1, 21, 23.
Sestianus: 44. 10.
Sestius: 44. 19, 20.
Silenus: 64. 252.
Silo: 103. 1.
Simonideus: 38. 8.
Sirmio: 31. 1, 12; Intr. 5, 10, 14,
36.
Socration: 47. 1.
Sol: 63. 39; 64. 271.
Somnus: 63. 42.
Sopor: 63. 37.
Stymphalius: 68. 113.
Suffenus: 14. 19; 22. 1, 10, 19.
Sulla: 14. 9.
Syria: (n.) 45. 22; 84. 7; (adj.)
6. 8; 66. 78; cf. Assyrius.
Syrtis: 64. 156.

Tagus: 29. 19.
Talasius: 61. 134.
Talus: (58b. 1).
Tappo: 104. 4.
Taurus: 64. 105.
Telemachus: 61. 229.

Tempe: 64. 35, 285, 286.
Tethys: 64. 29; 66. 70; 88. 5.
Teucrus: 64. 344; cf. Troicus,
Troia (adj.).
Thallus: 25. 1, 4.
Themis: 68. 153.
Thermopylae: 68. 54.
Theseus: 64. 53, 69, 73, 81, 102,
110, 120, 133, 200, 207, 239, 245,
247.
Thespius: 61. 27.
Thessalia: 64. 26, 33; cf. Ema-
thius.
Thessalus: 64. 267, 280.
Thetis: 64. 19, 20, 21, 28, 302,
336; (64. 329).
Thia: 66. 44.
Thracius: 4. 8.
Thyias: 64. 391.
Thynia: 31. 5; cf. Bithynia.
Thynus: 25. 7.
Thyonianus: 27. 7.
Tiburs: 39. 10; 44. 1, 3, 5.
Torquatus: 61. 216; cf. Manlius.
Transpadanus: 39. 13.
Trinacrius: 68. 53.
Triton: 64. 395.
Triuia: 34. 15; 66. 5; cf. Diana,
Luna.
Troia: (n.) 68. 88, 89, 90, 99;
(adj.) 65. 7; cf. Teucrus, Troi-
cus.
Troicus: 64. 345; cf. Teucrus,
Troia (adj.).
Troiugena: 64. 355.
Tullius: 49. 2.
Tyrius: 61. 172.

Varus: 10. 1; 22. 1; Intr. 66.
Vatinianus: 14. 3; 53. 2.
Vatinius: 52. 3; Intr. 7.
Venus: 3. 1; 13. 12; 36. 3; 45.
26; 55. 20; 61. 18, 44, 61, 198,
202; 63. 17; 66. 15, 56, 90; 68.
5, 10; 86. 6; (68. 17); cf. Ama-
thusia, Erycina.
Veraniolus: 12. 17; 47. 3.
Veranius: 9. 1; 12. 16; 28. 3;
Intr. 68 f.
Verona: 35. 3; 67. 34; 68. 27;
Intr. 5, 11, 14, 15.

INDEX TO THE NOTES.

———•◦•———

270